The Responsa Anthology

by
Avraham Yaakov Finkel

TEMPLE EMANU-EL
HaSifriyah
Haverhill, MA 01830

JASON ARONSON INC.
Northvale, New Jersey
London

Copyright © 1990 by Avraham Yaakov Finkel

10 9 8 7 6 5 4 3 2 1

All rights reserved. Printed in the United States of America. No part of this book may be used or reproduced in any manner whatsoever without written permission from Jason Aronson Inc. except in the case of brief quotations in reviews for inclusion in a magazine, newspaper, or broadcast.

Library of Congress Cataloging-in-Publication Data

Finkel, Avraham Yaakov.
    The responsa anthology / Avraham Yaakov Finkel.
      p.   cm.
    Includes bibliographical references and index.
    ISBN 0-87668-773-7
     1. Responsa. 2. Responsa—History and criticism. I. Title.
BM522.A1F56 1991
296.1'8—dc20   90-39600

Manufactured in the United States of America. Jason Aronson Inc. offers books and cassettes. For information and catalog write to Jason Aronson Inc., 230 Livingston Street, Northvale, New Jersey 07647.

This book is dedicated to my dear parents, שיחיו
Yehoshua Mattisyahu (Max) and Ida Finkel,
who have raised a dynasty of five generations of *ovedei Hashem*.
May Hashem Yisbarach grant them *arichas yamim veshanim*
in good health with simchas and nachas
from all their offspring.

CONTENTS

ACKNOWLEDGMENT xv

INTRODUCTION xvii

I. THE RESPONSA OF THE GEONIM: 589-1038 1

    Rav Poltoi Gaon 3
        Doing Business on the Intermediate Days of a Festival 3
        Annual Fair Dedicated to an Idol 3

    Rav Netronai Gaon 4
        A Religious Divorce by an Apostate? 4
        An Apostate's Right of Inheritance 4

    Rav Amram Gaon 5
        False Messiah 5

    Rav Nachman Gaon 6
        Captive Jewish Women 6

    Rav Sherira Gaon 7
        Creating Fire from Water 7
        The History and Development of the Oral Law 7

    Rav Hai Gaon 9
        An Arrogant Kohen 9

II. THE RESPONSA OF THE RISHONIM: 1038-1492 11

    Rabbi Moshe ben Maimon—Rambam (Maimonides) 13
        Destroying a Tree 14
        Dismissing a Cantor on the Basis of a Rumor 15
        A Dishonest Shochet 15
        Playing with Pebbles on Shabbat 15
        A Ransomed Torah Scroll 16
        A Young Man Who Bought a Slave Girl 16
        Brit Milah on a Fast Day 16

    Rabbi Meir of Rothenburg—Maharam 17
        Two Captives 18
        Preface to Maharam's Responsum 250 18
        Preventing Someone from Leaving Town 18
        Mourning for an Apostate? 18
        Book Destroyed by Fire 19
        Was It Lead or Silver? 19

Rabbi Shelomoh ibn Aderet—Rashba 20
  The Converted Slave 21
  Sprouted Wheat Kernels 21
  Disputation with a Christian Scholar 21
  A Wife Who Wants to Take Fertility Drug 22
  The Weak-Willed Gambler 22
  Unfair Competition 22

Rabbi Asher ben Yechiel—Rosh 23
  Must He Obey His Father? 24
  Death Penalty for a Slanderer 24
  Decorate a Synagogue with a Moslem Prayer Rug? 24
  What Should Be Done with the Ransom Money? 25
  Can This Teacher Be Dismissed? 25
  The Noisy Blacksmith's Shop 25

Rabbi Yom Tov ibn Ashvili—Ritva 26
  Refusal to Return Security 26
  Can a Gambler Be Forced to Divorce His Wife? 27
  Dispute about Access Road 27
  Is This Torah Scroll Unfit for Use? 27
  The Repentant Thief 28
  Must He Pay His Wife's Medical Expenses? 28

Rabbi Nissim Girondi—Ran 29
  The Stolen Security 29
  A Vow to Move to Eretz Yisrael 30
  A Shipment of Lamb's Meat 30
  May He Marry Two Wives? 31

Rabbi Yitzchak ben Sheshet Perfet—Rivash 32
  A Question Concerning Marranos 33
  A Philosophical Question 33
  Riding a Camel in a Caravan on Shabbat 33
  Rescue from a Wine Vat 33
  Bruised in a Fistfight 34

Rabbi Shimon Duran—Rashbatz 35
  Death in the Desert 35
  Can a Wife Be Compelled to Move? 36
  An Islamic Sacrificial Sheep 36
  The Importance of Torah Teachers 37
  Love of Eretz Yisrael 37
  Who Gets Custody of the Little Girl? 37
  Remove Shoes before Entering Synagogue? 38

Rabbi Yisrael Brunna—Mahari Brunna 39
  Unable to Go to Eretz Yisrael 39
  Attend Horse Races? 40
  Double Pay for Delivering Twins? 40
  Who Supplies the Clock? 40
  A Non-Jew Made a Gift to the Synagogue 41

CONTENTS

       A Chazzan's Voice   41
       An Ungrateful Husband   41

Rabbi Yosef Colon—Maharik   42
       Rescuing the Jews of Regensburg   42
       Donations for the Synagogue in Jerusalem   43
       No Tax Exemption   43
       Is a Jew Permitted to Wear a *Kaffiyeh*?   44
       A Dispute between Doctors   44
       Disrespect toward Rabbis   44
       One Who Reneges on His Obligation   44
       Should a Jew Pay This Tax?   45

Rabbi David ibn Zimra—Radvaz   46
       Karaites   47
       Ethiopian Jews   47
       Exorbitant Medical Fees   47
       Milk Used in Processing Sugar   48
       Egyptian Mummies   48

III. THE RESPONSA OF THE EARLY ACHARONIM: 1492–1648   49

Rabbi Meir Katzenellenbogen—Maharam of Padua   51
       The Case of the Two Prisoners   51
       Can This Vow Be Annulled?   52
       Must This Student Pay Tuition?   52
       Their Father Renounced the Jewish Faith   52
       He Promised His Mother . . .   53

Rabbi Yosef Karo—Beit Yosef, Shulchan Aruch   54
       Is the Slave Girl Permitted to Marry a Jew?   55
       Placing a Statue of a Lion on an Aron HaKodesh   55
       A Dispute between Neighbors   56
       Opposition to the Rabbi's Appointment   56
       A Judge under Forty Years of Age?   57
       A "Marriage" of Minors?   57

Rabbi Moshe di Trani—Mabit   58
       By Giving Her Grapes, Did He Marry Her?   58
       Shipwrecked   59
       The Lost Necklace   59
       The Wicked Son   60
       Must the Agent Suffer the Loss?   60
       A Former Marrano   61
       He Wants to Break Away from the Community   61

Rabbi Shemuel di Medina—Maharashdam   62
       Quarreling Neighbors   62
       A Problem for Travelers   63
       May the Son Marry the Girl of His Choice?   63
       The Brother's Vow   63
       Freeing Captives   64

Who Is Responsible for the Fire? 64
Can He Evict the Tenant? 65
She Doesn't Want to Sell Her Slave Girl 65

Rabbi Moshe Alshich—Alshich Hakadosh 66
A Ship Sank with a Load of Iron Ingots 66
A Dispute about a Will 67
Wife Refuses to Move to Husband's Hometown 67
Should the Wealthy Pay a Proportional Tax? 68
Is a Hybrid *Etrog* Fit to Be Used? 68
Is the Rabbi Exempt from Paying This Tax? 68
He Overcharged for the Wine 69

Rabbi Shelomoh Luria—Maharshal 70
Consult Sorcerers? 71
Recovery from Childbirth 71
Should the Blind Light the Menorah? 71
May the Landlord Evict His Tenant? 71
Pangs of Conscience 72
Fry an Egg on a Hot Roof on Shabbat? 72

Rabbi Betzalel Ashkenazi—Shittah Mekubetzet 73
A Man Lost at Sea 73
Dispute about a Pirated Shipment 74
Where Should Reuven Pay Taxes? 75
Firing an Unqualified Rabbi 75
Is the Synagogue Entitled to the Bequest? 76

Rabbi Avraham di Boton—Lechem Mishneh, Lechem Rav 77
Dismiss the Chazzan? 77
Can Yaakov Francis Serve as Chazzan and Shochet? 78
A Pearl-Studded Wedding Ring 78
The Rabbi's Parents Are Marranos 78
May He Pray in Another Synagogue? 79
Can He Cancel the Sale? 79
He Took Him to the Civil Court 80

Rabbi Meir of Lublin—Maharam Lublin 81
Someone Accidentally Shot and Killed a Man 82
A Marrano Betrayed a Mohel 82
The Nobleman's Promissory Note 83
Synagogue Destroyed by Fire 83
Must Hatziplatz Help Tziltz? 83
Creditors Press Murder Victim's Widow for Payment 84

Rabbi Yoel Sirkes—the Bach 85
The Marriage Broker's Fee 86
Does He Have to Share the Profit? 86
The Agnostic Doctor 86
Is This Widow Allowed to Remarry? 87
A Boisterous Wedding Feast 87
He Wants to Break His Engagement 88
Sing Secular Melodies in the Synagogue? 88

Rabbi Yaakov Sasportas 89
Can Reuven Collect This Debt? 90
Competing Money-Changers 90
Marrano Returned to the Jewish Faith 91
Abolish a Custom Established by Shabbetai Tzevi? 91
Excerpt from the Opening Chapter Relating the History of Shabbetai Tzevi 92

Rabbi Shmuel Abohab—Dvar Shmuel 93
Is Prayer in the Vernacular Permitted? 93
Biblical Illustrations of Angels 94
Seek a Cure through Exorcism? 94
Ascetic Old Rabbi Practices Self-Mortification 94
Freeing a Slave 95
Enlarging the Synagogue 95

Rabbi Yair Chaim Bachrach—Chavat Yair 96
Cutting Down a Fruit Tree 97
A Rabbi-Musician Performing at Weddings? 97
Transform an Apron into a Mantle for the Torah? 97
Are Incantations Superstitions? 97
Disposing of the Property of Others 97
Incident during the Cholera Epidemic 98

IV. THE RESPONSA OF THE LATER ACHARONIM: 1649–Present 99

Rabbi Tzvi Ashkenazi—Chacham Tzvi 101
God and Nature 101
Is England a Private Domain? 102
Who Has to Pay for the Disabled Horse? 102
What to Use for Maror at the Seder 103
The Stolen *Etrog* 103
The Nobleman's Loan 103
Man Created by Means of Kabbalah 104

Rabbi Yaakov Reischer—Shevut Yaakov 105
Siamese Twins 105
Who Has to Pay for the Wasted Food? 106
Did Shimon Cause the Fire? 106
A Husband Abused His Wife 106
Mail a Letter on Friday? 107
Should They Die for the Sanctification of God's Name? 107
Victims of the Plague in 1713 107
Terrorized by Bandits 108

Rabbi Yechezkel Katzenellenbogen—Kenesset Yechezkel 109
Can a Chazzan Accept a New Position? 109
Conflicting Chanukah Customs 110
Brit Performed before the Eighth Day 110
Wife Objects to Husband's Profession 111
The Tenth Man Refuses to Come to the Minyan 111

Rabbi Yaakov Emden—Yavetz 112
    Sister Deterred Brother from Sinning 113
    Anatomy Lessons on Shabbat? 113
    Should We Ransom the Boy or the Girl? 113
    He Went to the Stock Exchange on Shabbat 114
    Are Portraits Permissible? 114
    Reading Newspapers on Shabbat 114
    A Question on Abortion 115

Rabbi Yechezkel Landau—Noda biYehudah 116
    A Government Official's Problem 117
    A Kohen Who Married an Indian Woman 117
    Circumcision on a Child Who Died 117
    Hunting Wildlife 118
    A Philosophical Question 118

Rabbi Chaim Yosef David Azulai—Chida 119
    A Sephardi Who Made Fun of an Ashkenazi Song 120
    Husband Feigned Death 121
    No Tombstone on Rabbi's Grave 121
    When Must He Pay Back the Loan? 122

Rabbi Akiva Eiger 123
    Husband Drowned 123
    Wife Affected with Epilepsy 124
    The Battered Wife 124
    Dispute about Rent 125

Rabbi Moshe Sofer (Schreiber)—Chatam Sofer 126
    The Emperor Visits the Synagogue 127
    Lost Purse 127
    Son Supporting Parents 128
    Transfer of Graves 128
    The Poisoned Maid 128

Rabbi Yehudah Assad 129
    Naming a Baby after a Living Person? 129
    Problem in Painting the Synagogue 130
    An Abandoned Wife 130
    The Preacher Did Not Get Paid 130
    Who Gets the Torah Scroll? 130
    The Weighted Bracelets 131

Rabbi Moshe Schick—Maharam Schick 132
    A Bible Published by Missionaries 132
    Preach in the Local Language? 133
    The Torn-Down *Mechitzah* 133
    The Chapel in the Castle 133
    An Abortion to Save the Mother's Life 133
    Can This Gift Be Accepted? 134
    A Case of Murder 134

Rabbi Avraham Shemuel Binyamin Sofer (Schreiber)—Ktav Sofer 135
    Winding the Clocks on Shabbat? 135

CONTENTS

    Apostate Returned to the Fold   136
    Forced to Light Candles during Procession   137
    Student Wants to Sue His Rebbi   137
    A Charitable Prince   138
    A Marriage Made in Jest   138

Rabbi Moshe Weinberg of Volbrum—Ohel Moshe   139
    Dismantle the Old Reading Platform?   140
    Break the Engagement?   140
    Selling to a Non-Jew on the Second Day of Yomtov?   140

Rabbi Yosef Shaul Halevi Nathanson—Sho'eil Umeishiv   141
    Relations between Jews and Gentiles   141
    The Widow's Rent Dispute   142
    An Unwanted Gift   142
    Did He Donate the Sefer Torah?   142
    Who Has Precedence?   143
    What Is the Price of the Cow?   143

Rabbi Naftali Tzvi Yehudah Berlin—Netziv   144
    Selling Nonkosher Meat to an Apostate   144
    Reading from the Torah on Sunday?   145
    Polluted Drinking Water?   145
    Placing the *Bimah* in Front of the Ark   146
    Flour for Matzot from a Steam-Powered Mill   146

Rabbi Yitzchak Elchanan Spector   147
    Convert a Mosque into a Synagogue?   147
    Can He Break His Vow?   148
    Men Lost at Sea   148
    The Treacherous Husband   149
    The Faulty Scales   149

Rabbi Yitzchak Aharon Ettinger—Mahari Halevi   150
    Transfer Charitable Contributions?   150
    Can He Be Considered of Sound Mind?   151
    Tax Revolt   151
    Who Is Entitled to the Insurance Money?   151
    He Wants to Break Their Engagement   152
    Competing Tavern Owners   152
    Dispute about an Inheritance   153
    Conflict of Interest for the Shochet?   153

Rabbi Yosef Chaim Al Chakkam of Baghdad—Ben Ish Chai   154
    Which Bread Is Preferred?   155
    Did He Violate a Torah Decree?   155
    Healing by Cauterization   156
    Give His Son the Name of a Hebrew Letter?   156
    Testing a Servant   156
    Interpretation of a Dream   156
    A House or a Garden in Eretz Yisrael?   157
    Her True Age Was 32   157

Rabbi Shalom Mordechai Schwadron—Brezaner Rav, Maharsham 158
    Lost at Sea 158
    Wife Refuses to Move to Eretz Yisrael 159
    Eating through a Tube on Yom Kippur 160
    He Sold His Sins 160
    Circumcise Moslem Children? 160
    Contribute Money for a Church? 160
    The Butcher's Penalty 161
    The Borrowed Wedding Ring 161

Rabbi Avraham Borenstein of Sochatchov—Avnei Nezer 162
    Hand-Made or Machine-Made Matzot 162
    Does a Hospital Room Need a Mezuzah? 163
    Buying Land in Eretz Yisrael 163
    Unfair Competition? 163
    Lumber from a Demolished Church 164
    Sterilization 164

Rabbi Yonatan Steif 165
    Must She Keep This Promise? 165
    Should the Soldier Travel on Yomtov? 166
    Wearing Chasidic Garb? 166
    Visiting the Sick by Telephone 167
    Proper Pronunciation 167
    The Torah Scroll Fell Down 167

Rabbi Moshe Feinstein—Reb Moshe 168
    Heart Transplants 169
    Buying Insurance 169
    Auditor for the Internal Revenue Service 170
    Forced Baptism 170
    A Statue for President Kennedy 170
    Teaching Mythology 171
    Paper Cups for Kiddush? 171

Rabbi Mordechai Yaakov Breisch 172
    With Left Arm in a Cast, Where Should Arm Tefillin Be Placed? 173
    Fertility Drug Made of Blood 173
    Take Appetite Depressant Pill before Yom Kippur? 173
    A Soldier's Dilemma 174
    Guilt Feelings over a Brother's Death during the Holocaust 174
    Question Concerning Jewish Army Chaplain 175

Rabbi Yitzchak Yaakov Weiss—Minchat Yitzchak 176
    Tefillin on Tattooed Arm? 176
    Incident in a Concentration Camp 177
    Girl Born of Non-Jewish Mother 177
    Faith Healers 178
    Exaggerations at Fund-Raising Appeals 178
    Conflict between Yeshivah Students and Parents 178
    Report Careless Drivers to the Police? 179

Rabbi Menashe Klein—Ungvarer Rav 180
    Use Postage Stamp on Which God's Name Appears? 181

CONTENTS *xiii*

        Letter with Uncancelled Stamp   182
        Tragic Incident during the Holocaust   182
        Kidney Transplants   183
        Practice Birth Control?   183
        Discovery of a Valuable Book   184
        Bar a Photographer from Taking Your Picture?   184

GLOSSARY   185

NOTES   187

APPENDIX OF ADDITIONAL PROMINENT HALACHIC AUTHORITIES   201

SUBJECT INDEX   205

INDEX OF AUTHORS AND PERSONALITIES   207

ACKNOWLEDGMENT

I thank Hashem with all my heart (Psalm 111:1).

It is with deep gratitude to Hashem that I offer this work as a follow-up to *The Great Torah Commentators*. The thought of presenting a selection of the she'eilot and teshuvot of the foremost *meshivim* (writers of responsa) was generated by my good friend Arthur Kurzweil, vice-president of Jason Aronson Inc. An original thinker of deep faith and unerring judgment, he guided the production of this book through all its phases. For his encouragement and enthusiasm I thank him from the bottom of my heart.

My children and grandchildren have been a constant source of joy and nachas to me. Their lively interest in the work was heartening and inspiring. My special thanks to them all: to Moshe and Brenda, Motty, Tzvi, Rivkie, Shlomoh, Eliyahu, Eliezer, and Gavriel Finkel; to Berish and Elisheva, Moshe Levi, Devorah, Yehudis, Shlomoh, Chaim, Mordechai, and Sarahle Weinberg; to Moshe and Judy, Gedalyah, Akiva, Refael, Elisheva, Eliezer, and Yossie Klein; to Chaim and Naomi, Gavriel, Eliezer, Daniel, Yechezkel, Sarahle, and Yechiel Aryeh Finkel.

I am very grateful to Adelle Krauser for her caring attention and meticulous editing. My appreciation also to Nancy D'Arrigo, Art Director, for designing the impressive cover design, and to the entire dedicated staff of Jason Aronson Inc.

I am thankful to Yeshivah Emunas Yisroel and the Torah Library of Borough Park, whose extensive libraries of responsa literature were extremely helpful to me.

And finally, I would like to express my gratitude to my dear wife, Suri, whose wisdom, wit, affection, and devotion have helped me greatly in the completion of this book.

INTRODUCTION

Ever since the days of Moshe Rabbeinu (our teacher Moshe), the Jewish people has looked to Torah sages for answers to their questions and problems relating to all phases of life. As long as the main body of the Jewish nation was concentrated in Eretz Yisrael, where great academies and celebrated scholars were close at hand, answers were easily obtained. With the dispersal of Jewish communities to the far reaches of the Middle East, Northern Africa, Europe, and America, the people secured halachic solutions to vital questions by writing queries, she'eilot, to the most eminent scholars of the age. The rabbis replied in detailed responsa, teshuvot, rendering decisions and setting forth the halachic sources on which their rulings were based.

Halachah is the God-given system of the Oral Law as it was revealed on Sinai, transmitted from generation to generation, and subsequently written down in the Mishnah and the Talmud. It deals with all facets of Jewish life and has been expounded by great sages throughout history. In his teshuvah, the *poseik* (halachic authority) analyzes the question, breaks it down into its elements, and with pure inductive reasoning compares these components with analogous cases in the Talmud or in the teshuvot of earlier scholars. This process is called *medameh milta lemilta*, Aramaic for "comparing one case to another." Only a sage of prodigious Torah greatness, who has assimilated the entire Talmud into his thinking, can seek out the correct precedents, draw the right inferences, and arrive at the proper solution to the she'eilah at hand. With discernment, compassion, and utmost sensitivity he weighs all aspects of the she'eilah, dispensing justice to litigants, guidance to the bewildered, and solace to the bereaved. The teshuvot literature deals with a tremendous range of subjects such as kashrut, rituals, laws, vows, excommunication, marriage and divorce, commercial disputes, inheritance, torts and damages, and halachic decisions on new scientific discoveries and inventions, to name just a few. Many she'eilot are of a theoretical nature, the questioner seeking clarification of difficult topics in the Talmud or of apparent contradictions in the rabbinic writings. The majority of the teshuvot, however, reflect the everyday life of the average Jew at home and in the synagogue, celebrating Shabbat and Yomtov; they deal with a kaleidoscopic variety of his vexations, disputes, marital problems, and relations with non-Jewish neighbors. On the pages of the teshuvot the past comes alive, as we are transported to different worlds: From a marketplace in ancient Babylonia to a pirates' den in North Africa; from a wedding feast in a small shtetl in Poland to a modern military base in the United States. As the panorama of Jewish life unfolds before our eyes, we stand in reverent awe of the profound wisdom, the boldness and originality, and, above all, the burning *ahavat Yisrael* (love of the Jewish people) that emerge from the rabbis' responses. Such wisdom and love could flow only from saintly men—accomplished talmudists rendering justice tempered with mercy, according to the dictates of the Torah.

The responsa literature has traditionally been divided into three periods: the Geonic period, the Rishonim (the Early Great Sages), and the Acharonim (the Later Great Sages). The Geonic period began in 589 and ended with the death of Rav Hai Gaon in 1038, which led to a decline of the yeshivot in Babylonia. It was followed by the era of the Rishonim, who lived in North Africa, Spain, France, and Germany, and who introduced a system of codification of the laws of the Talmud.

The period of the Acharonim began with the expulsion of the Jews from Spain in 1492 and extends into the present. Generally, the Acharonim have all accepted the rulings of the Rishonim as final and binding. However, defining the era of the Acharonim as ranging from 1492 to the present would lead us to group the Torah scholars of our century with men of such incomparable greatness as the **Ran**, the **Rivash**, the **Radvaz**, and Rabbi **Yosef Karo**.* Although the scholars of our century certainly are eminent men, they cannot be placed in the same category with the earlier authorities, any more than the Geonim can be grouped with the much greater Tannaim of the Mishnah. Therefore, an additional demarcation point was needed, separating Early Acharonim from Later Acharonim, whereby the Later Acharonim will not contradict the rulings of the Early Acharonim. The year 1648, the date of the Cossack uprising under Chmielnitzki and the attending massacres and devastation of Polish Jewry, is generally considered as the point of transition between the Early and Later Acharonim.

In making our selections, we have chosen those responsa that illustrate Jewish life of the period in which they were written. It should be understood that these are only brief excerpts. We have omitted the lengthy, highly technical, intricate halachic discussions that constitute the main portion of every teshuvah, expositions in which the *poseik* defends his ruling and explains the process by which he arrived at his decision. In presenting the essence of these teshuvot, we hope to spark in the reader an appreciation of the wisdom and the beauty of our Torah and a deeper interest in studying the commentaries of the great rabbis.

A word of caution is in order. Since each individual case has many nuances that may have affected the halachic decision that was rendered, no parallels should be drawn from a given teshuvah to any current problem or question. Each question that arises must be judged on its own merits by a qualified halachic authority.

Many of the teshuvot we selected can be better understood if they are seen against the historical background of the period in which the questioner lived. To this purpose we provide the following brief synopsis of the major events that shaped Jewish history in the countries of the Diaspora.

---

*The names of people whose responsa are included in this book are printed in boldface for the reader's convenience.

SPAIN AND NORTH AFRICA

It is not known when Jews first settled in Spain. The Biblical prophet Obadiah, referring to the destruction of the First Temple (423 B.C.E.), states in verse 20 of his chapter, "And the captivity of Jerusalem that is in Sepharad." Sepharad is the Hebrew word for Spain.

Under Roman rule the Jews of Spain enjoyed equal rights with all the inhabitants of the Iberian Peninsula. They tilled the soil and were engaged in commerce. In the fifth century, after the fall of the Roman Empire, Spain was invaded by the Vandals and Visigoths. When in 589 C.E. the Visigoth king Recarred converted to Catholicism, he launched a policy of forced conversions of Jews.

There followed a century of persecutions, which reached a climax in 694, when the Jews of Spain were declared slaves and their children were taken from them at age 7 to be raised as Christians. In 711 the Moslem Moors invaded Spain, crossing the Straits of Gibraltar from Morocco. The Jews welcomed the invaders as liberators and became their allies. The arrival of the Moors marked the beginning of the Golden Age of Spanish Jewish scholarship, which produced such immortal greats as exemplified by the liturgical poets Rabbi Yehudah Halevi and Rabbi Shelomoh ibn Gabirol. Talmudic scholarship flourished, and the rabbis would send their halachic questions to the Geonim in Babylonia; months later, the responsa would arrive and their Aramaic text would be carefully studied.

This spiritual dependence on the faraway Geonim would change with the arrival of the "Four Captives." In 955 four great Torah scholars set out on a sea voyage to collect money for their yeshivot in Italy. They were captured by pirates and ransomed by the communities of Cordova, Kairouan, and Cairo. The scholars then established yeshivot in these cities, raising new generations of superior Torah scholars who were qualified to answer questions without having to consult the Babylonian Geonim.

In 1148 a series of rebellions brought to power the fanatic Moslem sect of the Almohads. The Jews were forced to convert to Islam and many fled the country. One who fled was a 13-year-old boy named Moshe ben Maimon who became known as the **Rambam** (Maimonides), the great codifier of Torah law who ultimately settled in Fostat, a suburb of Cairo. During the thirteenth century the Moslem rule declined, and gradually the Christians regained the territory they had lost. In 1236 they conquered Cordova; Seville fell in 1248. While the reconquest was in progress, the Christian rulers permitted the Jews a degree of autonomy, and many Jews held high government offices. The eminent talmudists Ramban (R. Moshe ben Nachman), **Rashba** (R. Shelomoh ibn Aderet), **Ritva** (R. Yom Tov ibn Ashvili), **Rosh** (R. Asher), and **Ran** (R. Nissim), lived and wrote their monumental halachic works and responsa during that era. Tragedy struck in 1391, when a wave of violence spread throughout Spain and 50,000 Jews were massacred. Many Jews saved their lives by professing to convert to Christianity while secretly remaining Jewish. These were the so-called Marranos, also called Anussim or Conversos. In the wake of these persecutions, the great scholars **Rivash** (R. Yitzchak Perfet) and **Rashbatz** (R. Shimon Duran) fled to Algiers, North Africa.

In 1478 the Inquisition was initiated in Spain with the purpose of ferreting out Marranos who were secretly practicing Judaism. Its victims were cruelly tortured and put to death in public burnings called *autos-da-fé*. In 1492 Granada, the last Moorish stronghold, fell to the Christians, ending 800 years of Moslem rule in Spain. During that same year King Ferdinand and Queen Isabella signed the edict expelling all Jews from Spain. Most of them settled in Turkey, Greece, Eretz Yisrael, North Africa, and Italy. When the Inquisition came to Portugal in 1531, the Marranos left that country; they were welcomed in the Netherlands, where they established thriving Sephardi communities in Amsterdam and The Hague.

Since the expulsion, no Jews lived in the Iberian Peninsula until the recent past.

ERETZ YISRAEL

Ever since Israel crossed the Jordan, entering Canaan under Joshua's leadership in 1273 B.C.E., the Jewish nation has resided in Eretz Yisrael. There, the Jews were successively ruled by judges and kings; they were exhorted by prophets and guided by the Sanhedrin and the rabbis of the Mishnah— the illustrious teachers of the Oral Law, who are known as the Tannaim.

In about 189 C.E., after Rabbi Yehudah HaNasi completed the editing of the Mishnah, the center of Jewish life and learning shifted from Eretz Yisrael to Babylonia. The communities in Eretz Yisrael then suffered under centuries of religious persecution, and were all but wiped out in 1099 when the Crusaders conquered Jerusalem, destroying most of the last remnants of the Jewish population. When Ramban (Nachmanides) settled in Jerusalem in 1267, he could not even find a minyan (quorum of ten adult males required for communal prayer). Rabbi Ovadiah Yarei of Bertinora reported that in 1480 the Jewish population of Jerusalem numbered seventy families, all of whom were destitute.

This changed with the arrival of the Spanish exiles in 1492, when new communities sprang up in Jerusalem, Safed, and Hebron. Safed became the focal point for the study of Kabbalah (mysticism). Among the all-time great kabbalists of Safed are Rabbi Moshe Cordovero, Rabbi **Yosef Karo** (author of the *Shulchan Aruch*), Rabbi **Moshe Alshich**, Rabbi Yitzchak Luria (the Ari), Rabbi Chaim Vital, and Rabbi **Moshe Trani** (Mabit).

Gradually, Jerusalem began to gain prominence. However, the governors of the city, who were appointed by the Turkish Ottoman Empire in Constantinople, were free to impose taxes at whim. They taxed the Jewish community of Jerusalem beyond its limits, a fact reflected in many of the responsa of that time. Rabbi **Betzalel Ashkenazi**, who was the author of *Shittah Mekubetzet* and who settled in Jerusalem in 1588, traveled to Egypt, Syria, and Turkey to raise funds for that impoverished community. In 1621 Rabbi Yeshayah Horowitz, renowned rabbi of Prague and author of the *Shelah*, settled in Jerusalem, but in 1625 the greedy pasha of Jerusalem arrested him along with other leaders. After he was ransomed he fled to Tiberias.

Gradually, Jerusalem experienced a revival of Torah scholarship; yeshivot were built and students streamed to them from near and far. But it received a mortal blow in 1720 when the Ashkenazi community fell victim to a cholera epidemic. Not until the onset of the twentieth century did Eretz Yisrael and, in particular, Jerusalem, begin to blossom again. Today, with God's help, Eretz Yisrael is again the spiritual center of world Jewry, taking pride in its prodigious talmudists and venerable chasidic rebbes, its thousands of yeshivot and girls' schools teeming with eager students from virtually every country in the world. Torah is vibrantly alive again in Jerusalem, in fulfillment of the prophecy: "For from Zion the Torah will come forth and the word of God from Jerusalem" (Isaiah 2:3).

TURKEY, GREECE, AND ITALY

The earliest records of Jewish settlements in Turkey and Greece date back to the time of the Second Temple (349 B.C.E.–69 C.E.), but they were small communities, and little is known about them. The Jewish population of the region increased markedly when, during the fourteenth century, Jews from Hungary, Germany, and Italy, who had been oppressed in and finally expelled from their native lands, escaped to Greece and Turkey.

It was during that century that the foundations were laid for the Ottoman Empire, which was to extend Turkish rule over Greece, Southeast Europe, and Northeast Africa. In 1453 Constantinople, the mighty capital of the Byzantine Empire, was conquered by Mehmet II and renamed Istanbul. Mehmet II invited all Jews to settle in Turkey, and when the Jews of Spain and Portugal were expelled in 1492 and 1497, respectively, many of them settled in Constantinople, Salonica, and Smyrna, where they began to prosper and established yeshivot and synagogues. A new language evolved that was called Ladino, spoken by the émigrés from Spain and still used by their descendants today. It is a mixture of Spanish and Hebrew, in the same way that Yiddish is a blend of Old German and Hebrew. This group of Jews produced outstanding Torah scholars; foremost among them is Rabbi **Yosef Karo** who wrote his commentary to the *Tur*, called *Bet Yosef*, in Adrianople, Turkey, and who later wrote the *Shulchan Aruch*. Rabbi **Shemuel di Medina (Maharashdam)**, the prominent halachist who lived in Salonica and wrote more than a thousand responsa, also was an offspring of Spanish exiles, as was his disciple Rabbi **Avraham di Boton**. The rulers of the Ottoman Empire during the first two centuries of its existence treated the Jews with benevolence, and many Jews attained influential positions at the Sultan's Court. In this peaceful environment Turkish Jewry prospered and its Torah scholarship reached high levels.

In nearby Italy there have been Jewish communities since the days of the Second Temple (destroyed in 69 C.E.). The Jewish community of Rome is mentioned in the Mishnah and Talmud; this community grew larger after the destruction of the Second Temple, when 16,000 Jews were brought to Rome. With the advent of Christianity the first restrictions on Jews were imposed, although there is no record of expulsions or massacres by the emperor and rulers. Generally, Italian Jews continued to enjoy a considerable measure of freedom. Many of them turned to secular studies, attaining prominence in the fields of medicine, science, and the arts. In the fifteenth century many Ashkenazi Jews from Germany migrated to Northern Italy, bringing with them their advanced talmudic scholarship. A most influential Torah sage of that era was Rabbi Yehudah Mintz, who founded a yeshivah in Padua where he gave instruction to a new generation of Italian rabbis. The great *poseik* R. **Yosef Colon (Maharik)** immigrated to Italy from France. Toward the end of the fifteenth century the arrival of the exiles from Spain ushered in an era during which Italy became the leading center of Torah study in Europe. An important factor contributing to the rise of scholarship was the availability of a new invention, the printing press, which made it possible to reproduce thousands of copies of a book in a very short time. Many *incunabula* (books printed before 1500) were produced in Italy by the famous Soncino family, among others. The first existing Hebrew *incunabulum* is the commentary to the Chumash (Pentateuch) by Rashi, printed in Reggio di Calabria in 1475.

In the sixteenth century the contra-Reformation efforts of the Catholic Church gave rise to persecutions and anti-Jewish decrees. In 1553 Pope Julius III ordered the burning of the Talmud, and two years later Pope Paul IV ordered Jews confined to ghettos; men were to wear yellow hats and women yellow kerchiefs. He also decreed that twenty-five Marranos living in Ancona be burned at the stake.

In spite of such persecutions and the general hardship of Jewish life in Italy at the time, Jewish scholarship there survived. In the seventeenth century Italian Jewry was led by such great rabbis as Rabbi **Shmuel Abohab (Dvar Shmuel)**, rabbi of Venice, and in the eighteenth century by the towering giant Rabbi **Chaim Yosef David Azulai (Chida)**.

FRANCE AND GERMANY

The earliest known mention of Jews in this area dates back to Roman times. It is found in two edicts issued by Emperor Constantine, in 321 C.E. and 331 C.E., directed at the people of Colonia

INTRODUCTION

Agrippina, now Cologne in West Germany. By the year 1000 there were Jewish communities all along the Rhine and the Moselle whose members engaged in agriculture and worked vineyards. In the sixth century there were synagogues in Paris and Orleans.

Until the tenth century, Jews and non-Jews generally lived as friendly neighbors, and German Jewish communities such as Mainz took pride in their talmudic academies, which attracted students from as far away as Italy and Spain. One of these students was the French scholar Rabbeinu Gershon Meor HaGolah (the "Light of the Exile"). He introduced a method of learning that became the pattern for the major Ashkenazi yeshivot, and his enactments strengthened the communal and family life of Ashkenazi Jewry. Then in 1012 the Jews of Mainz were given the choice either to convert or to be expelled. In the year 1040, in the town of Troyes, southeast of Paris, the greatest of all commentators was born—Rabbi Shelomoh Yitzchaki, better known as Rashi. That era also gave us the Tosafists, scholars whose penetrating analysis of the talmudic text is truly breathtaking.

During the first crusade in 1096, Jewish communities along the Rhine were pillaged by the crusaders' peasant mobs, and tens of thousands of Jews were murdered when they refused to accept baptism. The years following the crusades were marred by continual blood libels, both in France and Germany. Jews were fiendishly accused of using Christian blood in their matzohs and of desecrating the wafer used in the Catholic mass. Expulsions and persecutions were the order of the day, and in 1242 twenty-four wagonloads of handwritten copies of the Talmud were burned in Paris. The last of the Tosafists was Rabbi **Meir of Rothenburg (Maharam)** (1215?–1293), leader and teacher of all German Jewry; he wrote numerous responsa, and he died in prison while being held for ransom.

The history of the Jews of Germany during the Middle Ages is a sorrowful lament of expulsions and massacres culminating in the Rindfleisch massacres in 1298; at this time some 150 Jewish communities were annihilated in Bavaria, and as many as 100,000 Jews were killed at the hands of a rabble led by a knight named Rindfleisch. Fifty years later German Jewry was decimated again when in 1348–1351 Europe was ravaged by the Black Death (bubonic plague), and Jews were maliciously accused of poisoning the wells. In the ensuing massacres and expulsions, over 300 communities were destroyed and many Jews migrated to Poland and Lithuania.

These were newly settled lands, and the local kings encouraged Jews to come to their countries. During the fifteenth century Jews sought a haven in Poland in ever-growing numbers because of the persistent persecutions in Germany, and the numerous expulsions. The emigrants took their scholars and also their language, Yiddish, a blend of Old German and Hebrew, planting the seeds of a revival of Torah study that was to reach unprecedented heights.

During the sixteenth century the Jews remaining in Germany were confined to ghettos and were required to wear special hats and "Jew" badges, but they found solace in their studies of Torah and Talmud and felt superior to their oppressors. In the seventeenth century, Western Europe produced such Torah giants as Rabbi **Yair Chaim Bachrach (Chavat Yair)**, Rabbi **Tzvi Ashkenazi (Chacham Tzvi)**, Rabbi **Yechezkel Katzenellenbogen (Kenesset Yechezkel)**, Rabbi Menashe ben Israel, and Rabbi **Yaakov Sasportas**. This was also the century that witnessed the rise and fall of Shabbetai Tzevi, the false messiah who appeared on the scene in 1665; and the deep disillusionment and confusion that followed in the aftermath of his conversion to Islam in 1666, culminating in the bitter controversy between Rabbi **Yaakov Emden** and Rabbi Yonatan Eibschutz. Rabbi Yaakov Emden suspected Rabbi Yonatan Eibschutz of writing kabbalistic amulets containing references to Shabbetai Tzevi, and although the charge was proven to be unfounded, the ensuing controversy caused a deep rift in the Jewish community.

The eighteenth and nineteenth centuries brought Enlightenment and emancipation to German Jewry, and with it came the advent of the Reform movement, which threatened to engulf traditional Torah-observant Jewry. However, under the inspired leadership of Rabbi Samson Raphael Hirsch, the rising tide of Reform was stemmed. But in addition, many German Jews saw themselves as Germans first, identifying themselves as *deutsche Staatsbürger jüdischen Glaubens*, "German citizens of the Jewish faith." Seeking total integration, they considered mixed marriage and/or conversion a passport into German society. For two centuries German anti-Semitism, hidden under a veneer of "Kultur," was seething beneath the surface, until it erupted in wild fury in the final orgy of the Holocaust, destroying most of European Jewry.

POLAND, LITHUANIA, AND AUSTRIA

Ashkenazi Jews migrated from Western Europe to Poland and Lithuania as early as the eleventh century, but they came in masses only after the era of the Black Death, in the fourteenth and fifteenth centuries. By 1648 their number in this region had grown to about 300,000. The territory of Poland reached from the Baltic Sea in the north down to the Dniestr River in the south and included Lithuania and much of what is now the Ukraine. The rulers welcomed the newcomers, using them as tax collectors and land administrators. Jews prospered. They were in the lumber business, and they bred livestock, planted crops, and owned taverns, flour mills, and distilleries. The Jewish communities, which had a great deal of autonomy, were governed by their rabbis, foremost among whom were Rabbi **Shelomoh Luria (Maharshal)**, Rabbi Moshe Isserles (Rema), **Maharam Lublin**, and Rabbi **Yoel Sirkes (Bach)**. One of the most illustrious figures of that age was Rabbi Yehudah Loew of Prague (Maharal), who lived from 1526 to 1609.

The peaceful existence of the Jews in Poland came to an abrupt end in 1648 with the uprising of the Ukrainian peasants under Bogdan Chmielnitzki—the so-called Cossack Revolt. The Cossack hordes savagely destroyed 300 Jewish communities and massacred between 100,000 and 300,000 Jews. An epoch of Jewish growth and grandeur had come to a cruel end. The Cossack uprising and the ensuing death of one fourth of the Jewish population, coupled with the disillusionment coming on the heels of the apostasy of Shabbetai Tzevi, initiated a decline of Polish Jewry that lasted into the eighteenth century.

Judaism then experienced a remarkable revival with the rise of Chasidism, a movement of religious ecstasy expressed in joyful prayer and devotion to Torah and mitzvot. Its founder, Rabbi Yisrael Baal Shem Tov, was severely criticized by Rabbi Eliyah of Vilna, the Vilna Gaon. Nevertheless, under the Baal Shem's successors the movement swept through most of Poland, Volhynia, Podolia, and Galicia. In the nineteenth century, Lithuanian Jewry was buttressed by the advent of the *mussar* (ethics) movement founded by Rabbi Yisrael Salanter, and by the growth of the Lithuanian yeshivot. Great halachists living during that period were Rabbi **Akiva Eiger**, Rabbi **Naftali Tzvi Yehudah Berlin (the Netziv)**, and Rabbi **Yitzchak Elchanan Spector (Ein Yitzchak)**. Austria and Hungary also became flourishing centers of Torah study during the nineteenth century under the leadership of illustrious scholars such as Rabbi **Moshe Sofer (Chatam Sofer)**, **Maharam Schick**, and Rabbi **Yosef Shaul Nathanson (Shoel uMeishiv)**. The nineteenth and twentieth centuries saw the growth of the Reform and *Haskalah* ("Enlightenment") movements, which were vigorously opposed by all the leading rabbis, and many responsa from that time reflect the fierce struggle that was waged against these movements.

The death of six million Jews in the Nazi Holocaust wiped out virtually all of European Jewry. With indomitable faith and courage, a few surviving *rashei yeshivah* (deans of Torah academies) began to rebuild new Torah centers in Eretz Yisrael and the United States. Their yeshivot and institutions have risen from the ashes, testifying to the everlasting bond linking God, Yisrael, and the Torah.

I

THE RESPONSA OF THE GEONIM: 589–1038

The sealing of the Babylonian Talmud by Rav Ashi (321–427 C.E.), marking the close of the Talmudic period, was followed by the Era of the Geonim, the rabbis who headed the Torah academies in Sura and Pumbedita. It lasted from the end of the sixth to the middle of the eleventh century. The title *gaon* (plural *geonim*), meaning excellence, is probably derived from the phrase *geon Yaakov* ("the majesty of Jacob" [Psalm 47:5]). During the life span of the two yeshivot, tens of thousands of scholars were led by the fifty-two Geonim of Pumbedita and the forty-two Geonim of Sura, men of indisputable greatness; these geonim guided Jewry in Babylonia and the Diaspora through the stormy years of the end of Persian rule and the rise of Islam, preserving the integrity of the Law in its pristine purity. Thanks to them, the Talmud became the authoritative criterion of Jewish daily existence. Thousands of halachic responsa by the Geonim have been discovered, replies to inquiries from as far away as Spain.

These responsa (*teshuvot*) deal with all phases of Jewish life. They offer guidance in matters of religious practice and they clarify talmudic passages that the questioner did not fully understand. They settle disputes on legal and financial affairs and give advice on domestic problems. The replies of the Geonim, which were often discussed at a *kallah*—a biannual conference of scholars—form an important part of Torah literature.

The Geonic period began with R. Chanan of Ashkana (589 C.E.), soon after the end of the Persian rule of Babylonia, and it ended in 1038 C.E. with the death of Rav **Hai Gaon**. Other famous Geonim were R. **Netronai** (Sura, from 853 to 858); R. **Amram Gaon** (Sura, from 858 to 876), who was the compiler of the first prayerbook (*siddur*); and R. **Bustenai** (Pumbedita, 660–689), who, in response to a question, created the first talmudic dictionary. R. Nachshon bar Mar R. Tzadok brought brilliant new insights into the calculation of the Jewish calendar (Sura, 876–884). Rav **Sherira Gaon** (Pumbedita, 968–1003) is the author of the famous *Iggeret Rav Sherira Gaon*; his son was Rav **Hai Gaon** (Pumbedita, 1003–1038). Rav Saadya Gaon (Sura, 928–942) was the author of the seminal philosophic work *Emunot Vedei'ot*. Rav Sheshna, many of whose responsa have been published, was the fourth Gaon of Sura, and headed that yeshivah from about 660 to 670. By that time Babylonia had been conquered by the Moslems, and the Geonim were recognized as the supreme authorities of world Jewry.

Very little is known of the personal history of the hundred or so Geonim whose teshuvot afford us an insight into Jewish life during the 450 years of the

Geonic period. Without exception they were illustrious scholars. According to Rabbi Shlomoh HaMeiri, who lived in Perpignan, France from 1249–1306:

> They were not accustomed to stir from the tent [of Torah] day and night, and they knew the entire Talmud by heart (or nearly all of it), and the words of the entire Torah, and of the Talmud, were as ready on their tongues as the Shema. And for this reason they did not consider it necessary to elaborate at length in their writings; since the entire explanation [of the Talmud] was so familiar to them; and in their eyes, to write out the explanation of the laws [of the Talmud] would be like one who in our days simply translated the words.... [*History of the Jewish People*, Mesorah Press, Brooklyn, N.Y.]

They were treated with enormous respect by the Jewish community, and their responsa were frequently referred to in its daily life. The responsa often ended with "... and this is the way it must be done, and it cannot be altered." *Teshuvot HaGeonim* is the title of their compiled responsa; the nine responsa that follow are a typical sample and will serve to illustrate how the Geonim have played an essential role in the decision-making process of Halachah throughout Jewish history and into the present time.

The Geonic period came to a climactic end in the person of Rav **Hai Gaon**, who was among the most brilliant scholars and most prolific writers that golden age of Torah scholarship produced. After succeeding his father as Gaon of Pumbedita, he attracted, by his leadership and erudition, thousands of students from all over the world to his yeshivah. He received halachic questions from all the great rabbis of his time, such as Rabbi Shemuel HaNagid of Egypt and Rabbi Yaakov of Kairouan. He wrote more responsa than any of the preceding Geonim—a total of many thousands—and answered each questioner in the language in which the she'eilah was phrased: Hebrew, Aramaic, or Arabic. When he died in 1038 he had reached the venerable age of close to 100 years. His writings were among those that made the most lasting impact upon the decisions of the Rishonim and Acharonim, the halachic authorities who led the subsequent generations.

RAV POLTOI GAON
רב פולטוי גאון

born: Babylonia, date uncertain
died: Babylonia, date uncertain
Gaon of Pumbedita, 842–858.[1]

Rav Poltoi Gaon wrote a great number of teshuvot, many of which have been preserved. When he received a request from the Jews of Spain for a copy of the Talmud, he sent that community a complete set of all the tractates along with a commentary that had been written under his guidance.

Doing Business on the Intermediate Days of a Festival
***Teshuvot HaGeonim*, no. 149**

Question: *Ashkenazi Jews*[2] *regularly call on us Babylonian Jews with their wares, during the summer and sometimes in the rainy season. They buy our garments and tell us that they are worthless. But when they hear that another caravan is approaching they quickly buy everything in sight and sell everything they brought with them.*[3] *On* Chol HaMoed *(the intermediate days of Passover and Sukkot) non-Jews come to trade with them. Are we allowed to buy from them on* Chol HaMoed? *And the women who made clothes to sell, are they allowed to sell to them on* Chol HaMoed?

Responsum: Our sages permitted us to perform work on *Chol HaMoed* in order to prevent a loss. Here we have a case of loss of business, and the Gemara in Moed Katan 10b says, "Any business activity, the nonperformance of which would entail a loss, is permitted on *Chol HaMoed*."

Annual Fair Dedicated to an Idol
***Teshuvot HaGeonim*, no. 104**

Question: *In a town there is an annual fair dedicated to a cerain deity, and it is called the "fair of* [*that idol*].*" May a Jew conduct business at this fair or not?*

Responsum: If the admission fee is given to that idol worship, it is forbidden to do business there. Regardless of whether they are dealers or private citizens, all are forbidden to enter. But a traveler who is passing through town is permitted to attend the fair. If it is called the "fair of the idol" but the admission fee does not go to a pagan establishment, everyone may attend. Thus we have learned in *Avodah Zarah* 12b, "If there is an idol in town and some stores are decorated in its honor whereas others are not, then the decorated ones may not be entered but the undecorated ones may be visited."

RAV NETRONAI GAON
רב נטרונאי גאון

born: Babylonia, date uncertain
died: Babylonia, date uncertain
Gaon of Sura, 853–858.[1]

Rav Netronai Gaon wrote more responsa than did any of the geonim who preceded him. Most of his teshuvot were directed to Spanish Jewry, with whose living conditions and customs he was thoroughly familiar. In contrast with the teshuvot of earlier Geonim, which generally clarified complex talmudic texts, Rav Netronai's responsa dealt with problems relating to prayer, the reading of the Torah, customs of mourning, and the like. During his rule, many Karaites (a heretical sect) had become disillusioned and wanted to return to Judaism. Rav Netronai Gaon advocated that they be accepted—after first being chided for their past misdeeds, and after promising not to revert to their former ways.

A Religious Divorce by an Apostate?
Teshuvot HaGeonim, no. 5

Question: *If a Jew has converted to another religion, can he give a halachically valid divorce to his wife?*

Responsum: It seems to me that he can divorce his wife, (give her a *get*). Since he married her lawfully, he can dissolve the marriage by means of a religious divorce. Furthermore [if we would not empower him to divorce her], what remedy is there for this unfortunate Jewish woman? She would forever be forbidden to remarry. We find that the sages were lenient when dealing with an *agunah*. They certainly would be tolerant in this case, where no other remedy exists.

An Apostate's Right of Inheritance
Teshuvot HaGeonim, no. 4:3

Question: *Halachah rules that an apostate (meshumad) does not inherit from his father. Why is this so?*

Responsum: When he defected from the Jewish faith, he turned his back on the sanctity of Yisrael and on the sanctity of his father–son relationship. An inheritance passes on only to a son of the Jewish people, to one who has a filial relationship with his father, as it is written: "To you and your offspring I will give the land where you are now living as a foreigner."[2] The phrase "to you and your offspring" implies that one's offspring is related to him; this excludes an apostate, who has broken relations with his father. . . . Thus, if a Jew lent money to another Jew and the latter became an apostate and subsequently died, then the Jew cannot collect the debt from money the apostate's father left his son, because an apostate has no right of inheritance to his father's estate.

RAV AMRAM GAON
רב עמרם גאון

born: Babylonia, date uncertain
died: Babylonia, date uncertain
Gaon of Sura, 858-876.[1]

Rav Amram Gaon was a student of Rav Netronai, and became his successor as the Gaon of Sura. He is best remembered for a very long responsum that he wrote. It contains the complete text of the *siddur* (prayerbook), and it is known as the *Seder* ("Order") *Rav Amram Gaon*.

With the dispersal of the Jewish people throughout North Africa and Spain, many different versions of the basic prayers had evolved. The prayers had been formulated by the Men of the Great Assembly, but since the text was transmitted orally, slight changes had crept in. Rabbi Yitzchak ben Shimon, a leader of Spanish Jewry, asked Rav Amram Gaon for the authoritative text. His responsum was the first written prayerbook, and forms the basis of the *siddur* that is currently in use in all communities.

False Messiah
Teshuvot HaGeonim, no. 261

Question: *Concerning the false messiah called Sharini, who declared himself to be the Mashiach, many people were duped by him and turned to heresy. They do not pray or observe the laws of kashrut, they work on Yomtov, and they do not write ketuvot phrased according to the rabbinical formulation. When these people return to traditional Judaism, do they require tevilah (immersion in a mikveh) or not? Some say they should not be admitted into the Jewish community because they do not adhere to the laws of marriage and divorce. Besides, this charlatan [Sharini] sanctioned adulterous unions, and if we accept them [his followers] they will intermarry with observant Jews. Do we have to be concerned?*

Responsum: These sinners, although they went wrong and denied the authority of the rabbis, rejected the festivals and the mitzvot, and defiled themselves by eating nonkosher meat—still it is better to befriend them than to shut them out. Bet Din should impose a penalty on them for their past sins; they should pledge in the synagogue not to return to their former ways. Then you should accept them and not rebuff them. They are Jews who have strayed. We must investigate whether they practiced adultery, and anyone living in an adulterous relationship must separate. Their *ketuvot* should be examined, and any *ketuvah* that is not written in accordance with your custom must be rewritten.

RAV NACHMAN GAON
רב נחמן גאון

No biographical data available.

Captive Jewish Women
***Teshuvot Geonei Mizrach uMaarav*, no. 47**[1]

The following responsum is quoted in *Teshuvot HaRosh* 32:5. The **Rosh** (Rabbi Asher ben Yechiel) attributed this responsum to Rav **Poltoi Gaon**, and (despite the fact that the words of these early sages were rarely—if ever—disputed by the later ones) the Rosh disagreed with this decision.

Question: *A general conquered a city and took many non-Jewish and Jewish women captive, among whom were wives of kohanim. The non-Jewish women, casually, in aimless, unpremeditated conversation,[2] mentioned that the general had not come near them. After the Jewish women were ransomed, the general swore by* Altallah *(possibly the holy stone* Kaaba *in Mecca)*[3] *that he had not touched them, and that in whatever he did he was only following the king's orders. He claims to speak the truth. [Are the wives of the kohanim permitted to return to their husbands?]*

Responsum: I tend to agree with this, because the non-Jewish women who were in captivity with the Jewish women and who said that the general had not touched any of them, made this statement during innocent, idle, purposeless conversation. In cases of captive women our sages take a lenient view.

RAV SHERIRA GAON
רב שרירא גאון

born: Babylonia, date uncertain
died: Babylonia, date uncertain
Gaon of Pumbedita, 968–1003; Father of Rav Hai Gaon.

Creating Fire from Water
***Teshuvot Geonei Mizrach uMaarav*, no. 145**

Question: *We are puzzled about the mishnah in* Beitzah *33a that states, "You may not produce fire from wood or stones, nor from sand or water [on Yomtov]. Stones and wood are commonly used to produce fire, but how do you create fire from water or from sand? Please enlighten us.*

Responsum: We frequently see people fill a clear glass with water and place it in the blazing sun. When the glass is very hot they touch it with a piece of cotton which catches on fire.[1] As for sand, there are several ways of producing fire. Some people take cow or sheep dung which they deposit in the sand so that its warmth does not dissipate. When it decomposes and becomes very hot it bursts into flame. Or, they take sand from a stone, which in Aramaic is called *nahurta* and in Arabic *nura* (calcium). They burn this substance and don't extinguish it. They then hide it away for several months. When they want to produce fire they run water over it, and when it ignites they use sulphur to transfer the flame.

The History and Development of the Oral Law

The following selection consists of brief excerpts from a book-length responsum by Rav Sherira

Page from a thirteenth- or fourteenth-century manuscript of *Iggeret of Rav Sherira Gaon.*

Gaon to a question posed by Rav Yaakov ben Nissim on behalf of the community of Kairouan, Tunisia. It was written one thousand years ago, in 987 C.E., and is called *The Iggeret (Letter) of Rav Sherira Gaon.*

The questioners wanted a clear understanding of how the Oral Torah had developed, from the beginning until their time. They needed this information to refute the claims of the Karaite sect, who denied the authority of the Talmud and its teachers, the Geonim. The *Iggeret* is an excellent guide to the serious study of Jewish history and offers a deeper insight into the transmission process of the Oral Law. An outstanding English annotated translation, written and published by Rabbi Nosson Dovid Rabinowitch,[2] is available.

Question: *The rabbis of Kairouan [Tunisia] have addressed a question to the yeshivah of our master and teacher Sherira.... They have asked: How was the Mishnah written?... Similarly: In what manner was the Talmud composed?... What is the chronological order of the Savoraim, the sages who lived after Ravina and the completion of the Talmud? Who was the controlling authority from that time to the present?*

Responsum [Rav Sherira's answer constitutes the contents of the *Iggeret*]: Rabbeinu HaKadosh (Rabbi Yehudah HaNasi, the Prince) arranged the six orders of the Mishnah just as they are now learned, law after law, and one cannot add or detract from them. As long as the *Bet HaMikdash* was standing, each one of the sages taught his students the explanations of Scripture, Mishnah, and Talmud.... The words of the Mishnah can be compared with the words of the Almighty to Moshe. Rebbe did not produce these words with his own mind; rather, they were the teachings of the early sages who preceded him....

Regarding your question about the Talmud: ... When the Mishnah was concluded and Rebbe died, the capacity for learning lessened, and they [the sages] had to collate their various Talmuds, to recite it [in a uniform version], and to add to it a number of other methods. They incorporated [the systems of exegeses of] those earlier sages in it, as we say [in the Talmud]: "From what is this derived?" and we answer by expounding verses....

Rava officiated for fourteen years, and he died in the year 352 C.E.[3] In all these years there was only one yeshivah, the one in Pumbedita [Babylonia]....

[The Geonic period:] There were years of persecution and suffering at the end of the Persian rule, and the rabbis could not deliver sermons, establish yeshivot, and carry on the normal duties of the Geonim.... After R. Mari Sorgo, R. Chanina officiated in Nahardea, and in his days Mohammed came forth into the world (613 C.E.) ... After him [ruled] R. Mari from Nehar Pakod, for eight years. And after him Mar Acha officiated for one half-year.... In the year 968 C.E., I was appointed to the Geonate. And about two years ago we appointed our son Hai[4] to the position of *Av Bet Din* [Chief Justice].... May Mashiach ben David come quickly in our lifetime, and in your lifetime, and in the lifetime of the whole house of Yisrael. May it be His will. Amen.

RAV HAI GAON
רב האי גאון

born: Babylonia, c. 938
died: Babylonia, 1038
Gaon of Pumbedita, 1003–1038; for further biographical data, see p. 2.

An Arrogant Kohen
Teshuvot HaGeonim, no. 132

Question: *Concerning a kohen who is a Torah scholar and has objectionable character traits. He regards himself as a wise man and has contempt for everyone. . . . He often publicly insults people, telling them what fools they are. He even curses his aged mother. He has a bad temper and would think nothing of killing a man. Most people know that he has these qualities, yet he pretends to be a virtuous man. He lectures people on the values of modesty and humility, on respecting the truth, and the like. Everyone says that he is a disgrace to God's name and that he is not qualified to be a kohen. We have found precedents in the writings of the rabbis where kohanim were disqualified. [Is this man unfit to officiate as a kohen?]*

Responsum: This is most certainly a case of desecration of God's name. A Torah scholar who does not act properly is discussed in the Mishnah,[1] where Rabbi Shimon interprets the verse "Do not take the name of God your Lord in vain"[2] to mean, "Don't wrap yourself in a tallit while you violate the Torah."

This kohen, by engaging in repulsive behavior, has tainted his holy calling and placed a blemish on himself.[3] He should not be first to be called to the Torah, nor should he bless the congregation, even if there is no other kohen present. He should be content to be considered a Yisrael.

Title page of *Teshuvot Hageonim*, Responsa of the Geonim. From the archives of the *Genizah*, a vast ancient storehouse in Cairo, where thousands of long-lost historic documents were discovered. Printed in Jerusalem, 1929.

II
THE RESPONSA OF THE RISHONIM: 1038–1492

Jewish history, which is inextricably linked with the development of Torah, took a decisive turn in 1038 with the death of Rav **Hai Gaon**, the last of the Geonim. The subsequent decline of the Babylonian yeshivot coincided with an astonishing blossoming of Torah in France, Germany, and Spain. The scholars of this period, which extended approximately from 1038 until 1492, are identified as the Rishonim, or early Torah sages, and include such giants as Rashi (Rabbi Shlomoh Yitzchaki), the Rif (Rabbi Yitzchak Alfasi), the **Rambam** (Rabbi Moshe ben Maimon, Maimonides), and the **Rosh** (Rabbi Asher ben Yechiel).

This was the era of the great codifiers, who sifted through the *yam haTalmud*, the ocean of the Talmud—extracting from the lengthy debates the various legal opinions, deciding in each case what the halachah should be, and arranging these halachot, according to subject matter, into numbered chapters and paragraphs. The responsa literature of this era reflects the eminence of the responders who respectfully quote the opinions of earlier authorities but do not hesitate to disagree with them occasionally and to render decisions based on their own analysis of the Talmudic and Geonic sources. The Rishonim were the instrument in the unseen hand of God for bringing about the transplantation of the Torah from Babylonia to the West, where it continued to grow despite the ravages of the Crusades and the expulsions and persecutions in England, Germany, and Bohemia. Through their works these sages guide our daily life to this very day.

RABBI MOSHE BEN MAIMON—RAMBAM (MAIMONIDES)
רבי משה בן מיימון — רמב"ם

born: Cordova, Spain, 1135
died: Cairo, Egypt, 1204
Popularly know as Rambam, the initials of his name.

Rambam received his early Torah education from his father, a noted scholar who traced his ancestry back to Rabbi Yehudah HaNasi, compiler of the Mishnah, and to King David. When he was 13 years old, Cordova was conquered by the invading Almohads, a fanatic Moslem sect. The family fled from the attackers, wandered about for twelve years, and finally settled in Fez, Morocco. In 1165 Rambam made his home in Cairo, where he found peace and religious freedom.

When he was 23, Rambam began writing his commentary on the Mishnah, *Peirush HaMishnayot*, in Arabic. This was later translated into Hebrew and was first printed in Naples in 1492. It is appended to the Vilna edition of the Talmud. The work analyzes each mishnah and provides an introduction clarifying the fundamental tenets of Judaism. Rambam's philosophical treatise in the introduction to tractate *Berachot* is known as *Shemonah Perakim*, "Eight Chapters." It deals with the diseases and cures of man's soul, prophecy, reward and punishment, free will, and the rule of the "golden mean." In his commentary on *Sanhedrin* 10:1, he enunciates the thirteen principles of the Jewish faith. In 1170 Rambam began to write his major work, *Mishneh Torah*, a fourteen-volume compendium of all laws extracted from the Talmud and the writings of the Geonim. Also called *Yad HaChazakah*, it was completed in 1180. It is written in a lucid and concise mishnaic Hebrew. In his *Sefer HaMitzvot*, written in Arabic, Rambam enumerates and explains the 613 precepts of the Torah. In 1185 he wrote a major

Rabbi Moshe ben Maimon (Maimonides), Rambam.

philosophical treatise, *Moreh Nevuchim*, "Guide of the Perplexed," which was translated from the Arabic by Shmuel ibn Tibbon. It is addressed to persons who were confused by the seeming contradictions between the teachings of the Torah and the then prevalent Aristotelian philosophy.

Rambam was the *nagid*, spiritual and political leader of the Jews of Egypt, but his influence as preeminent Torah scholar extended over the entire Jewish nation. Rabbis and simple folk presented their queries to him, and he responded to each according to the questioner's level of understanding. Scholars received detailed responsa, citing sources and precedents; others received a definitive reply of one or two lines. His responsa *Teshuvot HaRambam* were edited and published by Rabbi A. C. Freiman, Jerusalem, 1934.[1] In his responsa, Rambam's noble character traits come to the surface. More than any of his other works they express his glowing love for the Jewish people and the Torah. In his straightforward answers, this towering giant rises to even greater stature, and one truly comes to appreciate the inscription on his tombstone: "From Moshe (Moses) till Moshe (Rambam), no one arose like Moshe (Rambam)."

Destroying a Tree
Teshuvot HaRambam, no. 54

Question: *In the courtyard of a Jew there grows a date tree. It stands close to a wall that faces the street. Adjacent to the wall is a non-Jewish social hall. The date tree grows very rapidly and leans into the street. During the winter we have many fierce storms and we are afraid that the tree will be blown down, which would endanger the passersby. Additionally, when the dates are ripe, people throw stones into the tree to bring down the fruit. The ground is full of rocks and people are afraid to pass for fear of being struck by a rock. Are we permitted to remove this tree because it is a public hazard, or not?*

Responsum: You are *required* to uproot this tree, lest, God forbid, an accident happens because of it. You would be allowed to do it even if you merely needed the space it occupies. The Torah forbids only uprooting without any purpose, for that is wanton destruction. Purposeless destruction is what the Torah had in mind when it said, "You must not destroy its [a city's] trees."[2]

Title page of *Teshuvot HaRambam*, first published from the original Arabic text from fragments discovered in the *Genizah* in Cairo and from manuscripts. Translated into Hebrew. This edition printed in Jerusalem, 1986.

Dismissing a Cantor on the Basis of a Rumor
Teshuvot HaRambam, no. 85

Question: *A man is a well-known chazzan and a scholar. There is a rumor circulating that he committed a sin, which shall remain unmentioned. There are no witnesses, and the man is known to have enemies. Should he or shouldn't he be dismissed from his position? If witnesses bear out the rumor and he accepts the penalty that is imposed, must he be dismissed even though he accepted his punishment?*

Responsum: No appointee should be fired on the basis of a rumor, even if he has no enemies. But if he does have enemies in his town, then, even if witnesses confirm the rumor, he should not be dismissed if he accepts the penalty. For we do not demote a person from the rank of sanctity he holds, whether he is a member of the Great Sanhedrin or a chazzan in a synagogue, unless he publicly violated the law. The man who spread the rumor should be banned and flogged because of defamation of character.

Be respectful of the Torah, "for the mitzvah is a lamp and the Torah is light."[3]

A Dishonest Shochet
Teshuvot HaRambam, no. 112

Question: *Reuven is employed as a shochet (ritual slaughterer). It is common knowledge that he steals meat from the slaughterhouse and from the butcher stores. Witnesses have testified that he has contempt of the shechitah and is negligent in the examination of the slaughtered animals. Subsequently, he was caught in the act of stealing. Should a man like this be retained in public office?*

Responsum: Such behavior does not befit a person who represents the Torah of Moshe Rabbeinu. The sin of stealing and selling the stolen goods to the public is unforgivable, even if he would repent wholeheartedly of his sin, for there can be no greater desecration of God's name than that. Therefore, he may not continue to perform *shechitah* for the public. If he wishes to slaughter privately in someone's house, he may do so.

Title page of *Mishneh Torah*, also called *Yad HaChazakah*, Rambam's fourteen-volume compendium of all Torah laws. He wrote this, his major work, over a period of ten years.

Playing with Pebbles on Shabbat
Teshuvot HaRambam, no. 117

Question: *On Shabbat and on the festivals some people are in the habit of getting together to enjoy a game played with round pebbles. The winner gets a cup of wine to drink. Other people play with fruits, nuts, and almonds. Is this permitted on Shabbat and Yomtov?*

Responsum: Handling pebbles and stones is surely forbidden,[4] but playing with fruits or any other article that you are allowed to handle on Shabbat is permitted. Furthermore, the latter is not considered gambling.

A Ransomed Torah Scroll
Teshuvot HaRambam, no. 131

Question: *If someone bought, from the spoils taken by soldiers returning from battle, Torah scrolls or other holy books that came from a synagogue in another city, may he keep them or must he return them to the place from which they were taken? Can he collect the money he paid for these books? Must he return them specifically to this synagogue, or may he return them to any synagogue he chooses?*

Responsum: If these scrolls were confiscated on orders of the king, then he acquired title to them and the synagogue has no claim to them. We say this even about the vessels of the *Bet HaMikdash*: once they were captured, their sanctity was no more. But if the scrolls were taken without the king's permission, the buyer must swear how much he paid for them, and should be reimbursed for that amount. He should give the scrolls back to the place from which they were taken.

A Young Man Who Bought a Slave Girl
Teshuvot HaRambam, no. 132

Question: *Binyamin, an unmarried young man, bought a beautiful slave girl, and she lives in his house. His father's wife and her three daughters live in the same house. After three months the situation led to friction and quarreling. They denounced Binyamin to the judge, accusing him of having a non-Jewish slave girl in his house. The judge interrogated the girl, asking her about her nationality. She told him that she was Jewish and that she had been taken captive and brought there. The judge believed her and sent her back to Binyamin's house. Does the Bet Din have to remove her from this house because of yichud (the prohibition against a man being alone with a woman), even though he is not actually alone with her, since his father's wife and her three daughters are in the house?*

Responsum: Most certainly, he must send her away. It is the Torah's intent to curb our natural instincts. The Bet Din must do its utmost to expel this slave girl. Otherwise, he should set her free and marry her. May God in heaven forgive our sins, as He has said, "I will take away all your alloy."[5]

Brit Milah on a Fast Day
Teshuvot HaRambam, no. 63

Question: *If a circumcision occurs on Yom Kippur or Tisha Be'Av, are we permitted to recite the berachah (blessing) of the brit milah over wine; and since these are fast days, may we give the wine to a child to drink? Must we be concerned that when the child grows up he will continue to drink wine on Yom Kippur? Or should we recite the berachah, omitting the wine altogether?*

Responsum: The *berachah* of *koret brit*—the blessing said on the *brit milah*—does not require the drinking of wine. If you said the *berachah* over wine and gave the wine to a child, the *berachah* was said in vain, because you yourself did not consume the wine, and neither did anyone else who understands the meaning of the *berachah*, and neither is drinking the wine of any educational benefit to the child. Therefore, on these or any other fast days no wine should be used in the *brit milah* ceremony.

RABBI MEIR OF ROTHENBURG—MAHARAM
רבי מאיר מרוטנבורג — מהר"ם

born: Worms, Germany, 1215?
died: Ensisheim, Alsace, 1293
Popularly known as Maharam meRothenburg; the word Maharam is the acronym formed of the initials of Moreinu Harav Rabbi Meir

Maharam meRothenburg was one of the last Tosafists (authors of Tosafot, commentary to the Talmud). After studying under his father, Rabbi Baruch, rabbi of Worms, he traveled to France to study at the yeshivot of the French Tosafists, Rabbi Yechiel of Paris, Rabbi Shemuel of Falaise, and Rabbi Shemuel of Evreux. Returning to Germany as a rising star on the talmudic firmament, he served as rabbi of Rothenburg, where he established a yeshivah that attracted the most talented students. Maharam became the recognized leader of German Jewry, and thousands of queries on all phases of Jewish life were addressed to him. His straightforward, crystal-clear decisions were followed implicitly.[1] He presents his rulings without lengthy discourses on the underlying talmudic reasoning. Various parts of his numerous responsa have been published at different times.

In his later years conditions of the Jews in Germany worsened steadily. Harsh decreees, taxes, and persecutions made life unbearable. Maharam decided to leave Germany to seek a new home. En route he was taken captive and imprisoned in Ensisheim, Alsace. Emperor Rudolph I demanded a huge sum as ransom. Maharam, in keeping with the mishnaic dictum "We do not ransom prisoners for more than their worth,"[2] did not permit the Jewish community to pay ransom, since doing so would expose all Torah sages to abduction. His self-sacrifice serves as the model for a policy toward abductors and terrorists that is maintained in Israel today. While in prison, Maharam continued to study, teach, and respond to all questions. He died in

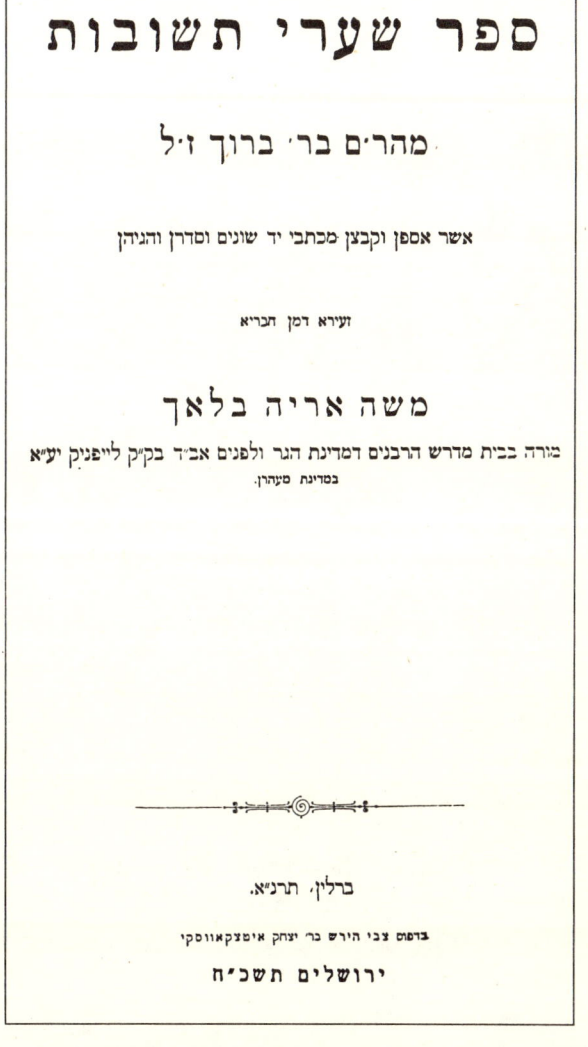

Title page of *Shaarei Teshuvot*, responsa by Rabbi Meir of Rothenburg (Maharam); published from unedited manuscripts, Berlin 1891 edition.

prison seven years later, but the authorities did not release his remains for burial. Fourteen years later, Rabbi Alexander Wimpen gave most of his vast fortune to bring Maharam's remains to a Jewish burial. As a reward he asked only to be buried next to the great rabbi. His request was granted.

Maharam wrote extensively on talmudic and halachic themes. He is the composer of the famous elegy *Shaali Serufah baEish* on the burning of the Talmud in Paris in 1242, which is recited on Tisha beAv, the Fast of the Ninth of Av.[3]

Two Captives
She'eilot uTeshuvot Maharam meRothenburg, no. 39

Question: *Reuven and Shimon were held captive by bandits. Reuven was a rich man, Shimon was poor. Through his mother, Reuven arranged to pay ransom to the bandits for the release of both of them. Now that they are free, Reuven wants to collect from Shimon his share of the ransom, stating that this sum was paid at Shimon's express desire. Shimon denies it, stating that he didn't say anything to that effect. What is the law?*

Responsum: The Gemara in Sanhedrin 73a states: "If you see a man drowning, it is your duty to save his life. Even if he says, 'Don't save me,' you must save him, and you may ask him to pay for any expenses you incurred in saving his life."

It is evident that Shimon must pay his share of the ransom. You cannot argue that the bandits would have set him free eventually without being paid a ransom. It is a known fact that no one captured by bandits ever escapes unscathed.[4]

Preface to Maharam's Responsum no. 250
She'eilot uTeshuvot Maharam meRothenburg

[This very personal note affords us a rare glimpse into Maharam's inner feelings while in prison. Not having any books to consult, he had to rely on his phenomenal memory in answering the queries from his cell.]

My spirit is gone, my strength has withered away, the light of my eyes fails me because of the oppressors who torment me exceedingly. . . . I have no access to any books to enlighten me and to give me understanding. May God avenge His people, and may He put an end to our suffering.

Preventing Someone from Leaving Town
She'eilot uTeshuvot Maharam meRothenburg, no. 1016

Question: *In a town where there are only ten Jews [a quorum of ten men, called a* minyan, *is required for prayer services] and one wants to leave the synagogue, can the others force him to stay?*

Responsum: It seems to me that if they have no *minyan* without him, the others can force him either to stay or to hire someone to take his place. *Tosefta Bava Metzia* 11:12 states that the people of a community have the right to compel one another to pay for building a synagogue or buying a Torah scroll. This is clear evidence that we may use coercion in order to satisfy the needs of the community. It is the universal custom to hire people when a community is short one or two men to complete the *minyan* on *Yamim Nora'im*, the High Holy Days.

This case is analogous to *Tosefta Bava Metzia* 11:13, which states if there is only one bathhouse keeper, barber, or baker in a community, and before Yomtov he wants to go home, then we can keep him from doing so until he appoints a substitute. Furthermore, **Rabbeinu Nissim (Ran)** cites a source in *Yerushalmi* (the Jerusalem Talmud) to the effect that those who leave must hire substitutes and are required to pay their share of the chazzan's salary.

Mourning for an Apostate?
She'eilot uTeshuvot Maharam meRothenburg, no. 544

Question: *Must the laws of mourning be observed for the death of an apostate?*

Responsum: It is written in *Sefer haGeonim*, "If a *meshumad* (an apostate, a person who defected from the Jewish faith) dies, the family need not observe the rites of mourning for him. Proof of this can be found in Sanhedrin 47a, which relates that relatives of people who were executed by the Bet Din did not mourn for them. Now, if they refrained from mourning even though the executed person's sin is forgiven by virtue of his death, then certainly no mourning period should be observed for a *meshumad* whose misdeed is never expiated. For it is said that even when all the fires of *Gehinnom* are doused, those burning for a *meshumad* are never doused. And to him the verse applies,[5] "And they shall go forth and look upon the carcasses of the men that have rebelled against Me; for their worm shall not die, neither shall their fire be quenched; and they shall be an abhorrence to all flesh."

Although Rabbeinu Gershom[6] mourned his son for two weeks, this is not the halachah. He did so out of his intensely bitter grief.

Book Destroyed by Fire
She'eilot uTeshuvot Maharam MeRothenburg, no. 140

Question: *Reuven borrowed a book from Shimon for exactly one hour. He told him, "Either I will return it to you or you come and pick it up." In the meantime a fire broke out in Reuven's house, and the book was destroyed. Reuven was forced to run away as soon as the fire started, for the gentiles are in the habit of throwing into the fire any Jew in whose house a fire breaks out. Must Reuven pay damages?*

Responsum: At first glance it would seem that Reuven is exempt from making restitution. He borrowed the book for one hour. The hour had passed when the fire broke out. Reuven was unable to return the book because he had to flee for his life lest he get thrown into the fire by the gentiles. Shimon did not come to pick up the book. Consequently, according to the Gemara in *Bava Metzia* 72a, it would seem that Reuven is exempt.

However, we must consider this: Granted that Reuven himself could not have gone into the house to save the book, for fear of the gentiles who throw into the fire the Jew in whose house a fire breaks out. But he could have hired other gentiles or Jews to save the book. Since he did not do this, he is responsible and must make restitution.

Was it Lead or Silver?
She'eilot Maharam MeRothenburg, no. 721

Question: *A Jew bought from a non-Jew two thalers worth of lead. Thereupon he sold the lead to another Jew for four thalers. After a while it was found that the lead was in fact silver. Now the Jew claims that he was cheated [by selling it too cheaply] and he wants to rescind the sale.*

Responsum: The seller cannot nullify the deal. We say to him, "Just as you bought it, so did you sell it." He bought it as lead, and he sold it as lead. His claim of being cheated has no validity.

RABBI SHELOMOH IBN ADERET—RASHBA
רבי שלמה אבן אדרת — רשב"א

born: Barcelona, Spain, 1235
died: Barcelona, Spain, 1310
Popularly know as Rashba, the title of his work and initials of his name.

Rashba, the undisputed Torah authority of his age, studied under the famous luminaries Rabbeinu Yonah Gerondi[1] and Ramban.[2] For more than forty years he served as rabbi of Barcelona, a city that had been an important center of Torah study since the ninth century. The vastness and depth of his Talmudic knowledge, coupled with a character of fearless rectitude, gained him the respect of all of the world's Jewish communities. He received queries from Germany, France, Bohemia, Sicily, Morocco, Algiers, Eretz Yisrael, Portugal, and, of course, Spain. Most of his responsa are brief and straightforward. The majority of them deal with everyday halachic problems, but in a number of them he expounds on philosophical themes. Rashba defended the **Rambam**'s[3] *Moreh Nevuchim*, "Guide of the Perplexed," but he opposed the trend toward allegorical interpretation of the Torah that was prevalent in Southern France and Spain. He headed a prominent yeshivah that drew students from many countries and from as far away as Germany. Best known among his disciples are Rabbeinu Bachya,[4] the Torah commentator, and the **Ritva**,[5] renowned for his commentary on the Talmud.

More than three thousand of his responsa have been published under the title *She'eilot uTeshuvot HaRashba*, in seven volumes.[6] His masterful commentary on fifteen tractates of the Talmud represents a synthesis of the analytical approach of the French Tosafists and the early Spanish Talmudists. To date it has seen ten editions.[7]

Title page of *Teshuvot Rashba*, responsa by Rabbi Shelomoh ibn Aderet (Warsaw 1884).

The Converted Slave
Teshuvot Rashba, no. 1:99

Question: *Reuven had an Arab slave. Shimon either persuaded or forced this slave to come with him to a Bet Din of three rabbis, who converted him to Judaism. Reuven demands from Shimon restitution for the loss of his slave. Please let us know whether Shimon must compensate Reuven and whether the slave did indeed gain his freedom, since his conversion was performed against his master's wish.*

Responsum: If the slave was converted against his own free will, he is no convert at all, if he is an adult. He does not become a convert unless he is told about the mitzvot and he freely accepts them. If Shimon persuaded him and he agreed to convert, then Shimon is not liable for anything, for he caused the master no loss. The slave converted voluntarily, and advising someone to convert is not punishable. As a matter of fact, halachically, dispensing counsel in any area of concern is not punishable by law, even if the counsel generates damage to someone.

Sprouted Wheat Kernels
Teshuvot Rashba, no. 1:120

Question: *We have had much rain during the past year. The rain has fallen on the heaps of wheat in the fields, and a few of the ears of grain have sprouted. Should we be concerned that the wheat of this harvest has become* chametz,[8] *or can we say that the rain has not penetrated the heap because it is stacked high like a wall? Or must we be apprehensive that the sprouted kernels will start a chain reaction among the other kernels, rendering them all* chametz?

Responsum: Common sense dictates that you should not be concerned about the wheat of that particular year. For if you would be concerned, you would never be able to eat matzah on Pesach, since there is never a year that it does not rain on the heaps of wheat in the fields. The Torah rules that we always follow the majority, and most of the harvest does not become *chametz*. And even if you saw rain fall on a given heap, we still are lenient because it is doubtful that the water penetrated the body of the heap; and even if you say that the water did penetrate, it is doubtful that it caused the kernels to become leavened.

Now this chain reaction that you spoke about, I have no knowledge of it. Even if you placed a piece of real *chametz* or sour dough in a heap of wheat, would it trigger the leavening process if you do not add water? To think that a kernel of wheat can start a chain reaction is simply absurd.... I think the matter is subject to doubt, and therefore it is permissible.

Disputation with a Christian Scholar
Teshuvot Rashba, no. 4:187

Question: *A non-Jewish scholar spoke to your congregation on matters of religion, and you want to know how to refute his arguments.*

Responsum: I will relate to you briefly the answers I gave to a Christian scholar regarding these issues.

My disputant asserted that the Messiah had come already. He cited as proof the blessing Jacob gave to his sons, telling them "what will happen at the end of days."[9] Speaking to his son Judah, Jacob said, "The scepter will not depart from Judah, ... until Shiloh will come."[10] And Shiloh refers to the Messiah, as *Targum Onkelos* translates it. Now, Jacob prophesied that the scepter of kingship will not depart from Judah until Shiloh's coming. Well, the Jews do not have a kingdom any longer. Consequently, the Messiah must have appeared.

I replied, ... the true meaning of the verse is as follows: "The scepter will not depart from Judah forever, since in the end Shiloh will come, and he will be a descendant of Judah." God promised Israel that the kingship over the nation is the inherited right of the tribe of Judah. And if there will be an interruption, it will not be permanent, for ultimately Shiloh, meaning the Messiah, will come, who will be of the lineage of Judah.

Then my disputant tried a different approach. He said that Scripture proves that after the destruction of the second Temple there will not arise a third Temple. For it is written, "The glory of this last house shall be greater than that of the first."[11] The prophet calls the second Temple "the last"; thus, there will not be another.

I replied: He calls it *acharon*, "the last," only relative to the first Temple [in the sense of "the latter"]. . . . God Himself uses the word *acharon* in this sense, speaking to Moses: "And if they do not believe you, and they do not pay attention to the first miraculous sign, then they will believe the evidence of the 'last' sign. And if they also do not believe these two signs . . . the water that you will take from the Nile will turn to blood."[12] God calls the second sign *acharon*, "the last," yet it is followed immediately by another sign, the sign of blood.[13] Clearly, in this context, *acharon* means "the latter."

A Wife Who Wants to Take Fertility Drug
Teshuvot Rashba, no. 4:122

Question: *A woman made a vow to take a medicine that will enable her to conceive. Her husband is against it. Does the husband have the right to annul her vow? The questioner thinks that the woman's vow can be characterized as a vow of "self-affliction" and as such it can be broken by the husband. You argue that every medication, however beneficial, has harmful side effects and by taking it she hurts herself. Furthermore, the husband fears that pregnancy will impair her beauty.*

Responsum: It seems to me that this husband has no right whatsoever to cancel her vow. Your argument of self-inflicted pain because every drug has harmful side effects does not hold water. If you were right, you should never eat bread or fruit because everyone knows that eating too much of it can be very hazardous to your health. If he is afraid that she may lose her beauty; . . . she only married him in order to bear children. Let him not be like Er, who did not want Tamar to become pregnant because he feared that it would spoil her beauty.[14] Let him raise a family, for "The heritage of God is children; the fruit of the womb is a reward."[15]

The Weak-Willed Gambler
Teshuvot Rashba, no. 74

Question: *A man swore not to gamble for a certain period. Now he asks that his oath be annulled, since he is afraid that he will succumb to temptation and that, by gambling, he will be committing a dual sin: the sins of wagering and of violating his oath.*

Responsum: It stands to reason that we don't accede to his request. Gambling is a sin, and we do not annul his oath in order that he may commit a sin. If he is afraid that his gambling urge will overpower him, let him place his gambling urge under oath. We do not allow a person to commit a minor transgression [gambling] in order to avoid violating a major prohibition [his oath]. However, if the Bet Din already annulled his vow, let the annulment stand *ex post facto*.

Unfair Competition
Teshuvot Rashba, no. 6259

Question: *For many years, Reuven, a tailor, has been a good friend of a local non-Jew, who ordered all his garments exclusively from him. He always paid Reuven two dinars for a garment. Now Shimon, also a tailor, moved into town. Wanting to ingratiate himself with this non-Jew, he offered to make his garments for one dinar. Reuven complains that Shimon is hurting his business and stealing his customers by undercutting his prices. He accuses Shimon of encroaching on his territory, and he says he could have earned so-and-so much if not for Shimon's competition. What is the law?*

Responsum: As in all such cases, legally the Bet Din is not empowered to extract compensation from Shimon, because the non-Jewish employer voluntarily paid him his wages. . . . Nevertheless, by enticing the non-Jew to let him do his tailoring, he took away Reuven's livelihood. Shimon should be scolded for that, and the Bet Din should issue a protest against such practices.

RABBI ASHER BEN YECHIEL—ROSH
רבי אשר בן יחיאל — רא״ש

born: Germany, c. 1250
died: Toledo, Spain, 1327
Popularly known as Rosh (Rabbi ASHer).

Rabbi Asher, one of the early great *poskim*, deciders of Halachah, was a descendant of a long line of eminent rabbis, one of whom was Rabbi Gershom Meor HaGolah. His mentor was **Maharam Rothenburg**, whom he succeeded as spiritual leader of German Jewry. In the wake of the Rindfleisch massacres, in 1298 (see p. 16), Rosh convened a rabbinical conference to determine the disposition of the property of the victims who had left no heirs. With the worsening situation of German Jewry, Rosh feared that he might be imprisoned and held for ransom, as was his teacher, Maharam, and so he left Germany. He arrived in Spain in 1306 and was welcomed by the great **Rashba** (Rabbi Shelomoh ibn Aderet), Rabbi of Barcelona, with whom he had corresponded while in Germany. Soon after his arrival in Spain, the community of Toledo, the capital of Castile, invited him to serve as its rabbi. In that capacity he assumed the leadership of the Bet Din, which was empowered by the government to enforce its own decrees by imposing judicial punishment—even to administer the death penalty.

After **Rashba**'s death in 1310, Rosh became his successor. He received thousands of halachic inquiries from Spain and all over the world. More than a thousand of his responsa were collected and published under the title *She'eilot uTeshuvot HaRosh*.[1] His teshuvot are a rich source of practical halachic decisions that deal with a wide range of problems and reflect Jewish life during his era. He was an independent thinker of illustrious greatness who on occasion respectfully disagreed with earlier authorities such as Rav **Amram Gaon**, Rav **Hai Gaon**, Rif, Rashi, Rabbeinu Tam, **Rambam**, Ravad, and oth-

Title page of *She'eilot uTeshuvot* of Rabbeinu Asher ben Yechiel, known as Rosh; he was the author of the monumental halachic code by that name, which appears in all standard editions of the Talmud. Published in Jerusalem, 1971.

ers. His yeshivah became a famous Torah academy, attracting students from far-off countries.

Rosh is best known for his monumental halachic code, which follows the Talmudic tractates. His decisions, in which he identifies his sources, are printed in all editions of the Talmud. He lists all the main opinions on each halachah, showing the process by which the final decision was reached. This was the seminal work on which **Rabbi Yosef Karo** based his authoritative code *Shulchan Aruch*. Rosh's disciples included his eight sons, the most famous of whom was Rabbi Yaakov Baal HaTurim, author of the halachic code *Arba'ah Turim*. **Rabbi Yosef Karo**[2] expresses his adulation for the eminence of the Rosh, stating, "The works of Rif, **Rambam**, and Rosh are the three pillars on which rests the entire structure of Halachah of the House of Israel."

Must He Obey His Father?
Teshuvot HaRosh, no. 15:5

Question: *A father told his son not to speak to a certain Jew and not to forgive him for what he had done. The son would like to patch things up but he is concerned about his father's command. What should he do?*

Responsum: Let me make it clear that it is forbidden to hate a Jew.... The father who told his son to hate this Jew had no right to order his son to violate a Torah decree. The verse, "Every person must respect his mother and father"[3] concludes with the words, "I am God your Lord," indicating that God's law must be obeyed even if a parent tells you to violate it. Besides, by giving such an order, the father was acting in an un-Jewish manner. This being so, the son is not required to obey him.

Death Penalty for a Slanderer
Teshuvot HaRosh, no. 17:1

Question: *What should be done with a person who is known to level false accusations with government authorities against individual Jews and against the entire community? He continually threatens them with dire consequences to their life and property. People are very afraid of him since he is a constant visitor with one of the influential Arab government officials. The Jewish community has been authorized by the government to put this man on trial and, if he is found liable to the death sentence, to execute him. A Bet Din was convened and a number of witnesses testified that this man is indeed an informer and also that one of the notables of the community warned him to cease and desist, and he refused to do so. Please tell us whether we may judge him as a* rodeif, *a pursuer, since he continues to make threats against us, and whether, pursuant to the law of* rodeif, *we are permitted to save our lives by taking the life of the* rodeif *as sanctioned by the government authorities.*[4]

Responsum: After the Sanhedrin left their site inside the Holy Temple, death sentences could no longer be passed. But in cases where a person is not on trial for past misdeeds, but in order to save a potential victim from his pursuer, the death sentence may still be carried out if the local government permits it. For we apply the verse, "Do not stand still when your neighbor's life is in danger."[5] The sages equate an informer who causes Jewish property to fall into the hands of oppressors with a *rodeif* who threatens to kill, because once an extortionist has had a taste of Jewish property, he wants more and more, until in the end he takes the Jew's life. The Torah permits you to save your life by taking the pursuer's life . . . for eventually he will endanger the lives of all Jews.

Therefore, in all countries of the Exile, drastic action was always taken against informers to set an example for others who might harbor such nefarious notions.

In the present case, where witnesses established that he was an informer, you did well in sentencing him.... "May all Your enemies perish like this, o Lord, and may they who love Him be as the sun when it goes forth in its might."[6]

Decorate a Synagogue with a Moslem Prayer Rug?
Teshuvot HaRosh, no. 5:2

Question: *When praying, Moslems use a small prayer rug, called* sagada *in Arabic, that is deco-*

rated with black designs. Is it permitted to hang such prayer rugs on either side of the Holy Ark for ornamental purposes, and of course not as an object of worship?

Responsum: I researched this matter, and I found out that here in Toledo[7] it has been the custom to forbid sitting on such rugs in the synagogue and certainly to bar displaying them alongside the Holy Ark. People say that the black design on the rugs represents the place in Mecca where Moslems worship. Others say that it represents Mercury and that they bow down to this idol. They also explained to me that in Arabic it is called *sagada*, a term related to the Aramaic *sagad*, to prostrate, because they use the rug to bow down on. In view of this, it seems to me that it is forbidden to display these rugs in the synagogue . . . they should be removed . . . articles intended to be used in Moslem worship have no place in our synagogue.

What Should Be Done with the Ransom Money?
Teshuvot HaRosh, no. 32:6

Question: *When Leah was abducted by Arabs, her mother collected 600 gold ducats for ransom from the surrounding communities and deposited the money with a trustee. Now it has been learned that Leah converted to Islam, married an Arab, and had two children by him. Her mother asserts that since Leah became assimilated among the Arabs, the ransom money she deposited with the trustee should be returned to her. The community wants to use the money to establish a fund for the redemption of captives.*

Responsum: . . . In this case, since she turned into an Arab, got married, and bore children, she certainly has no right to this money, for the donors did not intend their ransom money to be enjoyed by an apostate . . . We must regard this case as though the abducted woman had died and was never redeemed, for what difference does it make whether she died or converted. Therefore, she has no legal claim to the money. The correct thing to do would be to return the contributions to the donors. They gave the money for her ransom, and until she is ransomed the money is legally theirs. Failing that, the money should be used for the benefit of the public, preferably as a fund for the release of captives, as the community suggested. Perhaps with the passage of time this captive woman will repent and can then be redeemed with this fund.

Can This Teacher Be Dismissed?
Teshuvot HaRosh, no. 104:4

Question: *A man hired a teacher for his son for the term of one year, and during the course of the year he found a better teacher. Is he permitted to dismiss the first teacher and employ the second one?*

Responsum: Let me point out, since he hired the teacher for a fixed term, and the teacher started his employment, he cannot be dismissed during the term of his contract unless he is negligent in his work.

The Noisy Blacksmith's Shop
Teshuvot HaRosh, no. 18:14

Question: *A Jewish blacksmith rented a house from an Arab to use as a smith's shop. The shop is adjacent to the house of Shimon, who complains that he is distressed when the earth shakes each time the hammer strikes the anvil, that the noise does not let him sleep, and that the dust and smoke are harmful to his health. The blacksmith argues that Shimon cannot prevent the Arab from doing in his place anything he wishes, and since he, the blacksmith, is the Arab's tenant, Shimon cannot interfere with his activities either.*

Responsum: . . . It is the duty of every Jew not deliberately to inflict pain or damage on his fellow Jew. The dust and smoke that rise from the shop are the direct result of the blacksmith's willful and premeditated actions. Granted, Shimon cannot stop the Arab if he does these things in his own place, but when a Jew who abides by Halachah is doing them, he can indeed raise a protest against them.

RABBI YOM TOV IBN ASHVILI—RITVA
רבי יום טוב אבן אשבילי — ריטב"א

born: Spain, c. 1260
died: Seville, Spain, c. 1328
Commonly known as Ritva, the initials of his name.

Although the dates of Ritva's birth and death are under dispute, it is certain that his teachers were the illustrious **Rashba** (R. Shelomoh ibn Aderet) and Ra'ah (Rabbi Aharon HaLevi). He was an eminent scholar, admired by Jews and non-Jews alike, yet he remained humble and self-effacing. His halachic opinions were sought out by individuals, rabbis, and *Batei Din* (rabbinic courts). Even the Spanish ruling circles respected him as a great juridical authority. His responsa were collected by his son and remained in manuscript for more than 600 years, and 209 of them were published for the first time by Mossad HaRav Kook.[1]

Ritva is best known for his popular commentary on the Talmud. He interprets and analyzes the text, offering a condensation of the views of Rashi, Tosafot, Rif, **Rashba**, Ra'ah, and Ramban. This work can be found on the bookshelves of every advanced student of Talmud. He left a legacy of many other works, among which are *Sefer HaZikaron*, which is a defense of **Rambam**'s philosophical opinions, and a commentary on the Haggadah.[2]

Refusal to Return Security
Teshuvot Ritva, no. 58

Question: Reuven gave Shimon an object as a security for a certain amount of money. After a while Reuven came to redeem the security. Shimon concedes to holding the security but says, "I am retaining it because I rented you an animal on condition

Title page of *She'eilot uTeshuvot Ritva*, by Rabbi Yom Tov ibn Ashvili; this was published for the first time, from the only existing manuscript, by Mossad HaRav Kook in Jerusalem, 1959, and annotated by Rabbi Yosef Kapach.

that you feed it adequately, that only you would ride it, and that you would not overload it. When you returned the animal to me, it was lean and its back was lacerated from the heavy burdens you made it carry; it also lost a great deal of blood. As a result of all these factors it died. Therefore, I am withholding the security until you pay me the value of the animal."

Reuven contends, "I have witnesses who will testify that only I rode the animal, that I never overloaded it, and that I fed the animal as we agreed. It died through no fault of mine. Furthermore, I want to state that en route the animal was overcome by a spell of weakness, so that I was forced to dismount and continue on foot." Please enlighten us as to who is right.

Responsum: No one can simply hold an object belonging to someone else unless he has undeniable proof for his claim. Shimon's claim for damages done to his animal are based on conjecture. How does he know that Reuven did all the things he accuses him of? He was not there himself and he has no witnesses to substantiate his claims. Perhaps the animal died of other causes. It is clear to me that Shimon must return the security.

Can a Gambler Be Forced to Divorce His Wife?
Teshuvot Ritva, no. 122

Question: *What should be done in the case of a woman whose husband gambles and loses his money? The woman clamors that she wants to have a divorce, claiming that she despises her husband. Can the husband be forced to give a divorce when the wife says "I despise him," based on* **Rambam**'s *ruling[3] that Jewish women cannot be held captive by a husband whom they despise?*

Responsum: As you know, Ramban and a number of other authorities, including my teachers, disagree on this point with the great Master (**Rambam**), and so do I, though I am insignificant compared with these great lions.[4] Under no circumstances should you rule according to Rambam and in opposition to my teachers on a grave matter such as this. Thus, a gambler cannot be forced to divorce his wife unless he does not fulfill his matrimonial duties, that is, furnishing food and clothing to his wives and fulfilling his conjugal duties. But he cannot be forced to give a divorce merely because the wife claims that she despises him. . . . We can request that he do so but he cannot be coerced.

Dispute about Access Road
Teshuvot Ritva, no. 124

Question: *Reuven's vineyard is located inside of Shimon's vineyard. Reuven owns an access road running through Shimon's vineyard. Reuven acquired several other vineyards adjacent to his original vineyard, that have gates and access roads to the outside. Reuven closed these gates and wants to use the access road running through Shimon's vineyard to transport workers and produce to and from all the vineyards, causing considerable damage to Shimon's vineyard. Can Shimon prevent Reuven from doing this, and is Reuven required to pay for the damage that has been done . . . ?*

Responsum: Of course, Shimon can stop Reuven from using the access road for all but the original vineyard. . . . Therefore, if he has caused some damage he must indemnify him. Shimon should estimate the minimum amount of the damage. If Reuven agrees, that is what he should pay; otherwise he has to give a *shevuat heset*[5] (an oath required of one who is sued for a debt and who denies it entirely). . . . If Shimon is uncertain as to the amount of the damage, then Reuven is not required to swear.

Is This Torah Scroll Unfit for Use?
Teshuvot Ritva, no. 122

Question: *Is a* sefer Torah *that has words or letters missing fit for reading in the synagogue? We have noted that several scholars who came here from France are not concerned about this matter and read from a* sefer Torah *in which many words are missing.*

Responsum: I am very astonished about these scholars. On what do they base their position? We have a clear-cut halachic ruling dating back to the Geonic era,[6] stating that any *sefer Torah* in which there is even one superfluous or missing letter is unfit for use until the defect has been repaired. **Rambam** renders the same ruling.[7] I too received this teaching from my masters Ra'ah (Rabbi Aharon HaLevi) and **Rashba** (Rabbi Shelomoh ibn Aderet). Ramban in his introduction to the Torah offers a convincing reason for it, and Rashi also repeatedly mentions this law. [He proceeds to examine this subject at great length and from all possible angles, concluding:] These traditions we received from our great teachers really do not need any buttressing, and the holiness of the letters makes it imperative, as Ramban explained. I wrote my remarks only for the greater glory of the Torah.

The Repentant Thief
Teshuvot Ritva, no. 188

Question: *During the night, Avraham Midro and Avraham ben Flas broke into the ark of the synagogue in Daroca[8] in order to steal the silver Torah ornaments. They were apprehended and jailed, but both escaped. Thereupon the Bet Din barred them from living in Daroca. The Bet Din also decreed that [Avraham Midro's brothers] Oro, Tzavach, Nissim, Yosef, and their mother Jamilla are forbidden to live in Daroca for a period of time [five years], whereupon they all converted [to Christianity]. Now the mother of Avraham ben Flas petitions Bet Din to retract the decree banishing her son from Daroca, lest he too convert. She states that her son is willing to accept on himself any punishment or fine that the Bet Din imposes, if only he may live in the Jewish community of Daroca. She asks that the Bet Din have pity on her son in honor of his father, who cleanses and purifies all the corpses in the community as an act of kindness, preparing them for burial, and in her merit, as she is the midwife to all Jewish mothers in the community. "Do this favor for me," she asks, "so that he will not be tempted to convert as Jamilla and her sons have."*

Now we, the Bet Din, ask you, our Master and Ruler, is it proper for us to accept his repentance for his evil deed of laying hands on the holy Torah, and to nullify our decree before its five-year term has ended?...

Responsum: I have carefully studied your question, and I think that if it appears to you that this Avraham would renounce Judaism because of this decree, and that by your nullification he would repent and accept expiation, then you may cancel your decree so that he will repent and not turn to evil. For every sinner who repents is always accepted, as it is written, "Return, you wayward children, I will heal your failings...."[9] It is a great mitzvah to save a Jewish soul from the ruin of idol worship and turn him to repentance.... Had the community known that he would renounce Judaism, they would not have issued such a harsh decree.

Must He Pay His Wife's Medical Expenses?
Teshuvot Ritva, no. 151

Question: *A wife claims that while she was away from home she fell ill and borrowed money for medical expenses. She wants her husband to pay the medical bills. The husband refuses to pay, stating that he does not believe her. Who is right?*

Responsum: It seems plain to me that the burden of proof rests on her. You cannot compare this to a claim for payment for food. There is no question that she needs food, and everyone agrees that the husband must sustain her every day. But sickness is an unanticipated situation. Since her status is presumed to be healthy, it is she who has to prove that she has become sick.... Although by his marriage he has the obligation to pay for her medical costs, since this obligation arises only when she falls ill, and in this case he says that he does not know whether she was sick, she has to prove her claim.

RABBI NISSIM GIRONDI—RAN
רבי נסים גירונדי — הר"ן

born, Spain, c. 1290
died: Barcelona, Spain, c. 1380
Popularly known as the Ran, the acronym formed of the initials of his name.

The Ran, one of the foremost rabbinical scholars of the fourteenth century, served as rabbi and *rosh yeshivah* of Barcelona, Spain. In that capacity he received thousands of she'eilot from France, Italy, North Africa, and even from as far away as Eretz Yisrael. Only seventy-seven of his teshuvot have survived, and they were published as *Teshuvot HaRan*.[1]

His greatest claim to fame in the Torah world is his commentary to Rif's *Sefer HaHalachot*, printed together with the Rif in the Vilna edition of the Talmud. He reveals himself as an independent thinker who carefully examines the opinions of earlier authorities. Especially his running commentary on Tractate *Nedarim*, printed opposite that of Rashi, is extremely helpful in clarifying this complex Gemara. Rabbi Nissim made a valuable contribution to Jewish thought with his homiletic work *Derashot HaRan*,[2] in which he offers a classic exposition of the tenets of the Jewish faith. Many great philosophers after Ran, such as Rabbi Yosef Albo, the author of *Ikkarim*, used *Derashot HaRan* as the cornerstone of their system of thought.

The Stolen Security
Teshuvot Rabbeinu Nissim Girondi, no. 18

Question: *Reuven, who lives in Lardia, Spain, lent the congregation of Barcelona a silver cup. They*

Title page of *She'eilot uTeshuvot HaRan* by the Ran, Rabbi Nissim Girondi, acclaimed for his seminal commentary on the Rif and Tractate *Nedarim*. This edition was published in Jerusalem, 1960.

were in need of money, and the lender required an article of silver as a security. They in turn gave Reuven a woolen garment of equal value as a security. Reuven's house was looted and the woolen garment was taken. The Barcelona congregation demands the return of the garment before they will give back the silver cup. Reuven claims that it was not because of his negligence that the garment was lost, that in fact all his possessions were stolen. He therefore demands the return of his silver cup. Who is right?

Responsum: Reuven is right. The Gemara in *Bava Metzia* 82a states, "If someone lends and takes a security, he has the legal status of *shomer sachar*,[3] paid guardian." As such, the lender who holds the security is not responsible for an unavoidable accident.... In our case, since the security was lost through looting, an unavoidable accident, the borrower must repay and the lender is exempt.

A Vow to Move to Eretz Yisrael
Teshuvot Rabbeinu Nissim Girondi, no. 38

Question: *Reuven, Shimon, and Levi joined together in a venture to cross the Mediterranean Sea together to be closer to Eretz Yisrael. They made the following agreement which they signed under solemn oath:*

> Before us, the undersigned witnesses and before Rabbi Yosef of Marseilles and Rabbi Chaim Tzarfati, they [Reuven, Shimon, and Levi] agreed to sail in October or November on a vessel from the port of Barcelona, Spain, bound for that destination, for the purpose of settling in Eretz Yisrael or near it, in Cyprus or Alexandria, Egypt.

Now Shimon wants to recant his vow because his wife refuses to go along with him. Her relatives incited her not to follow her husband and to refuse to accept a get from him. Besides, he surmises that she is pregnant. He says that if he had known that she would not join him, he would not have sworn to emigrate. He is asking whether his vow can be annulled and, if so, whether he needs Reuven's and Levi's consent, since they swore to go together.

Responsum: This is indeed a severe oath, one that you should avoid like a snake.... But a man is not permitted to leave his wife, and he cannot demand that she follow him to the ends of the world.... I agree that this vow should be annulled.

As for the question whether the consent of Reuven and Levi is needed.... In this case, if Shimon received no consideration or favor from Reuven and Levi to induce him to make the vow, it may be annulled in their presence, even without their consent. But if he did receive a consideration or favor from them and because of it he made the vow, then he must do his utmost to obtain Reuven and Levi's agreement to the annulment. However, if they are unwilling to give their consent, the vow may be annulled in any event, for the reasons set forth.

A Shipment of Lamb's Meat
Teshuvot Rabbeinu Nissim Girondi, no. 50

Question: *Reuven, sailing from Majorca,[4] accompanied a shipment of lamb's meat, that was salted the way Jews salt it for commercial purposes. The lambs in question are eight days old, very lean animals. Several local Jews testified that they buy these newborn lambs for their hides, which they sell. Nevertheless they* shecht *(slaughter)[5] and salt them and sell the meat cheap. The Christian dealers buy the hides from the Jews. If these dealers buy live lambs they slaughter them, throw the meat to the dogs, and keep the hides. The non-Jews never eat this kind of meat, salted or unsalted. This load consisted of fifty quarters of such salted lambs and seven salted sides. All this meat was packed in canvas bags that were sewed and tied with cord. The knot was sealed with wax imprinted with several letters. Still, it would be possible to remove the meat by opening the seams and maneuvering the pieces between the loops of the cord. Reuven is certain that aside from his salted meat there was no other meat on the ship.*

When Reuven realized that the vessel would not reach its destination before Pesach he got off the ship in Palma (on Majorca), leaving the goods on the ship. After Pesach the ship arrived on the Island of Sardinia. The shipment was delivered to Reuven but he found the seams torn. There are some authorities who permit this meat, and others who fear that it may have been exchanged for meat from Castile, where the custom prevails of salting small lambs. *Those permitting it argue that the meat from Castile is fatter than the lean meat of Reuven's shipment. What is your decision regarding this meat?*

Responsum: I think that even if the lambs from Castile would be like these . . . [there follows a detailed analysis of the problem at hand] . . . It seems to me that this meat is permissible.

May He Marry Two Wives?
Teshuvot Rabbeinu Nissim Girondi, no. 48

Question: *Reuven married his wife in France, a country where the enactment of Rabbeinu Gershon Meor HaGolah against polygamy is accepted as law. [Rabbeinu Gershon Meor HaGolah, "The Light of the Diaspora," was born in Metz, France, c. 960, and died in Mainz, Germany, 1040. His enactments, which have had a far-reaching effect on Jewish family life, are accepted throughout Ashkenazi Jewry but are not accepted by Sephardi Jews.] Reuven now resides in Castile, Spain, where Rabbeinu Gershon's ban is not accepted, and where it is customary to marry two wives. Is Reuven permitted to take an additional wife?*

Responsum: We have a rule that when someone travels from one place to another he must observe the stringencies of both the locality he came from and the place where he now resides (*Pesachim* 50a). . . . Furthermore, Rabbeinu Gershon's ban was accepted by all the people of the Ashkenazi region as mandatory law for them and their offspring. It is binding on their *person*, regardless of the locale where they may be situated.

However, I am inclined to permit polygamy if the [first] wife gives her consent. For the ban was instituted for the woman's benefit, and if she declares that she does not want the protection offered her by the rabbinical enactment, we should abide by her wishes. But, on second thought, I am pondering the question of whether the ban against polygamy was instituted for the benefit of women, or perhaps it was also for the benefit of the men, to prevent the plague of constant bickering and recriminations in the home. If that is the case, the ban is not lifted even if the wife gives her consent. And even if we say that it was enacted solely for the benefit of women, I don't think it is enough that the wife give her consent, for there is the danger that the husband will pester her until she agrees to let him marry a second wife. Therefore, I defer to the rabbis of France and Germany, where the enactment originated. We should follow their directives in this matter.

RABBI YITZCHAK BEN SHESHET PERFET—RIVASH
רבי יצחק בן ששת פרפט — ריב"ש

born: Barcelona, Spain, 1326
died: Algiers, North Africa, 1407
Popularly known as Rivash, the title of his collected responsa and the initials of his name.

Rivash studied under the greatest luminaries of his age: **Ran** (Rabbeinu Nissim), Rabbi Peretz Ha-Kohen, and Rabbi Chisdai Crescas. At an early age he gained the reputation of being an outstanding scholar, but he refused to serve in the rabbinate, choosing to earn his livelihood as a merchant. In 1367 he was imprisoned on trumped-up charges; he laments his fate in responsum no. 376. After his release he became rabbi of Saragossa and Valencia, Spain, where he served until the frightful massacres of 1391; in the wake of these he fled to North Africa, where he was appointed rabbi of Algiers.

One of the refugees from Spain tried to undermine Rivash's authority. A bitter quarrel ensued which came to a head when a ship arrived from Majorca, Spain, carrying forty-five Marranos, Jews who had been forcibly baptized but who practiced Judaism secretly. Rivash's opponent asked the sultan of Algiers to deny admission to the refugees. Rivash, unable to contain his indignation at this treacherous act against his fellow Jews, excommunicated his enemy.

Rivash was the foremost authority of his day, and his halachic opinions were universally respected. In his responsa *Teshuvot Rivash*[1] he cites all previous opinions on similar cases before rendering his decision. His teshuvot range from problems dealing with the status of Marranos to questions of a purely philosophical nature. *Teshuvot Rivash* is one of the most important classics of the responsa literature.

Title page of *She'eilot uTeshuvot Rivash* by Rabbi Yitzchak ben Sheshet Perfet, known as Rivash. Printed in Jerusalem, 1975.

A Question Concerning Marranos
Teshuvot Rivash, no. 11

Question: *A woman obtained a get. Both she and her husband were Marranos,[2] as were all the witnesses to the divorce. Now this woman, by the grace of God and her own efforts, left the land of shmad[3] and came to the Arab lands to worship God in freedom, without fear. She says that the witnesses were known to observe the Torah, but because of many reasons, they had been unable to leave. Must these Marranos be considered transgressors and, as such, invalid witnesses, because it is evident that they remained in Spain only out of lust for money? . . .*

Responsum: It is clear that only a person who willfully and intentionally transgressed the law is invalid as a witness. If a person was forced to convert, then even if he worshipped idols and openly desecrated the Shabbat, since he did so under duress, he is still considered a Jew. We must ascertain if in private he refrained from violating the Torah laws to the best of his ability. But if he, even in private, violated prohibitions such as eating nonkosher meat, then he is invalid to be a witness.

Therefore, regarding the *get* whose witnesses were Marranos who remained in the land of *shmad*, we must investigate into which category they fall, since they have stayed there for a long time and, unlike many wealthy and poor people, they did not escape. A rabbi must determine if they belong to the Marranos who are valid witnesses. If they are valid witnesses, then the *get* is acceptable and the woman is free to marry. But if they are the kind of Marranos who are invalid witnesses, then we cannot permit her to marry.

A Philosophical Question[4]
Teshuvot Rivash, no. 370

Question: *What is the meaning of the rabbinic aphorism, "If you have no knowledge you have no understanding; if you have no understanding you have no knowledge" (Avot 3:21)?*

Responsum: The **Rambam** in his commentary to *Avot* writes that these are profound philosophical concepts that are very difficult to understand. He devotes an entire chapter to the subject in his work *Moreh Nevuchim*, "Guide of the Perplexed."[5] Its subtleties are beyond the comprehension of many philosophers; therefore, I will not write you his explanation.

However, the plain meaning is this: *Da'at* denotes knowledge of fundamental, axiomatic facts—for example, that the whole is the sum of its parts, or that a pair is two of a unit. *Binah*, understanding, signifies inductive reasoning—that is, deriving conclusions from a number of basic facts. Thus, without *da'at*, knowledge of facts, there can be no *binah*, logical thinking. Conversely, if there is no *binah*, deductive reasoning, then *da'at* is merely a sterile accumulation of knowledge.

Riding a Camel in a Caravan on Shabbat
Teshuvot Rivash no. 17

Question: *Jews are riding on camels as part of an Arab caravan, traveling through a great and awesome desert. All know that since they are not riding on swift horses, they will be forced to desecrate the Shabbat openly, riding with the caravan. Because of the hazards involved, they cannot stay back alone in the desert on Shabbat. They are in a quandary as to whether they should refrain from joining such caravans so as to prevent the desecration of Shabbat, even though they cannot earn a livelihood unless they ride in caravans.*

Responsum: If it is for the purpose of performing a mitzvah, such as saving a life, they may go out with the caravan, but for discretionary purposes it is forbidden. On Shabbat it is forbidden to ride an animal or to ride in a wagon that is pulled by an animal.

Rescue from a Wine Vat
Teshuvot Rivash, no. 310

Question: *Shimon stepped into a wine press to determine if the wine was ripe to be drawn. He was overcome by the fumes emanating from the vat, so he fainted and fell in. His friend Levi cried out and three non-Jews came to help; one reached out his* hand and pulled him out of the vat. Levi observed that the non-Jew did not come in contact with the wine. Rabbi Yosef ben David prohibited the wine in the vat, because of maga al yedei davar acheir, "indirect contact with the wine by a non-Jew."[6] What is the halachah?

Responsum: I would be inclined to permit this wine, because there was no contact, either direct or indirect, by a non-Jew. The Jew, who is a human being just as the non-Jew is, is the one who touched the wine; only he touched a non-Jew at the same time. There is no precedent for a Jew to cause wine to be prohibited because he is physically connected to a non-Jew—not even if the non-Jew has sacramental purposes in mind; not even if the non-Jew expressly says that with his indirect contact he intends to offer the wine as a libation to his deity. His words mean nothing.

Clearly, this seems to me to be the halachah. I am surprised that this has escaped your notice.

Bruised in a Fistfight
Teshuvot Rivash, no. 490

Question: *Submitted by the Honorable Governor Don Michael Di Gaudia concerning a case that was brought before the civil court regarding two Jews who were embroiled in a fistfight. The plaintiff charges that the defendant injured him during the fight. The defendant denies the charge, and states that he has two Jewish and two Arab witnesses who were present during the altercation, and who would testify that he did not lay a hand on the plaintiff. When the witnesses were questioned they testified against the defendant. Now the defendant recants and claims that the witnesses' testimony is invalid because the Jews who testified against him are enemies of his, and the testimony of the Arabs is not acceptable according to Torah law. The above-mentioned governor is asking whether the defendant's claim has any legitimacy according to Torah law.*

Responsum: In my opinion the claim of the defendant has no merit whatsoever. The civil judge may decide the case on the testimony of the witnesses. In the first place, the Jewish witnesses are not disqualified as alleged enemies, because no Jew will testify falsely out of hatred, as is set forth in Sanhedrin 27b. It was the defendant who suggested the witnesses in the first place; they came on his invitation; he agreed before the judge to abide by their testimony, and therefore he cannot go back on his word. For the same reason the judge may also accept the testimony of the Arab witnesses. The defendant agreed to accept their testimony, and therefore he cannot now disavow his earlier statement.

RABBI SHIMON DURAN—RASHBATZ
רבי שמעון דוראן — רשב"ץ

born: Palma, Majorca, Spain, 1361
died: Algiers, North Africa, 1444
Popularly know as Rashbatz, the initials of his name, Rabbi Shimon bar Tzemach.

Rabbi Shimon, a descendant of a prominent family in Provence, France, traced his ancestry to the Ramban (Nachmanides). He studied under Rabbi Vidal Ephraim and became an authority not only in Talmud but also in the sciences, mathematics, astronomy, and philosophy. During the massacres in Spain in 1391, Rashbatz escaped to Algiers, where he was received with open arms by **Rivash**, the rabbi of Algiers, himself a Spanish refugee. After Rivash's death in 1407, Rashbatz was appointed his successor, serving as rabbi of Algiers until his death in 1444. He was succeeded by his son, Rabbi Shelomoh (Rashbash).

Rashbatz was one of the great responsa writers, responding to queries from communities in all of North Africa and beyond. With great clarity he analyzes the questions, citing the sources on which he bases his decisions. More than 900 of his responsa have been published under the title *Tashbatz*,[1] an acronym of the initials of *Teshuvot Shimon ben Tzemach*. He also wrote commentaries on a number of Talmudic tractates, on Job, and on the Haggadah.

Death in the Desert
Tashbatz, no. 3:71

Question: *A Jew traveled through the desert in a caravan in the company of a group of Arabs and, according to the testimony of the Arabs, he was very thirsty for water until he died of thirst. The Jews of*

Title page of the collection of responsa by Rashbatz, Rabbi Shimon bar Tzemach (Duran), Rabbi of Algiers; it is entitled *Tashbatz*, an acronym for *Teshuvot Shimon bar Tzemach*, and comprises approximately 900 responsa. Published for the first time by Rabbi Meir Crescas (Lemberg 1891) after remaining in manuscript form for 320 years.

the town of Touggourt, Algeria,[2] *wrote that the Arabs told them they had seen his body. The Arabs also gave them the dead man's hat. When his wife wanted to remarry, the rabbi opposed the marriage. We are eagerly awaiting your answer.*

Responsum: . . . When the Arabs related that the Jew had died of thirst, they surely were speaking innocently, guilelessly, and without any ulterior motive. . . . It is clear that we should not prevent her from marrying since there is no reason to fear that the Arabs had any selfish motives in testifying.

. . . Therefore, this woman is permitted to marry, and it is forbidden to keep her in her present state of uncertainty. May the Merciful protect us from the sin of oppressing the unfortunates.

Can a Wife Be Compelled to Move?
Tashbatz, no. 3:86

Question: *A man married a woman in Bejaia, Algeria.*[3] *All his relatives live in Algiers. At the time of the wedding he agreed not to move away from Bejaia for the next ten years. The ten years have gone by. Now the husband has found business opportunities and the cost of living in other towns to be more advantageous than in Bejaia. Additionally, in Bejaia evil people have spread slanderous rumors about his wife. He wants to move to Algiers to be near his relatives. Can he compel his wife to join him?*

Responsum: If he expressly married her with the stipulation that he would be able to remove her from there after ten years, and the term has passed, then the halachah is simple that he can compel her to move. If she denies that this was what they had agreed, then she must declare so under oath.

Regarding his claim that he wants her to move away because evil gossipers are spreading false rumors about her, it is plain that for this reason, too, he can force her to move. We have a statement by the **Rambam**[4] to that effect in Laws of Matrimony, Chapter 13:15 "If a husband says, 'I do not want to live in this place because the people are evil or immodest or heathens, and I am afraid of them,' we support him, because our sages have said, 'Stay away from bad neighbors.' And even if their dwelling belongs to the wife, he has the right to remove her from there to go and live among decent people."

But we do not need all these arguments. The husband prefers living in Algiers to living in Bejaia, and everyone will agree that life in Bejaia is not more pleasant than life in Algiers. Predicated on this, the husband can force his wife to move with him to Algiers; as the Rambam states in the above-mentioned chapter, "If a man marries a woman in a given country, and he is a citizen of that country, he cannot force her to move to a different country, but he can make her move from one village to another or from one region to another within the same country." But the **Maharam of Rothenburg**[5] rules on the basis of *Yerushalmi, Ketuvot* 13:11 that if the husband wants to move to Eretz Yisrael and the wife refuses to move, he can compel her to move. . . . Thus, we have made it clear that she can be coerced to move from Bejaia to Algiers, as these are two comparable cities within the same country. . . .

An Islamic Sacrificial Sheep
Tashbatz, no. 3:133

Question: *Is a Jew permitted to slaughter a sacrificial sheep*[6] *for Moslems, and is he permitted to eat from it?*

Responsum: Moslems are not idol worshipers; thus their sacrifices are not offerings to idols. However, in the case of the "Festival of the sheep" it would seem that a Jew is prohibited from slaughtering it, because this is an established religious ritual with them. We do not want to assist non-Jews in adding commandments to the seven Noachide mitzvot[7] that they are obligated to observe. . . .

We are forbidden to rejoice with them on their festivals. Accordingly, even if this sheep were not a sacrifice, we would not be allowed to participate in slaughtering and eating it. . . . But since they are not idolators, we are allowed to have dealings with them before their festivals, as it is stated in *Avodah Zarah* 65a, "Rav Yehudah[8] sent a gift to Avidrana (a non-Jew) on his festival; Rava sent a gift to Bar Sheshak (a non-Jew) on his festival. He [Rava] said, 'I am certain that he does not worship idols.'"

The Importance of Torah Teachers
Tashbatz, no. 3:153

Question: *Is a teacher of the young exempt from paying the sultan's taxes and communal levies, as a rabbi is?*

Responsum: Every community has the duty to hire Torah teachers for the young, in compliance with the enactment of Rabbi Yehoshua ben Gamla in *Bava Batra* 21.[9] Since it is incumbent on the community to employ teachers, just as they must employ a chazzan, therefore, just as the chazzan is exempt from paying taxes, so is the teacher exempt from paying taxes. This holds true if there is no other teacher in town and there are fewer than twenty-five children, for then the townspeople can say that they need only one teacher. But if there is only one teacher in town, or there are more than twenty-five children and they have to hire another teacher or an assistant teacher, then both the teacher and the assistant are exempt. As the above-mentioned Gemara states, "If there are forty children, they must hire an assistant."

Now, the Gemara states that Torah scholars are tax exempt, even in a town where there are many Torah scholars and there is no great need for scholars. Then surely a teacher who is urgently needed should be exempt from paying taxes.

Love of Eretz Yisrael
Tashbatz, no. 3:288

Question: *Is it correct to say that upon entering Eretz Yisrael all of a person's sins of which he repents are forgiven? And can it be said that a person who died while on his way to Eretz Yisrael is considered as having lived in Eretz Yisrael if his intentions were upright?*

Responsum: To live in Eretz Yisrael is a great mitzvah. The Ramban[10] counts it as one of the 613 mitzvot of the Torah, and he writes that living in Eretz Yisrael is equal to all the mitzvot in the Torah. . . . Whoever lives in Eretz Yisrael lives without sin . . .[11] Whoever is buried in Eretz Yisrael is as though he were buried underneath the altar.[12] The great sages of Israel would risk their lives fording raging rivers in their attempts to reach Eretz Yisrael. They would say, "The land that Moshe and Aharon did not merit to enter, will we deserve to enter it?" They would kiss the stones and roll in the dust, in fulfillment of the verse, "For Your servants take pleasure in her stones, and love her dust."[13] You are permitted to leave Eretz Yisrael only for the purpose of learning Torah, if you cannot find anyone there to teach you, or in order to honor your father and mother.

From all this it is evident that if a person is a *baal teshuvah* (returnee to Torah observance) and wishes to move to Eretz Yisrael (although *teshuvah* [repentance] in itself brings about forgiveness), by moving to Eretz Yisrael he gains additional merit, and it will save him from sin all his life.

As for your question regarding a person who was unable to complete the mitzvah, our sages state[14] that virtuous thoughts count as deeds. As Rav Asi said, even if you planned to do a mitzvah but you did not perform it, you are deemed as though you had actually done the mitzvah. May God help you to carry out your good intentions.

Who Gets Custody of the Little Girl?
Tashbatz, no. 4:38
(This responsum was written by Rabbi Shelomoh Duran, the son of Rashbatz, but was included in his father's volume.)[15]

Question: *Leah died and left a 4-year-old daughter. Leah's mother wants to raise her as her own child. The father insists on keeping his child, since he is her closest relative. How is this case to be decided?*

Responsum: The Rashbatz was asked a similar question about a woman who died and left a little boy and the woman's mother wanted to have custody of the boy. The father resisted because he wanted to raise the child himself. The Rashbatz ruled that the father should keep the child in order to teach him moral values and instruct him in Torah, and to show him fatherly love as only a father can.

In this case, however, where the surviving child is a girl rather than a boy, we must ponder whether the same ruling applies to a girl as to a boy, or whether a girl innately requires motherly affection more than a boy, a need the grandmother can fill better than the father, and would it [therefore] be preferable for the girl to be placed with her grandmother rather than with her father. . . .

My opinion is that it would be a good thing if the girl would stay with her grandmother, who will love her as her own child. However, if this grandmother is married to a husband who is not the father of the deceased, then the girl should not be placed in her custody as it would cause unbearable anguish to the girl's father to see his daughter raised in the house of a stranger to whom she is a burden. And even if the [grandmother's] husband keeps silent and allows his wife to take care of her granddaughter, experience has shown that he might not be happy with the situation. Therefore, the halachah [in this case] would be that the father should take the girl home, even if he is married to a new wife, for he will zealously shelter his daughter day and night.

Remove Shoes before Entering Synagogue?
Teshuvot Rashbash, no. 285

(This responsum was written by Rabbi Shelomoh Duran [Rashbash], the son of Rashbatz, and was printed in his own volume [Livorno 1740].)

Question: *A congregation wants to introduce a new ordinance forbidding anyone to enter the synagogue wearing shoes, since in Moslem eyes wearing shoes in a house of worship is a disgrace. Some members oppose this on the grounds that the* **Rambam** *permits the wearing of footgear in a synagogue. What is your opinion on this matter?*

Responsum: Everyone knows that a synagogue must be treated with the utmost honor and respect, and any form of contempt or humiliation must be avoided at all cost. Honor and respect depend on what it is that people regard as a mark of distinction. For example, a synagogue building should be taller than the surrounding houses, if that is possible; a synagogue should be brightly illuminated with beautiful chandeliers; no casual snacks should be eaten there; it should not be used as a shelter from rain or sunshine; it should not be used as a passageway or a shortcut, or shown similar signs of disrespect. However, the question of what constitutes respect or disrespect depends on local custom.

Intrinsically, honor and dishonor are qualities of the soul. But there is also imagined honor and dishonor. If a person wears dignified clothes he is regarded as a respectable man; if he wears disheveled clothes people have contempt for him, although in truth the clothes do not reflect the soul of a man. It is all in the mind. In one place a certain garment confers great honor on you, while in another locality you will be a laughingstock for wearing it. . . . In Christian lands where wearing shoes is not a sign of disrespect, where you wear shoes even when you stand before the king, it is no disgrace to wear shoes in the synagogue. In our [Moslem] lands, however, where it is an insult to wear shoes in the presence of dignitaries, and certainly in the presence of the king, there you should not wear shoes in the synagogue. The fact that until now the rabbis have not forbidden it does not mean that it is permitted. The Mishnah and the Gemara and the writings of later authorities are full of examples of new enactment that were instituted to remedy situations that earlier *poskim* had not dealt with. And when the **Rambam** states in Chapter 5 of the Laws of Prayer that you should not pray barefoot, he means in localities where it is customary to wear shoes when standing in front of government officials. Therefore, in Christian countries it is forbidden to pray barefoot, whereas in Moslem countries you should remove your shoes. It is really self-evident, for how would it look if in a Moslem country no one may enter the home of even the lowliest Arab wearing shoes, while in the House of God shoes should be permitted?

RABBI YISRAEL BRUNNA—MAHARI BRUNNA
רבי ישראל ברונא — מהר"י ברונא

born: Germany, c. 1400
died: Prague, Bohemia, c. 1480
Popularly known as Mahari Brunna, the title of his responsa.

Rabbi Yisrael, one of the illustrious halachists of fourteenth-century Germany, studied under Rabbi Yaakov Weil, known as Mahari Weil, and Rabbi Yisrael Isserlin, author of *Terumat Hadeshen*. His first rabbinic post was in Brünn (Brno), Moravia,[1] hence Rabbi Yisrael's surname Brunna. In 1451 he moved to Regensburg,[2] where he was appointed rabbi. He established a yeshivah there that became a famous center of Torah study.

In 1454 Frederick III imprisoned Mahari Brunna as a means of forcing the Jewish community to pay the so-called *Krongelder*, "crown tax," which amounted to one third of their wealth. In 1474 he was imprisoned on a ritual murder charge brought against him by an apostate Jew. At the trial he proved his innocence, and his accuser was executed in his stead. Following this incident Mahari Brunna left Germany to spend his remaining years in Prague.

Two hundred eighty-four of his responsa were published under the title *She'eilot uTeshuvot Mahari Brunna*.[3] In his teshuvot he offers solutions to halachic problems dealing with all facets of daily life.

Unable to Go to Eretz Yisrael
Teshuvot Mahari Brunna, no. 77

Question: *Circumstances prevented a person from carrying out his planned trip to Eretz Yisrael. Is he still credited with the mitzvah?*

Title page of *Teshuvot Mahari Brunna*, responsa by Rabbi Yisrael Brunna. This was published in Jerusalem in 1987.

Responsum: If you have the intention of doing a mitzvah but circumstances prevent you from fulfilling it, then the Torah considers it as though you had performed that mitzvah. A case in point: Moshe Rabbeinu was eager to enter Eretz Yisrael so that he could fulfill those mitzvot that are associated with the Land. Said God to him, "Your only wish is to receive the reward these mitzvot entail. I will count it as though you had fulfilled them."[4]

Consequently, whoever attempts to go to Eretz Yisrael but is detained is considered as having gone there.

Attend Horse Races?
Teshuvot Mahari Brunna, no. 71

Question: *Is it permissible to attend gentile festivities when they have horse races, at which the owner of the horse that comes in first wins money or a prize? Should it be compared to hunting wild game, which is forbidden according to* Avodah Zarah *18b?*

Responsum: It is permitted. Essentially, this is not done for amusement but to learn horsemanship. It also enables buyers to purchase the swiftest horses, which they will need to escape from their pursuers. I am doubtful, however, whether it is permitted to attend jousting tournaments, where men take pleasure in racing toward each other on horseback while holding lances.

Hebrew text of Mahari Brunna's Responsum #71, regarding horse races; English translation of this responsum is at the left.

Double Pay for Delivering Twins?
Teshuvot Mahari Brunna, no. 115

Question: *A midwife demands a double fee for delivering twins. Is she entitled to it?*

Responsum: If both infants are born in one delivery, she should receive one fee in full and a partial fee for delivering the second baby. If they were born in two separate deliveries, even if both occurred on the same day—and surely on two consecutive days—she is entitled to two delivery fees. But if both are born within seconds of each other during the same episode of labor, it seems to me that the fee for the second baby should be split in half.

Who Supplies the Clock?
Teshuvot Mahari Brunna, no. 116

Question: *When a rebbi teaches a pupil, is it the pupil's responsibility to provide the clock or must the rebbi furnish it?*

Responsum: Mr. Isaac Levi reported to me that Mahari Weil[5] decided that the pupil is required to furnish the clock.

I am quite astonished. After all, a scribe furnishes the quill, a tailor supplies the needle; every craftsman provides the tools of his trade. Perhaps Mahari [Weil] reasoned that the rebbi can argue, "Look, I can estimate the hour without a clock. If you don't trust my judgment, go ahead and buy a clock and I'll teach your son in your house."

In the same way, in any business transaction it is the buyer who pays the fee for the scribe because he needs the deed or bill of sale, and it is the borrower who pays the scribe's fee because he needs the money. This matter requires further reflection.

A Non-Jew Made a Gift to the Synagogue
Teshuvot Mahari Brunna, no. 276

Question: *A non-Jew donated a cloth for the Torah reading desk. May we accept it?*

Responsum: The Gemara states[6] that in the Temple we accept pledges and free-will offerings from gentiles. The same applies in this case. Similarly, we read that the chest the Philistines sent as a gift to the God of Israel was placed beside the Holy Ark.[7]

However, [in this case] the donor is the daughter of a Jewish apostate mother. This puts a different light on the situation, for the halachah states that a child born from a union between a non-Jewish man and a Jewish woman has the status of the mother.[8] Thus, halachically, this daughter is a Jewish apostate. According to the Gemara,[9] we do not accept gifts from apostates. Therefore, we cannot accept the cloth she wants to donate, for "the sacrifice of the wicked is an abomination."[10]

A Chazzan's Voice
Teshuvot Mahari Brunna, no. 85

Question: *At what point does a chazzan's voice become unacceptable?*

Responsum: Song is a form of service to God. For example, the Levites would chant a daily song during the Temple service. The voices of the Levites had to be pleasing, as it is written, "when the trumpeters and singers were as one,"[11] which Rashi explains to mean that their music sounded harmonious.[12] When a Levite's voice ceased to be resonant, he was disqualified as a singer. Our prayers have replaced the service of the sacrifices in the Temple, and song continues to be an integral part of our prayer service, as it is said, "God, Who chooses musical songs of praise."[13] Therefore, as long as a chazzan's voice sounds smooth, he is acceptable, but if it sounds shaky, broken, and unsteady, he should not continue to officiate.

An Ungrateful Husband
Teshuvot Mahari Brunna, no. 236

Question: *David Setzer lodged a bitter complaint. He paid a ransom of 1,100 gold pieces to free Abraham Ezra's wife and granddaughter from prison. Abraham Ezra refuses to reimburse him. [Can he be made to do this?]*

Responsum: Mahari Weil[14] decided this case already, stating in his letter to Abraham Ezra, "Do not be ungrateful toward your benefactor. You must save David Setzer from suffering any loss, and you must compensate him for the ransom he paid, and any other expenses he incurred, even to the last penny." The words of this gaon are like the words of God.

Mahari Weil adduces proofs from sources in the Gemara and the responsa of **Maharam Rothenburg**.[15] In order to avoid any dispute by the litigant, I must explain the details of the case. [There follows a wide-ranging analysis of all relevant sources and their legal ramifications.] . . . A Jew who is held in prison is in danger of being forced to baptize and is likely to be tortured. Therefore, his life is threatened.

Regarding the statement in the Gemara[16] that we should not ransom captives for an exorbitant price in order not to encourage the taking of hostages, Tosafot[17] rules that this applies to captives in general, but not to a wife, for *ishto kegufo*, "your wife is like yourself," and halachah does not forbid you to spend even your entire fortune in order to save yourself. Moreover, Tosafot[18] rules that where the hostage's life is in danger, we do pay exorbitant amounts for ransom. And this clearly applies in our case, for they threaten to force the child to convert to their faith, and the woman is old. . . . It is for these reasons that Abraham Ezra is required to redeem his wife and to pay to David Setzer every penny he expended, according to the decision by Mahari Weil. . . . I fully concur with the decision of Mahari Weil in the above-mentioned case.

RABBI YOSEF COLON—MAHARIK
רבי יוסף קולון – מהרי"ק

born: Chambery, France, 1410
died: Pavia, Italy, 1480
Popularly known as Maharik, the title of his responsa and the initials of his name.

Maharik's first teacher was his father, Rabbi Shelomoh Tarbot, a descendant of Rashi. Maharik showed early signs of greatness, and while still a young man was recognized as a Torah giant. In the wake of anti-Jewish attacks he was forced to leave Chambery, and he wandered from town to town in northern Italy until he accepted a post as a Hebrew teacher for children. Soon thereafter he was appointed rabbi of the prominent community of Piamenta, Italy, where he founded a yeshivah that became a great Torah academy. For a variety of reasons a large number of Jews from southern Germany migrated to northern Italy at that time, establishing new Ashkenazi communities. They accepted the Maharik as their halachic authority. As a result, he was considered the leading Torah figure by both the Italian and the German Jews. The most famous of his many disciples is Rabbi Ovadiah Yare of Bertinora, author of the well-known commentary to the Mishnah.

Maharik wrote numerous responsa which he identified as *shoresh*, root. They were published as *She'eilot uTeshuvot Maharik*.[1] A new edition, annotated by Rabbi Shemuel Baruch Deutsch and Rabbi Elyakim Schlesinger, including a biography of Maharik, has been published by Oraysoh.[2]

Rescuing the Jews of Regensburg
Teshuvot Maharik, no. 4

Question: *There exists a very real and demonstrable danger that the incident[3] leading to the imprison-*

Title page of *She'eilot uTeshuvot Maharik* by Rabbi Yosef Colon. First printing in Venice, 1551; second printing in Cremona, 1557; third printing in Lemberg, 1798. The encircled name "Rabban Maharik z'l" has the numerical value of 1884, the year of the present Warsaw edition.

ment of our brothers in Regensburg is liable to occur in any other city. The rabbis of Nuremberg have been asked to organize a rescue effort for the innocent Jews who were condemned to death. Now, *there may be some individuals who do not recognize that the same fate may befall them and who say that the evil will never happen to them, thinking, "I will have peace, even if I follow my heart's desires."*⁴ *Therefore, I have been requested to remove this stumbling block and advise how to enlighten the people.*

Responsum: First and foremost, it seems to me that all the communities that are also likely to fall victim to the "cup of deadly poison"⁵ must share the burden of rescuing the Regensburg community, for the rescue of Regensburg means their own rescue. Although for the time being the blood libel is spread in Regensburg only, eventually it will reach them too. They are obligated to help Regensburg. As proof of this, we cite the Gemara in *Bava Metzia* 108a, which states that in the case of a stream overflowing its banks downstream during heavy rains, the people living upstream must help the people downstream in their efforts at digging a drainage ditch, for if the water has no outlet downstream, eventually the people upstream will be flooded too. The people upstream must help although no damage has as yet occurred to them. In this case, too, although the disaster struck Regensburg first, the other communities are also endangered, God forbid. Therefore, they must help Regensburg. You cannot argue that in the case of the flooding, the damage to the people upstream is inevitable whereas here the false accusations and blood libels may not spread to other communities. We see with our own eyes that their intent is to frame us and to convict us, and God in His mercy saves us from them. . . . We most certainly must be concerned about such a great danger. If someone is not fearful about something as frightening as this, he does not care about his Creator, and it is better if he had never been born.

Since the Jews of Nuremberg and many other cities in Germany cannot write about these matters for fear of dukes, princes, or whoever is in power, I emphatically decree herewith on all Jews living in Germany, on pain of excommunication, not to reject the decisions of the appointed rabbis of Nuremberg as to the amount for which they assess a community or an individual to pay to lift the false charges that have been leveled maliciously and fiendishly against our brothers in Regensburg. They should pay whatever they are assessed, no more and no less. If there is a man who rebels and refuses to listen to the rabbis of Nuremberg, he shall be separated from the community, may his insides turn to water, his bones to oil, and his name be cursed. Whoever obeys me will live in safety and will be blessed.

Donations for the Synagogue in Jerusalem
Teshuvot Maharik, no. 5

Question: *Concerning the funds that were donated for the poor people of Jerusalem. These funds have been administered for many years by treasurers who distributed the funds as they saw fit. The treasurers are upright men and faithfully fulfilled their task to everyone's satisfaction.*

Recently, the great synagogue of Jerusalem was destroyed. The Jerusalem community is forced to spend large sums of money to obtain permission from His Majesty the King of Egypt to rebuild the synagogue and for contruction costs. They had to borrow large amounts at interest from non-Jews, for which they pledged their lives and property. Since they are unable to repay, they fear their creditors' wrath. They sent two distinguished representatives to seek help from Jews living in the lands of the Exile. When the treasurers of our community were approached, they were inspired to donate the charity funds toward the building of the synagogue in Jerusalem. Being Godfearing men, they did not want to do so without prior permission from the rabbinical authorities.

Responsum: It is clear that it is permitted. . . . There is no greater mitzvah than building a synagogue in the holy city of Jerusalem, the place that is ideally suited for prayers to ascend to Heaven. . . . The money was entrusted to the treasurers to allocate according to the demands of the hour. They may give it to the synagogue, especially since the poor people of Jerusalem will also benefit greatly from it.

No Tax Exemption
Teshuvot Maharik, no. 2

Question: *Concerning Yehoshua and Shelomoh, sons of Rabbi Avraham Mintz, who lived here* under the rule of His Lordship the Duke when the agreement was made with the Duke to pay him a tax of 13,000 florins. Recently, Yehoshua and Shelomoh ran away to live in another principality, and they think that they are now exempt from paying this tax. The Jewish community of Lombardy[6] demands from them payment of their share of this tax to which they were subject before leaving.*

Responsum: The halachah states that those who move away to avoid paying a tax are not exempt from paying that tax. They are still linked to their former community. They were partners in the tax from the start. They are still partners and surely must pay their share.

Is a Jew Permitted to Wear a *Kaffiyeh*?
Teshuvot Maharik, no. 88

Question: *Concerning the kaffiyeh, which is a garment that is worn by Arab scholars. It is a long garment, reaching to the floor in front and back and open on the sides. Is a Jewish scholar permitted to wear it or does the wearer violate the law of "do not follow any of their customs"?*[7]

Responsum: It is plain that the wearing of a *kaffiyeh* is not forbidden. It is worn because it confers honor on the wearer, giving him the reputation of a scholar. It is evident that one does not wear it to emulate the non-Jews.

A Dispute between Doctors
Teshuvot Maharik, no. 181

Question: *A dispute arose between physicians who had entered into a partnership and had signed a notarized agreement and sworn a solemn oath to that effect. They maintained the partnership for a period of time but then one of the doctors [maestro Josef] withdrew from the partnership. Was he permitted to do so?*

Responsum: . . . It seems obvious to me that maestro Yosef benefited from being associated with these distinguished doctors, since he did not yet have the reputation of an eminent physician. Only through the partnership did he make a name for himself and learn from these expert physicians, Dr. Mordechai Nathan and maestro Nathan, following them on their rounds. The only reason these doctors accepted him as a partner was that they thought that although now he still is an intern, eventually he will become a qualified doctor and then they will benefit from having him as a partner. . . . Therefore, the agreements he entered into are binding on him.

Disrespect toward Rabbis
Teshuvot Maharik, no. 189

Question: *Concerning Elyakim, also known as Getzel, who made a disparaging remark to our rabbis in Germany, stating to Rabbi Meir Tzvi and Rabbi Baruch of Oppenheim that they should not think that he had come in compliance with their summons, for their summonses mean nothing at all to him.*

Responsum: This is a clear-cut matter, for this is the epitome of rebelliousness. A person who contemptuously insults a Torah scholar is placed under a ban. My thanks to the rabbis of Germany who placed him under a ban. I fully concur with them. His sin is too great to bear when he offends an angel of God and scorns his word.

I say, therefore, let this man remain under the ban until his heart bends and he turns from his evil path and seeks forgiveness from the rabbis he humiliated . . . then his curse will be transformed into a blessing, and all will be well with him.

One Who Reneges on His Obligation
Teshuvot Maharik, no. 172

Question: *Shimon was caught in a precarious situation and asked Reuven to intervene on his behalf. Reuven's efforts bore fruit, and Shimon's life was spared. Now that Shimon is safe, he does not want to pay Reuven the amount Reuven swore that he spent on Shimon's rescue unless Reuven divulges the names of the officials he bribed and how much he gave to each. Reuven does not want to reveal* their names since doing so would cause grave danger.

Responsum: It seems to me that undoubtedly Reuven is right. Obviously, any revelation of this nature would bring great harm, and the favor he did to Shimon would be repaid by evil. . . . Shimon, who was in serious danger, certainly must pay all of Reuven's expenses. Nevertheless, it is clear that Reuven has to declare under oath how much he spent, without having to disclose to whom he gave the money.

Should a Jew Pay This Tax?
She'eilot uTeshuvot Maharik, no. 192

Question: *In the past, in a certain community the government expended none of the tax revenues on church-related purposes. However, the new duke decreed that henceforth all taxes that are collected from Jews should be used to purchase priestly vestments and church ornaments. It should be mentioned that the Jews continued to pay the same taxes as before; no additional tax was levied.*

Is it permissible to pay a tax that will be passed on to the church?

Responsum: Since the Jews are paying no additional tax, the clerical vestments and religious articles are, in effect, paid by the prince's treasury.

Regarding this subject *Sefer HaTerumah* states, "In certain localities a surtax is collected which goes toward building a new church. If a merchant says to a Jew, 'This article costs one *florin* plus 10 cents tax for the church,' then the Jew may not buy the article. But if he says, 'The article costs 1.10 *florins*,' without specifically mentioning the church-tax, then it does not matter." So you see, even though it is a known fact that the 10 cents tax goes to the church, as long as the merchant did not expressly mention it, there is no objection.

Surely, in our case, where the Jews pay the same tax as they did before, and the money does not go directly from the Jews to the church . . . it is clear that it is permitted to pay this tax. In fact, this tax *must* be paid. Evasion of this tax would be tantamount to theft, for we have the rule "Shmuel says, *dina demalchuta dina*"—"The law of the government is binding, and must be obeyed."

RABBI DAVID IBN ZIMRA—RADVAZ
רבי דוד אבן זמרה — רדב"ז

born: Spain, c. 1480
died: Safed, Israel, 1573
Popularly known as Radvaz, the initials of his name.

When Rabbi David was 13 years old, his family fled Spain and came to Safed, Eretz Yisrael. After a stay in Jerusalem he moved to Egypt in 1513 and settled in Cairo, where he remained for forty years. Before long he was appointed Chief Rabbi of Egypt. Radvaz enacted a number of measures designed to promote peaceful relations between the various Jewish groups in Cairo. He maintained an important yeshivah, which produced many outstanding scholars, the most prominent of whom were Rabbi **Betzalel Ashkenazi**, author of *Shittah Mekubetzet*; the Arizal; and Rabbi Yaakov Castro, who later became Chief Rabbi of Egypt. In 1553 Radvaz left Egypt to settle in Jerusalem and subsequently in Safed, where he met Rabbi **Yosef Karo**, author of the *Shulchan Aruch*.

His responsa, *She'eilot uTeshuvot Radvaz*,[1] are an important contribution to Torah scholarship. His teshuvot, which are written in a terse and crystal-clear style, deal with the important issues of his day, such as the status of the Ethiopian Jews. This teshuvah formed the basis for the legal opinions of the Israeli rabbinical authorities on the issue of the Ethiopian Jews who had been brought to Israel. He also wrote *Magein David*,[2] a kabbalistic work; *Metzudat David*,[3] another kabbalistic work; and *Migdal David*,[4] a kabbalistic commentary to *Shir Hashirim*.

Title page of *She'eilot uTeshuvot Radvaz*, containing 3000 responsa by Rabbi David ibn Zimra, mentor of Rabbi Betzalel Ashkenazi (Shittah Mekubetzet) and the saintly kabbalist Rabbi Yitzchak Luria, the Ari Hakadosh. In the last lines the publisher thanks the officers of the Library of Warsaw for lending him the early editions, and Rabbi Naftali Tzvi Berlin, Rabbi of Volozhin (the Netziv) for lending him the very rare Livorno edition of the last volume.

Karaites
Teshuvot Radvaz, no. 1:73

Question: *Please let me know your opinion about a Karaite[5] who agreed to observe all the rabbinical mitzvot and not to violate any of the rabbinical prohibitions. Is he permitted to marry a Jewish woman? Is there reason to bar him from "entering into the assembly of God"?[6]*

Responsum: I have been asked this question a number of times and I have answered that they are permitted to enter into the assembly of God, if they become like us [and observe the Oral Law]. The reason for this is that their *kiddushin* (marriage ceremony) has no validity at all, and a union with one of their women does not confer on her the status of *eishet ish* (married woman). Therefore, even though their *get* has no legal consequence, there is no reason for concern regarding *mamzerut*, since their marriage had no validity to begin with.

A similar incident occurred when a large community of about 500 Karaites returned to the true faith in Egypt through the efforts of Rabbeinu Avraham HeChasid, son of **Rambam**. These families became known in Egypt as kohanim and Yisraelim of impeccable lineage and no one cast any aspersions on them. On the contrary, the most prominent rabbis of the Egyptian community intermarried with their families.

Ethiopian Jews
Teshuvot Radvaz, no. 2:1290

Question: *The question concerns an Ethiopian woman from the land of Kush (Ethiopia).[7] We call this land Alchabash. She was abducted together with her two sons. Reuven bought her [as a slave]. We asked her what her marital status is. She said that she had been married and that these were her two sons by her husband. The enemies had come and killed all the men who were in the synagogue . . . and took the women and children as captives. We established that she is a descendant of the people of Israel, specifically from the tribe of Dan, who live in the mountains of Ethiopia. . . . In the meantime, her master Reuven lived with her and she had a son by him. This son has now grown up and wants to marry a girl from the Jewish community. Is he eligible to enter into the Jewish community? And, if not, how can his status be rectified?*

Responsum: . . . It is a well-known fact that there always have been wars between the kings of Ethiopia, a country that consists of three nationalities: Arabs, and Arameans who observe their religion, and Israelites from the tribe of Dan. It seems that they [the Israelites] belong to the sect of the Sadducees, [forerunners] of the Karaites,[8] for they do not know the Oral Law and they don't kindle lights on Friday night. The wars between these groups never stopped and they constantly take prisoners from each other. . . . Furthermore, I have a general rule that Karaites are considered Jews. . . .

If they would agree to return to traditional Judaism and accept the authority of our sages, as we do, I would permit them to to enter the Jewish community, with the approval of the rabbis. The reason is that all their *kiddushin* (marriages) were contracted in the presence of witnesses who are halachically invalid,[9] and since the marriage has no legal foundation, its dissolution requires no divorce. . . . They were led astray by Anan and his companions. At the present time many of them are returning to Judaism, as happened when a large group returned on one day in Egypt through the efforts of Rabbeinu Avraham HaNagid (the prince).[10] It seems to me that this Rabbeinu Avraham was the son of the **Rambam**, and he had no qualms about accepting them.

Exorbitant Medical Fees
Teshuvot Radvaz, no. 1:986

Question: *Reuven is ill and needs a certain medicine that could be obtained from only one pharmacist. Taking advantage of Reuven's plight, the pharmacist charges an exorbitant price. Reuven also needs a doctor, and there is only one specialist but he demands an outrageous fee. Reuven agrees to pay the fee. Is Reuven obligated to pay this fee or is he permitted to pay him the standard fee for such procedures?*

Responsum: This case can be compared to the case of the man who escaped from captivity and must use a ferry to elude his pursuers. He says, "Take me across the river and I'll pay you a golden dinar." The law is that he must pay only the regular fare. Since he agreed to pay the excessive amount only because he was in a tight spot, he can say, "I didn't mean it." . . . The doctor is entitled only to the standard fee, but if the patient has already paid him, we have no power to recover the money.

Milk Used in Processing Sugar
Teshuvot Radvaz, no. 1:1032

Question: *In the processing of sugar, milk is added. The technician stated that the milk constitutes 2 percent (one fiftieth) of the sugar. The question is: How are we permitted to use sugar with meat dishes, since the mixture is less than sixty times the quantity of the milk?*[11]

Responsum: There is no reason for apprehension at all, for twice the amount of water is added to the mixture. It is impossible to process sugar unless water is added. Now you may ask, are we allowed to neutralize a forbidden substance? This presents no difficulty, for at the time when you nullify it, the substance (the milk) is not forbidden. The prohibition arises only when you eat it with meat, and by then the milk is already neutralized. Moreover, I say, even if no water had been used in the processing, the sugar would still be permitted because the heat evaporates the milk and only the sugar remains. I have never tasted the flavor of milk in sugar. . . . To summarize, there is no problem of eating sugar with meat dishes.

Egyptian Mummies
Teshuvot Radvaz, no. 1:979

Question: *You asked, on what basis do Jews use the flesh of mummies*[12] *for medicinal purposes, even in cases that are not life threatening? And how can they do business with mummies and derive benefit from them? Isn't it forbidden, since it is prohibited to derive benefit from the flesh of a corpse?*

Responsum: You don't have to be concerned regarding the prohibition against eating it, because a mummy has lost its identity of flesh and has turned into ordinary dust. These corpses have been embalmed with various substances to preserve the body, and as a result they turn into something like pitch. Thus, there is no prohibition against ingesting them. . . . So you see that it is permissible to heal diseases with a mummy, even by ingesting it, and even if the patient is not critically ill.

In our case, you are permitted to derive benefit from a mummy, because it is the corpse of a heathen from the days of the Egyptians, and it has lost its form, it is inedible, and it has become like dust of the earth.

III

THE RESPONSA OF THE EARLY ACHARONIM: 1492–1648

The dividing line separating Rishonim and Acharonim (the later Torah scholars) is not clearly defined. Generally, the events of 1492 are considered as marking the end of the period of the Rishonim. That was the year of the disastrous expulsion of the Jews from Spain, resulting in the dispersion of this once flourishing community to far-flung locations in Turkey, Greece, Italy, Eretz Yisrael, and North Africa. Simultaneously, in the wake of continuous persecutions, there occurred a mass migration of Jews from Germany, Bohemia, and France to Poland and Lithuania, where thriving new Torah centers emerged and reached unprecedented heights of scholarship. These parallel migrations are mirrored in the names of the cities in which the great rabbis of that era officiated. Among these sages were luminaries such as Rabbi **Yosef Karo** (author of the *Shulchan Aruch*), Safed, Eretz Yisrael; the Rema (Rabbi Moshe Isserles), Cracow, Poland; the Ari HaKadosh (Rabbi Yitzchak Luria), Safed, Eretz Yisrael; the Shelah HaKadosh (Rabbi Yeshayah Horowitz), Prague; and the **Bach** (Rabbi Yoel Sirkes), Cracow, Poland.

The Early Acharonim consolidated Halachah, spurred widespread interest in the study of Kabbalah, and wrote important commentaries to the Mishnah and Talmud. The major distinction between the Rishonim and the Acharonim may be seen in the fact that the Acharonim hold the opinions of earlier scholars in unqualified and utter regard. Thus, while a Rishon will occasionally contradict the ruling of a predecessor, an Acharon will never dispute the opinion of a Rishon. This attitude reflects the diminishing degree of divine inspiration of the successive generations of scholars: a Tanna (teacher of the Mishnah) occupies a higher level of sanctity than an Amora (teacher of Talmud), who in turn ranks higher than a Gaon, whose standing is greater than that of a Rishon, who in turn is treated with deference by an early Acharon, whose opinion, in turn, is treated with utmost respect by a later Acharon.

The era of the Early Acharonim came to an end with the tragic upheavals of 1648, the year of the Chmielnitzki massacres, when 300 Jewish communities in Poland were laid to waste and hundreds of thousands of Jews were brutally murdered.

RABBI MEIR KATZENELLENBOGEN— MAHARAM OF PADUA
רבי מאיר קצנאלבגן — מהר"ם פדבה

born: Katzenellenbogen, Germany, 1482
died: Padua, Italy, 1565
Popularly known as Maharam Padua, the title of his responsa.

Rabbi Meir, one of the great rabbis of Italy, was a disciple of Rabbi Yaakov Pollak of Prague (or, according to some, of Cracow); he subsequently studied at the yeshivah of Rabbi Yehudah Mintz in Padua, Italy, whose granddaughter he married. After the death of his father-in-law, Rabbi Avraham Mintz, who had succeeded his father as rabbi of Padua, Rabbi Meir became the rabbi of that city. He gained widespread recognition as one of the greatest talmudists of his time and corresponded with the foremost scholars, one of whom was his relative Rabbi Moshe Isserles,[1] the Rema, famous for his glosses to the *Shulchan Aruch*.

Rabbi Meir's responsa were published under the title *Teshuvot Maharam Padua*.[2] Included in this work are the responsa of his mentor Rabbi Yehudah Mintz (Mahari Mintz). Rabbi Meir is considered to be the progenitor of all the families named Katzenellenbogen.

The Case of the Two Prisoners
Teshuvot Maharam Padua, no. 40

Question: *Reuven and Shimon were held in prison awaiting their execution. A Jew with influence at the royal court undertook to rescue them. After depositing a huge amount of money into the royal treasury, he obtained from the king a royal edict*

Title page of *Teshuvot Maharam Padua* by Rabbi Meir Katzenellenbogen; it was printed together with *Teshuvot Mahari Mintz* by his wife's grandfather. This was published in Cracow, 1882.

ordering the release of the prisoners. However, before the edict arrived, Reuven, with the help of God, managed to escape from the prison, and only Shimon was still in captivity when the king's document arrived. Thereupon, Shimon was set free. It is clear that the amount of ransom was not affected by the fact that there were two prisoners. The same amount would have been demanded if only Shimon was held captive from the start. Our question is whether Reuven must pay his share of the ransom even though he escaped on his own, or must Shimon pay the entire amount because he is the only beneficiary, or should he pay half and the interceder bear the loss of the other half?

Responsum: [After comparing this case to similar cases in the Gemara, Maharam states:] The inescapable conclusion is that Reuven is exempt from paying anything, since he freed himself without any outside help and he did not enjoy any benefit from the ransom payment.... The interceder did not make a greater effort to save two people than to save one person. If he had known that one man escaped, he would have exerted himself just as much to gain the release of the remaining prisoner. Thus it is only Shimon who benefited. It is right, therefore, that the interceder should not have to suffer any loss, but Shimon should pay the entire amount....

Can This Vow Be Annulled?
Teshuvot Maharam Padua, no. 72

Question: *Three years ago, while in prison and in grave danger, a man made a vow. If he were liberated from prison, within two years [after his release] he would go to Eretz Yisrael on one of the fishing boats that regularly sail from Venice in May or August, that is to say in May or August of 1538 [at the present time]. A bloody war is [now] raging between Italy and the Moslem world, which makes any sea voyage extremely hazardous. This man, fearful of incurring heavenly wrath, is seeking to have his vow annulled.*

Responsum: On the one hand, a vow that was made in time of distress cannot be annulled; on the other hand, in an unavoidable emergency such as this case, no annulment is needed. We can argue, however, that although present circumstances prevent him from carrying out his vow, why should he be relieved of his vow completely? Perhaps he should fulfill his vow when the war is settled and the sea lanes are open again.... However, I found in **Teshuvot Rashba**, no. 84 that if a person made a vow to do something at a certain time, once that time has passed and he failed to do it, the vow is cancelled.

In our case, he vowed to go to Eretz Yisrael within two years [of his release]. Since unavoidable circumstances prevented him from going during that time, the vow is cancelled....

Must This Student Pay Tuition?
Teshuvot Maharam Padua, no. 86

Question: *A student fled from Venice at the time the plague was ravaging that city. Does he have to pay full tuition to his teacher or may he subtract the period of his absence?*

Responsum: It is a simple and unequivocal halachah that if an unavoidable situation prevents a teacher or a worker from performing his duties, the worker suffers the loss.

Our case is analogous to this. The student's absence due to his fear of the plague certainly can be termed an unavoidable situation. If you want to argue that not everybody fled the city and therefore it should not be considered an unavoidable emergency and the student should not have fled either, this is a fallacy. It is a well-known fact that those who are fearful and fainthearted are more likely to fall victim to the bubonic plague than the bold and the undaunted. People who are afraid are in mortal danger and must flee for their lives.

Their Father Renounced the Jewish Faith
Teshuvot Maharam Padua, no. 87

Question: *Two brothers, Avraham and Efraim, are living in the city of Oven. Their father, formerly known as Shnei'ur, renounced his faith and converted to Christianity. Since the day of his conversion, his decent and upright sons have not been* called up to the reading of the Torah. They are ashamed to be called up by the name of their grandfather; this would publicize their humiliation, since before that time they were called up by their father's name. Would it be permissible to call them by their father's name?

Responsum: I decide herewith that it is absolutely permitted. I am undaunted by the ruling of the Gaon Rabbi Isserlin[3] to the effect that the son of a *mumar*[4] should be called by his grandfather's name. After all, our Rabbis said in *Bava Metzia* 59a: "It is better for a man to be thrown into a fiery furnace than humiliate his fellow man in public." ... We find an example in Scripture of a *tzaddik* (righteous man) being named after his father who was a *rasha* (wicked man) in the case of King Chizkiyah (Hezekiah) ben Achaz.[5]

Their father is a powerful and influential government official ... and I have heard that he tries to do good for the Jewish people, helping them personally and financially. His actions prove that he feels remorse and fears God. We should bring him closer to us rather than repel him. For the above-mentioned reasons, the brothers should be called up to the reading of the Torah as "ben Shnei'ur," as before.

He Promised His Mother ...
Teshuvot Maharam Padua, no. 74

Question: *Before leaving home to study at an out-of-town yeshivah, Avraham gave his widowed mother a solemn oath not to get married without her approval. In the far-off city the young man fell in love with a beautiful girl, and in spite of his mother's protests he promised to marry the girl, ratifying his intentions by giving the girl's mother a firm handshake. Some say he even gave an oath. The learned men of the city are in a quandary; some think of excommunicating the young man if he does not live up to his handshake and refuses to marry the girl.*

Responsum: I cannot comprehend their convoluted logic. Inasmuch as the young man is under oath not to marry without his mother's permission, how can a handshake or another oath override the first oath? It is plain as day that a second oath cannot invalidate a prior oath; the second oath is a vain oath. ... This young man should repent his sin of uttering a vain oath. ... Those who pursued him and tried to make him violate his oath acted wrongly, for they knew that he was bound by a divine oath.

RABBI YOSEF KARO—BEIT YOSEF, SHULCHAN ARUCH
רבי יוסף קארו — בית יוסף, שולחן ערוך

born: Toledo, Spain, 1488
died: Safed, Eretz Yisrael, 1575
Popularly known as Beit Yosef and Shulchan Aruch, the names of his major works.

Rabbi Yosef Karo's family was forced to flee Spain in the wake of the great expulsion of Spanish Jewry in 1492. After years of wandering, the family settled in Constantinople, Turkey. When Rabbi Yosef was 24 years old, while living in Adrianople, Turkey, he began writing his famous commentary *Beit Yosef* on *Arba Turim* by Rabbi Yaakov, son of the Rosh. It took him twenty years to complete it.

Under the influence of the great kabbalist Rabbi Shelomoh Molcho, Rabbi Yosef Karo followed an ascetic lifestyle of fasting and pious devotion to God. In 1530 he moved to Safed, Eretz Yisrael, where he was appointed a member of the Rabbinic Court of Rabbi Yaakov Beirav. He established a yeshivah, counting among his many students the great Rabbi **Moshe Alshich** and the illustrious kabbalist Rabbi Moshe Cordovero (Remak). Upon the death of Rabbi Moshe Beirav, Rabbi Yosef Karo succeeded him as Chief of the Rabbinic Court in Safed, which served as the main Bet Din for worldwide Jewry. Through his monumental books he became the acknowledged preeminent Torah authority in the world, a reputation that has not waned with the passage of time.

In his *Beit Yosef* he compiles all the variant views on each halachah and renders a decision as to which opinion is to be the authoritative law. It is printed alongside the text of the *Arba Turim*.

After completing *Beit Yosef*, Rabbi Yosef Karo wrote the *Shulchan Aruch*.[1] As its title implies,

Rabbi Yosef Karo.

Shulchan Aruch, "The Set Table," presents all Jewish laws and customs relevant to the present time in clear and concise Hebrew, divided into four sections and arranged systematically according to topic.

This work is the cornerstone of authoritative Halachah to this very day: the Code of Jewish Law par excellence. Among his other writing is his commentary on the **Rambam**, entitled *Kesef Mishneh*.

Rabbi Yosef Karo received inquiries from rabbis in remote communities, all seeking his guidance and advice on Halachah. His responsa, which are clear and to the point, have been published under the title *Avkat Rocheil*,[2] "The Perfumer's Powders." Through his *Shulchan Aruch*, Rabbi Yosef Karo has become the guide and mentor of every Jewish home to this very day. He is one of the all-time Torah giants.

Is the Slave Girl Permitted to Marry a Jew?
Avkat Rocheil, no. 49

Question: *Reuven, arriving in Egypt from a country in the North, brought with him a young Christian girl whom he had bought, and placed her in the care of a [Jewish] woman. This woman stated that he planned to marry her [the girl] eventually. Reuven left for a western country and is reported to have died. The girl, who has been raised as a Jew, is now 20 years old and resides in Jerusalem. Can a way be found for this young woman to marry a Jew? Reuven has no known heir or relative [who will inherit her as a slave], and there is reason to fear that when the non-Jews learn that she has no master they will take her into a harem or that she will become promiscuous.*

Responsum: At first glance, there seems to be no way for this woman to enter the marriage group of Israel, since no one inherited her. If there were an heir, the Bet Din would compel the new master to release her so that she could marry a Jew. But since there is no known heir, there is no one to remove her impediment.... Therefore, in this case a Bet Din of three rabbis should appoint an executor for Reuven's estate who sells this maidservant with the stipulation that the buyer set her free. He places the money in escrow, and the buyer issues a document of release. She is thereby permitted to enter the marriage group of Israel.

Facsimile of the original title page of *She'eilot uTeshuvot Rabbi Yosef Karo* by the author of the *Shulchan Aruch*; published in Salonica "under the rule of the mighty Sultan Mehmet." The letters following Mehmet are an abbreviation of *yarum hodo*, "may his glory be exalted," an expression usually appended to names of benign kings and potentates.

Placing a Statue of a Lion on an Aron HaKodesh
Avkat Rocheil, no. 63

Question: *Someone wants to place on the Holy Ark a stone slab into which is carved the form of a lion. Rabbi Eliyahu Kafsali ruled against it and is asking whether we concur with his decision.*

Responsum: Anyone in whose heart stirs a love of God should put a stop to this. It is true that the **Rambam**[3] asserts that, except for statues of the

Title page of *Avkat Rocheil*, responsa by Rabbi Yosef Karo; the Hebrew words say, "Improved and beautifully arranged second edition, printed on good paper, with graceful letters, black ink, and carefully edited, as the reader will see. Leipzig 1859."

human form, all forms are permitted, but the **Ran**[4] rules that statues of all forms of animals are forbidden. In fact, Rabbi Elyakim ordered the forms of lions and snakes removed from the synagogue in Cologne (Germany). . . . When people gaze at these forms, they are distracted from their prayers . . . and there is the apprehension that, although the gentiles do not worship these forms, if they see the congregation bowing in the direction of a lion, which is one of the four living creatures of the *Merkavah*, "Divine Chariot,"[5] of Ezekiel, the wrong impression may be created.

The **Rosh**[6] was asked, concerning prayer rugs that Moslems use for their prayers, whether these may be displayed on the walls of a synagogue. He ruled against it.

To recapitulate, no one should place such an image on the Holy Ark. They should not disobey their rabbi, who adopted a stringent view in this matter.

A Dispute between Neighbors
Avkat Rocheil, no. 107

Question: *Reuven and Shimon live in houses that are facing each other on opposite sides of the street. Reuven's house has always had a second story with windows opening toward the street. Shimon now added a second story to his house with windows facing Reuven's second story. Reuven claims that Shimon can peek through these windows and watch the goings-on in his second story and this entails "damage from peeking." He contends that his windows were there first. Shimon asserts that, since the homes face the public domain, each may do as he pleases. Who is in the right?*

Responsum: Reuven is right since he has the right of priority. Shimon, who opened the windows afterwards, must be compelled to close them up and block them so that no "damage from peeking" ensues to Reuven.

Opposition to the Rabbi's Appointment
Avkat Rocheil, no. 196

Question: *The majority of the members of a congregation want to appoint a rabbi according to the accepted custom. A few individuals who oppose the candidate signed an agreement under oath not to allow this rabbi to be elected. A bitter dispute arose over this issue which led most of the opposing members to regret their defiance. However, they now say that their sworn agreement stipulated that their oath was to remain in force even if the majority of the signatories change their mind, as long as there is one dissenter. One of the signatories left for a faraway country. Can the oath of the others be annulled or must they wait for the absent member to return?*

Responsum: This oath may be annulled because it involves the great mitzvah of establishing peace in the community. Peace is an overriding concern, and this will put an end to the quarreling and strife.

There is another facet of mitzvah involved. Because of this dispute, they have appointed neither this rabbi nor any other. As a result, they don't study Torah. Furthermore, since the opposing individuals agree to the rabbi's appointment, the one who is abroad will not object. They should notify him of their decision, exhorting him not to withhold his approval. In essence, we are dealing here with two oaths: (1) The oath to oppose the rabbi's election, and (2) the vow not to permit the oath to be annulled as long as there is one dissenting vote. Let them begin by annulling the second oath and subsequently have the first oath annulled.

A Judge under Forty Years of Age?
Avkat Rocheil, no. 201

Question: *A group of rabbis convened and declared under pain of excommunication that no rabbi under forty years of age be permitted to act as a judge and arbiter or render halachic decisions, What is your view?*

Responsum: . . . Since the three pillars of the world, the Rif, the **Rambam**, and the **Rosh**, agree on this matter, the halachah is clear and unassailable, and who would not bow to their decision that anyone who is qualified to decide halachah, even if he has not reached the age of 40 years, is authorized to decide halachah and administer justice. The Tur[7] states that one is unqualified to administer justice until he is 18 years old. It is the accepted custom in all Turkish communities to appoint as judges and deciders of halachah unmarried young scholars who are qualified, and no one ever has raised objections to this. The **Rivash**[8] appointed in the city of Safed judges who had not reached the age of forty. In summation: Whoever is qualified, even if he is only 18 years old, may decide halachah and administer justice. Whoever prevents him from doing so prevents him from fulfilling the explicit command of the Torah, "Judge your neighbor fairly."[9] Not even a father is allowed to forbid his son, or a teacher his student, to serve as rabbi. If they do, he should pay no attention to them.

A "Marriage" of Minors?
Teshuvot Beit Yosef, no. 7

Question: *It happened in a tavern that a man who is the father of a little son was drinking with a friend who has a small daughter. Suddenly the father of the boy rose and took his friend's little daughter in marriage for his son by giving the girl's father a cup of wine. The girl's father accepted the cup of wine as* kiddushin [*a token of the consecration of a marriage*]. *Then they both sat down to drink. Will this "marriage" have any validity when the children grow up?*

Responsum: [After citing numerous sources from the Gemara, the Geonim, and later authorities, Rabbi Yosef Karo quotes] **Maharik**, who states in his responsa: "Even if the father had consecrated the little girl in marriage with a ring on behalf of his son, there is no marriage, for the Gemara states in *Kiddushin*, *Yevamot*, and *Ketuvot* that a minor cannot enter into a marriage. However, if, after the son grew up, witnesses saw him closeted alone with the girl, then the *kiddushin* are valid, as set forth by the Tur (*Orach Chaim*, no. 43), and then the marriage can be dissolved only by means of a *get*, a religious divorce. . . . In this case, where she was "married" through a cup of wine that her father drank, the *kiddushin* have no validity when the minor grows up. This is the law, and it is final. We have proved conclusively on the basis of the opinions of the Geonim, Rishonim, and Acharonim, by whose words we live, that this case presents no cause for any concern.

RABBI MOSHE DI TRANI—MABIT
רבי משה די טראני — מבי"ט

born: Salonica, Greece, 1500
died: Jerusalem, 1585
Popularly known as Mabit, the title of his responsa work and the initials of Moshe ben Yosef Trani.

Rabbi Moshe's father escaped the massacres in Spain and settled in Salonica, Greece, where Rabbi Moshe was born. His first teacher was his uncle, Rabbi Aharon di Trani, in Adrianople, Turkey. When he was 18 years old he came to Safed to study under the great Rabbi Yaakov Beirav, becoming his most outstanding disciple. In 1525 he was appointed rabbi in Safed, along with Rabbi **Yosef Karo**,[1] the author of *Beit Yosef* and the *Shulchan Aruch*. The Mabit served in that post for fifty-four years, teaching Torah to a great number of students and leading the community. After Rabbi Yosef Karo's death, the Mabit served as head of the Bet Din for five years. On halachic issues he often disagreed with Rabbi Yosef Karo, as is evident in his responsa.

As a leading halachic authority, he received numerous queries which were published, under the title *She'eilot uTeshuvot Mabit*,[2] in two volumes containing more than 800 responsa. They afford illuminating insights into the halachic decision-making process. The Mabit also wrote *Kiriat Sefer*[3] on the **Rambam** and *Bet Elokim*[4] on ethics, prayer, and repentance.

By Giving Her Grapes, Did He Marry Her?
Teshuvot Mabit, no. 1:14

Question: *Reuven was working for Shimon pressing grapes. Shimon told him that he was free to eat of*

Title page of *Mabit*, responsa by Rabbi Moshe di Trani, Rabbi of Tzefat (Safed). The phrase following the name Tzefat is *Galil ha'elyon tibaneh vetikonen bimehera beyamenu* ("in the Upper Galilee, may she be rebuilt and established speedily in our days").

the grapes and to give some away. A woman passing by asked Reuven to give her some grapes. He replied, "If you'll marry me, I'll give you this bunch of grapes." She answered, "Yes," and he gave her the cluster of grapes. She took the grapes and went on her way. . . . There were several people who witnessed the incident. Please let us know if there is reason for concern that this constitutes kiddushin, *a legal marriage?*[5]

Responsum: It seems to me that there is no reason to fear that this constitutes *kiddushin*, for a number of reasons: To begin with, the Gemara in *Kiddushin* states that if a man marries a woman by giving her a stolen article, the *kiddushin* is invalid. In this case, even if Reuven's boss gave him permission to eat or give away some grapes, he did not really mean a full cluster . . . possibly a few loose grapes. Giving a bunch of grapes is theft, and thus the *kiddushin* is not valid.

Second, Reuven did not use the standard formula. If he had said, "With these grapes I marry you," there would be a marriage, but he said, "If you'll marry me," which means, "If you will marry me some time in the future," and to this she said "Yes." But she did not accept the grapes as *kiddushin* to be married then and there. . . .

I say, in view of all these doubts, in this case there is no reason for apprehension that this constitutes *kiddushin*, and no *get* is needed. May God lead me on the path of truth.

Shipwrecked
Teshuvot Mabit, no. 1:186

Question: *A number of Jews sailed on a large ship together with several hundred Arabs. Most of the passengers and the freight were in the hold of the ship. There was only one exit door leading from the hold to the upper deck. A howling storm blew up which turned the ship on its side, and water began to enter the hold. Three or four Jews and some Arabs were on deck, and when they saw that the ship was about to capsize, the Jews went below and pleaded with their brothers to save themselves. But they were weeping and confessing their sins as they saw that their death was imminent. Suddenly the ship began to list and the men who were above fell overboard and swam in the raging waters. Slowly the ship went down to an unknown watery grave. A few of the survivors, two of whom were Jews, made it to a lifeboat. One of them reported that all the men that did not make it to the lifeboat drowned and that their bodies washed ashore on the island of Chio, where they were buried. He also reported that the Jews who were in the cabin below must have perished since there was no way for them to escape, because the ship was overturned when it went down, and neither Arab nor Jew of the passengers below was seen afterward. The question is whether the men who were in the cabin may be considered as drowned at sea.*

Responsum: It seems that we may permit the wives of those who were in the cabin to remarry. . . . As another reason, we can cite the fact that they did not want to leave their cabin and were preparing to die, since they wept and confessed their sins as the water came bursting in. They wanted the cabin to be their grave rather than fall prey to the sharks. Also, the fact that neither the bodies nor the belongings of any of those in the cabin washed ashore while the bodies of some of the men on deck were recovered proves that they did not escape from the cabin but died there. For if the door was closed, they could not get out, and if the door was open, the water would have poured in.

The Lost Necklace
Teshuvot Mabit, no. 1:241

Question: *It happened at a wedding that Mrs. Reuven noticed that the bride was not wearing any jewelry. She took off her gold necklace and placed it on the bride's neck, fastening it securely. She told Mrs. Levi, a relative of the bride, "I beg of you, please keep an eye on this necklace. It is a very valuable piece of jewelry. See that I get it back." After the week of feasting had ended, Mrs. Levi asked the bride, "Please give me Mrs. Reuven's necklace. She asked me to get it for her, and I went out of my way to pass by your house to pick it up." The bride bent down, asking Mrs. Levi to unfasten the necklace. As she untied the knot, the young husband came in, shouting angrily, "Leave the necklace alone. I don't want to return it right now." Mrs. Levi replied, "I have been asked to bring it back, and I'm afraid it might get lost or stolen." Said the young man, "That's none of your concern.*

If it is lost or stolen, I'll pay for it. Besides, show me your written authorization."

Not long after that the necklace disappeared. Now Mrs. Reuven claims that the young husband should have trusted Mrs. Levi and should have returned the necklace to her, and that it was lost through his negligence since he did not watch it properly. Furthermore, the young man had said that in case of loss he was going to pay for it. Rabbi, please give us guidance in this matter.

Responsum: First we must establish if the bride has the status of a borrower.[6] On the one hand, she made use of the necklace, since it made her look beautiful, but on the other hand, she did not ask for it. And if indeed she is a borrower, we must determine if the husband is responsible for her losses.

... In this case, even though she did not ask for the necklace, since it was placed on her neck and she did not refuse it and it enhanced her appearance as a bride, she is considered a borrower and is responsible for all losses. The fact that she used the necklace is not sufficient to place responsibility for it on her husband. The statement by the husband that he was going to pay in case of loss does not obligate him. He just said that to answer the woman, and besides, he did not say it at the time the borrowing took place and in the presence of the lender. He must declare under oath that the necklace is not in his possession and that he did not hide it and that it was not stolen through his negligence. She too must swear, and an order of Bet Din should be issued that if and when she has the means she is responsible for paying for the necklace.

The Wicked Son
Teshuvot Mabit, no. 2:38

Question: *Reuven has a son, Shimon, who has a sick mind and who continually taunts and humiliates his father in front of other people and demands from him money for unnecessary expenses. The more money his father gives him, the more abusive Shimon becomes and the more outrageous are his demands. He threatens to denounce his father to the government and to abandon the Jewish religion. He shamelessly strikes his father and pulls his beard.*

A number of people who could not bear to see the father suffer advised him to write Shimon a promissory note for a substantial amount, payable at a later date, so that he will leave his father alone and stop beating, threatening, and abusing him. Reuven should write another note stating that the promissory note was written under duress, so that he would not have to pay it when it came due. The friends were going to confirm and certify the second note. Reuven followed their advice and wrote the promissory note and also the second note. Shimon now sues in a Din Torah *(rabbinical court) to collect the note, and the father showed his "declaration of duress." Rabbi, please let us know whether according to halachah, Reuven is obligated to pay this promissory note. May you be doubly rewarded from Heaven.*

Responsum: Although generally we say that people have a tendency to exaggerate, and their threats should not be taken seriously, in this case the son actually carried out his threats. He abused his father, who gave him money repeatedly, to the point of striking him and pulling his beard. Thus his father was forced to write this note and he does not have to pay it. . . . This holds true especially in this case where the note was a gift, since the father did not owe the money. Therefore, Reuven is exempt from paying the promissory note he wrote to his son.

Must the Agent Suffer the Loss?
Teshuvot Mabit, no. 2:156

Question: *Reuven appointed Shimon as his agent to buy for him a certain house from a non-Jew. Shimon negotiated the deal, and he and the seller agreed on a price. In the meantime, Reuven backed out. The non-Jew took Shimon to court. Shimon asserted that he was only the agent and that they had only a verbal agreement. The non-Jew brought witnesses to support his claim that Shimon was the principal and that he had never mentioned another buyer. The judge ruled that Shimon had to buy the house and pay the money to the non-Jew. Shimon now sues Reuven for his loss. Reuven declines any responsibility, saying the loss is Shimon's bad luck. Rabbi, please decide who is right.*

Responsum: In *Teshuvot Ramban*,[7] no. 2, he writes that one who sends an agent is not responsible for the losses the agent incurred, especially if he was a paid agent. . . . It seems to me that the principal is not responsible if the loss was not the principal's fault—for example, if the agent was taken captive while on the mission on behalf of the principal. For if the agent had passed that location on his own business, he would also have been taken captive. Thus the principal is not liable. But if the bandits were the sworn enemies of the principal and abducted the agent because they knew that he was his representative and was carrying his money, then the principal would have the duty to ransom him, because his capture was the principal's fault. . . .

In our case, since the agent suffered the loss as a result of Reuven's change of heart, it is clearly Reuven's fault, since the agent did his job properly. Therefore, Reuven must pay for the loss.

A Former Marrano[8]
Teshuvot Mabit, no. 1:170

Question: *Is the testimony of a former Marrano regarding events that occurred while he was a Marrano acceptable in a Bet Din?*

Responsum: If a person commits even the most severe transgression because he is forced to do so, he is not disqualified from testifying as a witness . . . as stated by the **Rivash**,[9] responsum no. 4 . . . and it is a known fact that the majority of these Marranos did not violate the Shabbat and did not adhere to Christianity in the privacy of their homes. Therefore, the fact that they publicly practiced Christianity and violated the Shabbat does not disqualify them as witnesses, for they were compelled to do so. Thus they were acceptable witnesses even while still in Spain, and surely now, that they resumed to serve God openly. It seems to me that by returning to Judaism they proved retroactively that they never believed in Christianity and that they were not disqualified as witnesses from the start.

He Wants to Break Away from the Community
Teshuvot Mabit, no. 151

Question: *A group of people formed a mutual society for the purpose of praying together and assisting each other, to share in each other's joys and sorrows, and to help one another in case of distress. The members took an irrevocable oath not to rescind this mutual pledge, and not to withdraw from the society unless all other members gave their consent. Now one of the members wants to leave the society. He claims that in his moment of trouble the other members did not come to his aid. Therefore, he contends, the agreement was broken and is now null and void, and he wishes to join another synagogue. Please, Rabbi, let us know, if he leaves, what should be his punishment. Also, may another synagogue accept him as a member?*

Responsum: The society was formed primarily for the purpose of praying together. It is too much to expect that a group of people should be associated with each other for any length of time without an occasional disagreement. Therefore, although he may have a grievance about not receiving help in a time of need, this does not release him from the obligation to pray in that synagogue. The clause regarding assisting each other is not linked to the agreement of praying together. They are two independent clauses; the abrogation of one does not cancel the other.

A Bet Din must decide whether the members violated the agreement by not coming to his aid. If they are found guilty, they must be punished and warned henceforth to live up to their pact. And if they fail to do so, the members must permit him to leave the community. But before the matter has been clarified by the Bet Din, he has no right to resign. If he does, he is subject to the fines that are spelled out in the agreement, and he is not permitted to pray in any other synagogue.

RABBI SHEMUEL DI MEDINA—MAHARASHDAM
רבי שמואל די מדינה — מהרשד"ם

born: Salonica, Greece, 1506
died: Salonica, Greece, 1589
Popularly known as Maharashdam, the title of his work and initials of his name.

Rabbi Shemuel di Medina was one of the great *poskim* of the sixteenth century. He was born into a family of Spanish exiles and studied under Rabbi Levi ibn Chaviv. He served as rabbi of Salonica, Greece, and of several communities in Turkey, returning to Salonica toward the end of his life. He gained fame as an outstanding halachic authority, and rabbis from near and far wrote their queries to him. His responsa exhibit his great humility and his peace-loving nature. Close to a thousand of his responsa were published by his son, Rabbi Moshe, under the title, *She'eilot uTeshuvot Maharashdam*.[1] The loss of both his sons-in-law placed the responsibility for his daughters and their children on his shoulders. Despite this personal tragedy, he served his community with undiminished vigor, teaching Torah until the last day of his life.

Title page of *She'eilot uTeshuvot Maharashdam* by Rabbi Shemuel di Medina of Salonica. Maharashdam is an acronym of the initials of his name. First printed in 1596, Salonica.

Quarreling Neighbors
***Teshuvot Maharashdam, Orach Chaim*, no. 5**

Question: *Reuven and Shimon, living in the same house, became embroiled in a bitter quarrel. Shimon was reprimanded three times by the Bet Din for offending Reuven. Shimon told friends that he had a way to get rid of Reuven. Since he lived above Reuven's apartment, he was going to drill a hole in his floor over Reuven's bedroom and pour water on his bed. That would surely make Reuven move out. One Shabbat, having returned home from the synagogue and having had his Shabbat meal, Reuven wanted to take a nap but found his bed soaked with water.*

A short while later someone in Shimon's apartment heard a commotion and, upon inspection, found Shimon's dishes broken in pieces. They suspected Reuven but no one had seen him break the dishes. Shimon, angry and provoked, denounced Reuven to the authorities, leveling false accusations against him. Reuven was forced to pay 13 grossos to ransom himself. He claimed that he did not do it and that Shimon, by accusing him without witnesses, had caused him serious losses. The matter was subsequently adjudicated before a Bet Din, which found Reuven guilty and imposed a fine on him. Reuven thinks that the Bet Din treated him unfairly.

Responsum: If there were witnesses, Reuven should be duly punished. But the matter should not have been brought before the civil court, particularly since there were no witnesses. . . . Quite the contrary, Shimon, who poured water on Reuven's bed, should be penalized. He was the one who provoked Reuven's sin, and as if that were not enough, he also sued him in civil court. And if he made the hole in the floor on Shabbat, his transgression is very grave indeed. In fact, the sin of making a hole in the floor is much graver than Reuven's trespass of breaking the dishes. . . .

I am astonished at the Bet Din for fining Reuven. What made them find Reuven guilty and acquit Shimon? It is a topsy-turvy world! Shimon commits a sin and Reuven is punished! If it were up to me I would punish the Bet Din that rendered such a verdict, and I would sentence Shimon to compensate Reuven for the ransom he had to pay, for no money in the world can make restitution for Reuven's mental anguish.

May the Rock of Israel save us from great and small errors.

A Problem for Travelers
Teshuvot Maharashdam, Orach Chaim, no. 7

Question: *People traveling to Egypt and other distant places usually sew their money into their clothing for fear that otherwise it would be stolen. Are they permitted to go out in these garments on Shabbat?*[2]

Responsum: It seems to me that it is permitted, just as it is permitted to go out on Shabbat wearing a garment that has cotton padding. [There follows a detailed analysis of the relevant sources.]

May the Son Marry the Girl of His Choice?
Teshuvot Maharashdam, Orach Chaim, no. 95

Question: *It happened in Salonica, Greece, that before his death, Reuven told his son that under no circumstances was he to marry a certain young lady. The questioner asks, since this young lady appeals to Reuven's son, whether he should be concerned about violating the command of honoring his father.*

Responsum: The *Chacham*[3] Rabbi Chaim Ovadiah wrote about this at great length. I received his decision and I concur. Reuven's son is permitted to marry the woman he favors and his father's command constitutes no impediment whatsoever. If she is a decent Jewish girl and he loves her, then he should marry her, for with her, God will give him upright children; this would not be the case if he married another woman whom he did not desire, for the children of an unloved wife are unloved by God.[4]

There are two instances where a son need not obey his father: if a father wants to deter his son from leaving the country in order to study Torah, and most assuredly if the son wants to marry the girl who appeals to him, then the very great mitzvah of marrying her overrides the mitzvah of honoring one's father and mother.

The Brother's Vow
Teshuvot Maharashdam, Yoreh De'ah, no. 77

Question: *Concerning two brothers, of which the older one is married to a lady of a very distinguished family. When his younger brother reached marriageable age, it occurred to him to arrange a match for his brother with his wife's younger sister. He requested his father-in-law to give his other daughter in marriage to his brother. They swore a solemn oath that the young man would marry the girl. But evil people suggested another, very rich young woman to the brother. The brother, on the advice of his mother, took it under serious consideration and tried to find ways to have the vow annulled. When the older brother saw that a Jewish girl was being trifled with (especially since he had implored his* father-in-law to give his consent), he made an oath, saying, "I will be a nazir like Samson,[5] son of Mano'ach, husband of Delilah, whose eyes were put out by the Philistines, if my brother marries this other girl without my father-in-law's approval." The question is, if the younger brother does marry the other girl, must the older brother remain a nazir for the rest of his life, or is there a way that he need not fulfill his oath?

Responsum: There is no need to go into great detail, because everyone knows that the older brother must fulfill his vow if, God forbid, the younger brother marries another woman without the father-in-law's permission. . . . It is clear that it is an irrevocable vow. Let the younger brother not transgress and cause such anger and distress to his older brother. The vow cannot be annulled. . . . I do not believe that any rabbi in Israel will rule contrary to anything I have said.

Freeing Captives
Teshuvot Maharashdam, Choshen Mishpat, no. 344

Question: *Rabbi Yosef ben Shelomoh was sailing in a fishing vessel together with a group of Jewish merchants when they were taken captive and their merchandise seized. Among the merchandise that was taken there were bales of silks belonging to Yechiel Shaki. With the help of God and the intervention of His Majesty the King of Venice and the police authorities, some of the pirates were arrested, and they are being held in prison until the captive Jews are freed and their goods returned to them. The pirates are willing to release the Jews in order to gain freedom for their accomplices, but they say that the silks and the goods are irretrievably lost. The fifty Jewish captives want to be released even without receiving one penny for their merchandise. Only Yechiel Shaki objects and does not allow the imprisoned pirates to be released unless they return his silks. Rabbi Yosef and the Jewish captives are crying out, "Is it fair that we should die for a few bales of Yechiel's silk?" They ask if Yechiel is obligated to renounce his claim to the silk, so that the government will release the pirates and the captive Jews will thereby regain their freedom, or do we* say, *"This is not Yechiel's concern. Why should he forfeit his money?"*

Responsum: Yechiel is, in essence, threatening the life of the Jewish captives, for if the silk were not his, the Jews would be free. Only because of his silks are they still in prison. He is pursuing and threatening the lives of these unfortunate Jews. And their life is indeed in jeopardy. The **Rambam** says that if anyone is pursuing and threatening to kill someone, all Israel has the duty to save the intended victim, even if it means killing the pursuer. . . . Each day Yechiel is violating the command of "Do not stand still when your neighbor's life is in danger."[6] I don't understand, if this Yechiel is a Jew, how could he even entertain a doubt in this matter. Moreover, the merchandise is not even here, and there is only a very small chance that it will ever be recovered, while at the same time people's lives are at stake. It is self-understood that Yechiel should renounce any claim he has to his silks and let him not be a *rodeif*, a pursuer of the captives, who are in the right, as I have mentioned.

Who Is Responsible for the Fire?
Teshuvot Maharashdam, Choshen Mishpat, no. 266

Question: *Reuven rented a house to Shimon. On Friday, Shimon's wife used the stove for baking, as Jewish woman usually do, and placed pots in it to keep the dishes hot for Shabbat. As a result, a fire broke out on Friday night and the house burned down. Reuven now sues Shimon for damages, as it is written, "the one who started the fire must make restitution."*[7] *Shimon contends that he owes nothing since Reuven did not tell him that the stove was defective, and it is Reuven who caused the loss. Who is right?*

Responsum: First we must establish whether Shimon is considered a *shomeir chinam*, an unpaid guardian,[8] who is exempt from damages in case of any accident, or a *socheir*, a renter.

It is clear that a tenant falls under the classification of *socheir*. As such, he is exempt from damages only in case of an unavoidable accident. . . . Shimon was guilty of negligence. . . . He should have watched the fire in the stove, especially since the fire did not break out when he lit the stove but only on Friday night. He was very negligent in failing to size up the situation when he placed the pots in the oven. He should have checked to see whether the clay on the walls of the stove had caught fire. This was something he could have determined, yet he failed to do so. He was negligent and he must pay the damages.

Can He Evict the Tenant?
Teshuvot Maharashdam, Choshen Mishpat, no. 300

Question: *Reuven rented one of his houses to Shimon for a term of three years. It was stipulated that Reuven could not cancel the lease before the end of three years. It happened that after one and a half years some Turks falsely accused Reuven of a crime which is punishable by lashes, according to Turkish law. After this denunciation Reuven sold the house to Levi, and then he ran away. Now Levi took Shimon, the tenant, to the Bet Din, demanding that he vacate the house, since he, Levi, is the new owner. Shimon countered, "Levi, you bought the house subject to my lease. You cannot evict me before the lease is terminated. I will pay the rent to you, and when the term of the lease is completed I will move out voluntarily."*

Please, Rabbi, let us know who is right.

Responsum: It seems obvious to me that the buyer has no right to evict the tenant before the completion of the full term of the lease which runs three years. [The Maharashdam proceeds to treat the question from a variety of angles, arriving at the same answer and refuting all arguments to the contrary. He ends:] These are the proofs as I see the case, and my views are supported by the Tur. No court or judge will remove the tenant before the term of the lease is concluded.

She Doesn't Want to Sell Her Slave Girl
Teshuvot Maharashdam, Even Ha'ezer, no. 211

Question: *Reuven bought for his wife a young slave girl. She grew up in the house, and now that she has reached the age of 18, Reuven went ahead and sold her. When his wife found out, she cried that she would not sell the girl even if she were offered a thousand gold ducats. Does the wife have the power to rescind the sale?*

Responsum: ... When a wife brings a dowry into the marriage, the husband has the obligation to buy a slave girl for her. Surely, since the husband bought the slave girl for his wife, he has no right to sell her.

RABBI MOSHE ALSHICH—ALSHICH HAKADOSH
רבי משה אלשיך — אלשיך הקדוש

born: Adrianople, Turkey, 1508
died: Damascus, Syria, 1593

Rabbi Moshe Alshich, a descendant of Spanish exiles, studied under Rabbi Shelomoh Taitatzak in Salonica and received *semichah* (rabbinical ordination) from Rabbi **Yosef Karo** in Safed. An acknowledged halachist, he devoted his days to answering questions of practical Halachah and adjudicating cases of law, while his nights were occupied with the study of Torah. One hundred and forty of his responsa have been published by his son, Rabbi Chaim Alshich, under the title *She'eilot uTeshuvot Maharam Alshich*[1]; the word Maharam is the acronym formed of the initials Moreinu HaRav Rabbi Moshe.

Rabbi Moshe Alshich is best known for his homiletic commentary on the Torah, *Torat Moshe*,[2] also known as *Alshich Hakadosh* (the saintly Alshich). When Rabbi Yitzchak Luria, the saintly kabbalist, arrived in Safed, Rabbi Moshe Alshich joined his inner circle of devoted disciples. He was a preeminent kabbalist in his own right, although this is not evident from his commentaries. His most famous student was Rabbi Chaim Vital, author of the kabbalistic work *Etz Chaim*.

In 1857 Rabbi Moshe Alshich was forced to leave Safed in the wake of the epidemic that ravaged that city, and he found refuge in Damascus. He was one of the greatest luminaries in an age that was blessed with a large number of outstanding Torah scholars.

Title page of *She'eilot uTeshuvot Moshe Alshich*. Facsimile of the original Venice edition printed in the year "keMoshe," which is the last word of the phrase *Mimoshe ve'ad Moshe lo kam keMoshe* ("Since Moshe [Rabbeinu] until Moshe [Alshich], no one has arisen to equal Moshe [Alshich]"). The numerical value of keMoshe is 365—5365 being the Jewish year corresponding to 1605, the year of its publication.

A Ship Sank with a Load of Iron Ingots
***Teshuvot Maharam Alshich*, no. 10**

Question: *Reuven bought from Shimon two thousand iron ingots. Shimon told Reuven that the iron was on board a ship and that he had instructed the* non-Jewish owner of the ship to transfer ownership of the ingots to him. Reuven agreed to buy the iron without any legal form of acquisition.[3] Subsequently Reuven sold the shipment to Levi, again without any legal form of acquisition. He merely told him that the iron ingots were aboard the ship. Levi made a partial payment, the balance to be paid in instalments.

En route, on the high seas the freighter was shipwrecked and sank, so that Levi did not receive any of the ingots. Reuven now demands from Levi payment of the balance he owes him, whereas Levi wants a refund from Reuven for the partial payment he made, contending that he never received the merchandise and that the deal was not legally consummated in the first place. Please, Rabbi, tell us who is right.

Responsum: The question is framed in terms of a dispute between Reuven and Levi, and the questioner evidently assumes that Reuven had legal title to the ingots. But this is not so. Even if Reuven had paid Shimon in full for the ingots, he has not taken title to them, and even after the freighter has gone down Reuven can back out of the deal and demand the return of his money from Shimon. . . . Thus, since Reuven did not legally acquire the ingots from Shimon, it goes without saying that Levi did not acquire them from Reuven, for the mere transfer of money does not constitute a legal transfer of ownership. . . .

For all of the above-mentioned reasons, Reuven can renege on his deal with Shimon and get his money back from him, and surely Levi can collect from Reuven the payment he made to him.

A Dispute about a Will
Teshuvot Maharam Alshich, no. 12

Question: *Reuven died and left a will in which he divided his estate. Among other things, he mentions that he owes Ploni ["John Doe"][4] 100 ducats. Ploni is to take all of his books in payment of this debt. . . . Ploni took the books, as stipulated in the will. Now the heir demands the difference between the value of the books and the amount of the debt, since the value of the books exceeded the 100 ducats by a sizable amount. . . .*

Responsum: It follows that in the present case the creditor acquires only as many books as equal the amount of the debt. The fact that the deceased stipulated that he was to take "all the books" was modified by the statement "in payment of this debt." Now you may infer from the term "he is to take all the books" that he is to receive the surplus as a gift. This is not so. You may be right if the deceased had stated, "Let Ploni, my creditor, take all the books." But since he added "in payment of my debt," he clearly indicated that when he stated, "take the books," he did not mean a gift, but a payment.

. . . The creditor is entitled only to the payment of his debt; the heir is entitled to the surplus.

Wife Refuses to Move to Husband's Hometown
Teshuvot Maharam Alshich, no. 55

Question: *Reuven, a resident of Cavalia, married Dinah from Adrianople. One year later he wanted to move to his hometown but she refused to join him, because the water in Cavalia is unhealthy, the land causes women to abort, and periodically the town is invaded by looting and pillaging mercenaries, and she does not want to live with danger hanging over her head. Besides, the inhabitants of Cavalia are* surgunish, *meaning that by governmental decree neither they nor their children may ever move to another city, and Dinah does not want to be tied down to that city forever. Reuven contends that he married her with the understanding that they would live in Cavalia and that she agreed. Who is right?*

Responsum: . . . The questioner does not mention what Dinah claims—whether she admits or denies that she agreed to move. Neither does he mention whether Dinah knew the bad features of Cavalia: its unsound water, its poisonous earth, the threat of the mercenaries, and the trouble of the *surgunish.*

. . . And even if she agreed to join him and took an oath to that effect, since she was not informed of the drawbacks of Cavalia, her oath was not given with full knowledge of these negative factors. . . . Therefore Dinah is right. Her husband cannot make her move away from her hometown.

Should the Wealthy Pay a Proportional Tax?[5]
Teshuvot Maharam Alshich, no. 56

Question: *In our town there are some rich people and a few who are much wealthier than the others. The community wants to levy a proportional tax, making each member pay according to his income. The very wealthy oppose the plan. They claim that until now there was a cap on the tax, and a rich man had to pay tax only on 3,000 gold florins, even if he earned 10,000 florins. They want things to remain the way they were. The other members of the community argue that this is unfair: a man earning 1,000 florins would pay tax on his entire income, while a man earning 10,000 florins pays tax on only one fifth of his income....*

Responsum: It seems quite obvious that justice dictates that each person should pay according to his income....

Therefore, because of all the above-mentioned reasons, the community can assess everyone to pay according to his income. But in the interest of preserving the peace, the right thing to do would be not to insist on levying taxes on the entire amount of the income. For example, a person earning 15,000 florins should pay tax on only 12,000 florins, and so forth.

Is a Hybrid *Etrog* Fit to Be Used?
Teshuvot Maharam Alshich, no. 110

Question: *This year, 5346/1586 in the holy city of Safed, we were asked if on Sukkot we may fulfill our obligation with a hybrid etrog.[6] The question does not arise if you implant a young shoot of a lemon tree into an* etrog *tree, for such a shoot produces only lemons, as all gardeners will attest, and as Rashi states (Sotah 43b), "... if you make a hole in a tree and you take a soft young shoot from another tree and you insert it into the hole so that it becomes a branch, then that branch will bear the fruit of the tree from which it was taken." The question is relevant only if you implant an* etrog *shoot into a lemon tree, for then the shoot produces a fruit that looks like an* etrog. *The only difference is that a genuine* etrog *has a thicker peel....*

Responsum: All the previous rabbis of Safed prohibited the use of this hybrid fruit.... In the Gemara in *Sukkah* 34b we learn that an *etrog* that is smaller than the size of an egg is invalid. Now, if this hybrid *etrog* were the size of an egg, how can we say that it is valid? After all, the *etrog* portion of the fruit comprises only half the size of an egg. Furthermore, the halachah states that if even the slightest part of an *etrog* is missing, it is invalid. Now this hybrid *etrog* lacks the portion that is made up of lemon. Moreover, the Gemara (*Sukkah* 36a) states that a round-shaped *etrog* is invalid. Does it make sense for a round-shaped *etrog* to be invalid and for an *etrog* half of which is another species to be fit for use?

To cite another reason: our sages expounded that the *etrog* with which you fulfill the mitzvah must be entirely yours, and not belong to someone else. This being so, then surely the *etrog* itself must be entirely an *etrog* and not half *etrog* and half lemon. Unquestionably, a hybrid is invalid and you cannot fulfill your obligation with it.

Is the Rabbi Exempt from Paying This Tax?
Teshuvot Maharam Alshich, no. 52

Question: *A Torah scholar is living abroad, where he devotes his time to Torah study. Since he owns a house in his hometown, he occasionally returns there, staying only a few days. The people of his hometown appointed a rabbi as their spiritual leader and judge and promised to pay him a certain salary. They never approached the Torah scholar for a contribution toward the rabbi's salary. Indeed, the rabbi agreed that the Torah scholar should not have to pay since he is engaged in Torah study all day.*

Five years had gone by in which the Torah scholar did not contribute toward the rabbi's salary, when one day a collector of the community came to his yeshivah demanding payment of 50 ducats. The Torah scholar asked him to leave, telling him, "Never before have I been asked to pay. Did you come here to give me trouble?" The collector became very abusive, insulting the Torah scholar, calling him names, and humiliating him publicly.

This collector has been known to act in this manner. In the past he has denounced many people to the Turkish authorities and he has been placed under a ban for this. Please, Rabbi, tell us if this boor has a right to treat a Torah scholar in such a contemptuous manner, and whether he has to pay him punitive damages. Also whether the Torah scholar is required to contribute toward the rabbi's salary, since he has no need for him and the Torah exempts Torah scholars from paying taxes (Bava Batra 8a).

Responsum: The Torah scholar exhibited an extraordinary degree of humility and forbearance by the fact that he did not place this collector under a ban. But it is the duty of the Bet Din to defend his honor by banning the collector and punishing him.

In regard to your other question, the Torah scholar is not required to pay toward the rabbi's salary. Since he studies Torah all day, he has no need for the rabbi's services. . . . It is the universally accepted custom that Torah scholars are exempt from paying the rabbi's salary.

However, I want to call your attention to a different aspect. If the community appointed the rabbi mainly to adjudicate legal disputes, then it is not right to assess each member according to his income. The rabbinic judge, knowing how much each person contributed toward his salary, cannot avoid favoring the one who paid more. His salary should be paid out of the general *tzedakah* account, so that he will not know who paid more and who paid less. Then the Torah scholar will also be a contributor toward the rabbi's salary, for there is no doubt that he is giving *tzedakah* according to his ability. In so doing, you will avoid any discord and resentment.

In summation, I want to state that the Torah scholar should not be charged with paying for the rabbi's salary.

He Overcharged for the Wine
Teshuvot Maharam Alshich, no. 75

Question: *A community prohibited, on pain of ban, anyone from selling wine for more than 5 dinars per liter. It was decreed that the ban and an attending fine would be imposed only on the offending seller, but not on the buyer. Reuven violated the decree, selling wine to Shimon for 7 dinars per liter. The Bet Din forced Reuven to pay a penalty for violating the ban. Reuven paid the penalty before Shimon had an opportunity to pay him for the wine. Reuven now demands that Shimon pay him the price of 7 dinars per liter, as he was charged. He [Reuven] claims that he received his due punishment. Shimon will pay only 5 dinars per liter. Please let us know who is right. Also, if Shimon had already paid him the 7 dinars, would Reuven have to refund the 2 dinars he overcharged, or could he keep the payment since he received his punishment?*

Responsum: [After citing decisions of Rav **Hai Gaon**, the Rif, and the **Rashba** in comparable cases, Maharam Alshich continues:] The Ramban and the Rashba state that violating a ban instituted by the community is as serious an offense as violating an oath, which is a biblical injunction.

Consequently, in this case, the sale remains intact and is not canceled, but Reuven must return the sum he overcharged.

RABBI SHELOMOH LURIA—MAHARSHAL
רבי שלמה לוריא — מהרש"ל

born: Brest-Litovsk (Brisk), Poland, c. 1510
died: Lublin, Poland, 1573
Popularly known as Maharshal, the abbreviation of Moreinu HaRav Shelomoh Luria.

Maharshal was born into a prominent family whose roots reached back to Rashi, and he was also related to such Torah giants as the Ari (Rabbi Yitzchak Luria), the Rema (Rabbi Moshe Isserles), and Rabbi **Meir Katzenellenbogen**, the Maharam of Padua. He received his early education from his maternal grandfather, Rabbi Yitzchak Kloiber. Later, he married the daughter of the rabbi of Ostroh, and when his father-in-law moved to Eretz Yisrael, Maharshal succeeded him in that post. Even as a young man, his vast erudition was universally recognized and he received halachic queries from near and far. He was an independent and creative thinker. At that time the prevailing method of talmudic study in Poland was *pilpul*, an intricate system of relating a wide range of subjects to the text being studied. In contrast, Maharshal's approach was to try to understand clearly the subject at hand on the basis of the correct text of the classic commentaries of Rashi and Tosafot.

His most important work is *Yam shel Shelomoh*,[1] a commentary on sixteen tractates of the Talmud of which only seven are available to us. An equally important work, *Chochmat Shelomoh*, is composed of glosses on the Talmud and is printed in all standard editions of the Talmud. Many of his responsa were published as *Teshuvot Maharshal*;[2] they manifest his penetrating thoughts and vast knowledge. Although he criticized many of his great contemporaries, he was full of praise for his relative Rabbi Moshe Isserles, the Rema. However, he did take him to task for studying philosophy. In a detailed reply in *Teshuvot Rema* no. 6, the Rema defends

She'eilot uTeshuvot Maharshal by Rabbi Shlomoh Luria, "who responded to every question on Halachah, our eminent Rabbi and Gaon, *rabban shel kol benei hagolah* (teacher of all Jews in exile), who illuminated the eyes of Israel with his Torah and wisdom, pillar of fear of God, on whom all Israel depends, and by whose word we live." Lemberg edition, reprinted in Jerusalem, 1977.

himself. Maharshal influenced the thinking of his numerous disciples, many of whom went on to become leading rabbis of the next generation.

Consult Sorcerers?
Teshuvot Maharshal, no. 3

Question: *Is a sick person permitted to ask a non-Jew to consult a sorcerer on his behalf?*

Responsum: The Ari (Rabbi Yitzchak Luria) has answered this question already, stating that the Torah does not expressly forbid consulting sorcerers. The prohibition of the Torah is limited to the specific forms of witchcraft of *ov* and *yidoni* (mediums and oracles).[3]

Consulting a sorcerer constitutes only a violation of the commandment, "You must remain totally faithful to God your Lord,"[4] and is no actual transgression. . . . Nevertheless, I say, since these practices are deceptions, trickery, and quackery, without a shred of substance, consulting sorcerers should not be permitted, except in life-threatening situations, because sometimes they make a wild guess and arrive at a correct remedy . . . but I can find no reason for permitting it on behalf of a patient who is not critically ill.

Recovery from Childbirth
Teshuvot Maharshal, no. 45

Question: *It is customary for women to stay in bed from three to four weeks after giving birth. One such woman demanded that her husband furnish specially prepared sumptuous meals and that he hire a nurse to serve her. The husband refused. Can he be forced to comply with her wishes?*

Responsum: It seems reasonable to consider her a seriously ill patient for the first thirty days after her delivery. Indeed, our sages postulated that women in this condition need not fast, except on Yom Kippur and Tisha Be'Av.[5] And if they have a craving for food they should not fast at all. Likewise, with regard to Shabbat, until thirty days after childbirth a woman is considered a noncritical patient, and all her needs may be met by a non-Jew. . . . And we know that many women become infertile or chronically ill if they don't eat and drink properly after giving birth. The husband must take care of her according to the prevailing standards of his community.

Should the Blind Light the Menorah?
Teshuvot Maharshal, no. 77

Question: *Does a sightless person have to light the menorah on Chanukah? Since we do not recite the* berachah *for* viewing *the Chanukah lights but rather "to* kindle *the Chanukah lights," should he therefore be required to light the menorah? Or, since we light the menorah in order to proclaim the miracle of Chanukah and he cannot proclaim something he cannot see, should he be not required to light the menorah?*

Responsum: If a blind person is in a house where other people are lighting the menorah, he should give a coin and acquire a share in the oil and the wick. If he is married, his wife should light the menorah for him. If he has no wife and lives by himself, although he cannot see the lights, he should kindle the menorah with someone's assistance. The mitzvah of Chanukah certainly is not inferior to the mitzvah of *tzitzit*, about which it says, "that you may see them";[6] and yet a blind person who cannot see them is required to wear *tzitzit*.

May the Landlord Evict His Tenant?
Teshuvot Maharshal, no. 38

Question: *Reuven rented his house to Shimon with the understanding that he was moving to Tiberias, where he was going to stay for three years. He had leased a mill there from the local sultan for the customary term of three years. Reuven departed, but he returned after only one and a half years, since the sultan had repossessed the mill, depriving him of his livelihood. He wants Shimon to vacate the house. Shimon refuses to leave, claiming that he rented it for three years. Who is right?*

Responsum: . . . Since the landlord was forced to return by circumstances beyond his control, the tenant must vacate the house.... This is analogous to the case of a landlord who rents a house for one year during which his own house burned down. In this case we rule that the tenant must relinquish his rights and vacate the house. If this holds true in the case of a fire, for which no provisions were made at the time of the rental, then surely in the present case, where the landlord rented the house with the understanding that he was going to establish himself elsewhere, and this did not come to fruition, the tenant must yield to the landlord.

Pangs of Conscience
Teshuvot Maharshal, no. 96

Question: *Moshe Lipschitz sent his servant Hirsch on a mission for him. On the way, Hirsch became involved in a fight with several non-Jews and punched one of them. Filled with rage, the others wanted to avenge their friend, but Hirsch managed to escape. Running for his life, he accidentally fell into a deep well and drowned. Moshe Lipschitz, distressed about his servant's death, saw to it that he received a proper Jewish burial. He wants to know whether he has to repent and atone for the death of his servant.*

Responsum: ... This young man indirectly caused his own death. The fact that he fell into the well is not Moshe's fault. When the sages say that ordinarily people don't watch where they are going, they mean, in general, people who are preoccupied with other matters. But this fellow's mind was focused on getting away. He should have concentrated on his escape route and avoided an open well.... Furthermore, bear in mind that it was he who initiated the entire episode by hitting the non-Jew. The non-Jew's friends then threatened to kill him, which impelled him to flee for his life.

Therefore, Moshe Lipschitz does not have to repent. I declare on pain of ban and excommunication that no one is to blame him or shame him for this.

Fry an Egg on a Hot Roof on Shabbat?
Teshuvot Maharshal, no. 61

Question: *In the tropics, are you permitted to roll an egg on a hot roof as a means of frying it on Shabbat, inasmuch as you are using solar heat and not fire?*

Responsum: [Following a lengthy and brilliant dissertation on this subject, Maharshal concludes:] Solar heat is permissible on Shabbat. Therefore you are allowed to roll an egg on a hot roof on which there is no sand. But if the roof is covered with sand it is forbidden to bury the egg in the hot sand [since in the process you are making a groove in the sand, which is forbidden on Shabbat]. You may not place it in the sand even before Shabbat, and not even if the egg is already hard [cooked] and you just want to keep it warm.

RABBI BETZALEL ASHKENAZI— SHITTAH MEKUBETZET
רבי בצלאל אשכנזי — שיטה מקובצת

born: Eretz Yisrael, 1520?
died: Jerusalem, 1594?
Popularly known as Shittah Mekubetzet, the title of his work.

Rabbi Betzalel was born in Eretz Yisrael after his family had moved there from Germany (hence the name Ashkenazi, which refers to a person originally from Germany). Little is known of his early years. The family moved to Egypt, where Rabbi Betzalel studied under the eminent **Radvaz**, Rabbi David ibn Zimra. After the Radvaz left for Eretz Yisrael, Rabbi Betzalel was appointed to succeed him as Chief Rabbi of Egypt. The most famous of his students was the great kabbalist Rabbi Yitzchak Luria, the Ari'zal.

In the wake of a bitter dispute, Rabbi Betzalel was forced to renounce his high post. He moved to Jerusalem, where he was elected Chief Rabbi of both the Ashkenazi and Sephardi communities. Because he was fluent in Arabic, he became the spokesman for the community before the sultan. He was like a father to the poor and the oppressed. His most famous work is *Shittah Mekubetzet*, a collection of commentaries on the Talmud by early scholars.[1] He became renowned also for his responsa, *Teshuvot Rabbi Betzalel Ashkenazi*,[2] which attest to his vast knowledge and keen insight. In clear, unencumbered language he analyzes the problem in the light of halachic precedent and then arrives at a clear-cut decision.

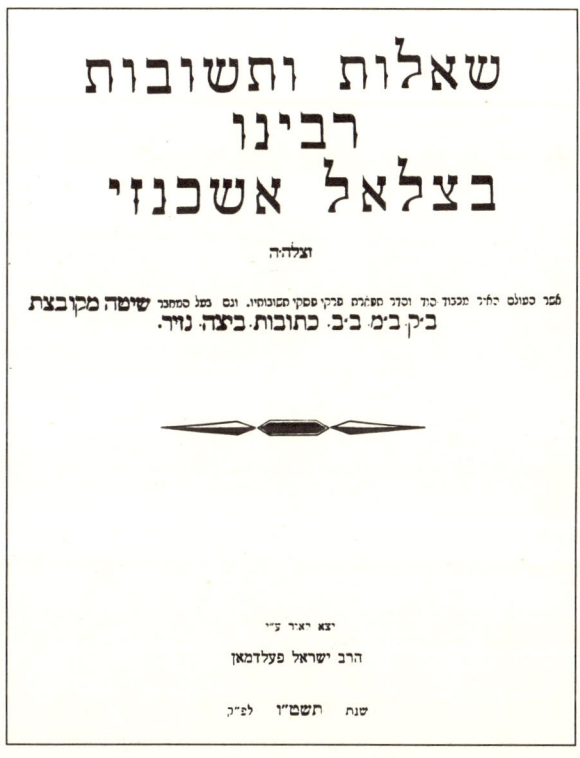

Title page of *She'eilot uTeshuvot Rabbeinu Betzalel Ashkenazi*, by the author of the widely studied talmudic commentaries *Shittah Mekubetzet*. This was printed in Jerusalem, 1955.

A Man Lost at Sea
Teshuvot Rabbi Betzalel Ashkenazi, no. 20

Question: *Concerning Reuven who drowned in the ocean. A non-Jew, casually and with genuine sincerity, told several Jews what he had seen. One of these men related the account of the non-Jew to the Bet Din, which issued the following report:*[3]

Mr. Nissim Cohen appeared before us, a Bet Din of three judges, and officially testified that on the Shabbat following the reported sinking of a ship that was boarded by Reuven, son of Ploni (John Doe), he, Nissim Cohen, and a number of other Jews met a non-Jew who came from the port from which the above-mentioned ship had sailed. They asked this non-Jew, "Have you heard any news of that ship?" The non-Jew replied that the ship had gone down and the passengers' bodies had washed up on the beach, that they had buried them, and that the Jew who had boarded had also been found on the beach and had been buried. End of testimony.

Mr. Nissim Cohen mentioned also that, aside from Reuven, no other person from that town had boarded the vessel.

This testimony was recorded this day, the 5th of Nisan 5345/1585.

Our question is whether or not Reuven's wife must be considered an eishet ish *(married woman).*

Responsum: We must consider two questions:

(a) Can the non-Jew's account be termed an unqualified *meisi'ach lefi tumo* (unpremeditated, casual statement), since the Jew initially asked him, "Have you heard any news of the ship that sailed from here?" You might argue that to qualify as an unguarded, sincere statement it may not be elicited by a prior question, however offhandedly that question is posed.

(b) Since the non-Jew did not state that he actually saw Reuven being expelled by the sea, we have reason to fear that the body had been lying there for an hour or more and his facial features may have changed. Although the non-Jew claimed that he recognized him, the dead man may in fact be someone else. . . .

It seems logical to say that the non-Jew was *meisi'ach lefi tumo*, because he did not intend with his story to free the wife from the bonds of marriage, nor did he mean to offer legal testimony. [There follows an exhaustive study of *meisi'ach lefi tumo*.]

[He concludes:] There is no doubt that this woman is free to remarry. . . . It is clear that anyone taking a more stringent position is frowned upon by the sages.

Dispute about a Pirated Shipment
Teshuvot Rabbi Betzalel Ashkenazi, *no. 28*

Question: *A dispute arose in the city of Rhodes (on the island of Rhodes, off the southwest coast of Turkey). The case is that of Yosef against Yekutiel and Meshullam. Yosef, who lives in Rhodes, sold to Yekutiel and Meshullam, also living in Rhodes, a shipment of cut stone, called* aspros cordatos, *for 315 grossos.*

The stone blocks were to be shipped from Rhodes to Salonica (Greece). The buyers deposited with Shelomoh Gabbai of Salonica a number of articles of gold and silver as security for their payment of the 315 grossos.

Yosef declared before the Bet Din that he had accepted liability for the stone blocks if the vessel that carried them should be shipwrecked or captured by pirates, God forbid. In that event, Yosef would release without delay the items that had been placed in escrow. Signed, Rhodes, Thursday, 5th of Sivan 5343/1583.

But it was God's will that when the ship came into the open seas, the crew of the ship, accursed and perfidious heathens, killed all the Jews aboard the ship, men, women and children. Only one Jew escaped, who reported the massacre, may Hashem, the God of vengeance, avenge them and repay our neighbors sevenfold.[4] *Among the murder victims was the above-mentioned Yekutiel, and the money was lost.*

And now Meshullam and Yekutiel's widow demand that Yosef release the jewelry they deposited with Shelomoh Gabbai, for Yosef had accepted liability in case of unspecified pirates, which means both outside pirates and pirates that were on board the ship. Yosef countered that he had accepted liability only in case of outside pirates attacking the vessel, but not if the crew itself turned into pirates who rob and kill. He refers to the contract that states "in case of shipwreck or pirates who should come and attack the ship, God forbid." Clearly, this means outside, not internal pirates.

Please let us know who is right in this case.

Responsum: At first glance it appears that Yosef is right in this case. It might be comparable to Responsum no. 7 of Rabbi **Yosef Colon**, (Teshuvot Maharik) . . . [There follows a thorough analysis of Yosef's intent when he spoke of unspecified pirates attacking the vessel. The conclusion is:]

But we must make a distinction between large ships and a small boat. A large vessel that regularly carries passengers and freight and whose crew is well known, has established a good reputation that it wants to maintain. It is not likely to spoil its good name. A small boat, however, that is not regularly used by merchants, is manned by sailors who are unknown and who should be under suspicion of being pirates and murderers. Our sages warned us to give such people a wide berth. . . .

When Yosef in his contract mentioned unspecified pirates he did not know whether Yekutiel was going to board a large or a small vessel. When he learned that Yekutiel had boarded a small vessel that had never before carried Jewish passengers he again accepted liability against unspecified pirates, meaning *any pirates* that are likely to attack this vessel. In the case of this small vessel it was more likely that there would be a mutiny by the crew than an attack by outside pirates. Thus, Yosef's liability extends to these internal pirates as well.

The law is clear in this case that Yosef must release the items that were deposited as security and return them to their rightful owners. Case closed.

Where Should Reuven Pay Taxes?
Teshuvot Rabbi Betzalel Ashkenazi, no. 36

Question: *Reuven, a resident of Gaza, Eretz Yisrael, conducts his business there, and his property and material assets are located there. He pays his taxes in Chevron (Hebron), because his ancestors lived in Chevron, where they are recorded in the town register as local taxpayers. In the past, the Gaza Jewish community did not require Reuven to pay the local tax, but recently the community demanded that Reuven, as a Gaza resident earning his livelihood in Gaza, pay the community tax.[5] Reuven asserts that, since he pays taxes in Chevron, he should be exempt from all Gaza taxes, all the more so since the Gaza people over the years never billed him for taxes. This clearly proves that they exempted him from paying taxes. He asserts that his case is analogous to that of a widow who for twenty-five years has not claimed her* ketuvah[6] *and who has forfeited her right to it.*

Please let us know who is right in this case.

Responsum: The Gaza community is right. Reuven's claim is without foundation. The matter of the widow has no bearing on this case whatsoever. The law is simple. Reuven, who lives and earns his living in Gaza, must share in the upkeep of the Gaza facilities as do all citizens of Gaza. He cannot claim exemption by virtue of the fact that he pays taxes in Chevron. . . . If he obeys our ruling, he will be blessed by the One Who dwells on this Wall. . . .

Firing an Unqualified Rabbi
Teshuvot Rabbi Betzalel Ashkenazi, no. 24

Question: *A congregation, after taking a vote, agreed to appoint Rabbi X as their spiritual leader. They gave him a contract stipulating that he was to guide them, teach them the Torah and its commentaries, adjudicate their disputes, and decide their questions, for the term of X years. The majority of the members signed this contract in the presence of two witnesses, who affixed their signatures.*

Some time later, the entire congregation decided to dismiss this rabbi. They said to each other, "We are thirsty to hear the word of God, and this rabbi does not teach us anything. He does not know the halachah at all, and if he should involve himself in issues of marriage and divorce, he would, God forbid, cause illegitimate children to be born." After consulting with each other they decided to hire another rabbi, who would establish a yeshivah, deliver a sermon every Shabbat, and teach them the law. As they were all assembled at the meeting, the above-mentioned rabbi X entered and said, "What are you doing here? You are committing a sin. You are humiliating me!" The rabbi summoned the congregation to Bet Din.

[*There follows a detailed record of the legal arguments presented by both sides to the dispute.*]

Responsum: [*After a thorough and learned exposition of all halachic aspects and precedents of the case, Rabbi Betzalel Ashkenazi summarizes:*]

Therefore the congregation is free of any guilt. On the contrary, they are to be commended for removing an unqualified person from the rabbinate. In so doing, they raise the banner of the Torah. Ever since such so-called rabbis have appeared on the scene, ignorance has replaced knowledge, the truth has been perverted, and justice has been distorted . . . and the Torah demands from young and old, "Why don't you raise your voice in protest against this conspiracy to break God's covenant?"

It is plain as day that the congregation is innocent and blameless, and the new rabbi whom they will appoint, who will bring back the high standards of

Torah observance, is not guilty of any infringement whatsoever. . . . May God grant us peace in serenity and safety forever, with the coming of Mashiach and the rebuilding of the Bet HaMikdash.

Is the Synagogue Entitled to the Bequest?
Teshuvot Rabbi Betzalel Ashkenazi, no. 16

Question: *Reuven's wife brought into the marriage a dowry of 30,000 dinars. Husband and wife agreed that if she would predecease him, he would distribute 20,000 dinars to the heirs and he would inherit 10,000 dinars. On her deathbed the wife reconsidered and stipulated that of the 20,000 dinars she bequeathed to her heirs, 10,000 should be donated to the synagogue. Our question is whether the synagogue is entitled to the bequest of 10,000 dinars, or did the heirs acquire title to the 20,000 dinars at the time the husband and wife made their original agreement, and thus the wife had no right to reduce the heirs' share of the inheritance?*

Responsum: My hands are tied because I don't have my books with me. They are in Jerusalem. My heart and my thoughts are there in the holy city all the time. However, in order to bolster the cause of the synagogue I will express my opinion. May God help me that the truth will emerge. [After a prolonged and detailed discussion of all ramifications of this question, and an analysis of the opinions of the **Rosh**, Rabbi **Yosef Karo**, the Baal HaTurim, the **Ran**, and others, he concludes:] The words of the eminent Rabbi Yosef Karo are as though they were given on Sinai, to the effect that when a husband and wife make an agreement concerning a will, the heirs do not take title while the wife is still living. The law in this case is undisputable. The synagogue is entitled to the bequest. This is my modest opinion; may God protect us from erring in answering halachic questions.

RABBI AVRAHAM DI BOTON— LECHEM MISHNEH, LECHEM RAV
רבי אברהם די בוטון — לחם משנה, לחם רב

born: Salonica, Turkey (now Greece), 1545
died: Salonica, Turkey (now Greece), 1588

Rabbi Avraham, a disciple of Rabbi **Shemuel di Medina (Maharashdam)**, is the author of *Lechem Mishneh*,[1] one of the most important commentaries on **Rambam's** *Mishneh Torah* and printed in all its standard editions. He corresponded on topics of Halachah with the greatest authorities of his time, such as Rabbi **Moshe Trani**, who mentions him in his responsa **Teshuvot Mabit**. Rabbi Avraham also wrote *Lechem Rav*,[2] a collection of 230 responsa.

He became a victim of the epidemic that swept Salonica in 1588, and he died at the young age of 43. His three sons were all prominent scholars. The oldest, Rabbi Meir di Boton, is the author of *She'eilot uTeshuvot Maharam di Boton*, a collection of his own responsa.

Dismiss the Chazzan?
Lechem Rav, no. 2

Question: *For a number of years, a chazzan has been leading the services in a congregation to everyone's satisfaction. Presently, the majority of the members do not want to keep him any longer, while a few of the members want to maintain him. The majority took the initiative and hired as chazzan one of the local young men who is a relative of one of the members. Please let us know whether the minority members can block the appointment of a new chazzan.*

Title page of *Lechem Rav*, responsa by Rabbi Avraham di Boton, famous for his commentary on the Rambam entitled *Lechem Mishneh*. Printed in Jerusalem, 1968.

Responsum: **Rashba** writes in one of his responsa that a chazzan cannot be dismissed unless he has been guilty of something that disqualifies him. . . . Rashba continues that in his days it was customary to appoint synagogue officials for a fixed term, and when the term expired they left office and others would take their place. . . . To recapitulate, appointments of chazzanim and synagogue officials are made by the majority of tax-paying members. If a majority of tax-paying members prefer the second chazzan, he should be appointed, although it would seem that Halachah rules in favor of the first one. Therefore, I say that a compromise should be found whereby both men should serve as chazzan.

Can Yaakov Francis Serve as Chazzan and Shochet?
Lechem Rav, no. 3

Question: *Fifteen years ago Yaakov Francis suddenly renounced Judaism and converted to Christianity. He immediately regretted his deed and repented. He has kept his face covered for the last fifteen years as a sign of remorse and has been steadfast in his repentance ever since. Is he qualified to be appointed as chazzan and shochet?*

Responsum: **Rambam** writes in *Hilchot Tefilah*, Chapter 15 [in speaking of a kohen who worshipped idols] that no matter whether he was forced to do so or did so unintentionally, a kohen may never again go up to bless the people. And furthermore, he states that a kohen who became an apostate, even if he repented, may never again go up to bless the people. . . .

However, in this case of a chazzan [and shochet] we must say that if he repented he can officiate again because, according to **Maharam** [R. Meir of Rothenburg, 1215–1293], the halachah is less rigorous for a chazzan leading in prayer than for a kohen blessing the people. . . . Therefore I say, even though compared with the great rabbis I am no more than the hem of their garment, that based on this statement, Yaakov Francis is qualified to serve as chazzan and shochet.

A Pearl-Studded Wedding Ring
Lechem Rav, no. 20

Question: *During the wedding ceremony a groom gave the bride a ring that was set with two pearls. Before the ceremony he showed the ring to a rabbi, who permitted him to use it. Please let us know if the rabbi acted properly in permitting him to marry the bride with this ring, and also whether the wedding ceremony should be repeated with a ring that is not questionable.*

Responsum: Of course, in the first instance a ring like that should not be used. . . . Rabbeinu Tam states that since the average person cannot appraise gemstones and pearls, it is the custom to marry with a smooth wedding band.[3] . . . In our case, Rabbeinu Tam would rule that if he married her with a ring that had a pearl in it, he should repeat the marriage ceremony. To be sure, not all authorities agree with him on this point.

Therefore I say, to be on the safe side, he should repeat the ceremony in a manner that is beyond question; but the *berachah* should not be repeated. This is in keeping with responsum no. 82 by **Rivash**, who states, "If the husband, to be on the safe side, wishes to repeat the marriage ceremony, he may do so, but the *berachah* of *eirusin*[4] should not be repeated."

The Rabbi's Parents Are Marranos
Lechem Rav, no. 5

Question: *Forty years ago Yaakov and his family, refugees from Portugal, found a safe haven in Turkey. They were Marranos, Jews forced to convert to Christianity by the Portuguese government, and upon arriving in Turkey they settled in Salonica. There they were blessed with two upright sons, Reuven and Shimon, who went to yeshivah in Salonica. About five years ago Reuven was elected to serve as rabbi in another city. One of the members of that community, who deems himself a scholar and feels overshadowed by the new rabbi, began to malign him, stating that Reuven was not qualified to be a rabbi because only Reuven's father was a*

Marrano but his mother was in fact non-Jewish.[5] He is spreading this libel wherever he goes, to the point that some of the members of the community are beginning to have doubts about their rabbi. They want to ask you what is Reuven's status. In Salonica it was always assumed that both his parents were Marranos, and that even his grandparents were Marranos. If indeed you find this rumor to be unfounded, how shall we deal with the man who spread this false rumor?

Responsum: My great rabbi and teacher Rabbi **Shemuel di Medina** (Maharashdam) wrote in his responsum no. 193 that a person can be disqualified only on the testimony of two valid witnesses, and that the testimony of only one witness should be dismissed. . . . Since for many years Reuven and his parents have been presumed to be full-fledged Jews, how does this man have the audacity to cast aspersions on his ancestry? And even if we did not have such long-time presumption and they had arrived from Portugal only today, and we would know that his father was a Marrano, then his mother is presumed to be Jewish also. . . . This is based on the statement by Rabbi Tzemach, grandson of the **Rashbatz**,[6] to the effect that we assume that the mothers of all Marranos who came from these countries are Jewish, because they have preserved the sanctity of their family and not one of them married a non-Jew. Thus, if Reuven's father presented himself today and we knew that he is a Marrano, we surely would hold his wife to be a Marrano too. Therefore, the thought of disqualifying Reuven on the basis of a contemptible rumor should not even enter your mind.

To summarize, Reuven is fully qualified to officiate as rabbi, may the likes of him increase in Israel. The person who slandered him will have to render justification and reckoning before the Heavenly Tribunal, and he must beg Reuven's forgiveness.

May He Pray in Another Synagogue?
Lechem Rav, no. 64

Question: The community of Avilona made an agreement under pain of ban that no member was permitted to pray in another synagogue for more than three days. The agreement was signed by some of the members of the community. A talmid chacham (scholar) left the synagogue to pray in a yeshivah where he has been engaged as a lecturer. He claims that it is a mitzvah to pray at the place where one studies and that a mitzvah overrides the community's agreement. He also asserts that in the yeshivah they pray faster and the classes begin immediately after the prayer session. If he prayed in the synagogue, he would be late for his lecture, and the yeshivah would object to this and would cut his salary. Besides, he argues, he did not sign the agreement in the first place.

Responsum: It seems to me that if the majority of the members signed the agreement, the scholar may not leave the synagogue [to pray]. His arguments that he is doing it for a mitzvah, either the mitzvah of praying in a yeshivah or that of being on time for the lecture, do not hold water. . . . We must conclude that the ban does apply to him.

As for his contention that he did not sign the agreement, my great rabbi and mentor [**R. Shemuel di Medina**, 1506–1589] ruled in his responsa *Maharashdam* 2:18 that in matters of communal enactments we follow the majority. He concludes by stating, ". . . any enactment or ordinance that was instituted by the majority of the community must be complied with by all members. The minority cannot exclude itself from the ban. All this has been said, provided the enactment has the approval of the rabbis and the lay leaders of the community. Otherwise, the agreement has no validity whatsoever." Since this is my master's statement, we must comply with it. . . .

Can He Cancel the Sale?
Lechem Rav, no. 226

Question: Reuven sold Shimon a piece of jewelry set with jewels and pearls. Since there were no expert appraisers in Shimon's town, he sent a messenger to another country to have it appraised. The expert valued the piece at less than half of what Shimon had paid. Shimon, who says he was overcharged exorbitantly, wants to cancel the sale and return the jewelry for a full refund. The reason he waited so long before returning it was that he had to send it to *another country to determine its value. May Shimon cancel the sale?*

Responsum: Although I am mourning today the passing of our crown, my great rabbi and master [**R. Shemuel di Medina**, 1506–1589], nevertheless, I will respond to your question. This case is very plain and simple. **Rambam** states in *Hilchot Mechirah* 12:11, "... Similarly, if he bought an article from a bookseller or a jeweler, the buyer may ask for a refund until he has had it appraised by a dealer who is an expert, no matter where this expert may be, because as a rule people are not familiar with these matters. Therefore, if there was no appraiser in his town and he had to take it to another place, or an appraiser came to him much later, he may return the article." Thus, it seems clear to me, the fact that a long time has passed since he purchased the jewelry does not matter at all. If he was told that he has been overcharged, he may renege on the deal.

He Took Him to the Civil Court
Lechem Rav, no. 89

Question: *Reuven had a claim against Shimon. Shimon stated two or three times in front of witnesses that he is willing to have the dispute settled by a Din Torah [rabbinical court]. Reuven refused. Instead, he sued him in civil court where he presented trumped-up charges that he backed up with false witnesses. As a result, Shimon lost the law suit. How should Reuven be dealt with?*

Responsum: . . . Even if both litigants agree to have their dispute adjudicated in civil court, it is forbidden [to Jews] to do so, because thereby you lend prestige and stature to their religion. . . . From all the foregoing it is apparent that it is reprehensible to sue a fellow Jew in civil court, even if the civil law in the case in question coincides with Torah law, and most certainly in the present case where Reuven accused Shimon falsely and hired spurious witnesses; his sin is too great to bear. . . . I really don't know how he can atone for this sin, for he reviled and raised his hand against the Torah. He and all his possessions should be placed under a ban until he repents and returns the stolen goods and begs Shimon's forgiveness, as the **Rivash** sets forth in responsum no. 120.

RABBI MEIR OF LUBLIN—MAHARAM LUBLIN
רבי מאיר — מהר"ם לובלין

born: Lublin, Poland, 1558
died: Lublin, Poland, 1616
Popularly known as Maharam Lublin.

Rabbi Meir was the scion of an illustrious rabbinical family. His grandfather, Rabbi Asher of Cracow, was a renowned kabbalist. Maharam's mentor was Rabbi Yitzchak Shapira, *rosh yeshivah* of the yeshivah of Cracow, who chose the brilliant young scholar as his son-in-law. When Maharam was only 24 years old he was appointed *rosh yeshivah* in Lublin. Five years later, after the death of his father-in-law, Rabbi Meir was elected to succeed him as rabbi of Cracow and to lead its yeshivah. After several years at this post he became the rabbi and *rosh yeshivah* of Lemberg, where he remained for nearly twenty years. In the wake of dissension in the community he was forced to leave Lemberg, and he returned to Lublin where he served in the rabbinate until his death in 1616.

The yeshivah he led attracted the finest minds and counted among its students such eminent scholars as Rabbi Yeshayah Horowitz, author of the *Shelah*, and Rabbi Natan Shapira, author of *Megaleh Amukot*. Halachic inquiries were directed at Rabbi Meir from communities as distant as Italy and Turkey. His sons compiled 140 of his responsa, which are popularly known as *She'eilot uTeshuvot Maharam Lublin*.[1] His major work, *Me'ir Einei Chachamim*,[2] is one of the most important commentaries on the Talmud and is printed in all of its standard editions. Maharam voiced serious reservations about deciding Halachah solely on the basis of the *Shulchan Aruch*. In his view, in-depth study of talmudic sources and the commentaries of early rabbinic sages were indispensable in crystallizing the correct decision. He was well versed in Kabbalah, as is evident in his responsum no. 83, which deals with

Title page of *Teshuvot Maharam Lublin*, responsa of Rabbi Meir of Lublin. The letters *kuf-kuf* before Cracow and Lublin are an abbreviation of *kehillah kedoshah*, "holy community." This edition was printed in Jerusalem, 1977.

the proper pronunciation of the four-letter Divine Name, the tetragrammaton.

Someone Accidentally Shot and Killed a Man
Teshuvot Maharam Lublin, no. 43

Question: *A broken-hearted, sick man came to me and related the following tragic incident.*

During the upheaval in Volhynia, by order of the Duke and his ministers every citizen was required to be armed and ready to go to war against the enemy. One day, during target practice, he fired his rifle from his window at a target on the wall of his courtyard. A passerby entering the courtyard walked in front of the target and was struck and killed by the bullet. The man firing the rifle did not see the victim, and a corporal who was standing outside the courtyard warning people not to enter angrily lashed out at the victim for disobeying his orders.

The unintentional murderer is crying bitter tears and wants to do penance for the accident he caused. I see before me a man who has only recently recovered from a case of leprosy; he is crippled and cannot do penance by wandering from town to town.[3] *Moreover, he has many children who depend on him, and he lives among non-Jews in a small village. Therefore, I will do my best to find precedents in the writings of the sages on the basis of which I can exempt him from going into exile.*

Responsum: I find support for my view in the Mishnah, "If one throws a stone into a public domain and kills, he is exiled. Rabbi Eliezer ben Yaakov says: If, after the stone left his hand, the other put his head out and received the blow, he is exempt."[4] Our case is analogous with that in the Mishnah because the victim placed himself in the line of fire. Additionally, since the victim did not heed the warning of the guard, the accident was unavoidable and he brought about his death himself.

Taking note of the man's frail physical condition, I want to ease his exile in that he should wander only to nearby towns.[5] . . . On weekdays he should not eat meat or drink whiskey, except on Shabbat and festivals. He should not sleep on a pillow or cushion on weekdays. He should change shirts only once a month . . . he should not attend any festive meals, nor should he have his hair cut. I am making it easier on him in view of his poor physical condition and the children who are dependent on him.

A Marrano Betrayed a Mohel
Teshuvot Maharam Lublin, no. 61

Question: *It happened in Italy that a Marrano*[6] *was arrested by the Inquisition, who investigated him and found that he was circumcised and practiced Judaism. The verdict was for the Marrano to recant, renounce Judaism, and beg the priests' forgiveness. He would then have to confess his "sins" against their religion and divulge the identity of the person who had performed the circumcision. Thereupon the Inquisition would go after the mohel with all their might. The Marrano did indeed return to their faith; he revealed the name of the mohel, and the Inquisition pursued the mohel with their customary methods.*

The mohel, who had learned of the impending danger, fled to a distant country and sent for his wife and children. Since he was highly skilled at his profession and also taught milah *to others, he had been earning his livelihood in this manner. By betraying the mohel, the Marrano deprived him of his source of income. Is the Marrano responsible and can his property be attached to pay for the mohel's expenses in saving himself and having his family join him, and for the mohel's being prevented from earning his livelihood?*

Responsum: [After a thorough discussion of all facets of this case, Maharam concludes:] The outcome of all of the above is that the Marrano must pay to the mohel all the losses enumerated in the question, except for the expenses the mohel incurred in moving his wife and children. These he does not have to pay, for the aforementioned reasons.

All this applies if the Marrano could have saved himself without revealing the identity of the mohel—if he could have said, for example, that another mohel had performed the *milah*, one who at that time was in a faraway country. But if the Marrano had no alternative and was forced by the Inquisition to give the name of the mohel, then he does not have to make restitution. This Marrano was in danger of his life. . . . I don't have time to elaborate, as I am very busy with the concerns of the yeshivah students. . . .

The Nobleman's Promissory Note
Teshuvot Maharam Lublin, no. 22

Question: *Reuven owed money to a* poritz *(Polish nobleman) for which he had given a promissory note. The nobleman joined the army and went to war. Before leaving, he paid a visit to Shimon and, in the presence of several witnesses, said, "It says in this note that the money Reuven owes me is payable on this and this date. I am giving you this note as a gift." When the note was due, Shimon presented it to Reuven, demanding payment. . . . Reuven replied, "I admit that this is my handwriting. I also acknowledge that I owe this amount. But, my dear Shimon, I don't owe it to you. I have had no dealings with you. The note is made out to the* poritz, *and you have no power of attorney from him, and besides, it may even be that you found the note. . . ."*

Said Shimon, ". . . and as far as finding the note is concerned, I have qualified witnesses who will testify that the poritz *gave me the note as a gift. . . ."*

Responsum: . . . To summarize, if the civil courts rule that a promissory note can be sold by merely handing it over, and they require no other formality, then Shimon, who received the note as a gift from the *poritz*, is judged accordingly. He has a legal right to the note and Reuven, the debtor, must pay him. However, if this *poritz* is a tyrant and there is reason to fear that he may go back on his word, disavow the witnesses, and again demand payment from Reuven, then it is only fair that Shimon should insure him against any losses he may incur.

Synagogue Destroyed by Fire
Teshuvot Maharam Lublin, no. 59

Question: *As you know, the synagogue in Lukva was destroyed by fire. The community's efforts to rebuild it were thwarted by the municipal authorities and by the Catholic clergy with the pretext that it would be too close to their church. The matter was referred to the government ministry, with the result that the Jewish community was forced to abandon the original site and build a new synagogue at a location that suited the mayor and the church officials. The old site remains desolate and empty. Our question is whether the leaders of the community are permitted to profane the sacred character of the old site by selling it to members of the community for the purpose of building homes on it. The proceeds of the sale will be used toward the construction of the new synagogue, since the members of the community are short of funds at the present time and cannot finance the building with their own resources.*

Responsum: . . . In light of the above, if the synagogue is sold according to Halachah, by seven elected representatives of the community in the presence of the people, and with the agreement of the Bet Din, then the buyers may use the land to suit their needs. Nevertheless, the preferred way of disposing of the land would be to divide the parcels on which the homes will be built in such a manner that the site on which the men's section was located, which is the holiest part of the synagogue, remains vacant. It should be turned into a garden. . . .

Must Hatziplatz Help Tziltz?
Teshuvot Maharam Lublin, no. 40

Question: *The king had issued an irrevocable decree by which all Jews living in Silesia[7] were expelled. The only exception was the community of Tziltz, who paid off their oppressors and managed to defer the expulsion until, with God's help and the intervention of the leaders of the Prague community, the expulsion decree for the Jews of Tziltz was lifted upon payment of 2,000 gold pieces. The Jews of the neighboring provinces of Poland agreed to contribute one fifth of this sum, and both Bohemia and Moravia likewise offered to donate one fifth each of the 2,000 gold pieces. The remaining two fifths, that is, 800 gold pieces, were to be raised by the community of Tziltz and its neighbor Hatziplatz. The question is whether the Jews of Hatziplatz are indeed required to contribute toward this fund and, if so, what amount must Hatziplatz raise in order to help Tziltz?*

Responsum: We base our ruling on the decision rendered by **Maharik**[8] in his responsum no. 4 [see pages 42–43] with regard to a similar incident that occurred in Regensburg. He ruled that all communities to whom the "bitter cup of poison" is likely to pass, God forbid, must share the burden of rescuing their brethren, even though as yet they have not fallen victim. Predicated on this we find, since both of these communities share a common destiny, they must come to one another's aid. Therefore, it is our ruling that the community of Hatziplatz is required to pay toward the expenses relating to the expulsion of Tziltz, the sum of 200 gold pieces, which is one half of the sum each of the provinces in Poland is contributing. I also rule that if, God forbid, at some point in the future there will be an expulsion of the Jews of Hatziplatz, the Jews of Tziltz must come to the aid of their brethren according to their ability at that time and according to the ruling of the judges at that time.

Creditors Press Murder Victim's Widow for Payment
Teshuvot Maharam Lublin, no. 86

Question: *Chavah, a lonely and dejected widow, was married to Simchah of Pinsk, who recently was killed by a vile murderer. Determined to avenge her husband's death, she brought the murderer to justice. To her great sorrow, the civil judge did not condemn him to death but only sentenced him to pay damages for taking her husband's life.*

Her husband had owed money to several people, and his creditors now want the murderer's money to be paid to them to settle her husband's debts. As a result, her orphan children would be left penniless and be reduced to hunger and deprivation.

Responsum: As I saw this poor woman standing before me, I could not control my emotions. . . . It is clear as day that the creditors have no claim to the restitution money of the murder victim. . . . The **Rosh**[9] rules that a creditor cannot lay claim to what is termed *ra'ui*, that is, what is due to come after the death of the father (as, for example, a debt that is payable to the father on a certain date but the father has died before that date). . . . Our case is a clear-cut case of *ra'ui*. Consequently, it is plain and simple that no creditor has any claim whatsoever to the compensation funds of the murder victim. These funds should be given to the orphans and no other person has any right to them.

RABBI YOEL SIRKES—THE BACH
רבי יואל סירקש — ב"ח

born: Lublin, Poland, c. 1561
died: Cracow, Poland, 1640
Known as the Bach, the acronym formed of the initials of Bayit Chadash, *his monumental commentary on the Tur.*[1]

The Bach's first teachers were his father, Rabbi Shemuel, and Rabbi Shelomoh, the rabbi of Lublin. Later he studied in Brisk under Rabbi Meshullam Feivush and Rabbi Tzvi Hirsh Shor, a disciple of the Rema. As a young man he was invited to serve as rabbi of Pruszany, Lithuania, and later he held rabbinical posts in Lukov, Lubomil, Medziboz, Belz, Shidlow, Brisk (1615–1618), and Cracow, where he stayed from 1619 until his passing in 1640. A man of great affluence, he lavished much of his wealth on his yeshivah, generously supporting many needy students. Among the outstanding scholars who studied under him were Rabbi David Halevi, author of *Turei Zahav* (the Taz); Rabbi Menachem Mendel Krochmal, author of *Tzemach Tzedek*; Rabbi Gershon Ashkenazi, and Rabbi Mendel Auerbach.

Rabbi Yoel Sirkes is best known for his commentary on the Tur, called *Bayit Chadash*, abbreviated as *Bach*. It is a penetrating analysis of all the halachot presented in the Tur, and it is printed in all standard editions alongside the main text. He also wrote *Hagahot HaBach*, critical notes on the entire Talmud and on the commentaries by Rashi, Tosafot, **Rosh**, and Rif, in which he presents corrected versions of the text. These notes are printed in the outside margin of the standard Talmud editions. His responsa were published in two sections: *She'eilot uTeshuvot Bayit Chadash Hayeshanot*[2] and *She'eilot uTeshuvot Bayit Chadash Hechadashot*.[3]

The Bach was a strong-willed and independent thinker who did not hesitate to express his opinions

Title page of *She'eilot uTeshuvot Bayit Chadash* by Rabbi Yoel Sirkes, known as the Bach for his major commentary on the *Tur Shulchan Aruch*. This was printed in Ostroh, Poland, 1834.

even if they ran counter to the views of the majority. For example, he ruled that *chadash* (grain that had taken root before Passover) could be eaten outside of Eretz Yisrael, in opposition to the decision of the Rema and many other halachists. The Bach was highly proficient in Kabbalah, considering it "the wellspring and foundation of Torah" (responsum no. 4). He wrote a kabbalistic commentary on prayers and a commentary on *Pardes Rimonim*, the kabbalistic work by Rabbi Moshe Cordovero. Both still exist in manuscript form.

The Marriage Broker's Fee
Teshuvot HaBach Hayeshanot, no. 28

Question: *A man promised to pay a* shadchen[4] *so-and-so-much if he should succeed in arranging a certain match. The* shadchen *put his heart into it and made the match. Now the man recants and says that he was only joking and that he owes him only the standard fee. Is the* shadchen *entitled to the amount he was promised?*

Responsum: ... He must pay the *shadchen* the amount he stipulated. The standard fee was instituted only for cases where no fee was agreed upon in advance. This was done in order to avoid quarreling and haggling about the *shadchen*'s fee. But when the man explicitly agreed to pay a certain amount, it is clear that he must pay all he promised and he cannot say that he meant it only in jest. Besides, it is quite logical. The man knows full well that the *shadchen* could arrange the same match with someone else and still receive the standard fee. With that in mind he promised to pay him more, in order that the *shadchen* should do his best on his behalf. Therefore, he cannot now say that he was only joking.

It is the accepted practice in all matters, if you are eager to obtain something, to offer an incentive to a broker to obtain the desired item before someone else gets it. Or if you want a job done quickly, you offer the workers a bonus, and you cannot say afterwards that you did not really mean it. This is surely true of a *shadchen*, where it is the accepted custom to offer him a larger than the standard fee. Therefore, he must pay the *shadchen* all that he promised to pay, even if it is in excess of the standard fee.

Does He Have to Share the Profit?
Teshuvot HaBach Hayeshanot, no. 19

Question: *Reuven knew of a quantity of wheat in the silo of a* poritz *(landowner) but he did not have the money to buy it. He approached Shimon and told him, "I know of a batch of wheat on which a profit can be made. I don't have the money to buy it. Let's buy it with your funds and share the profit." Shimon agreed. They negotiated with the* poritz *but could not close the deal, and both returned home. Some time later Shimon went to the* poritz *by himself and bought the wheat with his money. He contends that he bought it on his own acount. Reuven demands his share of the profit, according to the initial agreement with Shimon.*

Responsum: It seems to me that Reuven is right, and Shimon must divide the profit with him. He initially agreed to the deal and he did not abrogate the agreement in front of witnesses before he bought the wheat.... No doubt if Reuven had not relied on Shimon buying the wheat in partnership with him, he would have tried to find another partner. Reuven was sure that no one else would buy the wheat on his own, since only he knew that the *poritz* had wheat for sale. Therefore, even if Shimon had kept quiet and then bought the wheat, Reuven would get half of the profit, and surely now that Shimon explicitly stated his agreement, he must give him his share....

It is unequivocally clear that Reuven is right. Shimon, by verbally agreeing with Reuven's proposal and by going jointly to the *poritz* and negotiating with him, manifestly demonstrated that he consented to buying the wheat for both of them. Even though at first the deal did not materialize, he cannot now say that he bought it on his own account, for if he disavowed his earlier agreement, he should have declared in front of witnesses that he was going to buy the wheat on his own account. Since he did not do so, he must divide the profit with Reuven.

The Agnostic Doctor
Teshuvot HaBach Hayeshanot, no. 4

Question: *A dreadful thing happened in the distant city of Amsterdam. A doctor in that city had the* audacity to ridicule the Talmudic aggadot *(parables and tales with homiletic and ethical content)* and to scoff at the teachings of Kabbalah. To his mind only secular philosophy is worthy of contemplation and everyone should engross himself in its speculations. He is attracting a circle of decent people, seducing them with his nefarious ideas.

Additionally, since he is one of the leaders of the community, he licensed a man to be a shochet (ritual slaughterer). When this man was examined by two rabbis on the laws of shechitah, he proved to be totally ignorant as to what is permitted and what is forbidden. Thereupon an announcement was made in the two synagogues that all the meat that was slaughtered by this man is nonkosher and the utensils in which this meat was cooked may not be used. The doctor then mounted the rostrum shouting that this announcement was to be ignored and that on his responsibility the meat may be eaten. Some of the people heeded his call and, not fearing for their soul, ate the nonkosher meat. Should this doctor be excommunicated until he turns from his evil ways and repents completely?

Responsum: Without a doubt, this man should be banned and excommunicated since he is a person who mocks the words of our sages and reviles the Kabbalah, which is the wellspring and foundation of the Torah and is permeated with the fear of God. Moreover, he is drawn to philosophy which is intrinsically heretical, and by tempting others he is "placing a stumbling block before the blind," for which he deserves to be placed under a ban.

Furthermore, for speaking out against the rabbis who declared the meat to be nonkosher, he deserves to be banned. For it is stated in *Chullin* 44, "No rabbi may permit something another rabbi has declared unfit." According to Ravad, he may not do so even if he is more learned than the rabbi who prohibited. . . . And surely it applies in this case where this little man disputes the decision of accomplished scholars, permitting what they prohibited. He is prompting the people to eat nonkosher meat, and for that alone he deserves to be banned.

In light of the foregoing I agree that the above-mentioned doctor from Amsterdam should be placed under a ban throughout Israel until he repents of his evil ways. However, since I have not seen any statement from the doctor, there exists the possibility that he may claim that the rabbis are his enemies and he might want to prove his innocence before a Bet Din. Of course, if the Bet Din finds that he did not do the things he is accused of, the ban and excommunication do not go into effect.

Therefore, if the doctor agrees to appear before a Bet Din and to accept in advance any verdict they may render, the ban and excommunication will not go into effect. He should immediately set a time at which he will appear in the Bet Din, where guilt and innocence will be brought to light. However, if he declines to appear or plays for time, then the ban and excommunication shall be effective as of today until such time as he repents properly.

Is This Widow Allowed to Remarry?
Teshuvot HaBach Hayeshanot, no. 103

Question: *Two Jews testified that they overheard a group of non-Jews in casual conversation talking about a Jew by the name of Chaim Zimbalisti, who owed this strange name to the fact that he played an instrument called* tzimbel.[5] *They mentioned that this Chaim Zimbalisti had converted to Christianity, joined the army of General Wallenstein,[6] and died of the plague. They also stated that they had buried him where he died. Is his wife permitted to remarry?*

Responsum: This woman is permitted to remarry. There are no grounds for concern that the non-Jews spoke of someone else. Although they did not mention his hometown Turbin, Poland, they did mention that he was named Chaim Zimbalisti after his musical profession. There is no other person in our region who bears this name. Moreover, since the name Zimbalisti is a Polish name and the husband of the woman of Turbin bore that name, we are not afraid that there is someone else by the same Polish name who is also a cymbal player who came out of nowhere to join the Wallenstein army. Therefore, I am lenient in this case.

A Boisterous Wedding Feast
Teshuvot HaBach Hayeshanot, no. 62

Question: *Reuven, in high spirits at a wedding banquet, dizzily threw a glass at the wall, the way drinkers do in a tavern when they are in a happy* mood. Shimon contends that he damaged his eye, which became completely sightless.

Responsum: Evidently, a glass splinter flew into Shimon's eye and he claims that it was blinded. This case has been decided in *Bava Kama* 32b: "If someone entered a carpenter's shop without permission and a splinter flew into his face and he died, then the carpenter is exempt. But if he entered the shop with the carpenter's permission, the carpenter is liable. What is he liable for? Said Rabbi Yosi bar Chanina, 'He is liable for "the four things" (compensation for damage, pain, medical expenses, and loss of work), but he is exempt from going into exile." The Rif, the **Rosh**, and the **Rambam** rule that regardless whether the victim entered the shop with or without permission, the carpenter is liable for "the four things." Since the carpenter saw him, he is guilty of negligence.

So too, in our case, it is clear since he saw the victim, and especially in a wedding hall where there is a crowd of people, and he threw the glass without anyone's permission, he should have been careful.

Now, if you would argue that the breaking of the glass was a permissible act because it was meant to enhance the festive mood, this is not a custom of serious people but of good-for-nothings and rascals. Not only do they endanger people's lives but they also intentionally desecrate the Shabbat. If they think that breaking glasses enhances the festivities, that was taken care of by the breaking of the glass under the chupah. Therefore it is clear that the fellow who broke the glass is liable for "the four things." As for his contention that he was intoxicated, this is no excuse. A drunk person is considered legally sane in all respects, except that he is exempt from prayer. . . .

To recapitulate, the one who caused the damage is liable to pay "the four things" (damages, pain, medical expenses, and loss of work). If he cannot pay immediately, he should pay later. . . .

He Wants to Break His Engagement
Teshuvot HaBach Hayeshanot, no. 8

Question: *Two respected members of the community, Reuven and Shimon, made a solemn agreement according to the local custom to the effect that Reuven's son was to marry Shimon's daughter on a certain date. In the meantime, a rumor began to circulate that the prospective groom's niece had committed adultery. In view of this rumor, Shimon reneges on the agreement, claiming exemption from having to pay damages for breaking the engagement because the rumor blemishes his family's reputation.*

Responsum: Shimon's argument is baseless, although the **Rosh** in his responsum no. 34, rules that a young man may break his engagement and is exempt from paying damages if his fiancée's sister renounced Judaism and converted to Christianity. . . . This exemption applies only in a case of conversion to another religion, since this taint is conspicuous public knowledge, but the blemish in the present case is not universally accepted for she may have been framed by enemies and the charges may be fictitious. And even if there are witnesses who testify to seeing the adulterous act and she denies it, the reputation of the family still is not tainted, since we know of many cases where witnesses have been paid to testify falsely. And even if she admits to having had an affair, she may have repented, so that the family's reputation still is not impaired. She is quite unlike the person who converted and openly persists in her defilement and who transgresses the entire Torah every moment of her existence.

Thus, in our case the family name has not been blackened. . . . In view of all the aforementioned reasons, it is beyond question that Shimon must fulfill all the conditions of the engagement agreement. If he breaks it, he must pay the prescribed damages. . . .

Sing Secular Melodies in the Synagogue?
Teshuvot HaBach Hayeshanot, no. 127

Question: *Are we permitted to sing in the synagogue melodies that are sung in church?*

Responsum: I think that only liturgical melodies are forbidden that have been specifically composed for church worship. Since they are strictly religious compositions, they may be likened to a religious statue that is prohibited to be used because it was designed for the purpose of religious worship. . . . But if the melodies were not specifically created for church music, I see no reason to forbid them to be sung in the synagogue.

RABBI YAAKOV SASPORTAS
רבי יעקב ששפורטש

born: North Africa, 1610
died: Amsterdam, 1698

Rabbi Yaakov Sasportas, an eleventh-generation descendant of Ramban, is best known for his fearless stand in the battle against Shabbetai Tzevi, the false messiah. When Rabbi Sasportas was only 18 years old, he was appointed a member of the Bet Din of Tlemcen, Algeria, an important center of Torah study in North Africa. Six years later he became the rabbi of that city. In 1647 he was arrested on false charges and imprisoned in Tlemcen. After his release he lived in Salé, Morocco. In 1650 he moved to Amsterdam, which had become a haven for refugees from the Spanish Inquisition, and there he was invited to serve as *rosh yeshivah*. Before long he became a member of the renowned Rabbi Menashe ben Yisrael's inner circle, and when in 1655 Rabbi ben Yisrael traveled to London to confer with Oliver Cromwell and members of the British Parliament, Rabbi Sasportas was in the delegation accompanying him. He settled in London, and in 1664 he was elected rabbi of the London community. When an epidemic broke out two years later, he was forced to leave the city and find refuge in Hamburg. Toward the end of his life, in 1693, he returned to Amsterdam where he was appointed rabbi of the Sephardi community.

During much of his lifetime Jewry was in turmoil in the wake of the emergence of the false messiah Shabbetai Tzevi. In 1665, in Eretz Yisrael, the Smyrna-born Shabbetai Tzevi declared himself to be *mashiach* (messiah). Jews all over the world, including many rabbis, were swept up in the blind hysteria triggered by the impostor and his apostle Nathan of Gaza. Rabbi Sasportas was one of the few voices crying out with all his might against the Shabbatean hallucination that threatened to engulf

Portrait of the gaon and kabbalist Rabbi Yaakov Sasportas. Painted from life by a famous painter of the British Royal House. The painting is on display in the Museum of Israel in Jerusalem.

the Jewish people. The communities of Hamburg and Amsterdam were especially intoxicated with the wild dreams of messianic redemption. They offered excuses for all of Shabbetai Tzevi's bizarre excesses and violations of Halachah. Rabbi Sasportas, recognizing the dangers inherent in the messianic tide, sent forth a stream of letters to rabbis and communal leaders in which he expressed his skepticism about the so-called messiah. Shabbetai Tzevi was arrested in 1666 by the Turkish authorities as the leader of a revolt. At his trial in Constantinople he was given the choice between death and conversion to Islam. He chose Islam.

Rabbi Yaakov Sasportas wrote a record of the rise and fall of Shabbetai Tzevi entitled *Tzitzat Noveil Tzevi*.[1] It also contains a number of Rabbi Sasportas' letters as well as letters written by Shabbetai Tzevi and Nathan of Gaza. In a later edition this work was appended to a compilation of Rabbi Sasportas' responsa, called *Teshuvot Ohel Yaakov*.[2]

Can Reuven Collect This Debt?
Teshuvot Ohel Yaakov, no. 45

Question: *Reuven holds a note stating that Shimon declares under oath that he owes him 100 ducats, to be paid before Shimon's death. Years went by, and Reuven never demanded payment from Shimon. But now he notes that Shimon is squandering his money, and he is afraid that by the time Shimon dies there will be no money left for him to fulfill his oath. Therefore, he demands payment now. If he cannot collect at the present time, he wants the debt to be deposited with the Bet Din until one hour before Shimon's death. Shimon contends that as long as he is alive, the note is not due and Reuven has no right to demand payment.*

Responsum: At first sight it would seem that Shimon can stall for time by telling Reuven that as long as he has a breath of life in him he still has time to pay. He can say, "Although 'before my death' can be interpreted as 'any time before my death' or 'immediately before my death,' I choose the latter interpretation, and there is a rule that in case of doubt the burden of proof is on the lender."

[After a thorough evaluation of all pertinent opinions, Rabbi Sasportas concludes:] Shimon has the obligation of the oath, and he must be certain that he will not violate his oath. . . . Whichever way we look at it, Reuven has the right to demand payment now, especially since he claims that Shimon is wasting his money. It seems to me that there is no doubt about the matter.

Title page of *Kitzur Tzitzat Noveil Tzevi*. Written by R. Yaakov Sasportas in the form of questions and answers about the writings and beliefs of Shabbetai Tzevi, and containing some of the writings themselves, it was a major source for the study of the movement and a fierce attack upon it. First printed in Amsterdam in 1734.

Competing Money-Changers
Teshuvot Ohel Yaakov, no. 56

Question: *In Holland, the government decreed that money-changing could be carried on only by licensed money-changers. Reuven applied for and receive the exclusive right to conduct a banking business. He has been running a bank for a number of years. Recently Shimon put in a bid for a*

Title page of *Teshuvot Ohel Yaakov and Kitzur Tzitzat Noveil Tzevi* by Rabbi Yaakov Sasportas of Amsterdam. This was printed in Amsterdam in 1737.

banking license with the Ministry of Finance. Reuven is trying to invoke the ban of Rabbeinu Gershom[3] against unfair competition. Can Reuven prevent Shimon from engaging in this business?

Responsum [*to Mr. Joseph de la Pina of Rotterdam*]: It seems to me that Reuven cannot claim *chazakah* (claim based on undisturbed possession during a legally fixed period). The exclusive license was issued at the good will of the Ministry. It did not thereby relinquish its right to amend its rules and issue additional licenses. Who can dictate to the king what to do? . . . On the basis of these considerations, we can say that Shimon may attempt to gain favor with the governmental authorities so that they will permit him to engage in this business.

There is no sin in this. According to halachah, Reuven may not stop him.

Marrano Returned to the Jewish Faith
Teshuvot Ohel Yaakov, no. 3

Question: *A young man, Avraham Bueno, was taken captive by Christians, together with his uncle Yaakov Bueno. They applied pressure on him to convert, torturing him for three years, but he did not give in and persisted in his belief in the true God. But when he saw that they poisoned his uncle for refusing to convert, and he found himself in prison all alone, he professed to convert, but in his heart he remained a Jew. After three years of trying to escape, he risked his life swimming to a ship in the open sea, belonging to Jewish traders sailing for the West. His actions prove that his was a forced conversion. How can he repent?*

Responsum: . . . He does not have to repent the fact that he worshipped other gods, for he was forced to do so. . . . For desecrating God's name and eating forbidden foods, he should give himself lashes and accept the pain as a form of atonement. . . . And God's Hand is outstretched to receive those who repent . . . and after the completion of three years he may be considered a full-fledged Jew.

Abolish a Custom Established by Shabbetai Tzevi?
Teshuvot Ohel Yaakov, no. 70.

Question: *From the students of Yeshivah Keter Torah in Amsterdam:*
When the reports about the Mashiach (Messiah) and the prophet began to circulate, our congregation adopted the custom of having the kohanim (priests) bless the congregation[4] each Shabbat. Heretofore, this was done only on Yomtov. Now that the great error (the speciousness of his claim to be the Messiah) has been revealed, some of the leaders of the community want to return to the old custom in order to wipe out any trace of the memory of the impostors who originated the custom. Others maintain that Nesiat Kapayim *(the priestly*

blessing) is a mitzvah, and once we have begun to observe it, we may not abolish it. What is your opinion on the matter?

Responsum: Surely the priestly blessing must not be taken lightly. But it has been reestablished on the basis of false doctrine, and it has led to quarrels within the community. Therefore, I side with those who want to put a stop to it and return to the previous custom of reciting *Nesiat Kapayim* only on Yomtov.

. . . Even though blessing the people every Shabbat is a worthwhile practice, it should not be continued, because it was instituted by a false prophet, one who misled and enticed the Jewish people away from God. The Torah says about him, "Do not show him any mercy, and do not cover up for him."[5] It is better for now to recite it on Yomtov only. . . .

Excerpt from the Opening Chapter Relating the History of Shabbetai Tzevi
Tzitzat Noveil Tzevi

In the year 5426/1665, on 22 Kislev we received reports from Egypt that in Gaza, which is near Jerusalem, a prophet arose bringing good tidings, announcing salvation [Nathan of Gaza]. He stated that a certain scholar by the name of Shabbetai Tzevi from Smyrna, and presently in Jerusalem, is the Mashiach who will within a year and a few months seize power from the Sultan of Turkey. He will overthrow him peacefully, since the Sultan himself will place the royal crown on his head. . . . These words were accepted by the masses, and they even impressed some rabbis. . . . They held these words to be the truth, and whoever did not believe them or harbored doubt about them was considered as denying God and His Torah. . . .

I, unconcerned for my honor or the loss of my life, zealously took up the fight for the honor of God and His Torah, and the glory of the Kingdom of the House of David. I publicly announced that all his words are lies and deception. Although I have been cursed and my life has been threatened, no fear has entered my heart. The merit of my sainted ancestors and my honest intentions have stood by my side.

. . . He proclaimed himself as the Mashiach and performed bizarre and detestable acts which to the people appeared as mystical manifestations. He pronounced the complete Divine Name, abolished the Fast of the tenth of Tevet, changing it into a day of joy and feasting.

. . . Here in Hamburg they pronounced in his honor the blessing that is said for a king. People rise before him in awe and fear as if they were standing in the presence of royalty. They respond with amen to every praise that is uttered. And whoever does not rise or fails to answer amen places his life in jeopardy. . . .

He declared that Moshe is alive today and lives on the Sambatyon River, where he got married and had a daughter who is destined to marry the Mashiach. These fabrications were accepted by the people without verification. . . . The city of Amsterdam was buzzing with excitement. There was music and dancing in the streets and in the synagogue . . . without concern of arousing the resentment of the non-Jews.

. . . The guards at the prison of Gallipoli handed Shabbetai Tzevi over to the Sultan, and he found no other way to save his life than by renouncing Judaism.

RABBI SHMUEL ABOHAB—DVAR SHMUEL
רבי שמואל אבוהב — דבר שמואל

born: Hamburg, Germany, 1610
died: Venice, Italy, 1694

Rabbi Abohab's father, a wealthy philanthropist who founded a yeshivah in Safed, sent young Shmuel to study Torah in Venice when he was 13 years old. Shmuel became highly proficient in Talmud, science, and languages and was admired for his sterling character, humility, piety, and generosity toward the needy and oppressed. Initially he served as rabbi in Verona, where he established a yeshivah. From 1650 until his death he was the rabbi of Venice, where he led an important yeshivah and headed the Central Bet Din. He received queries from rabbis throughout Italy, and gained fame for his relentless opposition to the followers of the false messiah Shabbetai Tzevi.

His personal life was marred by the tragic deaths of several of his children when they were young. Of his four surviving sons, Avraham, David, Yaakov, and Yosef, it was Rabbi Yaakov who succeeded him at his rabbinical post, assisted by his brothers Rabbis Avraham and David, while Rabbi Yosef took his father's place as *rosh yeshivah*. At 80 years of age Rabbi Shmuel Abohab took it upon himself, as a form of ascetic self-mortification, to go into exile, wandering about from town to town for two years. He died in 1694, shortly after his return to Venice. His responsa were published by his son R. David under the title *She'eilot uTeshuvot Dvar Shmuel*.[1]

Is Prayer in the Vernacular Permitted?
***Teshuvot Dvar Shmuel*, no. 321**

Question: *Ten Jews, none of whom knows Hebrew, live in a community where there is no one who can*

Title page of *Dvar Shmuel*, responsa by Rabbi Shmuel Abohab, printed in Venice in 1702.

93

recite the prayers for them in Hebrew. Are they permitted to pray together and recite Kaddish and Kedushah in their own language?[2]

Responsum: Although it may sound strange, most *poskim* permit praying in any language. Proof of this is the Kaddish prayer, which is recited in Aramaic, and most *poskim* hold that Aramaic is inferior to any other language. An additional proof can be inferred from the verse, "Speak to Aharon and to his sons, saying: 'This is how you must bless the Israelites.'"[3] The implication is that the priestly blessing must be recited in Hebrew. It follows that were it not for this special injunction, even the priestly blessing could have been said in any language, just as can the Shema, the Shemoneh Esreih,[4] and Birkat Hamazon (Grace after Meals). I have heard from reliable sources that in the great city of Salonica there is a full-time chazzan for women who do not understand Hebrew, who prays for himself and for them in their language.

Biblical Illustrations of Angels
Teshuvot Dvar Shmuel, no. 247

Question: *What is your opinion of the drawings of angels that appear in Bibles?*

Responsum: I will not suppress my sentiments, and I will tell you that all my life I have deplored the making of such pictures to illustrate the stories of our holy Torah—not because of halachic objections, but because they manifest a disrespect of sacred beings. The drawings are supposed to be representations of divine angels as the artist imagines them to be, yet hardly anyone has ever beheld an angel. How can a mere mortal dare depict them according to his whim and paint them in false and deceptive images according to his momentary illusions? These pictures serve no useful purpose; they do not add to our knowledge or understanding of the Torah. I am afraid that these illustrations are a symptom of our emulating the non-Jews,[5] as it is written, "They mingled with the nations and learned their works."[6]

Seek a Cure through Exorcism?
Teshuvot Dvar Shmuel, no. 359

Question: *May a patient suffering from epilepsy or one possessed by demons seek healing from a Catholic priest who exorcises spirits by uttering religious incantations?*

Responsum: . . . We have a general rule that in life-threatening situations any method or cure is permissible except idol worship. You must give up your life rather than worship idols. Included in this category is seeking a cure through idolatrous incantations. All present-day priests and clergy mention the name of their deity in their incantations, and as the Baal HaTurim states (*Yoreh De'ah* 155), "their 'cures' are ineffective and futile because they are nothing but meaningless babble."

In the merit of staying away from all these so-called cures, with the intent of sanctifying God's Name and His Oneness, the patient will be healed from his afflictions. "For all the nations walk each one in the name of its god, but we will walk in the name of the Lord our God for ever and ever."[7] To Him we will pray that he may be healed speedily, and all his relatives will rejoice. May God protect them so that they will not stumble into sin. . . .

Ascetic Old Rabbi Practices Self-Mortification
Teshuvot Dvar Shmuel, no. 344

Question: *A venerable old rabbi has been fasting and practicing self-mortification for more than thirty-five years, except on Shabbat, Yomtov, and Rosh Chodesh (first day of the Hebrew month). He has now reached the age of 80 and, although he realizes that he cannot go on like this, he wants to maintain his life of pious self-denial. If, God forbid, something should happen to this man [as a result of these practices], wouldn't he be guilty of suicide? Shouldn't we do our best to convince him to have his vow annulled so that he will not endanger his life?*

Responsum: This question was answered by our sages long ago in the Gemara *Taanit* and in *Tur*

Orach Chaim, no. 571, where two contradictory statements by Amoraim[8] are reconciled. One Amora says, "He who fasts is considered a saint." The other Amora says, "He who fasts is a sinner." The first Amora has in mind a person who can endure the distress, the second Amora refers to a person who is too weak to fast. Both Amoraim agree that a person who is feeble, either because of advanced age or because of sickness, is committing a sin if he fasts or afflicts himself. It is the prevailing custom in all Jewish communities for pious men to have their vow annulled under such circumstances. Therefore, this fine Torah scholar should do likewise. Just as in the past he received a reward from Heaven for abstaining, so will he be rewarded for refraining from fasting, and in his old age God will not abandon him.

Freeing a Slave
Teshuvot Dvar Shmuel, no. 369

Question: *Reuven bought a black slave girl from a government official, who had bought her from a captain who had captured an Arab freighter loaded with dates, other merchandise, and male and female slaves to be sold at the slave market. The slave bore Reuven a son. After Reuven's death, his heirs inherited the slave and her son. The slave and her son underwent immersion for the purpose of conversion to Judaism. Our question is, do they require a letter of emancipation before they can be considered converts?*

Responsum: In order to remove all doubts, we should be stringent and require a letter of emancipation before permitting them to enter the community of Israel. The mother and her son both need separate letters of emancipation, for no two slaves can be set free with the same letter of emancipation.

The text of the letter of emancipation reads as follows:

On this . . . day of the week, the . . . day of the month . . . of the year . . . of Creation, in the city . . . , I, . . . , son of . . . , set you free from being my slave . . . and you are now a free woman. You are permitted to enter the community of Israel, to marry, and to teach your children the Torah and bring them into the community of Israel. From this day forward no one shall raise objections to you or your offspring. This is my letter of emancipation I am giving you herewith according to the law of Moshe and Israel.

Enlarging the Synagogue
Teshuvot Dvar Shmuel, no. 346

Question: *The synagogue of the Italian Jewish community of the city of Ancona is overcrowded, especially on Shabbat and Yomtov, a situation that has led to many quarrels over seats. The leaders of the community want to enlarge the synagogue, and to that end they consulted an engineer, who informed them that any extension of the existing synagogue would entail tearing down the two study halls in which the boys and young men are studying Torah. The question is whether it is permissible to demolish the walls of the two study halls if they will be reconstructed as part of the larger synagogue.*

Responsum: We should not be rigorous in this case. We have a precedent here in our own community where several synagogues have been enlarged and the study halls in their basements were moved to other locations, and none of the rabbis raised any objections. In the present case all doubts are removed, since in the projected new synagogue space has been set aside for a yeshivah to be used exclusively for the study and teaching of Torah, Mishnah, Halachah, and Aggadah. It will be a grand edifice and should be named "The Great House of Prayer," for in it prayer and Torah will be united.

RABBI YAIR CHAIM BACHRACH—CHAVAT YAIR
רבי יאיר חיים בכרך — חוות יאיר

born: Mezritz, 1638
died: Worms, Germany, 1702
Popularly known as Chavat Yair, the title of his responsa work.

After having studied under his father, Rabbi Moshe Shimshon, and in the yeshivah of Rabbi Mendel Bess in Frankfort on-the-Main, the Chavat Yair was chosen rabbi of Koblenz, Germany, in 1656, and four years later he was called to serve as rabbi of Mainz. In 1670 he came to Worms, and when in 1689 that city was occupied by the French army, he fled to Metz, France. From there he moved to Frankfort, where he published his important collection of responsa. In 1699 he returned to Worms to become its rabbi, and he stayed there until his death in 1702.

He was one of the most prominent Torah scholars in the Germany of his time, distinguishing himself for his keenly analytical approach to problems in Halachah. He had a thorough knowledge of the secular sciences, with a predilection for astronomy, mathematics, geometry, and world history. He had an aversion to *pilpul*,[1] calling it a "waste of time" (*Chavat Yair* no. 123). He was well versed in Kabbalah but discouraged his students from delving into its mysteries, "for the road to mastering it is very dangerous" (*Chavat Yair* no. 210). His collection of responsa, *Chavat Yair*,[2] comprises inquiries that were directed at him from all parts of the world. He chose the title to memorialize his grandmother Chavah, the learned daughter of Rabbi Yitzchak Katz; Chavah herself was an author of comments on the Torah.

Title page of *She'eilot uTeshuvot Chavat Yair* by Rabbi Yair Chaim Bachrach. This edition was annotated by Rabbi Baruch Frankel, Rabbi of Leipnik, author of *Baruch Taam*, and father-in-law of the Divrei Chaim of Sanz. Printed in Jerusalem, 1973.

Cutting Down a Fruit Tree
Chavat Yair, no. 195

Question: *A peach tree growing in a man's backyard shuts out the sunlight. Is he permitted to cut it down?*[3]

Responsum: It is clear that he is allowed to cut it down. If he needs to do so for his physical comfort, no prohibition applies. The Torah forbids only wanton destruction that has no purpose. We say, for example, if a fruit tree detracts from the taste of the fruit of a better tree or weakens it, then you may cut it down. Similarly, if it obstructs the sunlight, you may also cut it down. For what difference does it make whether the tree impairs the sense of taste or the sense of vision? Besides, the impairment of vision is constant and is a greater source of irritation.

However, if he can improve the brightness in his house by cutting down several branches, he should not cut down the entire tree, even though with the passing years they grow back and he will have to cut them again.

A Rabbi-Musician Performing at Weddings?
Chavat Yair, no. 205

Question: *A Talmudic scholar who is an accomplished muscian asks if he is permitted to perform at weddings, playing the violin, or if it is forbidden because it is degrading to his status as Torah scholar.*

Responsum: The mitzvah of gladdening the groom and the bride is not degrading to an older person or to a Torah scholar. Anyone acting playfully for the sake of God in the performance of a mitzvah is to be commended and is worthy of blessings.

Transform an Apron into a Mantle for the Torah?
Chavat Yair, no. 161

Question: *A woman, during her illness, vowed to donate her apron, which was embroidered with silver and gold threads, to the synagogue to be used as a sacred article. Should she make it into a mantle for the Torah scroll or a cover for the prayer lectern or for the lectern used for reading the Torah?*

Responsum: It seems clear to me that the greatest mitzvah would be to make a mantle for the Torah scroll out of it. The mantle is a sacred article that clings to the Torah scroll itself.

You cannot argue that it would be improper because an apron is a garment worn on a woman's body. Quite the contrary, it is a garment worn for modesty. It was precisely for this reason that Moses accepted the women's body ornaments to be used in the building of the tabernacle, for they were designed for modesty.[4]

I once was asked concerning a Jew in Eretz Yisrael who had bought an exquisitely embroidered cloth. This cloth is used by the Turks when they carry their children to their clerics to be initiated into their faith. He wanted to use it as a cover for the Torah scroll, and I forbade it. Since the man happened to be a mohel, he used it to wrap the infants he circumcised. I did not object to that.

Are Incantations Superstitions?
Chavat Yair, no. 234

Question: *Some women know certain incantations that they use against aches and pains and certain diseases. Is this considered superstition?*

Responsum: Halachically, it seems to me advisable to let the women do whatever they are practicing. It probably is a tried and proven remedy, and a previous authority must have sanctioned it. Thus, we cannot forbid the practice of describing a circle, with a ring taken from a dead person, around a child who is running a fever and developing blisters, or similar procedures. I also think that there is no harm in refraining from doing something; for example, some people refrain from slaughtering geese, thinking this will effect a cure.

Disposing of the Property of Others
Chavat Yair, no. 136

During the upheaval in the wake of the war with France, the villagers fled to the cities, either lodging with relatives or renting space. One of the landlords, whose house was filled wall to wall with refugees, would inspect their boxes and bundles to see to whom they belonged. He came upon one bundle whose ownership he could not determine and concluded that someone had deposited it without his knowledge. After trying without success to find the owner, he threw the bundle into the courtyard. Several days later the owner appeared and found much of the contents of his bundle stolen and several garments ruined by the rain. The owner of the bundle sued the landlord. The rabbinical judge decided that according to Halachah the landlord had no liability in this case but, for the sake of peace, the landlord should keep this bundle [under his protection] for six months. Both parties agreed: the landlord because he did not lose anything, and the owner of the bundle because of what the judge had decreed for the landlord.

When I heard this I spoke to the judge and he explained his reasons. I told him that the compromise was in error. It was based on incorrect assumptions and comparisons.

The *Chavat Yair* now explores in great detail all halachic implications of the theme *avid inish daina lenafshei*, whether a person can take the law into his own hands.

Incident during the Cholera Epidemic
Chavat Yair, no. 60

Question: *The following incident reportedly happened in Worms during the great cholera epidemic in the year 1630. The only daughter of a wealthy and prominent member of the community fell victim to the disease, and since most townspeople were similarly stricken, the only nurse to be found for her was the butcher's helper, a handsome, tall young man who told the girl's father that he loved his daughter and had pity on her. He said, "If you give me your word that, if she lives, you will give her to me in marriage, I will take care of her with all my strength, without pay." The father agreed with a handshake. The girl also promised to marry him. The butcher's helper faithfully attended to her needs and nursed her back to health. Then he fell ill with cholera and she cared for him, since she was deeply in love with him. He also recovered. The wealthy father recanted, for he was ashamed to let his talented only daughter marry a lowly butcher's helper. He argued that his own and his daughter's promise were given under duress. The daughter, however, against her father's wishes, remained faithful to the young man and insisted on marrying him. The father told her, "Except for a few ordinary dresses, you will not get one penny as dowry from me." The butcher's helper married her without a dowry.*

[*I was asked, if the helper had sued the father, how would I have ruled?*]

Responsum: Legally, the helper could force both the father and the daughter to fulfill their promise, which was binding like an oath. If the father had said, "Marry her, but I will give no dowry," we could not have forced him to give her money. However, since the butcher's helper was willing to risk his life to nurse this cholera patient, the father was obligated to keep his word.

IV

THE RESPONSA OF THE LATER ACHARONIM: 1649–PRESENT

The year 1648, also known as the tragic *Shenat Tach*, 5408 of Creation, the year of the bloody Chmielnitzki massacre, marks the conclusion of the era of the Early Acharonim and the emergence of the Later Acharonim, an era that extends into the present. It is a period that has produced a wealth of illustrious Torah sages, such as the Magen Avraham (Rabbi Avraham Gombiner), the **Chacham Tzvi** (Rabbi **Tzvi Ashkenazi**), Rabbi Yaakov Emden, Rabbi Yonatan Eibschutz, the Vilna Gaon, Rabbi **Akiva Eiger**, the **Chatam Sofer** (Rabbi **Moshe Sofer**), the Baal Shem Tov, the Chafetz Chaim, and more recently, Rabbi Aharon Kotler and Rabbi **Moshe Feinstein**.

The responsa of the Later Acharonim afford an insight into the major problems that have concerned the Jewish people of their time, such as the disillusionment that followed the fall of the fraudulent messiah Shabbetai Tzevi, and the advent of the Reform movement. The rabbis' responsa attest to the wisdom and resolve with which they guided their flock. The Holocaust, which ended in 1945, marks another milepost in the tragic history of our people. We mourn the deaths of most of our greatest modern sages and their students; we mourn the deaths of six million Jews who were brutally murdered.

Yet the Torah lives on. The recent incredible resurgence of Torah learning and teaching, the miraculous return to Torah of masses of alienated Jews, the astounding revival of Torah study and observance in the Soviet Union are proof of the eternal bond that exists between God, the Torah, and the Jewish people. The amazing exodus of masses of Soviet Jews to Israel that we have been witnessing daily, as this book is being written, is a vivid testimonial to the divine spark of Judaism that seventy years of Communist suppression were unable to extinguish. Having tasted their newly gained freedom, Soviet Jews eagerly turn to Torah values to satisfy their spiritual hunger. And, finally, the ever-increasing number of yeshivot in America, Israel, and the entire world, the multitudes of young Torah scholars clamoring to study Torah, the Talmud, the Geonim, the Codes, the Rishonim and the Acharonim, are living proof of the fulfillment of the prophecy that "[The Torah] will never be forgotten by their children" (Deuteronomy 31:12).

RABBI TZVI ASHKENAZI—CHACHAM TZVI
רבי צבי אשכנזי — חכם צבי

born: Moravia, 1660
died: Lemberg, 1718
Popularly known as Chacham Tzvi.

Tzvi Ashkenazi received his early Torah education from his father, Rabbi Yaakov Sak, and from his maternal grandfather, Rabbi Efraim HaKohen. As a young man he was sent to the Sephardi yeshivah of Salonica, Greece, where he adopted the Sephardi customs and studied the languages of the Sephardi Jews. It was there that he received the title of *chacham*, the Sephardi equivalent of rabbi. Chacham Tzvi was married in Budapest but soon was forced to flee when, in 1686, in the wake of the siege of that city by the forces of the Austrian Kaiser, his home was destroyed by a bomb that killed his wife and infant daughter.

After years of wandering he settled in Altona, near Hamburg, Germany, where he founded a yeshivah that he headed for the next eighteen years. During that time he remarried and had a son who became the famous Rabbi **Yaakov Emden** (1698–1776). In 1706 Chacham Tzvi was elected rabbi of the tri-cities Altona, Hamburg, and Wandsbeck. (These cities are commonly referred to as AHU, the acronym formed of their initials.) In 1710 he became the rabbi of the Ashkenazi community of Amsterdam. Soon afterward, he published his responsa *She'eilot uTeshuvot Chacham Tzvi*,[1] a work that won him the respect of the rabbinical world. On the heels of an acrimonious quarrel between the Ashkenazi and Sephardi communities, Chacham Tzvi left Amsterdam to become the rabbi of Lemberg, Poland, where he remained until his death.

Strength, truthfulness, and independence were the hallmarks of his character. He did not shirk from battle when the purity of Torah was at stake.

Rabbi Tzvi Ashkenazi, the Chacham Tzvi.

God and Nature
Teshuvot Chacham Tzvi, no. 18

Question: *Rabbi Nito of Congregation Shaarei Shamayim in London delivered a sermon in which he stated that God and nature are one and the same. Certain members of the congregation are up in arms* *about this, claiming that his statement is heretical. What is your opinion on this matter?*

Responsum: The rabbi's words can be found in the Kuzari[2] 1:15, which states, "God is called *teva* ['nature'; *teva* also denotes stamp or hallmark],[3] because He places His stamp and seal on all of Creation. For God nourishes and sustains all living beings, from the mighty bison to the egg of a flea." I do not understand those people who protest against their rabbi's sermon. Do they think that equating God with nature is demeaning to God's honor? Well, the illustrious giant of Torah scholarship, Rabbi Yeshayah [Horowitz][4] in his work *Shelah*,[5] which is accepted in all Israel, writes that reward for the performance of mitzvot and punishment for transgressions are natural consequences flowing from the deed. And anyone who has eyes and studies the wisdom of Kabbalah agrees with this. . . .

Therefore, this criticism is not directed against this rabbi but against all the saintly kabbalists by whose words we are guided. There is no basis for protest, for equating God with nature does not mean nature as an independently acting force, but nature as an expression of God's will. We should be grateful to Rabbi David Nito for his sermon, for he cautioned the members of his congregation not to stray after the views of the secular philosophers,[6] since this leads to many pitfalls. He enlightened them in the true tenets of the faith, that everything is guided by Divine Providence. I say to him, *Yasher ko'ach*, "More power to you!" . . .

Title page of *She'eilot uTeshuvot Chacham Tzvi* by Rabbi Tzvi Ashkenazi, "Rabbi of the Ashkenazic Congregation in the great city of Amsterdam." First printed in Amsterdam in 1712.

Is England a Private Domain?[7]
Teshuvot Chacham Tzvi, no. 37

Question: *It is a well-known fact that an area that is fenced by partitions is considered a private domain, even if that area encompasses thousands of square miles. In view of this, can all of England be considered a private domain, since it is "fenced in" on all sides by the sea?*

Responsum: Instead of asking me about England, why don't you ask about the entire world? After all, all the continents are "fenced in" by oceans!

Tosafot in *Eiruvin* clearly answers your question, to the effect that England and similar places that are surrounded by the sea cannot be considered a private domain, because the sea is a natural barrier and not a man-made partition, as required by halachah.

And now all your doubts are laid to rest, and your soul can be at peace like a fresh olive tree.

Who Has to Pay for the Disabled Horse?
Teshuvot Chacham Tzvi, no. 68

Question: *A nobleman bought horses from two Jews, Reuven and Shimon. Shimon misled the noble, since one of the horses he sold to him had a* defect. *After a while, the noble noticed the defect, and he returned the disabled horse to Reuven, demanding a refund. Reuven is suing Shimon, claiming that it was Shimon's horse and that Shimon should return the purchase price of the horse to the noble, since the noble mistakenly is demanding the money from him. Shimon contends that Reuven has no case against him, since he committed no wrong against Reuven.*

Responsum: It seems clear that Reuven has no claim against Shimon. Halachah states, "No one can be held accountable for a charge leveled at someone else." Whether the noble returned the horse to Reuven inadvertently or intentionally is immaterial. In either case Shimon is exempt from making restitution to Reuven. Reuven, however, has the right to inform the noble that it was Shimon who had sold him the defective horse. This does not constitute robbing Shimon, as halachically Shimon is obligated to return to the duke the purchase price of the horse.

What to Use for Maror at the Seder
Teshuvot Chacham Tzvi, no. 119

Question: *What species should be used for maror (bitter herbs)?*

Responsum: For the benefit of the public I think it is useful to let everyone know that the *chazeret* mentioned in the Mishnah as the preferred species to be used for maror at the seder is the plant known in German as *Salat* and in Spanish as *salada*. Its scientific name is *latuga*, and so it is called in all languages I know: Turkish, Italian, German, Spanish, and Portuguese, and it is called this in medical and science books.[8] There is no doubt about its identity, and it has all the characteristics that are mentioned in the Gemara.

Since in the regions of Germany and Poland, because of their cold climate, it is not available at the time of Passover, people are not accustomed to use it for the mitzvah of maror; or perhaps they do not use it because they are not as familiar with the names of the plants as the people of the Middle Eastern countries are.[9] Instead, they use *chrein*, horseradish. This has had detrimental results, because many people eat less than the required minimum of a *kazayit*[10] because of the pungent flavor of the horseradish. Thus they are neglecting the mitzvah of maror. And the meticulously observant Jews who do eat a *kazayit* of the horseradish are endangering their health. To use horseradish in places like Amsterdam and Hamburg where this *latuga* is available is a hazard and no mitzvah. Whoever is God-fearing should buy *latuga–Salat* for maror, even if it is costly.

The vegetable that is called *Endivien* in Hamburg (in German) and *andijvie* in Amsterdam (in Dutch)[11] is also valid for use as maror if no *latuga–Salat* is available.

The Stolen *Etrog*
Teshuvot Chacham Tzvi, no. 120

Question: *Reuven bought a beautiful* etrog,[12] *for which he paid a large amount. Shimon stole the* etrog. *How much restitution must Shimon pay?*

Responsum: When this question was put to Maharam Mintz,[13] he replied in his responsum no. 113 that the thief is required to pay only the replacement price of an ordinary *etrog* that qualifies for the mitzvah.

I think his decision is erroneous. A beautiful *etrog* has intrinsic value, and it can be sold for a higher price. The fact that the increased value is due to people's desire to glorify the mitzvah is irrelevant. Proof of this is that if someone steals a Torah scroll worth 1,000 *zuz* because its parchment is beautiful and its writing exquisite, would anyone dream of asserting that the thief can wipe the slate clean by replacing it with a Torah scroll that is not esthetically crafted and worth only 50 *zuz*, just because it is acceptable for the purpose of the mitzvah?

It is a simple fact that if someone grabs an *etrog*, either before or on Sukkot, for which the owner paid a high price, he must pay the value it has in terms of fulfilling the mitzvah in a glorious manner.

The Nobleman's Loan
Teshuvot Chacham Tzvi, no. 144

Question: *A nobleman asked for a loan from the Jews living on his estate, to be repaid after one or* two years. The loan was extended to him, each Jew contributing according to his means. When the loan was due and the representatives of the community came to demand payment, the noble vilified and abused them and sent them away, calling down curses on their heads.

As time went by, the Jews gave up hope of ever collecting the debt. "How can we sue the nobleman?" they wondered. In the course of time, the wealthy people who had contributed the money for the loan became poor, while many poor people became rich, as often happens when the wheel of fortune turns. Many years later the nobleman died and his son succeeded him. The son, wishing to reinstate his father's good reputation, told the Jews that he would repay his father's debts by reducing the annual tax they owed him.

Who should be the beneficiary of this reduction: the formerly rich people who are now poor, who actually paid the money for the loan, or those who are presently wealthy, although they did not pay for it? On the other hand, the original donors gave up long ago on ever collecting the debt.

Responsum: The **Maharik**[14] in responsum 3 rules in a similar case in favor of the people who are currently wealthy, and he explains his position at great length. . . . I disagree with the Maharik. . . . The fact that they gave up on ever collecting is of no consequence in this case. Therefore, it seems to me that the halachah is in favor of the people who originally extended the loan to the nobleman. Each should be repaid according to his contribution.

Man Created by Means of Kabbalah
Teshuvot Chacham Tzvi, no. 93

Question: *I have speculated on the theoretical question as to what would be the legal status of a man who was created by using the formulas found in Sefer Yetzirah [The Book of Creation, an ancient esoteric text] like, for example, the man who was created by Rava as mentioned in Sanhedrin 65b, or like the man who reportedly was created by my grandfather, Rabbi Eliyahu, the Rabbi of Chelm.*

Could such a man be counted as the tenth man in a minyan [the quorum required to recite the Kaddish or Kedushah]? Shall we say that he is not really one of the children of Israel, and therefore should not be included in the minyan? Or should we argue that, since he is the handiwork of a tzaddik, he is like the tzaddik's child and should be included?

Responsum: It seems to me that the answer can be adduced from the abovementioned Gemara: "Rava created a man (by using the formulas of *Sefer Yetzirah*—Rashi) and sent him to Rav Zeira. Rav Zeira spoke to him but received no answer. Thereupon Rav Zeira said to him, 'You were created by the use of mystical power. Return to your dust.'"

In other words, Rav Zeira killed him. Now, if this creature could have served any useful purpose, such as being included in a minyan, then Rabbi Zeira would not have removed him from this world. It should be understood that killing such a "man" is not considered murder. This is derived from the verse, "He who spills a man's blood shall have his own blood spilled by man" (Genesis 9:8)—[which means that] only killing a man born of a mother's womb is punishable as murder. Nevertheless, Rabbi Zeira would not have taken the life of this "man" if he could have been counted as one of a minyan. I conclude therefore that a "man" who was created with the *Sefer Yetzirah* cannot be included in a minyan.

RABBI YAAKOV REISCHER—SHEVUT YAAKOV
רבי יעקב רישר — שבות יעקב

born: Prague, c. 1661
died: Metz, France, 1733

Rabbi Yaakov was born into a prominent family that numbered many distinguished rabbis in its ranks. At a young age he was appointed dayan (judge) in Prague. His first rabbinical appointment was in Reishe (Rzeszow), Galicia; hence the surname Reischer. He served as rabbi in a number of other communities, and his most fruitful years were spent as rabbi of Worms, Germany, and of Metz, France.

He was a prolific writer, and his books, which manifest his deeply penetrating mind, found wide acclaim. He wrote *Minchat Yaakov*[1] and *Chok Yaakov*,[2] and halachic novellae, as well as *Iyun Yaakov*,[3] a commentary on the aggadic compendium *Eyn Yaakov*. The collection of his responsa, published under the title *Shevut Yaakov*,[4] is considered one of the major works of its kind.

Siamese Twins
Teshuvot Shevut Yaakov, no. 1:4

Question: *I want to report an amazing sight. Two non-Jewish twin boys were brought here who were attached to one another at the back of their heads. Each of them had all his limbs and organs, just like a normal person. They had two faces, but the backs of their heads were joined together so that it appeared as though they had one wide head. In all other respects they were like two individuals. They were a little over one year old, and I recited the proper* berachah.[5] *My question is, what would be their halachic status if, God forbid, a case like that should occur with Jewish children?*

Title page of *Shevut Yaakov*, responsa by Rabbi Yaakov Reischer, volume 1. Published anew in Jerusalem, 1972. The abbreviations on the last line stand for *Be'ir hakodesh*, "In the Holy City Jerusalem," *tibaneh vetikonen bimhera beyamenu*, "may she be rebuilt and established speedily in our days."

Responsum: . . . In this case we have two individuals who are attached to each other. There is nothing new under the sun, for the Gemara and the Midrash relate that Adam and Eve were created as one individual with two faces, for it is written, "He created them male and female and called them Adam."[6] Furthermore, we read in Psalm 139:5, "You created me back and front." Now, since they are two separate individuals, it is obvious that each must put on his own tefillin. As for inheritance rights, they receive two shares of the inheritance. However, they are forbidden to marry. . . . May the Merciful One protect us from such misfortunes.

Who Has to Pay for the Wasted Food?
Teshuvot Shevut Yaakov, no. 1:61

Question: *A man sent a messenger to his rabbi with a pot of meat into which some milk had spilled accidentally, asking whether the meat dish may be eaten. The rabbi ruled that the food was forbidden to be used, whereupon the messenger threw away the food. Subsequently, it was discovered that the rabbi had erred and that the food was actually permissible. The man demands payment for his food from the rabbi and the messenger. Who has to make restitution?*

Responsum: The rabbi who inadvertently rendered a wrong decision is surely exempt. Although indirectly he triggered the loss, this was not his intention. The messenger is at fault for discarding the food too quickly. But on further reflection I find that the messenger also is exempt because the matter was beyond his control, since his act was prompted by the rabbi's erroneous decision. I cite as proof for this the **Rashba,** responsum no. 1189.

Did Shimon Cause the Fire?
Teshuvot Shevut Yaakov, no. 1:136

Question: *Reuven and Shimon were riding together on a wagon, which was loaded with bales of cotton belonging to Reuven. As they were riding along, Shimon pulled out his pipe and began to smoke. When Reuven saw sparks coming out of the pipe he warned Shimon not to smoke, for he might set fire to the cotton. Shimon, paying no attention to him, continued to smoke. An hour or two later, a sudden gust blew up. A few sparks jumped into the cotton, setting the entire load on fire. Is Shimon responsible for paying for the damage, or should it be attributed to the wind?*

Responsum: . . . Shimon should be held accountable for the damages, since as soon as the strong wind blew up, he should have thought of the consequences and should have stopped smoking, especially since Reuven had warned him. Since he continued smoking, he did, in effect, ignite the fire. He is required to pay the damages as prescribed by Halachah.

A Husband Abused His Wife
Teshuvot Shevut Yaakov, no. 1:113

Question: *A woman, sobbing bitterly, complained that her husband had beaten her savagely. He had been warned repeatedly by the Bet Din to stop abusing her or else he would be forced to give her a get* as set forth in Even Ha'ezer *154:3. One day, only the wife, her husband, and his male servant were at home, when he brutally beat her. When her screams attracted people from the street, she showed them her bruised back, covered with bloody welts. The husband denied everything and said that he never touched her, that perhaps she inflicted these wounds herself, or perhaps his servant did it. . . . She countered that it was impossible for her to cause such wounds on her back, and anyway, that it was absurd even to think that she would hurt herself so severely, and that it certainly never entered the servant's mind to strike her. [She also said that,] on the other hand, her husband had beaten her numerous times in the past and the servant would testify to that. Who is right?*

Responsum: . . . In this case, even though the bruises and lacerations were on her back, in a way that she could not possibly have inflicted them herself, nevertheless, since there was someone else present, that is, the servant, we must consider the possibility that she told the servant to beat her in order to force her husband to divorce her because she has become enamored of someone else. The servant's testimony cannot be believed because he is an interested party. . . . On the other hand, the husband has beaten her before, and there is the presumption that he is also guilty this time.

Nevertheless, since this case involves the possibility of divorce action, and divorce is an extremely serious matter, . . . and the presumption of the husband's guilt is not altogether clear-cut, therefore she should be placed under oath. Without an oath she should not be believed, since this case leads to a divorce. It would be best if it were possible to reconcile them, because bringing peace between husband and wife is a great virtue.

Mail a Letter on Friday?
Teshuvot Shevut Yaakov, no. 2:42

Question: *Is it permitted to mail letters on Friday?*[7]

Responsum: I don't understand what is the problem. Since you did not ask the letter-carrier to deliver the mail, there is no reason to forbid it, as set forth in *Shulchan Aruch, Orach Chaim* 307 . . . "If a non-Jew is going someplace of his own accord on Shabbat, a Jew is permitted to give him along a letter." Similarly, in this case, the letter-carrier goes on his rounds by order of the King and the postal authorities.

However, it may be forbidden to send a special delivery letter that will be delivered on Shabbat, because doing this would amount to telling a non-Jew to deliver this letter on Shabbat. Still, I think that even this may be permitted if you do not personally direct the mail carrier to deliver the letter but rather you instruct the postmaster. Then the mail carrier does not act on your instructions but follows the postmaster's orders.

Anyway, every few miles the mail is transferred from one carrier to another. See also *Teshuvot Chavat Yair* no. 43, where he expressly rules that telling one non-Jew to relay a request to another is permitted on Shabbat.

Should They Die for the Sanctification of God's Name?
Teshuvot Shevut Yaakov, no. 2:106

Question: *In a certain city the Jews were given the choice between baptism and death. It is clear that they must choose death rather than convert. However, there are some who have an opportunity to escape. Are they required to flee and save their lives, since remaining in the city would be suicidal, or should they sacrifice their lives for the sanctification of God's name, like all the other Jews?*

Responsum: At first glance it would appear that they should not flee, based on *Pesachim* 53 where the question is asked, "What prompted Chananiah, Mishael, and Azariah to throw themselves into the fiery furnace?" This is inferred from the frogs that during the second plague willingly jumped into the ovens (Exodus 7:28). And Rabbeinu Tam explains that Chananiah, Mishael, and Azariah had the opportunity to escape, yet they chose death in the furnace.[8]

However, on further reflection it becomes clear that this reasoning does not apply to our case. Certainly it is preferable by far if you can both avoid violating the law and save your life. We can learn this from Rabbi Shimon ben Yochai and his son Elazar, who hid from the Romans in a cave for thirteen years.[9] . . . However, if someone wants to adopt a stringent attitude by offering his life in order to sanctify the Name in public so as to set an example for others, his memory will be blessed, and surely his act is not considered suicide.

Victims of the Plague in 1713
Teshuvot Shevut Yaakov, no. 2:104

Question: *A dying man stipulated that part of his money be left to a fund for the release of captives. At present, in the year 5473/1713, now that the bubonic plague is raging, many Jews find themselves in dire straits. Is it permissible to give this money to these unfortunate people, or would that constitute a violation of the will?*

Responsum: The Gemara in *Bava Batra* 8a states that the mitzvah of redeeming captives is paramount, surpassing even the mitzvah of saving people from the plague, for it is written, ". . . Thus says the Lord, 'Those that are marked for death, to death; those that are marked for the sword, to the sword; and those that are marked for famine, to famine; and those that are marked for captivity, to captivity.'"[10] The curses in this verse are going from bad to worse, so that captivity is the worst fate of all, because, as Rashi explains, the captor has the power to do as he pleases, to maim, to kill, or to starve his captives. Convincing proof that captivity is worse than the plague.

Nevertheless, I think that this held true only in ancient times, when God's rule was recognized in the world and the non-Jewish world looked with favor on the Jewish people. But now things are different. Today we live under the heavy yoke of the exile and our enemies concoct false accusations and spread the libel as if it were the Jews who caused the plague. And when in 1713 the plague erupted, in most places where Jews resided they sealed off the ghettos. No one could enter and no one could leave. Only with the greatest difficulty did they permit food to be brought in. In some localities Jews were forced to hide in the forests and in caves. A Jew who was found on the road or in a field was literally in danger of his life. Such conditions certainly qualify as the worst kind of captivity. The mitzvah of saving the victims of the plague undoubtedly can be characterized as redeeming captives; it might even be a greater mitzvah than that. Giving the money to the victims of the plague does not change the designation of the will, for this is an extreme emergency.

Terrorized by Bandits
Teshuvot Shevut Yaakov, no. 2:117

Question: *A group of Jews were traveling together. One of them was accompanied by his wife. Toward evening, as they sought shelter at an inn at the edge of the forest, they were confronted by a band of merciless bandits who were ready to kill them for their money. Their pleadings fell on deaf ears. The wife, seeing that they were all doomed to die, offered herself to the bandit and thereby saved their lives. Now her husband wants to know if he must separate from her. Or is he permitted to continue living with her, because she was forced to give herself by the death threat that was hanging over them, and a wife who was forcibly violated is permitted to live with her husband.*

Responsum: A similar case was decided by the **Maharik,** responsum no. 168, who compares the violated wife to Yael[11] and to Esther, who gave themselves to save the Jewish people. Even though they did not commit the slightest sin, subsequently they were forbidden to live with their husbands. [There follows a lengthy discussion of the Maharik's ruling and of the circumstances under which it applies. Maharik makes the following distinction: If the wife was raped after being overwhelmed by fear and terror of the rapist, then she is permitted to return to her husband. But if she willingly offered herself, although through her acquiescence many people were saved, she is forbidden to continue living with her husband. He concludes:] Since she was raped, she is permitted . . . to live with her husband. The husband has no grounds for observing stringencies for reasons of piety. He should not, God forbid, separate or abstain from his pure wife. . . .

RABBI YECHEZKEL KATZENELLENBOGEN— KENESSET YECHEZKEL
רבי יחזקאל קצנאלבוגן — כנסת יחזקאל

born: Lithuania, c. 1670
died: Altona, Germany, 1749
Popularly known as Kenesset Yechezkel, the title of his collected responsa.

Rabbi Yechezkel, a noted *poseik* (decider of Halachah), was a descendant of Rabbi Binyamin Aharon Solnick of Podayetz, author of the responsa *Masat Binyamin*. Initially, Rabbi Yechezkel served as rabbi of Keidan, Poland, but in 1614 he was appointed rabbi of the prominent community of the German tri-cities Altona, Hamburg, and Wandsbeck, known as AHU, the acronym formed of their initials. His son-in-law, Rabbi Yissachar, succeeded him as rabbi of Keidan. In the bitter controversy that erupted between the two Torah giants Rabbi **Yaakov Emden** and Rabbi Yonatan Eibschutz, both of AHU, Rabbi Yechezkel sided with the latter, much to Rabbi Emden's chagrin.

Rabbi Yechezkel corresponded with the foremost rabbinical figures of his time and published a compilation of his responsa under the title *Kenesset Yechezkel*.[1] Among his other works is a homiletic commentary on the Torah called *Mayim Yechezkel*.[2] Four generations of his descendants served in rabbinic posts in Poland.

Can a Chazzan Accept a New Position?
Teshuvot Kenesset Yechezkel, no. 8

Question: A chazzan gave a solemn promise to the community of Metz to become their new chazzan. The community of Bing, where he is presently employed, prevents him from leaving. The chazzan is clamoring, but they turn a deaf ear to his outcry.

Title page of *She'eilot uTeshuvot Kenesset Yechezkel* by Rabbi Yechezkel Katzenellenbogen, who served as rabbi of the tri-cities Altona, Hamburg, and Wandsbeck (known by the acronym AHU) in northern Germany. First printed in Altona in 1732.

The Bing community has a responsum by Rabbi Judah Meiler justifying their stand. This question was submitted by Rabbi Gershon Koblenz of Metz.

Responsum: ... When a community appoints a rabbi or a chazzan, they do so with the understanding that if the rabbi or chazzan receives a call from another community he will accept that position. Otherwise, no rabbi or chazzan will accept a position in a small community. ... In this case, the small community of Bing, compared with Metz, is like a drop in the ocean. ... The chazzan is crying out to keep the promise he made to the great community of Metz. I am astonished that my friend Rabbi Meiler does not support him in this matter. ... I am utterly surprised that Rabbi Meiler permitted the communal leaders of Bing to prevent the chazzan from leaving. They are acting contrary to Torah and halachah. ... I am asking my friend Rabbi Judah Meiler to forbid the community of Bing to employ the chazzan and to tell them that he [the chazzan] must serve in Metz. ... He who resides in Heaven knows that I love Rabbi Meiler with all my heart ... may He lead us on the path of truth.

Conflicting Chanukah Customs
Teshuvot Kenesset Yechezkel, no. 17

Question: *According to Sephardi custom, only the head of the household lights the menorah, and no one else. The Ashkenazi usage is for each member of the family to light the menorah. It happened that an Ashkenazi Jew lived in a Sephardi household, and the Sephardi forbids the Ashkenazi to light the menorah because he wants to adhere to his own custom. Does the Sephardi have a right to do so, and has the Ashkenazi fulfilled his obligation if he did not light the menorah himself?*

Responsum: Both customs are based on rulings of halachic giants. The Sephardi custom is founded on the *Shulchan Aruch*,[3] whereas the Ashkenazi custom is predicated on the annotations of the Rema.[4] Their source is the Gemara in *Shabbat* 21b: "The mitzvah of Chanukah is that the head of the household kindles a light. Among the devout each member of the family lights the menorah. ..." However, if the Sephardim do not want to abolish their custom in favor of ours, the Sephardi does not have the right to force the Ashkenazi to deviate from our custom, which is the accepted usage in these regions.

The claim of the Sephardi of wanting to prevent divisiveness which would result from divergent customs is specious. We can ask him why he deviates from the custom of the Ashkenazim who have lived in these countries before he arrived. And although the Sephardim settled in our community of Hamburg before the Ashkenazim came, they did not light the menorah at all until the Ashkenazim settled in Altona, at which time the Sephardim too began to be inspired with the fear of God. ... The truth is that this is not a question of creating divisiveness.

Brit Performed before the Eighth Day
Teshuvot Kenesset Yechezkel, no. 42

Question: *A young Jewish man who since childhood has lived only among non-Jews and was completely alienated from Judaism married a girl of similar background. They had a son, and since* milah *was the only thing they knew of Judaism, they performed the* milah *themselves—but they did so before the child was eight days old.*[5] *Driven by the desire to return to Torah Judaism, they [left Spain and] came to Holland to live freely as Jews. Should they make a symbolic* brit milah *by drawing a drop of blood? ... The child is two years old and very frail.*

Responsum: Let us begin by establishing that this child is Jewish in all respects. Even if the father had been a non-Jew, the child would be Jewish; this surely holds true in this case where both parents are Jewish. Even though they violated the Torah, they are still considered Jews. ...

... In our case, even though the father violated the entire Torah, he upheld the commandment of "You must keep My covenant: You must circumcise every male" (Genesis 17:9,11). He did not break the commandment of *milah*; it is the mitzvah on which everything depends. His subsequent actions prove that even at the time he made the circumcision he had in mind to return to Torah Judaism. Therefore, in this case where there is concern for the health of the child, we should not be stringent and no drawing of a drop of blood is required. When the child will grow up and will be a God-fearing Jew, perhaps he will voluntarily perform a symbolic *milah*. But as for now, no such action is needed.

Wife Objects to Husband's Profession
Teshuvot Kenesset Yechezkel, no. 74

Question: *After his marriage, a man decided to become a scribe of Torah scrolls, tefillin, and mezuzot. He also wants to process the parchment himself, which involves the use of dog's excrement. His wife objects to his profession. Can he be forced to divorce her?*

Responsum: The Mishnah in *Ketubot* 7:10 states that men in the following categories of repulsive physical conditions or loathsome professions may be forced to divorce their wives: a leper, one who has an offensive breath, one who gathers dog's excrement, a coppersmith, one who processes leather [all of the above emit an offensive odor]. . . .

Based on the views of the Rif,[6] the **Rosh**,[7] and Rashi,[8] we must conclude that if this is the only profession a husband is successful in, then his wife has no right to object to it, especially in the bitter exile in which we live, when it is so difficult to support a family. All the more so as his profession of scribe is a sacred one, and he wants to process the parchment himself for that holy purpose because he does not trust others. . . .

The Tenth Man Refuses to Come to the Minyan
Kenesset Yechezkel, no. 19

Question: *It has been an age-old custom of Jews living in small villages to assemble for prayer services on Yom Kippur and Purim in one of the villages where there is a Torah scroll. This year, on Purim, one man decided to stay at home and read the Megillah*[9] *by himself, refusing to join the minyan. As a result, no services could be held, and the others were unable to fulfill the mitzvah of reading the Megillah with a minyan. Should this man be fined?*

Responsum: [After a lengthy and thorough discussion of the various aspects of the question, Rabbi Yechezkel concludes:] In the final analysis, he did fulfill the principal mitzvah of reading the Megillah; he negated only the mitzvah of "proclaiming the miracle of Purim" by failing to read it with a minyan. Therefore, he is not liable to being banned, but he is liable to receive lashes. However, we all know that the **Maharam of Rothenburg, Maharshal,** and Rema stated that lashes can be redeemed with money. Therefore, he should pay a fine to be assessed by the leaders of the minyan. When determining his fine, they should be guided by piety and rid themselves of any feelings of revenge. He should promise never to act like this again. If he transgresses again, he and all his possessions should be placed under a ban.

RABBI YAAKOV EMDEN—YAVETZ
רבי יעקב עמדין — יעב"ץ

born: Altona, Germany, 1698
died: Altona, Germany, 1776
Popularly known as Yavetz, the initials of his name Yaakov ben Tzvi.

A son of the renowned **Chacham Tzvi**, Rabbi Yaakov Emden was an illustrious scholar in his own right. Only once in his life did he serve in the rabbinate, in Emden, Germany, but because of his tempestuous and strong-willed character he was forced to abandon his post after a few years. In 1733 he settled in Altona, where he opened a Hebrew printing press. A very acrimonious controversy broke out when Rabbi Yonatan Eibschutz, a prominent scholar and expert in practical Kabbalah, became the rabbi of the combined communities of Altona, Hamburg, and Wandsbeck (called AHU). The Jewish world was still suffering the aftershocks of the episode of Shabbetai Tzvi, the false messiah (see the section on Rabbi **Yaakov Sasportas,** beginning on p. 89); and Rabbi Yaakov Emden interpreted amulets written by Rabbi Yonatan as having Shabbatean overtones. A bitter battle ensued, with accusations, mud-slinging, and recriminations, which persisted even after Rabbi Yonatan was cleared of all charges and suspicions. The rancorous dispute sparked a deep rift in German Jewry. Yet even Rabbi Yaakov Emden's opponents agreed that he was a great man who only sought the truth and followed the dictates of his conscience. He wrote *She'eilot Yavetz,* a compilation of his responsa[1]; *Mor uKetziah,* novellae on *Orach Chaim*[2]; and a famous commentary on the siddur.[3]

Title page of *She'eilot Yavetz* by Rabbi Yaakov Emden, son of the renowned Chacham Tzvi. (Yavetz is an acronym of *Yaakov Ben Tz*vi.) This was published in Altona in 1739.

Sister Deterred Brother from Sinning
She'eilot Yavetz, no. 1

Question: *A man who was about to commit a dreadful sin was given a large sum of money by his married sister as an inducement not to carry out his nefarious plan. The sister is asking that her younger brothers, who are orphans, pay a proportionate share of the bribe. She asserts that if the older brother had carried out his wicked intentions, he would have adversely affected their chances to find suitable marriage partners. Aside from that, as brothers, they have the moral duty to save him from stumbling into sin.*

Responsum: It seems obvious to me that, even if the brothers were adults, in this case they cannot be charged with paying part of their sister's expenditures. The wicked brother did not plan to hurt them physically or damage their property. His sinful act would have given them a bad name, but they can say, "We don't care about our reputation." Thus we cannot force them to pay. . . . It is clear as day that the orphans do not have to pay, not only while they are minors but even when they have reached adulthood.

Anatomy Lessons on Shabbat?
She'eilot Yavetz, no. 41

Question: [*Questioner is a young Jewish medical student*] . . . *Sometimes as part of an anatomy lecture, a dog is killed and we are taught how to dissect it and what instruments to use in the process.* [*He suggests a number of reasons for permitting dissecting on Shabbat, then asks:*] *Is it permissible to participate in these procedures on Shabbat?*

Responsum: Even though there is no question at all that it is forbidden, I will give you a very comprehensive reply, and I will address all the arguments you advance so that you will recognize that I have considered all the points you made and I don't ignore them. . . . The dissection of a cadaver involves two of the principal labors that are forbidden on Shabbat:[4] skinning an animal, and cutting it into pieces.

[There follows a seven-page discussion in which R. Yaakov Emden refutes all arguments the young doctor advanced to prove that dissection is permissible on Shabbat. He concludes:] My beloved son, listen to me and don't attend anatomy classes on Shabbat. For attending such classes is in itself forbidden because of the sanctity of the day. Don't throw up a smokescreen saying that you are just watching the dissection as a form of entertainment. It is true, I would permit anyone else to watch it on Shabbat because I am not in the habit of imposing rigorous rules on people, but to *you*, I forbid it, because you are observing it in order to learn surgical procedures from it, and that is definitely prohibited on Shabbat. . . .

And now, my son, be careful not to violate any Torah laws. You need special vigilance since you entered a dangerous field, which has many pitfalls. Therefore, if the occasion arises that you must dissect and study the anatomy of cadavers, always keep the words of the Torah in mind. Fear the Lord your God and worship Him. Thereby you will attain your aspirations, honor, and glory. . . .

Should We Ransom the Boy or the Girl?
She'eilot Yavetz, no. 68

Question: *A malicious non-Jewish creditor threatens to take two Jewish children and convert them. We have enough money to redeem one child. Since they are a boy and a girl, who has priority? Should we be more concerned about the girl not being lost to the non-Jews because her offspring will be pure and Jewish?*[5]

Responsum: I don't know the basis on which your question is predicated. The Mishnah in *Horayot* states that in questions of life and death, a man takes priority over a woman . . . and surely this applies in a case of forced conversion, for "causing someone to sin is worse than killing him."

The point you raised regarding her future offspring . . . , even if she were forced to marry a non-Jew, her children would still be pure Jews. And even if these children would be forced to violate the Torah, God forgives them. There is reason for hope that they will escape, either with their mother or on their own. They are not irretrievably lost. By contrast, if the boy were to convert, his children would be non-Jews. It is plain that his fate would be worse than hers. Therefore, it is the boy who should be redeemed. However, when it comes to ransoming prisoners, a woman takes precedence over a man, provided she is an adult and there is no question of forced conversion.

He Went to the Stock Exchange on Shabbat
She'eilot Yavetz, no. 167

Question: *A young man went to the stock exchange on Shabbat to look for a non-Jew who owed him a great deal of money. He found him and forced him to guarantee payment of the loan. The Jewish community wants to punish the young man for creating the false impression among the non-Jews that Jews don't observe the Shabbat properly. This will result in Jews being forced to do other forbidden things on Shabbat. The young man contends that he did not transgress any law. He was just trying to protect himself from a great loss and should not be punished for that. Please let us know whether he is innocent. . . .*

Responsum: . . . The young man went there to protect his investment. It is quite true that he did not violate any law. . . . You brought up the point that he gave Jews a bad reputation of not observing Shabbat properly, and the inherent danger that non-Jews will force them to desecrate the Shabbat, for example, by demanding that they appear in court on Shabbat. . . . It depends on the local circumstances. If the Bet Din decides that he should be punished, they have a right to do so, because by his action he slandered Jews. . . .

I remember an analogous case in Amsterdam when a ship was late in arriving, and the owners were afraid that it had been shipwrecked. The freight it carried was worth a fortune, and there was still time to insure it, but it was Shabbat. In deference to Shabbat the owners did not insure it. Some people scoffed at them, calling them overly pious, but I praised their conduct very highly. . . . I didn't see it as piety, but as refraining from transgressing a clear-cut prohibition. Even though they stood to lose an enormous sum of money, I can find no permissible aspect in that. Although it involved only an oral agreement and no writing at all, it still was a business transaction, which is forbidden.

Are Portraits Permissible?
She'eilot Yavetz, no. 170

Question: *When Rabbi Elazar of Brody was installed as the rabbi of Amsterdam, someone struck a silver coin showing his image. [What do you think of this?]*

Responsum: I have seen it, and in my opinion it is absolutely prohibited, either to make an image yourself or to have someone do it for you. It is a violation of the commandment "Do not make a representation of anything that is with Me."[6] However, the **Rosh** holds that a replica of a head without the body is permitted. But I disagree with him. . . . In light of this I am sure that the above-mentioned rabbi did not know that this coin was being made and did not give his consent.

In this connection, let me relate an incident that took place when my sainted father[7] was invited to visit the Sephardi community in London. He was received by a huge crowd with great pomp, joy, and honor as he made his entry on the royal barge. To commemorate his visit, they wanted to have a portrait made of him. They implored him to pose for a painting, explaining that the overwhelming majority of halachists do not object to the painting of images. He turned them down repeatedly but they did not give up. They found a noted artist who, unbeknownst to my father, quickly drew a sketch of his face. From this sketch he painted an exquisite true-to-life portrait of my father. Copies of the painting sold for a very high price.

Reading Newspapers on Shabbat
She'eilot Yavetz, no. 162

Question: *Is it permitted to read a newspaper on Shabbat?*

Responsum: It seems to me that it is not forbidden. Newspapers carry mostly news stories that affect the public, particularly during times of war, when it is important to know which side is winning. Being informed of such events may prevent loss of life or loss of property. . . . Also, denying a newspaper to someone who thirsts for news would cause him distress. Therefore, in my opinion it is permitted.

However, there is one aspect that leads me to be stringent about this matter. For on the back pages there usually is business news, and it is certainly forbidden to read that on Shabbat. Now you may say, let people beware of reading the business section, and let us permit reading world and local news. That would be too tempting, especially to businessmen who read the papers only for the financial news. Therefore, it is proper to forbid the reading of newspapers altogether.

A Question on Abortion
She'eilot Yavetz, no. 43

Question: *Is it forbidden to abort a fetus that was conceived in an adulterous relationship?*

Responsum: This question concerns a married woman who commited adultery. It seems to me that in this case we should be lenient regarding abortion. The mother's crime of adultery is punishable by death according to Torah law. Although at the present time the Bet Din does not administer capital punishment, nevertheless, since she acted willfully and intentionally, she is condemned to death by the Heavenly Court. It is quite true that a *mamzer* (a child born of a forbidden union), once he is born, is considered a kosher child, and killing him is murder. However, while he is in the womb he is part of the mother, and if we would carry out the death penalty we would execute her together with her unborn child.

Therefore, it seems clear that there is no prohibition against aborting this fetus, even though the mother remains alive. As a matter of fact, if the mother, out of deep remorse, committed suicide, she would receive no heavenly retribution. Quite the contrary, it would be a commendable deed. . . . Furthermore, we cannot be certain that this fetus will become a full-term normal baby; perhaps it will be stillborn. . . .

To reiterate, it is obvious that in this case it is permissible, a priori, to perform an abortion; perhaps performing an abortion under such circumstances constitutes a mitzvah. We make no distinction whether the father of the fetus is a Jew or a non-Jew. As a married woman, the mother is liable to the death penalty, and the rights of the fetus certainly do not exceed those of the mother.

RABBI YECHEZKEL LANDAU—NODA BIYEHUDAH
רבי יחזקאל לנדא — נודע ביהודה

born: Apta, Poland, 1713
died: Prague, Bohemia, 1793
Popularly known as Noda biYehudah, the title of the collection of his responsa.

The Noda biYehudah was one of the illustrious Torah personalities of his generation. Until his thirteenth year he studied under Rabbi Yitzchak of Ludmir. The local rabbi, Rabbi Moshe Yaakov, who loved the young boy and recognized his brilliant mind, discussed with him the knottiest talmudic themes. When he reached the age of 14 he went to Brody, a city known for its outstanding scholars, where he studied in the great *kloiz*, a school for advanced students. After his marriage at 18 he settled in Brody. In 1734 Rabbi Yechezkel Landau was appointed as one of that city's dayanim (judges) and in 1746 he became the rabbi of Yampoli, Podolia. In 1755 he received the call to serve as rabbi of the renowned community of Prague, where he headed a yeshivah that attracted a large number of the most advanced scholars of the surrounding countries.

He was a man of indomitable spirit, fighting valiantly for the welfare and advancement of his people. In 1757, during the Seven-Year War between the forces of Queen Maria Theresa of Austria and King Friedrich II of Prussia, the Prussian army laid siege to Prague. The Noda biYehudah, against the advice of his communal leaders, remained at his post and guided his flock through the difficult times. He pronounced a ban of excommunication against anyone lending aid to the enemy and instituted a special prayer for the welfare of the government, to be recited at every public prayer session. At the war's end the queen publicly thanked Rabbi Yechezkel for his faithful dedication to his country.

He was an illustrious talmudist whose responsa, *Noda biYehuda*,[1] attest to his great erudition and

Rabbi Yechezkel Landau, Noda biYehudah.

clarity of thought. Almost all of his opinions became accepted as Halachah. He also wrote *Tzelach*,[2] novellae on Talmud; *Ahavat Tzion*,[3] sermons; *Dagul Meirevavah*,[4] novellae on *Shulchan Aruch*, and many other works.

116

A Government Official's Problem
Teshuvot Noda biYehudah, Orach Chayim, no. 33

Question: *The distinguished Yisrael Henigsberg asked the following question: Often on Shabbat he has to participate in cabinet meetings in the government administration offices, where he has to sign documents. If he had a facsimile of his signature made into a stamp, would it be permissible for him to tell a non-Jew to place this signature stamp on the documents he must sign?*

Responsum: ... The Mishnah states expressly, "If you write two letters [characters of the alphabet] in any language [on Shabbat] you are punishable (*Shabbat* 12:2).... Since the present case, according to most authorities, is a biblical prohibition, you are not allowed to tell a non-Jew to do it for you, not even in order to prevent a serious loss.[5] Therefore, it is difficult to find a way to sanction this matter.

A Kohen Who Married an Indian Woman
Teshuvot Noda biYehudah, Yoreh De'ah, no. 10

Question: (*Erev Shabbat, 21 Marcheshvan, 1778*) *Concerning the she'eilah from London, concerning a kohen who married a heathen woman in India in a pagan ceremony performed by a pagan priest. Reputedly, the man had to kneel during the ceremony and repeat after the priest the name of the deity. A while later the man regretted his deed, left the heathen woman, and did* teshuvah *(repented) according to the instructions of rabbis. Is this man permitted to go up to the platform in front of the Ark to bless the congregation?*[6]

Responsum: (*To my friend R. Leib Bumsla*) According to *Shulchan Aruch, Orach Chaim* 128, after a kohen repents, he may fulfill all the functions of a kohen.... Furthermore, even if during the marriage ceremony this kohen did acknowledge the idol as his god, this does not make him an apostate (one who renounced Judaism). He did so only because otherwise the woman would not have agreed to marry him.... If this kohen pledges not to return to his foolishness and sincerely repents, then immediately after agreeing to repent he is qualified to

Title page of *Noda biYehudah*, responsa by Rabbi Yechezkel Landau. Noda biYehudah means "Known in Judah," taken from Psalm 76:2, "God has made Himself known in Judah, His name is great in Israel." The words in the semicircle at the top of the page are, "The scepter will not depart from Judah..." (Genesis 49:10), a play on the title "Known in Judah." This was first published in Prague in 1776.

bless the people and he is entitled to all privileges pertaining to *kehunah*, to be called as the first to the reading of the Torah, as are all kohanim. There is no need to elaborate further.

Circumcision on a Child Who Died
Teshuvot Noda biYehudah, Yoreh De'ah, no. 164

Question: *A child, born in the eighth month of gestation, died before it was eight days old. They forgot to perform the* milah *before burial. Should the grave be opened in order to circumcise him?*

Responsum: . . . Each person, from the moment he has intelligence, and even small children once they understand the meaning of sin, must after death bear the consequences of their deeds. However, this applies to a child who has some degree of understanding of mitzvot and *aveirot* (sins); to a child of 1, 2, or 3 years, the concept of punishment is irrelevant.

According to the kabbalists, however, there are souls who are reincarnated (*gilgul*).[7] Accordingly, the soul of every infant stands in fear of Heavenly Judgment because of his deeds during his previous life. . . . I think, therefore, when it is immediately after burial and the body has not yet decomposed, the grave should be opened to perform the *milah* on him. For, whichever way you look at it, if he was not reincarnated then he has nothing to fear from the Heavenly Judgment. But if he was reincarnated and will rise at the time of the resurrection then it would be a disgrace for him to be uncircumcised, and it would be proper to perform the *milah* on him. However, if several days have passed since death, the grave should not be opened so as not to uncover his state of decomposition.

Hunting Wildlife
Teshuvot Noda biYehudah, Yoreh De'ah, no. 10

Question: *A man has large land holdings with villages and forests. The forests are swarming with all kinds of wildlife. Is he [as a Jew] permitted to hunt game with a rifle, or is a Jew forbidden to do this, either because of the prohibition against inflicting pain on animals or because of the prohibition against wanton destruction?*

Responsum [*to Gumpricht Oppenheim*]: I am very astonished that anyone should ask this question. The only hunters mentioned in the Torah are Nimrod and Esau. Hunting is not a sport for the children of Abraham, Yitzchak, and Yaakov. . . . How can a Jew go out and kill a living creature for no purpose other than for the pleasure of hunting? If you want to argue that there are bears and wolves and other wild animals . . . there is no mitzvah in chasing after them in the forest where they live if they don't come out and attack the villagers. This is only chasing after the lust of the heart.

. . . Aside from these considerations, there is a clear-cut prohibition against it. Hunters place their lives in jeopardy when they enter forests that are filled with wild beasts, and the Torah says, "Watch yourself very carefully."[8] There certainly existed no greater hunter than Esau, yet he said, "Here I'm about to die."[9] He meant, "I'm exposed daily to death by wild animals (this is Ramban's interpretation). Surely no Jew should endanger his life by exposing himself to bands of beasts of prey. Anyone going hunting violates the precept of "Watch yourself very carefully."

A Philosophical Question
Teshuvot Noda biYehudah, Mahadura Tanina, Orach Chaim, no. 107

Question: *You asked me to explain what the books on ethical thought mean when they speak in terms of "lamenting the exile of the Divine Presence." What do they mean by* shechinah *(Divine Presence), and how does the term "exile" apply to it?*

Responsum: In your letter you went into great detail outlining your question. By delving into mysteries, you acted incorrectly and you violated the dictum of our sages: "Don't inquire into things that are beyond your grasp." It is impossible to reveal these matters.[10] Nevertheless, I will explain some things that can be explained.

Moreh Nevuchim,[11] vol. 1, chapter 25, states, "I say that Divine Presence and Divine Providence are one and the same. When Israel is doing the will of God, then the focus of His Providence is on Israel and He bestows on them an abundant flow of goodness. But since there is an overabundance of bounty, it overflows to other countries and nations. We read in Numbers 26:9, [God says] "I will turn to you," and Rashi explains this phrase, "I will disregard all my other concerns in order to pay your rich reward." All this will happen when Israel is acting according to His will. But because of our many sins, we were banished from our land, where the Divine Presence is concentrated, and we were exiled to the lands of the nations of the world.

And then the situation was reversed. All the abundant bounty descends on the nations and from the overflow we receive just enough to get by.

RABBI CHAIM YOSEF DAVID AZULAI—CHIDA
רבי חיים יוסף דוד אזולאי — חיד"א

born: Jerusalem, 1724
died: Livorno, Italy, 1806
Popularly known as Chida, the acronym formed of the initials of his name.

The Chida, the son of Rabbi Yitzchak Zerachyah Azulai, descended from a line of famous rabbis in Spain. Studying under the great rabbis of Jerusalem—Rabbi Yonah Navon, Rabbi Yitzchak Rappaport, and the towering kabbalist Rabbi Chaim ben Attar (author of *Or HaChaim*)—he displayed early signs of genius. When he was only 20 years old he was acclaimed as one of the foremost Torah scholars in Eretz Yisrael and was invited to serve as a member of the Bet Din of Rabbi Raphael Meyuchas in Jerusalem.

In 1755 the leaders of the Jerusalem community sent him to Europe as an emissary on a fund-raising mission on behalf of the needy of the Holy City. On his travels through Italy, France, Germany, and the Netherlands, he gave sermons and lectures on Halachah and responsa. This led to many similar missions. Everywhere he went he was received with great honor by communal leaders and rabbis, who presented him with their unsolved questions. Even princes, dukes, and ambassadors paid homage to him, asking for his blessing. He used his years of traveling to study ancient manuscripts and long-lost books that he discovered in various collections and libraries. The product of his research is his famous work *Shem HaGedolim*,[1] an authoritative bibliography and the combined biographies of all the prominent Torah sages from the time of the Geonim until his time.

He wrote a large number of books on Halachah, aggadah, ethics, and Kabbalah, many of which are widely studied and quoted. Popular tradition credits him with authoring eighty-three books, one for each

Rabbi Chaim David Azulai, author of *Teshuvot Chida*.

year of his life. His responsa are entitled *Chaim Shaal*[2] and *Yosef Ometz*,[3] and deal primarily with practical halachic problems. One of the truly outstanding Torah personalities of the past two centuries, Chida has made an indelible imprint on Jewish scholarship.

A Sephardi Who Made Fun of an Ashkenazi Song[4]
Teshuvot Chaim Shaal, no. 28

Question: *At a gathering, in front of a group of people, a man ridiculed and made a mockery of the Haggadah chant "Chad Gadya,"[5] "One little goat, one little goat," which is sung by Ashkenazi Jews on the seder night. Outraged and appalled, one of the group pronounced a ban against him.*

Our question is whether this ban is legally in effect, or perhaps the man did not deserve to be banned and the one who pronounced the ban should be censured.

Responsum: The answer is quite simple. This person had the effrontery to scoff at a custom that is adhered to by millions of Jews in Poland, Germany, and the neighboring countries. In the past, the Torah giants and saintly personalities of each generation recited this liturgical poem, and also in our day it is chanted by numerous *rashei yeshivah* (deans of a yeshivah) and Torah luminaries. By making fun of "*Chad Gadya*," this evil man, in effect, insulted millions of Jews, their rabbis, judges, and scholars. His sin is grave, and he should be placed under a ban . . . especially a person who jeers and taunts, saying that anyone reciting this chant is a fool, uttering trivialities, should be banned. But that is not enough. He should also be fined according to his ability to pay, the fine to be distributed to the poor. He should be made aware of the gravity of his sin, and he should repent. May God have pity on him.

Now let me tell you that there exist many commentaries on this chant, some still in manuscript. It certainly is not just a simple rhyme. The grandeur and beauty of the German liturgical poems is well-known. The saintly Ari[6] attests that they are based on profound kabbalistic concepts. Rabbi Eleazar Rokeach of Worms[7] states that the literary techniques used in these poems have been transmitted from teacher to student in a chain reaching back to ancient times.

Regarding the disparity between the Sephardi, Ashkenazi, and Italian *minhagim* (ritual customs), the Ari wrote that this is attributable to the different spiritual roots of the ancient tribes of Israel. It touches on very lofty concepts. Therefore, no one should change from his traditional *minhag*. How-

Title page of *Shaar Yosef*, a commentary on Tractate *Horayot* by the Chida. Livorno, 1656.

ever, from a halachic perspective, if a Sephardi Jew prays according to the Ashkenazi custom, he certainly has fulfilled his obligation.

To recapitulate, if the man confesses his sin and asks forgiveness, the ban may be lifted. The rabbi should explain to him what he did wrong so that he will repent and be healed.

Husband Feigned Death
Teshuvot Chaim Shaal, no. 74:40

Question: *The following story happened in our own time. A non-Jew owed a large sum of money and was unable to pay his creditors. He thought of running away but dismissed the idea, knowing that his wife would report him to the police. At wit's end, he concocted a clever scheme. He colored his face with a greenish makeup and, pretending to be suffering from some exotic malady, he simulated a loss of appetite and lay on his bed, moaning that his strength was ebbing and his end was approaching rapidly. Just then he found out that someone in the neighborhood who resembled him both in appearance and size had died. He went to bed, pretended to be sleeping, and when he noticed that his wife was sound asleep he tiptoed out of the house, dug up the corpse that had been buried that day, dressed it in his night shirt, and placed it on his bed. Thereupon he made a quick exit and fled the country.*

When his wife woke up in the morning and found her "husband" dead beside her, she wailed and screamed and told the neighbors that her husband had died during the night without her noticing it. They all believed what they saw, mourned her departed husband, and buried him. She gave the creditors the little money she had in the house, and they wrote off the debt. After a few months she remarried and had a family.

Her first husband went to India, where he became a wealthy man within a few short years. One day, to everyone's utter surprise, he reappeared in his hometown and related all that he had done. When he learned that his wife had remarried, he wanted to have her back. The second husband argued that she was his wife and that he had seen with his own eyes how her first husband was buried. The king ordered the judges to study the legal ramifications of this case and to come up with a solution.

This is a brief summary of the reports as they appeared in the newspapers, called gazettas, *which also mention the locale and the date of the story. We wonder if, God forbid, something like this would happen among Jews, whether this woman, who acted unwittingly, would be permitted to return to her first husband.*

Responsum: We have a rule that if a Bet Din permitted a woman to remarry and subsequently her first husband reappears, she must divorce both husbands. However, it seems to me that this applies only to a lower court ruling, because we say that she should have ascertained the opinion of a higher court. However, if the High Court of seventy-one judges ruled that she could remarry, then she may return to her first husband, since she acted unwittingly.

Therefore, in this case, where she found him dead and he was buried in a public funeral, we may certainly say that she acted unwittingly. It is too far-fetched to think that there was collusion on her part. Neither can we say that she should have been more attentive, for that would have been impossible. The matter requires further study.

No Tombstone on Rabbi's Grave
Teshuvot Chaim Shaal, no. 71:6

Question: *A rabbi stipulated in his will that none of his titles or laudatory tributes should be mentioned in his funeral orations—rather, that he should have the funeral of an ordinary person. He also ordained that no monument be placed on his grave. The community leaders, thinking that a simple funeral would be disrespectful of their rabbi, want to change his will. Are they permitted to do so?*

Responsum: . . . Evidently this rabbi thinks that he is unworthy of the accolades that are being accorded in our days. He ordered the omission of all titles as a benefit to his soul. How could anyone dare violate his wish? Rabbi Moshe Chagiz in his *Mishnat Chachamim*, no. 186, also ordered that no titles should be mentioned in the eulogies for him. And I have heard that many rabbis in Eretz Yisrael have issued similar directives and they have been heeded. And even if we assume that he richly deserves all titles and tributes, perhaps his intention was to gain atonement by concealing his praises, "for there is not a righteous man on earth who does good and never sins."[8]

However, his wish not to have a tombstone placed on his grave, you should not follow to the letter. Rather, you should erect a small monument, for according to our rabbi, the Ari,[9] this brings about a restoration for the soul. Had this rabbi remembered that placing a tombstone has a mystical effect on restoring the soul, he would not have made his request.

When Must He Pay Back the Loan?[10]
Yosef Ometz, Teshuvot HaChida, no. 1

Question: *Reuven, a resident of Yerushalayim, borrowed from Shimon 1,000* arayot *which he swore to pay back on the night of the fifteenth of Adar, the night of the reading of the Megillah.*[11] *When the due date approached, he noted that in that particular year the fifteenth of Adar occurred on Shabbat. Whenever this happens the Megillah is read on Thursday night, because we may not read it on Shabbat.*[12] *Since the Megillah has been read, Shimon demands repayment of the loan. Reuven counters that he promised to repay on the night of the fifteenth, the night when the Megillah is read, and this did not happen; the two events did not coincide. The night of the fifteenth was Shabbat, whereas the Megillah was read on the night of the fourteenth. He assures Shimon, "Next year, when the reading of the Megillah will occur on the fifteenth, I will repay the loan. I never said in what year I would repay it." Who is right?*

Responsum: I am filled with trepidation as I begin to write, because I am young and unworthy, but it is Torah that I must study, and I have the duty to follow my master's [Rabbi Yonah Navon's] command. . . . In my modest opinion it seems that Shimon is right. I cite as proof the **Rosh** in his responsum 8:16, "Reuven swore to pay Shimon[13] a *manah* on the seventh of Nisan, and in that year the seventh of Nisan occurred on Shabbat. Reuven argues that since the date on which he swore to pay fell on Shabbat, he is exempt from paying. Shimon contends that he did not mean to be paid specifically on that day. What he meant was that he should not pay him later than on that date but that he should be paid before that date. Shimon is right. They both had in mind that Shimon should have payment in hand by the seventh of Nisan and not that he should be paid precisely on that day. . . ."

[In a lengthy dissertation, Chida cites opposing views and rebuts each of them. He concludes:] To summarize, it seems to me that Reuven must pay Shimon this year. Whatever I wrote is not meant to be a final halachic decision unless the great rabbis agree with me, for only they have the right to render decisions.

[*Chida's mentor comments on his student's responsum:*]

I read your lines with great pleasure, even though you did not draw the right conclusions. But such is the way of the Torah. The Mishnah says, "He who is bashful will never learn." [He proceeds to analyze the Chida's responsum, pointing out his errors. He ends:] In my opinion, the halachah is that he does not have to pay until the following year. This runs counter to your rationale, but all the proofs you cite have no bearing on the matter under discussion. . . . And you, my dear son, open your eyes and try better to understand the problem you are dealing with. Don't skim over it hastily but ponder it with deliberate judgment, and "he who has the will to do good receives help from God."

(signed) *Yonah Navon*

RABBI AKIVA EIGER
רבי עקיבא איגר

born: Eisenstadt, Austria, 1761
died: Posen, Poland, 1837

Rabbi Akiva Eiger, one of the greatest luminaries of the past two centuries, was born into a family of rabbis. He showed early signs of genius when, at the age of 13, he wrote a treatise on Tractate *Chullin*. In 1790 he became the rabbi of Friedland, where his outstanding leadership earned him the honor of being appointed chairman of the rabbinical conference in Warsaw. In 1814 he accepted the call to the rabbinate of Posen, where he led a yeshivah that attracted the finest minds in the country. He received she'eilot from all the great rabbis of Poland and beyond, and even many non-Jewish high government officials sought his advice. His piety and humility coupled with his vast Torah knowledge made him the foremost Torah personality of his generation. He wrote a collection of responsa called *Teshuvot Rabbi Akiva Eiger*,[1] *Gilyon Hashas, Tosafot Rabbi Akiva Eiger* on the Mishnah, and *Chiddushei Rabbi Akiva Eiger* on the *Shulchan Aruch*.

Rabbi Akiva Eiger.

Husband Drowned
Teshuvot Rabbi Akiva Eiger, no. 47

Question: *A witness testified that he saw a man drown in a large body of water. He waited for about half an hour, but the drowned man did not surface. According to the witness, the drowned man could not have survived. Is the wife permitted to remarry?*

Responsum [*to Rabbi Sender Leib of Gumbin*]: I agree that the witness should not be disqualified, ... although, by his own testimony, he saw the man drowning and did nothing to rescue him. This certainly is an unpardonable crime.... Concerning the length of time needed for death to set in, we only have the statements by **Rivash** (377, 380, and 416) that it is three hours.... The witness must stay there for as long as it takes for death to set in; otherwise his testimony is invalid, for we know of many cases where people surface and are still alive after being submerged under water for a long time. If the witness saw only that he fell into the water, who can say that he did not come up an hour later.

... It is doubtful whether Rivash meant the beginning or the end of the third hour. Therefore, I say, in our case, if the witness had waited for two hours, the man may be presumed dead. ...

You mention the case cited in *Teshuvot Mabit* 1:186.[2] There are many differences between the two cases; they are not analogous. ... I don't think we can rely on the witness's judgment that the man could not be alive any more. ... I can find no way of permitting this woman to remarry.

Wife Affected with Epilepsy
Teshuvot Rabbi Akiva Eiger, no. 84

Question: *It happened here in Friedland that a man married a woman from Zlatava and lived with her for one and one-fourth year. During that time he noticed that occasionally she would drop things for no apparent reason. He attributed it to her being startled by something. One time he found her lying motionless, flat on the floor, and moments later she got up as if nothing had happened. Thereupon, he took her to her father and asked him to get medical treatment for her condition. During one of the meals at her father's house she had another episode, and the husband began to suspect that she suffered from epilepsy. The doctors all confirmed his suspicion.*

When the disease progressed and the episodes recurred every other week, he wrote his father-in-law that he wanted to divorce his wife. He is a young man and has no children, and he is willing to pay whatever costs are due halachically. However, his father-in-law wants to take him to (civil) court and force him to continue living with his wife. He is also demanding an enormous amount for medical expenses.

Responsum: I agreed to accept the testimony of two witnesses who moved to a distant city, to the effect that the woman was afflicted with this sickness before she was married. One witness testified that he saw her fall down in a similar manner in front of a store eleven years ago. The other witness declared that he lived in the father-in-law's house for many years and he saw her have episodes of this disease when she was four years old. The parents covered it up, and when he would ask about her condition they would change the subject.

Title page of *Teshuvot Rabbi Akiva Eiger*. This edition was printed in Brooklyn, New York, in 1974.

Rabbeinu Gershon Me'or HaGolah[3] states in his responsa that an epileptic man may be forced to divorce his wife, and surely an epileptic woman may be coerced to accept a *get* from her husband, especially so in this case, where we have witnesses who testified that this was a preexisting condition of which the husband had no knowledge. ...

The Battered Wife
Teshuvot Rabbi Akiva Eiger, no. 107

Question: *Over the past ten years a woman periodically came to the Bet Din to complain about her husband beating her savagely. He threatened her with a knife, and she refused to live with him any longer; but upon the urging of the Bet Din she then agreed to reconciliation. She received written as-*

surance that if he ever struck her again, even upon her provocation, he must divorce her and pay her an alimony settlement. After four [more] years of continued beatings, she left her husband and went to live with her father. Before she went to the Bet Din, her husband came to her father's house pleading and cajoling, and persuaded her to come home.

Last Nisan she appeared again before the Bet Din crying that her husband beat her constantly, and she showed her arms covered with blue marks. She brought her maid to testify that he struck her three days before she gave birth, that she ran away, and that he pursued her, threw a brick at her, and broke a plate on her head so that she fainted. . . .

The husband heard the testimony and did not deny it. . . . He said, "There is no need for witnesses. I admit that I struck her. I only ask that I be given another chance."

Responsum: I recognize that a divorce would be extremely difficult since she has eight children, the youngest six months old. But she insists that she does not want to live with him any longer. Her relatives threaten to take the case to civil court if I do not render a decision. Therefore, I ruled that the husband cannot force the wife to live with him, and she cannot be considered a *moredet*.[4] . . .

I have serious doubts about the ruling of the Rema (154:63) that a husband can be compelled to divorce his wife if, after being warned, he continues to beat her. We may require independent witnesses, and not the testimony of neighbor women. Although he does not deny beating her, he states that she provoked him by humiliating and cursing him. . . . He must pay for her support, but he may pay it in weekly installments. . . .

It is impossible to hire an observer to determine who is at fault. Even if an observer should live with them for a few weeks, the husband would refrain from beating her during that time but afterward he would simply resume his practice. Therefore, my ruling is that he cannot force her to live with him under the same roof.

Dispute about Rent
Teshuvot Rabbi Akiva Eiger, no. II:39

Question: *A widow rented a room to another widow for 7 thalers per year. The tenant widow paid in advance 3½ thalers. After living there for three weeks the tenant died. Her daughter, who is her heir, demands a refund of the prepaid rent, and the widow who is the landlady wants to be paid the full year's rent of 7 thalers, claiming that she cannot find anyone else to rent it.*

Responsum: This case is clearly spelled out in the *Shulchan Aruch*, *Choshen Mishpat* 334:1: "If the tenant died, the landlord is entitled only to the rent for the time he lived there. If the landlord received the full rent, he is not required to repay it." Accordingly, in our case, it is simple that each of the litigants holds what he has.

The daughter claims that she wants to live in the room for the length of time the rent was prepaid. According to the *Sma*[5] 317:5, a tenant cannot sublet his apartment to someone else, for the landlord can say, "I want you but no one else as my tenant." So too, in this case, the landlady can say to the heir that she does not want her as a tenant.

RABBI MOSHE SOFER (SCHREIBER)— CHATAM SOFER
רבי משה סופר — חת"ם סופר

born: Frankfort on-the-Main, 1762
died: Pressburg, Hungary, 1839
Popularly known as Chatam Sofer, the title of his work. Chatam is the abbreviation of Chiddushei Torat Moshe, *his novellae on the Torah.*

Rabbi Moshe Sofer was a descendant of the author of *Yalkut Shimoni* (a midrashic anthology) and of Rashi. When he was 9 years old he entered the yeshivah of the illustrious Rabbi Natan Adler in Frankfort. He also studied under Rabbi Pinchas Halevi Horowitz, author of *Hafla'ah.* In addition to talmudic studies, he was proficient in biology, mathematics, engineering, and astronomy. In 1798 he was chosen as rabbi of Mattersdorf, Hungary, and in 1804 he became the rabbi of the prominent *kehillah* (community) of Pressburg, Hungary, where he founded a yeshivah that attracted students from many countries.

In 1819 the Reform movement was founded in Hamburg, Germany. Chatam Sofer vigorously opposed their attempts to introduce changes in Halachah and tradition. His uncompromising stand vis-à-vis Reform helped to stem the rising tide of the new movement. As a result he became the recognized leader of Orthodox Jewry, and questions on communal and personal problems were directed at him from near and far. These questions and his answers to them were published under the title *She'eilot uTeshuvot Chatam Sofer.*[1] They mirror his clear thinking, his understanding of human nature, his sensitivity, and his compassion. He wrote many novellae on the Talmud, a commentary on the Torah, *Sefer Zikaron*[2] (a chronicle of his ordeal during the siege of Pressburg during the war with France), and a Haggadah.[3]

Rabbi Moshe Sofer (Schreiber).

His son, **Avraham Shemuel Binyamin (Ktav Sofer)**, succeeded him as rabbi of Pressburg. Another son, Shimon, became rabbi of Cracow, Poland.

The Emperor Visits the Synagogue
Teshuvot Chatam Sofer, Choshen Mishpat, no. 190

Question: *Concerning the preparations for the visit to the synagogue by His Imperial Majesty, the benevolent Emperor.[4] Songs of praise and thanks to God will be sung in the synagogue for all the good that has been bestowed on us, and prayers will be offered for the long life of the Emperor and his children. The question is whether, on this occasion, it is permissible according to the Torah for men and women to sing together, as the women's voices carry from the ladies' section to the men's section.*

Responsum [*to R. Getz Oppenheimer, Vienna*]: It is our duty to perform the important mitzvah of rendering the utmost honor to a king. Failure to do this is like failing to don tefillin. We certainly must pay tribute to this benevolent Emperor under whose protection we and tens of thousands of Jews are living.

Were our mouths as full of song as the sea and our tongues as full of joyous song as its multitude of waves,[5] we could not sufficiently praise him for his countless good deeds toward us. Who would dare take this mitzvah lightly?

But let us remember that the Emperor allows us to practice our Torah laws freely. Now, if we did something contrary to the Torah, then instead of honoring him, we would in fact be showing disrespect for him. It would be tantamount to declaring that the Emperor wished to uproot our religion. Since mixed singing is forbidden to us, it would not be right to do so at the Emperor's celebration. The prohibition of mixed singing is explained in *Sotah* 48a. . . .[6]

It is incumbent on us to be vigilant that there be no mixed singing when the Emperor visits the synagogue, so that our prayers will be heard by the King of kings.

It is my opinion that mixed singing be barred.

Baden, 21 Sivan 1814

Title page of *Chatam Sofer*, volume 1, responsa by Rabbi Moshe Sofer (Schreiber). Chatam is an acronym of *Chidushei Torat Moshe*, Novellae by Rabbi Moshe Sofer. The abbreviation at the end of the second line of small print represents *rabbon shel kol benei hagolah*, "rabbi of all Jews living in exile," a designation reserved for the most illustrious rabbis. The abbreviation *kuf-kuf* stands for *kehillah kedoshah*, meaning community, congregation; *pei, pei, dalet-mem* stands for Frankfurt de Main; *pei-bet* stands for Pressburg. Reprinted in Jerusalem, 1972.

Lost Purse
Teshuvot Chatam Sofer, Orach Chayim, no. 42

Question: *Concerning the owner of a tavern where many non-Jews come to drink. The waiter found a bag containing money which evidently was lost by one of the customers. The question is whether the waiter may keep the bag or the owner can lay claim to it because it was found on his property.*

Responsum: In this case, the waiter acquired the

bag, on the basis of the rule that "whatever a worker finds belongs to him," unless the employer expressly said, "Pick up this found article on my behalf."

As for the people who say that it is the custom that whatever an employee finds belongs to the employer, this is nonsense. There is no legal basis for this, and there is no need for further discussion.

Son Supporting Parents
Teshuvot Chatam Sofer, Yoreh De'ah, no. 229

Question: *Concerning a son whose parents are respectable people who are unable to support themselves and cannot accept money from the charity fund. The son, who is burdened with heavy personal expenses, cannot support them adequately. The question is whether he may give his parents the entire sum of money he always sets aside for the poor. Would he not thereby go amiss of the rabbinical dictum that says, "Whoever gives all his tithes to only one poor man brings famine on the world"* (Yoreh De'ah 257:9).

Responsum: Quite the contrary. It is his duty to give them his tithe. He may not give his tithe to any poor person before his parents are adequately provided for . . . as it says, "to the poor man among you,"[7] and who is closer than his father? If the son is unable to support his father from his own funds, it is his duty to give him all his tithes and all the charity funds he has, until his father can take care of his own wants.

Transfer of Graves
Teshuvot Chatam Sofer, Yoreh De'ah, no. 334

Question: *Concerning the cemetery that was assigned to the Jewish community to bury their dead from the cholera epidemic. . . . This cemetery was not given in perpetuity. It is not surrounded by a wall, and it is unguarded. According to local ordinance, after six years the remains are removed and the field is then planted. Permission has been obtained from the authorities to transfer the remains to the old Jewish cemetery. Most of the victims of the epidemic were local residents whose relatives are buried in the old cemetery. Is it permissible to transfer these remains or not?*

Responsum [*to Rabbi Elazar Segal Horowitz, Rabbi of Vienna*]: It is quite obvious that it is permitted. It is a great mitzvah to participate in this undertaking. Not only the remains of those whose relatives rest in the old cemetery . . . but even those of other people who have no relatives in Vienna should be transferred. Since there is no wall and the cemetery is unguarded, eventually vandals will come and desecrate it.

16 Kislev 1832

The Poisoned Maid
Teshuvot Chatam Sofer, Orach Chayim, no. 177

Question: *Concerning a maid who was startled by a scoundrel. She fainted and appeared to be unconscious. Her mistress, being very alarmed, wanted to take a bottle of brandy and pour some of it into the girl's mouth in an attempt to revive her. In her excitement she grabbed a bottle of sulphuric acid and poured it down the maid's throat. As a result, the girl died.*

The question is whether or not the brokenhearted mistress needs atonement.

Responsum [*to Rabbi Yosef Moshe of Veretchvar*]: Basically, what we have here is a clear-cut case of murder. Since the maid was unconscious, it is as though she was tied down and then burned, because acid burns. On the other hand, the woman intended to do a mitzvah by trying to save her life. She does need a small atonement, because the accident happened through her. But don't overburden her, because she was agitated and bewildered. If we are too strict, we will cause people to stumble in the future [being overly cautious, they will be afraid to rescue a victim].

Don't be rigorous, especially with women, who are gentle by nature.[8]

RABBI YEHUDAH ASSAD
רבי יהודה אסאד

born: Serdahely, Hungary, 1797
died: Serdahely, Hungary, 1866

Rabbi Yehudah Assad received his early education from Rabbi Falk Sidyavitz of Serdahely. He soon graduated to the famous yeshivah of the eminent Rabbi Mordechai Banet of Nikolsburg in Moravia (now Czechoslovakia) and became one of his foremost disciples. After serving in the rabbinate of Rete and Semnitz, where he remained for twenty-one years, he became the rabbi of Serdahely, where he established a yeshivah and stood in the vanguard of the struggle against the Reform movement. His total dedication to Torah study was legendary, and his piety and his benevolent character won him universal admiration. The **Chatam Sofer,** with whom he corresponded on a regular basis, spoke of him with deep respect.

His responsa, which include many learned dissertations on difficult themes in the Talmud and the Codes, are known as *Teshuvot Mahari Assad.*[1] The work bears the approbations of the most prominent scholars of his age, Rabbi **Yosef Shaul Nathanson** of Lemberg, Rabbi Chaim Halberstam of Sanz, and Rabbi Shelomoh Kluger of Brody.

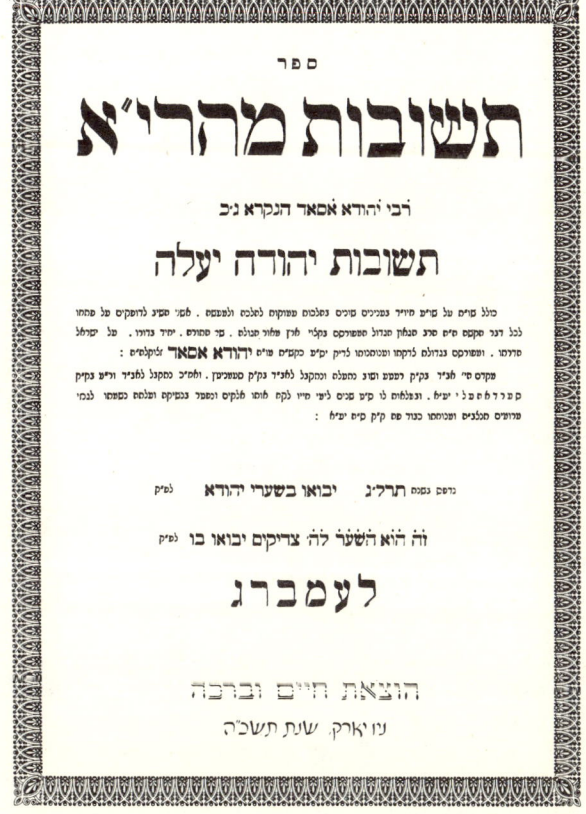

Title page of *Teshuvot Mahari Assad* by Rabbi Yehudah Assad. "After he served in the rabbinate of Rete, Semnitz, and Serdahely [Hungary] God took him in the 69th year of his life. His final resting place is in Serdahely." Published in Lemberg, 1873.

Naming a Baby after a Living Person?
Teshuvot Mahari Assad, no. 1:257

Question: *What is the source for the custom of not naming a baby after a living person?*

Responsum: *Sefer Chasidim*[2] states in paragraph 440 that non-Jews name their children after living parents but Jews object to this. Indeed, in some places they name the child only after a deceased person. I already pointed out to my student Rabbi Moshe Ber Schoen that in the past this custom was not known. Proof of this can be found in Chronicles 2:50: "These were the sons of Caleb son of Hur...." Rashi explains that Hur gave his son the name Caleb, naming him after his father while he was still living. I also cited [to my student] other proofs. At any rate, it is a custom to be observed only by those who object to naming the child after a living relative. However, inasmuch as nowadays everyone objects to it, it is clear that we should not change the custom.[3]

Problem in Painting the Synagogue
Teshuvot Mahari Assad, no. 1:304

Question: *All four walls of the synagogue in Semnitz are inscribed with Scriptural verses containing the Divine Name. Over the years the walls have become grimy. May we whitewash them, thereby fulfilling the mitzvah of enhancing the synagogue, or is it forbidden because we would be erasing the Divine Name?*[4]

Responsum: ... Just as it is forbidden to erase the four-letter Divine Name, the tetragrammaton, so it is prohibited to plaster it with whitewash. Neither may you have a non-Jew do it. It can be accomplished, however, by covering each Holy Name with a strip of heavy parchment, fastening it securely with nails and then painting over it.

An Abandoned Wife
Teshuvot Mahari Assad, no. 2:132

Question: *A woman from a highly respectable family got married. Her father, who is a famous rabbi, gave her a dowry of several thousand ducats. About one year after her marriage, her husband began misbehaving. He turned to gambling and drinking, lost his money, deserted his wife, and ran off to America. He has not been heard from for several years; his wife is thus an* agunah *(a woman tied to an absent husband). Recently he wrote to one of his relatives that he is planning to move to the West Indies. The wife's relatives want to know if they are permitted to take legal action through diplomatic channels to force him to give her a* get.

Responsum: The law in this case is crystal clear. Since he abandoned his wife many years ago and still persists in his recalcitrant behavior, leaving his wife an *agunah*, he is defying all marriage laws and may be coerced to divorce her by any means available, even by physically beating him, as set forth in the *Shulchan Aruch*. If they have the means to have him extradited to this country and to have him jailed, they should not allow him to be released unless he sends the *get* to his wife. See **Maharik**, no. 166. ...

The Preacher Did Not Get Paid
Teshuvot Mahari Assad, no. 2:244

Question: *It happened that the treasurers of the synagogue took their time paying the agreed-upon speaker's fee to a visiting preacher, a well-known rabbi. The preacher returned home without receiving his honorarium. What should the treasurers do with the money?*

Responsum: The answer is simple. First of all, according to most halachists you are not permitted to change *tzedakah* funds from one beneficiary to another, and most certainly not if the funds were verbally assigned to a specific purpose. At any rate, in this case, where the money had already been given to a messenger to hand to the rabbi, the messenger has taken possession of it on behalf of the rabbi. Haven't the rabbi and the Torah suffered enough humiliation? The treasurers are delinquent in their duty toward the community and toward Heaven until they forward the fee to the preacher's residence in an honorable way. This is not merely a moral obligation; it is their halachic duty.

Who Gets the Torah Scroll?
Teshuvot Mahari Assad, no. 1:46

Question: *A deceased man's will stipulated that his sefer Torah be given in his memory to the main communal synagogue. His son wants to keep it in the village synagogue and offers to donate [to the main synagogue] a sum of money as a perpetual charity fund in his father's memory. Who gets the sefer Torah?*

Responsum: A gift by a man on his deathbed is considered a firm and irrevocable gift—that is, if the beneficiary wants the gift and lays claim to it. . . . However, if the congregation does not ask for the sefer Torah now that they know of the will, they do not have title to it. Indeed, frequently congregations do not want to take advantage of such gifts, since they already possess a large number of Torah scrolls. To the contrary, very often they are not pleased with such gifts at all, because it burdens them with the expense of the care and repair of the sefer Torah. This being so, the congregation would much prefer to receive the money to establish a memorial fund for charity purposes on the deceased's Yahrzeit, as is the custom.

Furthermore, in the village the sefer Torah will be used regularly, whereas in the main synagogue, where there are many scrolls, it will rarely be read. . . . Giving the sefer Torah to the main synagogue would be like giving alms to a rich man. . . . It is preferable by far to leave the sefer Torah in the care of the son, provided he watches it properly and with due respect and makes a donation to the congregation, as promised.

The Weighted Bracelets
Teshuvot Mahari Assad, no. 2:223

Question: *A man sold a number of golden bracelets to a Jewish smelter. The total weight was four and one half ducats, the price amounting to 26 guilders. At the time of the sale the smelter said he suspected that the bracelets had been weighted with some base metal, because they weighed more than ordinary bracelets of that size. He probed deep inside the bracelets with a small instrument, inserting it through a small hole. Thereupon he paid the price of 6 guilders per ducat, a total of 26 guilders. Twenty-four days later the smelter appeared holding the bracelets. He said that he had sold the bracelets to a dealer in Tirnau, who had cut one of the bracelets and found the space inside filled with copper. The dealer had returned the bracelets to him, and now the smelter wants to return them to the seller for full refund or he wants to be repaid for the weight of the copper, which amounts to about one ducat.*

Responsum: [After a thorough examination of all relevant sources Mahari concludes:] The sale cannot be cancelled, because the smelter should have examined the merchandise . . . and according to all authorities the seller is guiltless, especially in this case where the seller did not have the slightest intention of committing fraud. The smelter had an inkling of fraud, which is quite common, and he expressed his suspicion, but since he proceeded with the purchase we must assume that he accepted that risk.

RABBI MOSHE SCHICK—MAHARAM SCHICK
רבי משה שי"ק – מהר"ם שי"ק

born: Brezove, Slovakia, 1807
died: Chust, Hungary, 1879
Popularly known as Maharam Schick, the title of his responsa work.

It is said that the name Schick is formed of the initial letters of *Shem Yisrael Kadosh*, "The Jewish name is sacred." The family chose it after the Austrian government made it obligatory for Jews to adopt surnames.

When he was 14 years old, Maharam Schick entered the famous yeshivah of the **Chatam Sofer**[1] in Pressburg, where he remained for six years. He served as rabbi of Vergin near Pressburg for twenty-four years, and in 1861 he accepted the rabbinate of Chust, where he established a yeshivah and developed the community into the most important Jewish center in northern Hungary. He fought ferociously against the encroaching Reform movement, advocating complete separation from the Reformers. Despite his vehement opposition to any religious innovation, Maharam Schick permitted preaching in the local language (see his responsum on p. 133).

He was a prolific writer of responsa, which mirror his fighting spirit and his vast knowledge of Talmud and Halachah. Almost one thousand of his responsa have been published: 345 on *Orach Chaim*,[2] 410 on *Yoreh De'ah*,[3] 155 on *Even Ha'ezer*,[4] and 62 on *Choshen Mishpat*.[5]

A Bible Published by Missionaries
Teshuvot Maharam Schick, Orach Chaim, no. 66

Question: *In London, a group of apostate Jews have become missionaries. In an effort to spread the Christian religion, they translated their New Testa-*

Title page of *Teshuvot Maharam Schick* by Rabbi Moshe Schick, comprising close to a thousand responsa. The letters at the very top of the page are an abbreviation of *Be'ezrat Hashem Yitbarach*, "With the help of God blessed is He." This latest edition was published in New York, 1961.

ment into Hebrew and published it along with our Tanach *(Jewish Bible)* in one volume. Is it permissible to study from this Tanach *after removing the New Testament section?*

Responsum [*to Rabbi Feish of Halitch*]: It is clear that it is a mitzvah to remove heretical books that contain harmful philosophies. . . . It appears that these missionaries are the publishers but not the actual printers of the book. The printers are simply people doing their job without any intent of proselytizing. If it can be established that the printing is indeed done by independent printers, then the books may be considered as any other books that were printed by a gentile, which may be used for study and may not be destroyed.

Preach in the Local Language?
Teshuvot Maharam Schick, Orach Chaim, no. 70

Question: *Is it permissible to preach in the local language?*

Responsum [*to Rabbi Wolf Sofer of Sangrut*]: Anyone familiar with history and the condition of the present-day generation knows that ever since the Jewish people drifted from the ways of their ancestors, turned to secular sciences, and spoke the vernacular, Torah learning has diminished and the observance of mitzvot has been forgotten by many young people. . . . Nevertheless, in the case of a God-fearing man who we are certain is a talmudic scholar and who preaches in the vernacular and whose sole purpose is to widen the border of our holy Torah and to attract those who have strayed and bring them closer to Torah and God . . . to fight God's battle against His enemies and to refute the lies they spread against the Torah . . . I see no reason to forbid him, where the congregation wishes to listen in the local language or where if he does not do so they will appoint another who is unfit.[6]

The Torn-Down *Mechitzah*
Teshuvot Maharam Schick, Orach Chaim, no. 77

Question: *The Reform-leaning Jews in the community of X until now kept their stores closed on Shabbat. Recently an incident occurred in which several wicked men tore down the* mechitzah *separating the women's from the men's section in the synagogue. The Reformers now say that they will secede from the community and open their stores on Shabbat. This may lead others to follow suit and also desecrate the Shabbat. Should we challenge them on this issue and take a stand against them, or shall we remain passive lest others follow their example and fall into their trap?*

Responsum: God forbid that you should acquiesce and back down in the face of the audacity of these shameless fellows. The Halachah requires a separation between the men's and women's section of the synagogue, similar to the separation that existed in the Temple, and every synagogue is a miniature Temple.

Anyone capable of putting a stop to this must fulfill the mitzvah of "you must admonish your neighbor."[7] And even if acquiescence will result in others keeping their stores closed on Shabbat, we have a rule that "we don't ask someone to commit a sin in order that his neighbor will benefit," especially in this case, where the rabbi's silence will be interpreted as approval. This would be a desecration of God's name, particularly so in this generation where transgressions are on the rise.

The Chapel in the Castle
Teshuvot Maharam Schick, Yoreh De'ah, no. 154

Question: *A Jew bought a castle in which there is a chapel containing [non-Jewish] religious statues. This chapel was used for religious services by the count who previously owned the castle. Is it permissible to use this chapel as a synagogue?*

Responsum [*to Rabbi Gottlieb Fischer of Stuhlweissburg*]: . . . You are permitted to use the chapel for secular purposes but it is forbidden to convert it into a synagogue.

An Abortion to Save the Mother's Life
Teshuvot Maharam Schick, Yoreh De'ah, no. 155

Question: *A woman is having a difficult pregnancy. Her obstetrician says that unless she has an abor-*

tion, both she and the fetus will die. Is she permitted to have an abortion?*

Responsum [*to Rabbi Chaim of Munkatch*]: . . . All of the above applies if we are certain that both will die. But we have only the doctor's word on that, and the **Chatam Sofer** [Maharam Schick's mentor] ruled that a doctor's statement is subject to doubt. However, according to *Ketuvot* 22b, if the doctor says, "I am sure beyond a shadow of a doubt," and he is willing to act on his diagnosis, we trust him and it is permissible to perform the abortion.

Can This Gift Be Accepted?
Teshuvot Maharam Schick, Yoreh De'ah, no. 231

Question: *A woman abandoned the Jewish faith and married a gentile. She wishes to make a contribution toward the building of the synagogue, but she wants to have her name inscribed in the synagogue on a memorial plaque. Is it permitted to accept her donation?*

Responsum [*to Rabbi Moshe Pollack of Bonyhad*]: . . . It seems to me that it is permitted only if her donation becomes part of a general building fund so that it becomes unidentifiable among the majority. But as for inscribing her name, aside from the fact that it is forbidden to inscribe the name of an apostate, such inscription would clearly identify her as the donor and then her money would not be neutralized by the other contributions in the fund. Since it is a sizable amount, there is also the apprehension about whether she is the rightful owner of this money or whether it belongs to her husband. Who knows! And God abhors stolen goods. In my opinion, it is very difficult to determine if it is really her money, for we cannot take her word for it, and who can testify on her behalf?

A Case of Murder
Teshuvot Maharam Schick, Choshen Mishpat, no. 50

Question: *The late Reb Mordechai died suddenly the day after Pesach, 1863. There is reason to believe that his wife poisoned him. There is circumstantial evidence and a partial admission of guilt on her part. She is also suspected of having an affair with a man who apparently was her partner in crime. The father of the deceased, a learned and pious rabbi, wants to keep the matter under wraps. Shouldn't this crime be reported to the police authorities so that justice will be done? The Torah says, "A life for a life,"*[8] *and "He who spills human blood shall have his own blood spilled by man."*[9]

Responsum: Of course, it is forbidden to have pity on someone who committed a crime that is punishable by death. The Bet Din is commanded, "Do not have pity in such a case"[10] and "You must destroy such evil from your midst."[11] . . . Nevertheless, the great rabbinical authorities should not actively involve themselves in making an effort to have her brought to justice. They should remain passive, and God will exact His retribution on the evildoers.

RABBI AVRAHAM SHEMUEL BINYAMIN SOFER (SCHREIBER)—KTAV SOFER
רבי אברהם שמואל בנימין סופר — כתב סופר

born: Pressburg, Hungary, 1815
died: Pressburg, Hungary, 1871
Popularly known as Ktav Sofer, the title of his work.

The Ktav Sofer was the oldest son of the illustrious Rabbi **Moshe Sofer** (Chatam Sofer) and the grandson of the great Rabbi **Akiva Eiger.** At his father's death in 1839, he succeeded him as rabbi and *rosh yeshivah* of the yeshivah of Pressburg (now Bratislava, Czechoslovakia), a position he held for thirty-two years. As his father had done before him, he forcefully resisted the growing Reform movement.

His responsa were published under the title *Teshuvot Ktav Sofer*[1] and are arranged according to the four sections of the *Shulchan Aruch*. He also wrote a homiletic commentary on the Torah, called *Sefer Ktav Sofer*, which was widely acclaimed, as well as novellae on numerous talmudic themes. Despite his frail health, he acted resolutely against any erosion of traditional Torah values and was the acknowledged leader of Austro-Hungarian Jewry during an era of confrontation with secularism and Reform.

Winding the Clocks on Shabbat?
Teshuvot Ktav Sofer, Orach Chaim, no. 55

Question: *A Jewish clockmaker was hired by the duke to wind all the musical clocks in his castle every day. By pulling the chains, he activates the clock movement and the machinery that makes the chimes ring a melody every hour. Some of the clocks must be rewound every seventeen hours, so*

Rabbi Avraham Shemuel Binyamin Sofer (Schreiber).

that even if he winds these clocks shortly before the onset of Shabbat, he still must pull the chains on Shabbat. What should he do on Shabbat and Yomtov? Losing this job would deprive him of an important source of income.

Responsum: In researching this problem, I found that the question of winding a watch on Shabbat has been dealt with in the responsa of many of the early halachic authorities. Some permit it while others prohibit it. [There follows a detailed analysis of the varying opinions.] . . . In our case, if the Jewish clockmaker can have a non-Jew substitute for him by pulling the chains on Shabbat and Yomtov while he supervises him, then, in my opinion, it may be permitted, in view of the financial loss he would otherwise incur.

Apostate Returned to the Fold
Teshuvot Ktav Sofer, Orach Chaim, no. 109

Question: *Several years ago a Jew converted to Christianity. Now that the king graciously has enacted legislation opening the way for anyone to return to his faith, this man immediately repented and came back to Judaism. He prostrated himself in front of the Holy Ark and wept bitterly. He is filled with remorse and grieves over his past. Ever since he has been behaving virtuously, fulfilling mitzvot, attending morning and evening services like any other member of the community.*

Currently, people in the community are trying to organize a society called Tikkun HaNefesh, *whose aim it is to study and pray for the souls of the departed during the first year after death and on the Yahrzeit. Two prominent members of the community stipulated that this man forever be barred from membership in this society. What is your opinion, did these members act properly?*

Responsum: I have no doubt that these men meant well. They think they are doing a mitzvah by closing the door on a man whose past was tainted with all manner of abomination. This is quite true. But now he is a *baal teshuvah*, a newly observant Jew, who is healed from his past; for *teshuvah* (repentance) wipes out any and all sins. . . . Rabbi Eliezer states (*Berachot* 80), "A *baal teshuvah* ranks higher than a perfect *tzaddik*." . . . **Rambam** in *Hilchot Teshu-*

Title page of *Teshuvot Ktav Sofer*, by Rabbi Avraham Shemuel Binyamin Sofer of Pressburg, Hungary. The abbreviation following the name Sofer is *zecher tzaddik vekadosh livrachah*, "of blessed and saintly memory." The words marked by asterisks have the numerical value of 600 and 633, corresponding to 1839–1872, the years of his tenure as Rabbi of Pressburg. Printed in Pressburg in 1873.

vah explains this seemingly paradoxical statement by the fact that a *baal teshuvah*, who has tasted sin, must overcome much greater temptations than the righteous man, who does not know what it is to sin. . . .

A person who has sinned and has become a *baal teshuvah* knows the burning desire he once had for committing a sin. He can apply this same overwhelming enthusiasm to performing mitzvot. We find, therefore, that a *baal teshuvah* performs mitzvot with greater zeal than an accomplished *tzaddik*.

We should also bear in mind that *teshuvah* has the power of converting intentional transgressions into merits. Thus, if a person repents, the deeper the abyss of his former evil deeds, the greater are his present merits for having conquered his cravings.

Our sages state that even if a person sinned all his life, if in the end he repented, he is forgiven.[2] . . . I am afraid that those individuals who want to bar him from membership are violating the law of "Do not wrong one another."[3] This prohibition refers to "wrong done by means of words," as, for example, you should not say to a *baal teshuvah*, "Remember your former deeds." These people should seek his forgiveness. They should immediately welcome him into their society and treat him as a respected member.

Forced to Light Candles during Procession
Teshuvot Ktav Sofer, Yoreh De'ah, no. 84

Question: *The priests and the gentile masses insist that the Jews light candles in their windows when they [the gentiles] march in procession on Christian festivals carrying crosses, which they revere as a deity. When the marchers fail to see candles in a Jewish home, they smash the windows and threaten the life of the inhabitants. Are we required to risk our life and refrain from lighting candles?*

Responsum: Exactly the same question was asked of my father of blessed memory. He responded in *Teshuvot Chatam Sofer, Yoreh De'ah,* no. 133. [There follows a detailed review of all relevant opinions.] . . . A better solution would be that someone tell the priests or the mayor or judge of the town, "It is impossible for us to light candles. We would rather suffer whatever may befall us. But if someone else lights the candles in our windows, we cannot stop him. We are not required to put up a fight and extinguish the candles."

. . . Another solution would be to light the candles in the windows several hours before the procession with the crosses begins and not to extinguish them until all the marchers have dispersed and returned home. This is in keeping with the Rema, who writes in paragraph 150 that when the officials and the clergy march in procession with the crosses, you should rise before they arrive so that it will not appear as though you rose in their honor.

Student Wants to Sue His Rebbi
Teshuvot Ktav Sofer, Yoreh De'ah, no. 107

Question: *A student who studied under his rebbi (teacher) for ten years has a legal dispute with him. Is he permitted to bring the case before a Din Torah (rabbinic court of arbitration)? Is the Bet Din permitted to try such a case?*

Responsum: . . . The respect due one's rebbi is greater than the respect due one's father.[4] This rule is applicable only if the respect does not entail a loss to the student. There is no halachist who holds that a student must suffer a loss in order to honor his rebbi. . . . If the student is convinced that the rebbi is wrong, he surely is permitted to seek redress in a Bet Din. But he should not discuss it with others, and before the Bet Din he should not speak disrespectfully against his rebbi.

All this is the purely legal aspect of the case. However, it would be preferable for the Bet Din not to get involved in a case like this. It is better to dissuade the student and to point out the ethical ramifications of his action. If he persists, it is advisable to listen to his allegations and see if they have any merit, before humiliating a rebbi. These allegations should be heard by one who is not a member of the Bet Din.

I call upon the student with the voice of my pen not to slight the honor of his rebbi, who taught him Torah and to whom he owes most of his knowledge, all the more so since I learned that he is also your father-in-law. . . . In today's generation it will create an appalling *chillul HaShem* (desecration of the Holy Name). People will say, "Look at this man. He studied Torah and now he abuses the honor of his rebbi and father-in-law." Please try to reconcile, and don't let rancor and resentment get the better of you. I hope that my words made an impact on you. Say to your rebbi, "The Torah of your mouth is better to me than thousands of gold and silver pieces."[5]

A Charitable Prince
Teshuvot Ktav Sofer, Yoreh De'ah, no. 114

Question: *Is it permitted to accept a charitable donation from a gentile prince?*

Responsum: . . . From all of the above you can infer that it is permissible to accept his donation. The fact that you advertise his gift in the press and publicly express your gratitude for his largesse does not constitute a shame and dishonor for the people of God. On the contrary, it raises their esteem in the eyes of the masses. However, you should make sure that you clearly state that it was the prince's own initiative to make this donation to buy clothes for needy Jewish children. No one asked him for it or suggested it to him.

A Marriage Made in Jest
Teshuvot Ktav Sofer, Even Ha'ezer, no. 35

Question: *Three youngsters, Amram, Yonatan, and Shimshon, went to a party at the house of a young girl, Dinah. They were having refreshments, laughing and chatting, when suddenly Shimshon called, "Someone give me a ring, and I'll marry Dinah!" One of the girls had a copper ring. Shimshon took it and walked over to Dinah. Squeezing her hands into tight fists, she cried out, "Let go of me!" As she cried, the boy grabbed her fist, forced her little finger, and, placing the ring on its tip, said, "Harei at mekudeshet li betabaat zo," "Behold, you are consecrated to me by means of this ring." Amram and Yonatan instantly jumped in, pulled him away, removed the ring, and yelled at him, "This is no way for a Jewish boy to act!" . . . Shimshon says that he did it only for fun and to demonstrate the marriage ceremony. The question is, does Dinah require a get from Shimshon?*

Responsum: . . . Since the subject of marriage was not discussed at all beforehand, there is no reason for concern that this act has any validity. It is not even a questionable marriage. Moreover, she clearly demonstrated that she rejected this "marriage." She cried out, "Let go of me!" What more could she have said to prove her sincerity? She could not have thrown the ring back at him, because one of the witnesses immediately took it off her finger. . . . This girl is free to marry anyone.

However, I wish to point out that this boy should be punished for his temerity in committing this deed. Things like this simply are not done in Israel.[6]

RABBI MOSHE WEINBERG OF VOLBRUM— OHEL MOSHE
רבי משה וויינברג — אהל משה

born: Pshedburzh, Poland, nineteenth century
died: Volbrum, Poland, nineteenth century
Popularly known as Ohel Moshe, the title of his work, or Volbrumer Rav.

Rabbi Moshe was a descendant of a well-known family of rabbis in Poland. On his father's side he traced his ancestry to Rabbi Yehudah, son of the **Rosh**, the illustrious Rabbi Asher ben Yechiel, the thirteenth-century author of the monumental halachic compilation that is contained in all full editions of the Talmud. Rabbi Moshe's maternal grandfather was the great Rabbi Yeshayah of Pshedburzh, who in 1815 was chosen to be a chasidic rebbe and was affectionately called the Rebbe Reb Shayale, and was one of the closest disciples of the giant of *chasidut*, the Chozeh of Lublin (the visionary).

Rabbi Moshe Weinberg, the Volbrumer Rav, was an eminent talmudic scholar and a man of great piety who led his community with wisdom and compassion. His work *Ohel Moshe*[1] bespeaks his passionate love for the Jewish people. The book comprises selected sermons, talmudic discourses, and a number of responsa that he introduces with the following words: "These are but a few of the responsa that remained after the fire that engulfed our city. Most of them were lost in the catastrophe. These are the ones I saved by the grace of God."

He was recognized as one of the foremost halachic authorities in Poland and corresponded with all the prominent rabbis, notably Rabbi Yisrael Yehoshua of Kutno, the author of the famous *Yeshuot Malko*. Rabbi Moshe Weinberg's descendants published a new edition of *Ohel Moshe* in B'nei B'rak, Israel, in 1975.

Title page of *Ohel Moshe*, responsa by Rabbi Moshe Weinberg of Volbrum. This was printed in Pietrkow, Poland, in 1908.

Dismantle the Old Reading Platform?
Teshuvot Ohel Moshe, no. 1

Question [*An inquiry from the city of Elkush*]: *A local benefactor built a beautiful* bimah *for the synagogue. Is it permitted to dismantle the old* bimah *in order to install the new one?*

Responsum: The source for this response is the Gemara in *Megillah* 26b: "Rav Chisda says, 'A synagogue should not be demolished until a new one has been built.'" Rashi explains the reason: "Lest people abandon the project and don't build a new synagogue."

Applying this to our case, in which the new *bimah* is already built, we must conclude that there is no reason for this concern. Consequently, the old *bimah* may be dismantled to be replaced with the new one.

Now there is the question of what to do with the old *bimah* and whether you are permitted to sell it. The lectern on which the Torah is read retains its sanctity, and it may not be used for any profane purpose. The rest of the *bimah*, its sides, floor, and steps, may be sold, and the buyer may use them as he pleases, except for shameful purposes.

These halachot can be found in *Shulchan Aruch, Orach Chaim*, chapters 152 and 153. It is all really very simple.

Break the Engagement?
Teshuvot Ohel Moshe, no. 14

Question: *Reuven betrothed his son to Shimon's daughter when they were still children. For three years the girl has been suffering from an incurable disease. She has consulted doctors, visited spas, and for a while her health improved, but before long the symptoms recurred. It is a disease that comes and goes. Both the young man and his fiancée are 18 years old now and should get married. The young man's father contends that he does not have to make his son wait until his fiancée recovers, if ever. He therefore wants to break the engagement. The father of the young lady asks him to be patient, saying that perhaps the treatments will restore her health. The young man's father asks whether his son is subject to a ban or penalty if he breaks the engagement.*[2]

Responsum: [After carefully weighing all halachic aspects of the case, the Ohel Moshe arrives at the following conclusion:] In summary I wish to state that certainly the father of the young man is permitted to find a new match for his son, and he is exempt from any penalties that might arise from breaking the current engagement.

Selling to a Non-Jew on the Second Day of Yomtov?
Teshuvot Ohel Moshe, no. 32 (part 2)

Question: *On the second day of Yomtov a non-Jew entered the store of a Jewish shopkeeper with whom he trades, wanting to buy merchandise. He claimed that he needed the goods urgently. He brought pressure to bear on the Jew, threatening that if he did not sell him the merchandise he would get even with him by not paying him the money he owed him, which was a considerable amount. The rabbi permitted the shopkeeper to sell the merchandise, provided the Jew does not hand any article to the buyer, who is to select the items he needs himself. They are not to negotiate a price, and the non-Jew is not to pay for the goods until after Yomtov. Now the rabbi has pangs of conscience whether he made the correct ruling.*

Responsum: I know of no precedent for this case, and nothing like this has ever happened to me on a second day of Yomtov. On the first day I would not have permitted it, but it seems to me that regarding the second day you made the right decision.

If you had asked me from the start, I would still have had to think about it, but since you already made your ruling, you need not have any qualms about it. In my humble opinion you did nothing wrong.

RABBI YOSEF SHAUL HALEVI NATHANSON— SHO'EIL UMEISHIV
רבי יוסף שאול הלוי נאטאנזאהן — שואל ומשיב

born: Brezan, Austria, 1810
died: Lemberg, Austria, 1875
Popularly known as Sho'eil Umeishiv, the title of his responsa.

Rabbi Yosef Shaul HaLevi Nathanson was the son of Aryeh Leib Nathanson, a wealthy businessman and accomplished talmudist. In 1857 he was appointed rabbi of Lemberg but did not accept a salary. He led a great yeshivah and instructed a large number of students from near and far. He was the outstanding *poseik* of his generation and queries reached him from all parts of the world. He tended to be lenient in his rulings, taking contemporary circumstances into consideration. For example, he was one of those who permitted the use of machine-baked matzot, in opposition to Rabbi Shelomoh Kluger's opinion and that of many other authorities. Although known for his permissive approach, he sometimes declared things forbidden simply as a precaution. He fought fiercely against the *maskilim*,[1] who wanted to introduce reforms in education.

His classic work is his responsa *Sho'eil uMeishiv*,[2] in six volumes, dealing principally with questions of practical Halachah. He also wrote *Divrei Shaul*,[3] which is a commentary on the Torah and the Five Scrolls, and many other works.

Relations between Jews and Gentiles
Teshuvot Sho'eil uMeishiv, no. 1:50

Question: *How should a Jew treat a non-Jewish servant?*

Responsum: Let me state in this regard the words of our greatest codifier, the author of *Mishneh Torah*,

Title page of *Sho'eil uMeishiv*, responsa of Rabbi Shaul Nathanson. The abbreviation after Nathanson stands for *Av bet din kehillat*, Chief Rabbi of the community [and district of Lvov (Lemberg)]. This was printed in Jerusalem, 1973.

Rabbeinu Moshe ben Maimon, who is much admired also among non-Jewish scholars. He writes in Laws of Servants 8:8 that a master should be compassionate and just. He should not overwork his servant or oppress him. He should give him plenty of food and drink. . . . He should not humiliate him by deeds or words. He should not shout angrily at him, but speak to him in a calm tone of voice. This halachah refers explicitly to a non-Jewish servant. . . .

It is a general principle that wherever the Talmud or the commentaries speak in derogatory terms of *akum,* heathens, the reference is to the ancient nations who did disgusting perversions and did not believe in divine Providence. They are the antithesis of the nations under whose protection we are living today. These nations observe their religion; they are men of high ethical and moral standards who maintain a judicial system that punishes lawbreakers. Although their religion is far removed from our faith, God forbid that we should entertain even the slightest thought of disrespect. . . . At the present, when the nations follow the tenets of their religion, it is self-understood that we must promote their welfare and treat them with respect. They are kind to us, and the shadow of their wings protects us.

The Widow's Rent Dispute
Teshuvot Sho'eil uMeishiv, no. 1:83

Question: *A widow rented space in front of a building, to open a stand on which to display her wares and to store the stand and the merchandise in the building at night. She paid the rent in advance for one year, and for about three months she used the rented space; but then the entire town burned down. The widow demanded the return of the unused portion of the rent. The landlord demurred, suggesting instead that when the house would be rebuilt she could reoccupy her space. The widow raised no objections to this.*

After the house was rebuilt, she again demanded the balance of the rent or that she be given the rented space. The landlord offered to give her the rented space but his wife refused to allow her to store her merchandise in the building.

Responsum: In my view, since the widow accepted the landlord's proposal, he cannot back down. If he permits her to store the merchandise in the house, he need not return the rent. This is so clear and simple that I do not have to elaborate on it.

An Unwanted Gift
Teshuvot Sho'eil uMeishiv, no. 1:299

Question: *A man donated a clock to the Bet Midrash and installed it on the wall. A number of people vehemently objected and removed the clock. Can he now withdraw his donation and use the clock for secular purposes, or has it become a consecrated object?*

Responsum: It is obvious that he can renounce his donation. His intention was to do a mitzvah by placing the clock in the Bet Midrash. Since his opponents removed it, he was forced to take it home. He certainly did not donate it to create dissension . . . if he would have known that people would be dead set against it, he would not have given it.

Did He Donate the Sefer Torah?
Teshuvot Sho'eil uMeishiv, no. 3:86

Question: *A venerable old man who had daughters but no son had a sefer Torah written that he gave to the synagogue as a memorial for himself. On numerous occasions he mentioned that he was donating the sefer Torah as an outright gift, and he promised to give the community a written statement to that effect in order to remove any doubt as to their right of ownership. He died suddenly, before having given the written declaration. His sons-in-law dispute the synagogue's title to the sefer Torah. They want to take it out and sell it.*

Responsum: . . . A person should not donate a sefer Torah as an unqualified gift, for if he does, he has not fulfilled the mitzvah of writing a Torah scroll.[4] Therefore, the father certainly did not mean to consecrate it as an outright gift. The fact that he publicly stated that he intended to give it as an absolute gift . . . he could have changed his mind. . . . Therefore, in my opinion, the community has no legal claim to this sefer Torah.

However, as far as selling the sefer Torah is concerned, the heirs are limited by the stipulations set forth in *Yoreh De'ah* 270 and *Even Ha'ezer* 1. Therefore, it is best if the sefer Torah remains in the synagogue and the heirs be paid a certain amount as compensation.

Who Has Precedence?
Teshuvot Sho'eil uMeishiv, no. 2:93

Question: *When arranging the seating order or the order of approbations for a book, who takes precedence, an aged Torah scholar or a young Torah scholar of more celebrated lineage?*

Responsum: *Tur Yoreh De'ah* 244:18 rules that seating order should be arranged according to age, but he does not apply the yardstick of lineage. But after a diligent search, I found the answer in Tosafot on *Ketuvot* 105a, listed under *dechashiv*. There the question is raised as to why the Haggadah of Passover, in the story of the rabbis in B'nei B'rak, mentions Rabbi Eleazar ben Azariah before Rabbi Akiva, even though Rabbi Akiva was the leading and most prominent Torah scholar and should have been listed first. Tosafot answers that Rabbi Eleazar ben Azariah had priority because he was a tenth-generation descendant of Ezra the Scribe and he bore the title of *Nasi* (leader of the Sanhedrin). Clearly, his prominent lineage was the deciding factor. Similarly in this case, the young scholar of distinguished ancestry should be accorded precedence.

What Is the Price of the Cow?
Teshuvot Sho'eil uMeishiv, no. 1:289

Question: *Reuven sold a cow to Shimon for a certain price. Before closing the deal, buyer and seller explicitly agreed that in the event the cow proved to be* treifah,[5] *the buyer would pay less. The buyer bought the cow with this stipulation and paid the price as if it were* treifah. *He would pay the balance if it proved to be kosher.*

Before the shechitah *(kosher slaughtering), the buyer sold the cow to a farmer, who bought it for stockbreeding and who paid the premium price. When the seller learned this, he demanded from the buyer the full price of a kosher cow. The buyer replied, "I don't know if I owe you the full price; maybe after the* shechitah *the cow would have been found to be* treifah.*" Who is right?*

Responsum: Nowadays we cannot say that the majority of the animals are found to be kosher, since we see as many *treifah* animals as kosher ones. Since the buyer does not know, he is exempt from paying the price of a kosher cow.

RABBI NAFTALI TZVI YEHUDAH BERLIN—NETZIV
רבי נפתלי צבי יהודה ברלין — נצי"ב

born: Mir, Poland, 1817
died: Warsaw, Poland, 1893
Popularly known as Netziv, the initials of his name.

The Netziv, one of the Torah giants of the last century, was a student of only average intelligence, yet with phenomenal diligence he managed to achieve the highest levels of scholarship. It is said that when he felt sleepy after many hours of study he would dip his feet in icy water to stay awake. In 1831 the budding Torah scholar married the daughter of Rabbi Yitzchak, the son of Rabbi Chaim Volozhiner (founder of the yeshivah of Volozhin, a small town near Vilna, Lithuania). In 1854 the Netziv became the *rosh yeshivah* of that institution. Under his inspired leadership the enrollment of the yeshivah grew to 400 students, each an accomplished talmudist. He headed the yeshivah for forty years and introduced a new approach to the study of the Talmud, based on the analysis of the text as it was interpreted by the Rishonim. He opposed the *pilpul* approach, whereby contradictions in unrelated themes are reconciled in flashes of pure genius.

In 1879 the *maskilim* (secularists) prompted the Russian government to convert the yeshivah into a modern seminary. The Netziv firmly opposed all attempts at changing the traditional character of the yeshivah, a stand that led to the closing of that institution by the Russian government in 1892. The Netziv was exiled. He moved to Minsk, Russia, and later to Warsaw, Poland.

His preeminence as a Torah scholar was undisputed, and questions from all over the world were addressed to him. His *She'eilot uTeshuvot Meishiv Davar*[1] is a collection of such teshuvot; it contains six teshuvot to American rabbis.[2] He also wrote the very popular commentary on the Torah, *Ha'ameik*

Rabbi Naftali Tzvi Yehudah Berlin.

Davar,[3] as well as a number of discourses on talmudic themes.

Selling Nonkosher Meat to an Apostate
Teshuvot Meishiv Davar, no. 2:31

Question: *Concerning a butcher who sells his nonkosher meat[4] to the households of the local noblemen. One of these noblemen is a Jew who is an* *apostate. You ask whether the butcher is permitted to sell him nonkosher meat on the grounds that if he did not sell him the meat the nobleman would buy it from a gentile butcher.*

Responsum [*to Rabbi Yekutiel Eliyahu of Hardok*]: We may rely on the statement of the **Rosh** and Tosafot in *Avodah Zarah* 6b to the effect that it is not forbidden to hand to an apostate a nonkosher item if he can obtain it any other way....

In this case it is the servant who is buying the meat, and if the Jewish butcher will not sell it to him, he will buy it from a gentile butcher. Therefore, selling it cannot be termed contributing to the nobleman's transgression. It is the unanimous view of all authorities that it is permitted.

Reading from the Torah on Sunday?
Teshuvot Meishiv Davar, no. 1:16

Question: *Concerning an incident that occurred in one of the synagogues in our city. A local society held a celebration in honor of the dedication of a new Aron HaKodesh (Holy Ark). After joyously carrying the Torah scrolls around the* bimah, *one of the members insisted on having a public reading of the Torah. Since this occurred on a Sunday, we did not permit the reading, explaining that Torah reading at times other than those designated by the rabbis[5] violates the injunction of* bal toseif, *"Do not add to the word that I am commanding you" (Deuteronomy 4:2). Did we act properly?*

Responsum [*to Rabbi ——— of Cincinnati, Ohio*]: I want to let you know that the prohibition of *bal toseif* does not apply to the reading of the Torah (see *Eiruvin* 96). Nevertheless, you did act properly, because it is forbidden to read the Torah on a day on which no reading was instituted.... I really don't understand what this person had in mind when he challenged you on this matter. If he had no halachic source to back up his contention, his behavior was nothing but foolishness, pride, and grandstanding. You acted correctly. Don't be concerned about hurting his feelings; he brought his humiliation on himself.

May HaShem grant us that "all your children will be students of HaShem and your children will have peace" (Isaiah 54:13).

Title page of *She'eilot uTeshuvot Meishiv Davar* by Rabbi Naftali Tzvi Yehudah Berlin of Volozhin, the Netziv, who also wrote *Haameik Davar*, a commentary on the Torah.

Polluted Drinking Water?
Teshuvot Meishiv Davar, no. 2:27

Zvinikradka, 3rd day of Chol HaMoed, Pesach, 1880.

Question: *Recently I was chosen rabbi of this city, and I have since become aware that the people do not drink the water from the river that flows through this town. They claim that many years ago they found in the water organisms tinier than sesame seeds. These organisms are almost invisible,* *and no more than one, two, or possibly three can be detected in a glass of water. By experimenting, they found that the organisms will pass through a fine cloth strainer. It is for these reasons that they prohibited the use of the water.*

The townspeople are in dire need of water, since there are only two good wells that lie beyond the city limits and the owner charges an exorbitant price for his water. The poor people complain that they cannot afford the water. They asked me to inquire of the great halachic authorities whether a way can be found to sanction the use of the water from the river. I myself have tested the water carefully and found it to be pure and clean, free of any polluting organisms. . . . From the distance, I herewith bow to you respectfully, awaiting your response.

Responsum: Regarding the river: if the water can pass a thorough inspection, you are permitted to use it. However, the water must be tested during the various seasons, in the winter and in the summer, because of the possibility that a change in temperature causes the organisms to emerge. It is important that the test be conducted at the point where the river exits the town. Testing at the point where the river enters the city yields inconclusive results, because pollutants that enter the stream as it passes through town may spawn these organisms. If the water is pure where the river exits, then there is no reason for concern.

Placing the *Bimah* in Front of the Ark
Teshuvot Meishiv Davar, no. 1:15

Question: *Concerning the fact that several members of the community want to remove the* bimah *from the center of the synagogue and place it in front of the* Aron HaKodesh *(Holy Ark).*[6]

Responsum [*to Rabbi ——— of Mitavi*]: Let me state at the outset that any innovation is forbidden. Especially in a synagogue where large crowds assemble, this would be disastrous. Many people who would be thrilled with the change would conclude that, God forbid, the Torah has changed and that its protective hedge has broken down.[7] Aside from this consideration, I think that according to halachah it is forbidden to make such a change. . . .

The **Rambam** states, "The *bimah* is placed in the center of the synagogue. . . ."[8] It seems to me that the main reason that the Torah reading must be done in the center of the synagogue is that the reading platform is compared to the altar in the Temple court. . . . Since the destruction of the Temple, the Torah is the source of the survival of our people in the diaspora. It is our mark of distinction, as the Temple was in years gone by. Now, just as the altar was situated a distance away from the Holy of Holies, so must we place the reading lectern far from the Ark. Subsequently, I found a similar explanation in *Teshuvot Chatam Sofer, Orach Chaim*, no. 28.

I pray to the Almighty that He may protect us from straying from the right path.

Flour for Matzot from a Steam-Powered Mill
Teshuvot Meishiv Davar, no. 1:30

Question: *Is it permitted to grind the wheat for Passover matzot in a mill that is driven by steam?*[9]

Responsum [*to Rabbi ——— of Prilavka*]: I must confess that I have never seen a steam-driven flour mill. Therefore, I cannot express a definitive opinion on this matter. . . .

You mention that in your town there are many flour mills that are powered by horses. It seems to me that flour produced by steam-driven mills is superior to that of horse-driven mills. Today times have changed, and people want to enjoy their "bread of affliction" in regal style, made with pure white flour. . . .

[Conclusion:] For people who wish to eat matzah made of choice flour that is produced by the large steam-operated mills . . . the local rabbi has the responsibility to appoint a qualified supervisor who follows the rabbi's instructions.

This is my modest opinion, considering, as I mentioned, that I am not familiar with the operation of a mechanized mill. Please consider carefully if it is worthwhile to impose stringencies on the public in this matter; and if there are some rabbis who permit it, under no circumstances should this be a source of friction and quarreling. May God protect us from the pitfalls of making decisions that are too strict, for the Torah is characterized as "Its ways are ways of pleasantness."[10]

RABBI YITZCHAK ELCHANAN SPECTOR
רבי יצחק אלחנן ספקטור

born: Lithuania, 1817
died: Kovno, Lithuania, 1896

Rabbi Yitzchak Elchanan was one of the foremost halachic authorities of the last century. He began his rabbinic career as a young man of 20, serving various communities in Eastern Europe. For the last thirty years of his life he was the rabbi of Kovno, Lithuania, gaining universal recognition for his communal activities and his great love for Eretz Yisrael which came to the fore in his efforts on behalf of the *Chibbat Tzion* movement.[1] One of his halachic works, which reflect his deep erudition and broad scope of knowledge, is *Ein Yitzchak*,[2] a collection of his responsa.

A prominent yeshivah, the Rabbi Isaac Elchanan Theological Seminary (RIETS) in New York, is named after this great Torah scholar.

Convert a Mosque into a Synagogue?
Teshuvot Ein Yitzchak, Orach Chaim, no. 11

Question: *Concerning the Jews of Kars,[3] a city that was conquered from Turkey by His Imperial Majesty the Czar. The Jews of Kars requested from the governor of the Kars district that they be given a house of prayer. The governor graciously made available to them a building that had been used as a Moslem mosque before the takeover of Kars by His Majesty. Are Jews permitted to pray there?*

Responsum: *Orach Chaim* 154:11, *Magein Avraham* 17, states that a mitzvah may not be performed with an article that was used in the worship of another religion. But this does not apply to a building, and especially not in this case, since the house

Rabbi Yitzchak Elchanan Spector.

itself was not the object of worship. Thus, it seems clear that Jews are permitted to pray there. . . . Moreover, Rema in *Yoreh De'ah* 146:5 states that Moslems are not considered idol worshippers. Also Tosafot in *Megillah* 6 agrees that it is permissible to pray and study in a Moslem house of worship.

Can He Break His Vow?
Teshuvot Ein Yitzchak, Yoreh De'ah, no. 24

Question: *A man made a vow not to reveal a certain thing to anyone in the world. Now he wants to reveal it, and he asks how he should go about having his vow annulled. The problem is that before having a vow annulled by a Bet Din, one must spell out to that court all the details of the vow. Thus, the moment this man specifies the particulars of his vow, he is breaking the vow, before the Bet Din has the opportunity to annul it.*

Responsum: . . . We may indeed permit him to reveal his secret to the Bet Din and they will immediately annul his vow. When they have annulled the vow, it is voided retroactively, so that he never violated it. . . . But before he reveals the secret, Bet Din should caution him that if the secret involves slander, defamation of character, or the like, they will not consent to annul his vow, so that if he does reveal such a secret he will then be breaking his vow. After issuing this warning, they can then proceed.

Men Lost at Sea
Teshuvot Ein Yitzchak, Even Ha'ezer, no. 1

Question: *The question has come from America concerning several observant women who have been agunot[4] for seven years. The ship on which their husbands sailed sank in the open seas, not far from Hamburg, Germany. The ship carried several hundred passengers, most of them non-Jews, and some Jews. Some thirty or forty passengers were saved. The marital status of the wives of those who perished is undecided. The name of the ship was "Dezember"; the shipwreck occurred in the month of Tevet of the year 5643/1883. There is valid testimony that the husbands of these wives were indeed on this ship. The above-mentioned thirty or forty survivors were saved in a lifeboat and it has been established that there were no other survivors. The ship sank one day after setting sail from Hamburg. The disaster victims were sleeping in their cabins before dawn. Divers who found the bodies stated that no one could have escaped by swimming away from inside the ship. The only doubt that remains is whether during the sinking these men were on deck*

Title page of *Ein Yitzchak*, responsa by Rabbi Yitzchak Elchanan Spector of Kovno, Lithuania, encompassing the four parts of the *Shulchan Aruch*. Printed in Vilna, 1889.

and jumped into the sea, and whether they could have survived.

Responsum: I truly do not have the strength to delve into this question, but because of the weightiness of the problem affecting several *agunot*, I will briefly review it, and may God help me. [Rabbi Yitzchak Elchanan's frail condition notwithstanding, he wrote a comprehensive four-part analysis of the problem, citing precedents and relevant opinions of other authorities. He concludes:]

. . . Since the accident occurred during the night while they were asleep in their beds, we assume that they did not leave their cabins but remained inside the ship. . . .

The gist of the foregoing is that the husbands were on the ship when it sank. A Bet Din of three judges should be convened and they should permit each and every one of these women to marry.

The Treacherous Husband
Teshuvot Ein Yitzchak, Even Ha'ezer, no. 44

Question: *A husband wanted to divorce his wife, who was sick and confined to the hospital. The husband, who was in a faraway place, sent an agent to deliver the* get. *Shortly thereafter, the husband appeared in the city where his wife and the agent resided, entered the agent's home, and asked him whether he had delivered the* get. *The agent replied that he had not. The husband then said, "You know, Kalman, I want to patch things up with her. I have had a child with her. Why should I make my life miserable?" The husband went to the hospital, placated his wife, and they agree to live again as man and wife. She remained in the hospital and he went to his wife's home. She expected him to visit her in the morning, but when he did not show up she left the hospital and went looking for him. Coming home, she found to her great consternation that the box where she kept her money had been opened. Her thirty rubles were missing and so was her husband. The scoundrel had run away to America.*

More than three months have gone by and she has not heard from him. The husband is known as a ne'er-do-well and wants to leave her as an agunah. The question is whether the agent can hand over the get. *The case is all the more serious since it involves America, a land of liberal attitudes.*

Responsum: At first glance it seems that the *get* was invalidated by the fact that they reconciled. However, his subsequent actions bear out his intent to steal the money and run away, and the fact that he never wanted to effect a sincere reconciliation. Since he never was alone with his wife, since she was in the hospital, we need not be concerned that this is an outdated *get*. . . . I therefore agree that the agent may deliver the *get*, and she is permitted to marry.

The Faulty Scales
Teshuvot Ein Yitzchak, Even Ha'ezer, no. 69

Question: *A man had a load of fish to sell and hired a fish-seller to bring his fish to market. He told him to borrow scales and weights from so-and-so. The fish-seller did as he was told, and sold some of the fish in the market. But since the scales were not certified by the Office of Weights and Measures, the police confiscated the scales, and the fish were also confiscated.*

What is the halachah concerning this fish-seller? Is he required to pay for the fish because he is at fault for using uncertified scales, or can the fish-seller argue, "You told me to borrow the scales from so-and-so; therefore, it is all your fault"? Or can the owner of the fish claim, "I did not know that these scales were unapproved; therefore, the fish-seller is responsible"?

Responsum: The halachah is that a worker is deemed a "paid guardian."[5] The fish-seller too, since he receives a salary, is considered a "paid guardian," and he should have inspected the scales to make sure they were certified. He is required to pay the value of the fish.

But the fish-seller surely need not pay for the scales that were confiscated. The owner of the scales knew that they were flawed by not having the government seal of approval. And if the owner is aware of a defect, the "paid guardian" is not liable; and he did lend the scales to be used for weighing. Likewise, the fine imposed by the laws of His Majesty the Czar on anyone harboring unlawful weights must not be charged to the fish-seller.

RABBI YITZCHAK AHARON ETTINGER— MAHARI HALEVI
רבי יצחק אהרן איטינגא הלוי — מהרי"א הלוי

born: Lemberg, Poland, 1827
died: Lemberg, Poland, 1891

Rabbi Yitzchak Aharon was born into a distinguished family of rabbis. His father was the famous gaon Rabbi Mordechai Zev Ettinger, author of *Teshuvot Maamar Mordechai* and other works. At an early age Rabbi Yitzchak Aharon exhibited amazing brilliance and a burning zeal to study Torah. At his bar mitzvah he was invited to deliver a halachic discourse in the large synagogue in Lemberg, which was filled with scholars who came to hear the young prodigy. Prominent in the audience was the bar mitzvah's uncle, Rabbi Yaakov Ornstein, the illustrious rabbi of Lemberg and author of *Yeshuot Yaakov*,[1] a commentary on the *Shulchan Aruch*. So impressed was he with the young man's halachic exposition that a few days later he sent him his rabbinical ordination.

Rabbi Yitzchak Aharon Ettinger served as rabbi of Premisla and Lemberg and was loved and admired for his vast knowledge, his kindness, and his humility. With clear penetrating thinking he replied to the numerous queries that were addressed to him by rabbis of other communities. His sons published his responsa, entitled *Teshuvot Mahari Halevi*,[2] in two volumes containing 362 responsa.

Transfer Charitable Contributions?
Teshuvot Mahari Halevi, no. 1:80

Question: *Charity funds have been collected for the purpose of building a shelter for the homeless in Jerusalem. Recently, a letter has been received from Safed, Eretz Yisrael, requesting assistance for a similar project in that city. Is it permitted to send the collected funds to Safed?*

Title page of *Teshuvot Mahari Halevi*, responsa by Rabbi Yitzchak Aharon Ettinger. This was printed in Lemberg, 1893.

Responsum: In my opinion you should not do this. . . . If this money is sent to Safed, no new collection will be taken up for the needy of Jerusalem. Therefore, it is forbidden to transfer the funds.

Additionally, it should be noted that residing in Jerusalem is a greater mitzvah than living in any other place in Eretz Yisrael. Therefore, supporting institutions in Jerusalem takes precedence over supporting other places in Eretz Yisrael. Consequently, by taking funds that were donated for Jerusalem and assigning them to Safed, you are downgrading the *tzedakah* and this is forbidden. . . .

Now, you may cite the Shach [his commentary] to *Yoreh De'ah* 259:11, stating that a lamp or a menorah that was donated to a synagogue may be used for a lesser purpose. This ruling applies if the synagogue has ample lamps and menorot. But in our case, everyone knows that all the donations that are sent to the Holy Land are not even enough to supply dry bread. Thus, since the original institution will suffer by the transfer, no change may be made.

Can He Be Considered of Sound Mind?
Teshuvot Mahari Halevi, no. 2:133

Question: *A man got married on the first of Kislev, and on Pesach he became psychotic. He jumped around irrationally, striking people. He refused to eat, alleging that his wife was trying to poison him. After some time he recovered. Now, several years have passed in which he speaks normally and eats the food his wife prepares, but his mind is not completely balanced. During prayer he will sit still without moving his lips, and when people ask him a question he will twist his hair and not respond. But whenever he does give an answer he is coherent. Can this man give a* get *to his wife?*[3]

Responsum: . . . Since he does not act abnormal and answers rationally, he must be considered mentally sound. Furthermore, the **Chatam Sofer** writes in *Even Ha'ezer*, 2:2, that if a person is mentally unbalanced but does not act in a deranged manner, he is not considered a *shoteh* (insane), but a *peti* (fool). . . .

Therefore this man, in his present state, is halachially sane, and if he divorces his wife, his *get* has validity.

Tax Revolt
Teshuvot Mahari Halevi, no. 2:46

Question: *In the city of Foltitchan, the Jewish community decided to levy a new tax on the sale of meat, amounting to one quarter franc per pound. The proceeds of the tax were meant to help the needy and businessmen who temporarily were in financial straits. It was decreed to declare unfit for use any meat that was sold without payment of the tax. Any shochet who came into town and slaughtered without collecting the tax would be excommunicated.*

Now the wealthy people in town refuse to pay the new tax. When the matter was brought to a vote, the rich were outvoted by 1,000 to 30. Thereupon, the rich brought a shochet from another city and are circumventing the tax, thereby disrupting the entire procedure. Are the wealthy within their rights, and is it permissible to eat the meat that was slaughtered by the new shochet?

Responsum: . . . In this case, since the ordinance regarding the meat concerns the entire community, it was legally instituted. *Teshuvot Chatam Sofer* no. 116, states that in matters of this nature we follow the majority, for if we waited for a unanimous decision, no decree would ever be passed and the community would go to ruin. Besides, this case involves a great mitzvah, that of supporting the poor and other people who are financially embarrassed. . . .

Now that we established that the enactment is legally valid, the shochet who with his actions thwarts this enactment violates a prohibition each time he slaughters an animal. Therefore, his *shechitah* is forbidden. I trust that my fellow Jews will not defile themselves by eating his rejected meat. Let them make peace with the majority of the Jews in town and pay the tax in accordance with the new ordinance. God found only one vessel capable of containing His blessing for Yisrael, and that vessel is peace.

Who Is Entitled to the Insurance Money?
Teshuvot Mahari Halevi, no. 2:126

Question: *Reuven rented his house to Shimon, who proceeded to buy fire insurance on it. Now Shimon* is asking Reuven to reimburse him for the premium he paid. Reuven refuses. Shimon says that he will subtract the amount of the premium from the rent, but Reuven demurs. In the meantime, the house burned down. Reuven asserts that he is entitled to the insurance money, since it is compensation for his house. Shimon contends that since Reuven did not refund the premium to him, the insurance money is his. Who is right?*

Responsum: You want to compare this case to *Choshen Mishpat*, no. 264, where Reuven's expensive honey is flowing out of a broken vessel, and Shimon, in an attempt to save the honey, empties his wine barrel, wasting his wine in order to capture Reuven's honey in the barrel. In that case, Shimon is entitled only to be reimbursed for his wine. He cannot claim that the honey would have been lost without his intervention and that he saved the honey for himself. Just as the honey had to be returned to the owner, so too, in our case, Shimon must return the insurance money to Reuven.

In my opinion, the two cases are not analogous. In the case of the honey, the honey itself was saved, and still exists. Since Reuven never renounced his ownership of the honey, by what right did Shimon acquire the honey? Therefore he must return the honey to the rightful owner, and receives only restitution for his expenses. In the case of the house, however, the house went up in flames; it no longer exists, and Shimon acquired the insurance money by virtue of the premium he paid. We are not dealing with the house itself, only with the insurance money.... In view of the above, Shimon is entitled to the insurance money.

He Wants to Break Their Engagement
Teshuvot Mahari Halevi, no. 1:148

Question: *A rabbi's daughter got engaged to a young man who subsequently began to lead an immoral life and turned his back on Torah and mitzvot. He traveled to Vienna, where he wrote a letter to the girl's father stating that he absolutely does not want to go through with the forthcoming marriage. In the event his parents would coerce him into marrying the rabbi's daughter, he would divorce her immediately after the wedding. The rabbi wants to know if his daughter is free to find another prospective match.*

Responsum: Permission for this has been granted already in a similar case by the gaon of Zlotchov. As for the penalty that must be paid by the party who breaks the engagement, far be it from me to decide on such a matter without listening to the claims of both parties. This concerns financial matters, and in such cases a judge is not permitted to listen to one side only. However, with regard to breaking the solemn promise that was made at the engagement, this is a religious matter about which a rabbi may respond to anyone. In this case, there is a clear-cut ruling in the *Shulchan Aruch*, *Even Ha'ezer*, 50:5; that if the fiancé has gone wrong, the young lady may break the engagement and is exempt from the promise she made.... In this case she is free to find another match since the young man wrote that if he would be forced to marry her, he would divorce her. Under such circumstances she is not even permitted to marry him.

In view of all these factors, it is clear that the father may marry off his daughter to someone else. I really would not have elaborated on a matter as simple as this. I did so only because I know how saintly and God-fearing you are. Therefore I laid out all the facts as clearly as possible.

Competing Tavern Owners
Teshuvot Mahari Halevi, no. 2:130

Question: *A tavern owner lodged a complaint against his competitor in the next village for underselling him on the price of whiskey. Attracted by the lower prices, all the gentiles from his village are going to his competitor. He cannot sell his whiskey as cheaply, because his competitor pays only 150 silver* reinish *annually for rent, whereas he pays 500 silver* reinish.

Responsum: In my opinion it seems obvious that he cannot prevent his competitor from lowering his price.... The competitor's tavern is in his own village and he lowers his price for the benefit of the local gentiles. It is only because the gentiles in the other village found out about the lower prices that they leave their village to frequent the other tavern. This is less than causing indirect damage, which is permitted according to all halachic authorities. Only if there are two merchants on the same street, and one competes unfairly, then we might say that he is taking away his competitor's customers, and that may be forbidden. But in this case, he is completely within his rights to lower the price in his village, and if the gentiles from other villages come to him, that is not his doing.

Dispute about an Inheritance
Teshuvot Mahari Halevi, no. 2:112

Question: *A prominent rabbi left a manuscript of his commentary on the Torah and willed that his sons publish it. After his death, the oldest brother refused to contribute toward the cost of publication, stating that he was short of funds. It was agreed that two of the [other] brothers would pay for publishing the manuscript, and after publication each of the three brothers who did not contribute toward the printing was to receive 250 copies of the Chumash (Pentateuch). The firstborn son stipulated that after publication a halachic authority should decide whether or not he is entitled to the firstborn's double share of the books.*

Responsum: [Preface: It should be noted that according to Deuteronomy 21:17, the firstborn son inherits a double portion of his father's property. Our sages explain that a firstborn does not receive a double share of what is due to come after the death of the father, such as, for example, when a debt is payable to the father on a certain date but the father died before that date. Such a debt is termed *ra'ui*. He does receive a double share of what is actually held in possession by the father. Such things are called *muchzak*.] . . . In this case it seems clear to me that the market value of the manuscript at the time of the father's death is considered *muchzak*. The added value by virtue of the printing is considered *ra'ui*. . . . Therefore, the firstborn is not entitled to a double portion of the published Chumash.

Conflict of Interest for the Shochet?
Teshuvot Mahari Halevi, no. 2:89

Question: *Is a shochet permitted to buy the animal hides from the butcher whose animals he slaughtered?*

Responsum: In your opinion, the shochet should not buy any hides. You state that since the shochet decides whether an animal is kosher or nonkosher he is like a judge, and a judge may not accept any favors from the litigants; he may not even borrow something from a party to a dispute. I must say that you did not think the matter through properly. . . . A judge is forbidden to accept a gift if it is offered by only one of the litigants, because he may give special consideration to the giver and bend justice. But if the judge is paid by both sides to the dispute, the issue of bribery does not arise.

Now, if the shochet bought only the hides of kosher animals and not of those that he found *treifah* [an animal with an organic defect, rendering it forbidden], there is the apprehension that he will tend to find an animal kosher since he would profit by it. That would be like a bribe. But in this case he buys the hides of both kosher and *treifah* animals. Thus there is no reason for concern. It is like the case of the judge who receives remuneration from both litigants.

I really don't understand what you are worried about. It is clear that this case does not resemble any of the precedents you cite from the Gemara in *Ketuvot*. There the judge accepts a fee from only one party, while in our case he receives the hides of both kosher and *treifah* animals. It is really very simple.

RABBI YOSEF CHAIM AL CHAKKAM OF BAGHDAD—BEN ISH CHAI
רבי יוסף חיים אל חכם — בן איש חי

born: Baghdad, 1834
died: Baghdad, 1909
Popularly known as Ben Ish Chai, the title of his work.

Ben Ish Chai was one of the most illustrious rabbinical personalities in Sephardi Jewry of the last century. In 1859 he succeeded his father, Rabbi Eliyahu, as rabbi of Baghdad, the capital of present-day Iraq. A holy and pure man of prodigious greatness in Talmud and Halachah, he was consulted by all the prominent rabbis of his time. He was also an accomplished orator and captivated his audiences with his spellbinding eloquence. Among Sephardi Jews there is a saying that Ben Ish Chai was originally destined to be one of the Tannaim,[1] but Heaven had compassion on us and sent him to our generation instead to enlighten us with the brightness of his Torah.

Ben Ish Chai's mastery of Talmud was matched by his vast kabbalistic knowledge, and he became the foremost exponent of the writings of Ari HaKadosh and Rabbi Chaim Vital.[2] He received inquiries from many countries ranging from questions on practical Halachah to requests for interpretations of disturbing dreams. His responsa, which are couched in gentle and compassionate terms, have been published under the title *Torah Lishmah*.[3] For unknown reasons the author signed his responsa with the pseudonym Yechezkel Kachli, which has the same numerical value as Yosef Chaim, his real name. He was a prolific writer but most of his books have not been published. His most popular work is *Ben Ish Chai*, homiletics with Halachah and Kabbalah.

In 1909 he fell ill while on a journey to pray at the tomb of the prophet Ezekiel in the village of Kifl, south of Baghdad, and he died shortly thereafter.

Portrait of Rabbi Yosef Chaim of Baghdad, the Ben Ish Chai. Made in 1860, when he was 26 years old.

He was laid to rest in Baghdad, having served as its rabbi for a half century. His fame has spread far beyond the Sephardi world to embrace the entire spectrum of Torah-observant Jewry.

Which Bread Is Preferred?
Teshuvot Torah Lishmah, no. 102

Question: *A person has two kinds of bread for Shabbat: One is savory and tasty but its appearance is somewhat unattractive, the crust a little dark; whereas the other looks exquisitely white, but since the dough did not rise properly it has a sour and moldy aroma. We wonder which bread should be placed on the Shabbat table for the berachah of HaMotzi.*[4]

Responsum: The good-tasting bread is preferred, even though it does not look quite as pleasing. In an analogous case in the Jerusalem Talmud, Tractate *Yoma*, Chapter 6, concerning the two goats of Yom Kippur,[5] if one is meaty and plump but not handsome-looking, and the other has a handsome appearance but is not as fat, . . . Rabbi Yirmiyah rules that the plump one is preferred; good quality takes precedence over outward beauty. So too, in our case the tastier bread should be used for the *berachah* at the Shabbat table.

Did He Violate a Torah Decree?
Teshuvot Torah Lishmah, no. 123

Question: *A Jew, while on a journey, was forced to spend Shabbat in a roadhouse for wayfarers. Since it was cold outside and he was not feeling well, he bedded down in the main public dining room. After two hours had passed, several tough-looking Arabs entered the dining room with the intention of spending the night there also. He knew that these men were vicious Jew-haters, and that if they would recognize him as Jew they would chase him out into the cold, which would surely aggravate his ailment. What did he do? He thought to outwit them by lighting a candle on Shabbat to make them think that he was not Jewish. Of course he had no need for the light; on the contrary, the light annoyed him, because he wanted to get some sleep. He lit the candle only to deceive them. He wants to know whether he violated the Torah law.*

Responsum: Since he did not light the candle in order to create light, his act was a labor that was not done for its own purpose.[6] He did not need the light,

Title page of *Rav Pe'alim*, one of the responsa collections by Rabbi Yosef Chaim of Baghdad, the Ben Ish Chai.

he only wanted to convey the impression that he was not Jewish, so that he would not be expelled from the room. According to Rabbi Shimon,[7] work that was not done for its own purpose does not constitute a violation of the Torah law. . . . In any event, the man requires atonement for lighting the candle, even according to Rabbi Shimon's view. He should have submitted to the distress of being evicted rather than actively desecrating the Shabbat. Surely, his eviction would not have involved any threat to his life.

Healing by Cauterization
Teshuvot Torah Lishmah, no. 119

Question: *A patient whose life is in danger was told by an Arab that he could be healed by being seared with a heated piece of copper or iron. According to the Arab, placing a red-hot branding iron on a certain spot on the body is a tried and proven therapy with them for this particular disease. Our question is whether we may rely on this advice and whether a Jew is permitted to administer this cauterization on Shabbat.*

Responsum: It has been reported that this branding therapy used by the Arabs is a tried and tested method and has produced astounding results for a number of various diseases whereby the patient has made a rapid recovery. Physicians practicing conventional medicine could not produce similar results even after many days of administering medication. Therefore, you should rely on these Arabs who have this remedy by tradition from their ancestors. Since this patient is critically ill, it is permitted for a Jew to give the treatment on Shabbat.[8]

Give His Son the Name of a Hebrew Letter?
Teshuvot Torah Lishmah, no. 405

Question: *It is a father's fondest wish to give his newborn son the name of a letter of the* alef bet, *for example, to call the baby Alef. Some people want to stop him from doing it because, they say, there is no precedent for it; it has never been done. Is there any reason for concern? If not, is he permitted to name his son for one of the letters of the Divine Name?*

Responsum: There is no reason for apprehension in this matter. Let him proceed to his heart's content, and let no one stop him. Those that oppose giving this name, claiming that there is no precedent for it, are in error. In the Mishnah in *Avot* 5:26 we find a saying by a sage named Ben Hei Hei. Furthermore, the Gemara in *Taanit* 22b mentions a sage by the name of Rami bar Rav Yud, and Rashi comments, "There was a sage named Yud." Both *hei* and *yud* are letters of the tetragrammaton and people were named for them. And if you think about it, you will notice that the name Yehudah contains all the letters of the Divine Name. So you see, the matter is not questionable at all.

Testing a Servant
Teshuvot Torah Lishmah, no. 417

Question: *A man wants to test his servant's honesty by making it appear as if he unintentionally left some money in a room. He then sends the servant to get something for him from that room. If the money has disappeared, he knows that the servant has taken it and that he cannot be trusted. If he brings him the money or leaves it in its place, he knows that the servant is honest. . . . Is it permissible to check out a servant by using such methods, or does the employer violate the prohibition of "Do not place a stumbling block before the blind"?*[9]

Responsum: It is forbidden to do tests of this kind. If the servant succumbs to the temptation and steals, the employer is guilty of placing a stumbling block in his path, causing him to sin. . . . Proof of this is the Gemara in *Bava Metzia* 75b, which states that he who lends money to someone without witnesses violates the law of "do not place a stumbling block before the blind." Rashi explains that by lending money without witnesses, the lender tempts the borrower into denying the loan. . . .

Therefore, it is surely forbidden to entrap someone and to lure his evil inclination into committing a sin.

Interpretation of a Dream
Teshuvot Torah Lishmah, no. 466

Question: *A man had a dream in which he was reciting the* alef bet *several times in succession. Each time, he skipped some letters and was unable to complete the entire* alef bet *flawlessly even once. He woke up feeling very upset, since he does not know what the dream portends. Please give us the true interpretation of the dream.*

Responsum: Our teacher, the Ari HaKadosh, in his *Shaar Ruach HaKodesh*, which we have in manuscript, writes, "The twenty-two letters of the *alef bet* are linked to the one hundred *berachot* a Jew recites each day. If a person fails to say a given *berachah*, the letter that is linked to that *berachah* is missing. If he did say the *berachah* properly but did not concentrate on its meaning, then the letter that is linked to it is obscure and unclear." Therefore, the interpretation of the dream is that he lacks one of the one hundred *berachot*. He is being guided from Heaven to exert himself to recite with concentration the full one hundred *berachot* each day. If he is careful to do that from now on, all will be well with him.

A House or a Garden in Eretz Yisrael?
Teshuvot Torah Lishmah, no. 387

Question: *A person living outside Eretz Yisrael bought there, out of love of Eretz Yisrael, a broken-down ruin that he wants to restore. He asks whether he should rebuild it as a dwelling and rent it, or convert the property into a garden in which to raise fruit and produce. He also wishes to know, if someone motivated by a love of Eretz Yisrael wants to buy property there, whether he should invest in a house or a garden.*

Responsum: Certainly, as for fulfilling the mitzvah of loving Eretz Yisrael, a house is preferable to a garden.... We have a ruling to that effect by **Rambam**[10]: "You should not demolish your house in order to convert it into a garden, neither should you turn your ruin into a garden, lest Eretz Yisrael be destroyed." Clear evidence that a house is preferred to a garden.

Her True Age Was 32
She'eilot uTeshuvot Rav Pe'alim, Even Ha'ezer, no. 1:8

Question: *A young woman was suggested to a talmudic scholar as a suitable marriage partner. The marriage broker told him that she was 24 years old, and since she came from a good family, he agreed to marry her. After the wedding he learned to his dismay that she was, in fact, 32 years of age. He accused the marriage broker of cheating him. The broker replied that her relatives had told him that she was only 24 years old. Now the husband wants to have the marriage annulled with the rationalization that if he had known her true age he would not have married her for all the money in the world. Thus, he argues, the marriage was contracted under false pretenses and has no validity. Please advise us as to whether the* kiddushin *are binding.*

Responsum: It seems to me that these *kiddushin* constitute a perfectly legal marriage. It was not she who deceived him; he fooled himself. This halachah was decided by the **Rambam** and in the *Shulchan Aruch* 38:24. At the time of the marriage the husband did not stipulate that he was marrying her with the understanding that she was 24 and not older. The woman did not mislead him, for he did not ask her for her age. True, the marriage broker gave him the information, but the woman had no knowledge of this. From the situation I can surmise who is the woman in question, and it is clear to me that she did not have the slightest inkling of these things. To recapitulate, she did not deceive him, neither did she ask others to misinform him. Instead of relying on the marriage broker he should have made his own investigation, just as he did after the wedding.

In short, there is not the slightest doubt about the legality of this marriage. They should always cling to each other with love. I would go into more detail, but the questioner urges me to respond without delay.

RABBI SHALOM MORDECHAI SCHWADRON—
BREZANER RAV, MAHARSHAM
רבי שלום מרדכי שבדרן — מהרש"ם

born: Zlotchov, Poland, 1835
died: Brezan, Galicia, Poland, 1911
Popularly known as the Brezaner Rav or Maharsham, the title of his work and initials of his name.

The Brezaner Rav, one of the foremost halachic authorities of the last century, served in the rabbinate of various communities in Galicia: Potek, Yislovitz, Butchatch, and Brezan. His fame as a *poseik* spread far beyond the boundaries of his native Galicia. He received queries from communities as distant as Hungary, Russia, Eretz Yisrael, and Western Europe. His lucid and well-documented responsa form a basic text that is consulted in deciding current halachic problems as they arise throughout the world.

His responsa have been collected and published in seven volumes as *She'eilot uTeshuvot Maharsham.*[1] The publisher is the author's grandson, Rabbi Shalom Mordechai Schwadron, a *rosh yeshivah* in Jerusalem.

Lost at Sea
Teshuvot Maharsham, no. 1:6

Question: *Moshe Leisten from Tarna traveled to Bremen, Germany, on the 2nd Shevat 1895. In Bremen he was to board a steamship sailing for America. Since he had previously lived in America, he carried a U.S. passport. Upon arriving in Bremen, he wrote to his wife that at noon on the following day he would sail on the "Elba." On January 30 the newspapers reported that the ocean liner "Elba" had gone down within fifteen minutes after colliding with another ship.*

Rabbi Shalom Mordechai Schwadron (Maharsham).

The steamship company notified his wife's relatives that the name Moshe Leisten, carrying a U.S. passport, appeared on the passenger list and that he was not among the survivors. On Thursday they received a death certificate stating "the third officer Theodor Stahlberg of Albenburg declares that the liner 'Elba' sank within a short time after colliding and that the entire crew and all the passengers drowned. Only he, twelve other crew members, and seven passengers survived. All the others perished, and among these is Moshe Leisten from New York, America, 32 years old." The press reported that the survivors were taken to an island. A few days later it was reported that fishermen had found a body that appeared to be Moshe Leisten. The family received a letter from the steamship company stating that the fishermen had found personal effects, documents, and cash in the amount of 20 pounds sterling. They demand 10 pounds sterling as a finder's fee. After agreeing to pay the fee, the family received a package containing the passport, a hatmaker's diploma, and other documents and letters in Moshe Leisten's handwriting. Among the articles was his golden pocket watch with chain, and a medal on which his name was engraved, given to him by an American organization whose president he was.

What is the marital status of his wife Reizel?

Responsum [*to Rabbi Naftali Tzvi Goldberg of Tarna*]: [After giving due consideration to a number of doubts as to the credibility of the steamship company and the testimony of the third officer and the possibility that the deceased had loaned his possessions to someone else, Maharsham concludes:] Since his passport, his diploma, and his steamship ticket were found, and it is inconceivable that he loaned these to someone else, and it is equally unthinkable that they were stolen or lost, for he would have notified the steamship company immediately, therefore, in consideration of all the above, I agree with you to free this woman from the status of *agunah*.

Wife Refuses to Move to Eretz Yisrael
Teshuvot Maharsham, no. 1:116

Question: *A man has been a* melamed *(teacher of the young) all his life. He feels his strength ebbing and wants to give up his position and move to Eretz Yisrael. His wife opposes his plan for fear that he will have no source of income there. She cannot be convinced to move, even though he can sell his house for 500 silver rubles, and the school officials promised to send him his full salary, and his wealthy relatives will support him there. She is afraid it may not be enough. He argues that since his strength is waning, he will eventually lose his income even if he remains here. Can he compel her to join him?*

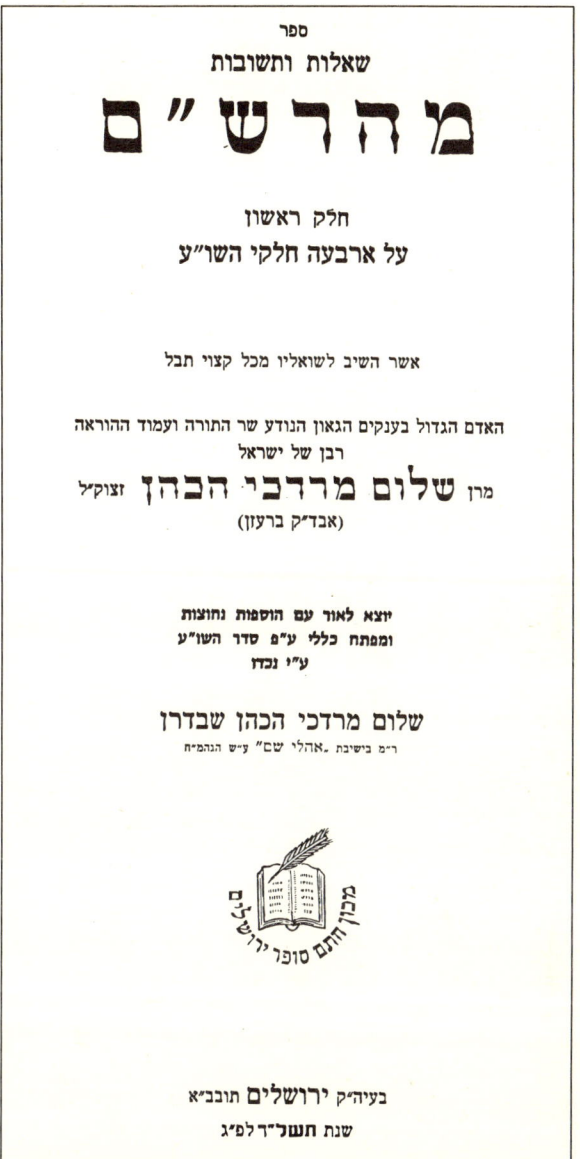

Title page of *She'eilot uTeshuvot Maharsham* by Rabbi Shalom Mordechai Schwadron of Brezan, responsa arranged to be consistent with the four parts of the *Shulchan Aruch*. Published in Jerusalem, 1974.

Responsum [*to Rabbi David Sperber of Ruspaliana, Hungary*]: . . . He certainly cannot force her to join him against her will, and he has no right to abandon her and free himself from his marriage obligations toward her, as long as he is capable of earning a living outside of Eretz Yisrael. If he is so weak that he is unable to teach any longer, he should move to Eretz Yisrael and then she is obligated to join him. But even if he feels that his energy is slackening and that eventually he will lose his ability to teach, since he is advancing in years, nevertheless, as long as he earns a living here whereas in Eretz Yisrael he is dependent on others, he cannot coerce his wife, and he has no right to release himself of his marital obligations.

Eating through a Tube on Yom Kippur
Teshuvot Maharsham, no. 1:124

Question: *A person's sickness prevents him from swallowing. The doctors in Kiev surgically inserted a tube in his throat and he receives his food through this tube. How should he conduct himself on the forthcoming Yom Kippur? The man's condition is very weakened; the doctors urge him to eat and drink a great deal in order to gain strength. There is hope that after some time his health will be restored and he will be able to eat normally again.*

Responsum [*to Rabbi Dov Ber Eliash of Kaminetz, Russia*]: . . . This case certainly cannot be considered a normal way of taking food . . . and eating forbidden foods in an abnormal manner is exempt. Thus, if he eats on Yom Kippur in an abnormal way, he is exempt. If it is possible for him to eat small quantities at intervals,[2] of course that would be best; otherwise he may take whatever he is served.

He Sold His Sins
Teshuvot Maharsham, no. 3:150

Question: *A man sold his sins to someone. The seller gave the buyer 30 silver rubles, and they shook hands to confirm the deal.*

Responsum [*to Rabbi Mendel Schwartz of Pomarin*]: . . . The sale was executed by means of transfer of money. In a sale, the buyer pays money to the seller. In this case the reverse took place, the seller paying the buyer. . . . Therefore, let the seller not take pleasure in the deal. Nevertheless, it is a sign of sincere remorse and it will help him in attaining atonement if he repents of his sins. . . . Let the buyer regret his evil deed. He should fear and worry for his soul, that he not be punished from Above. . . . They should nullify the entire transaction. . . . Still, he should be punished because he profaned the heavenly Name by making a joke out of the principle of Reward and Punishment. Every heart aches at hearing such jests.

Circumcise Moslem Children?
Teshuvot Maharsham, no. 7:93

Question: *A mohel who lives near a Moslem settlement has been asked by a Moslem father to circumcise his two sons.[3] He would pay him liberally for his services. Is the mohel permitted to perform the milah?*

Responsum [*to Rabbi Eliezer Moshe Horowitz of Cracow*]: You cite *Yoreh De'ah* 263:10 as well as Shach and Taz indicating that it is forbidden. . . . You also quote the Zohar that Yosef was punished because he circumcised the Egyptians. . . . But it is certain that the mohel is permitted to circumcise, for he is not performing the *milah* in fulfillment of Mohammed's command. . . . Therefore, he is permitted to circumcise these children, since otherwise he would suffer a serious loss.

Contribute Money for a Church?
Teshuvot Maharsham, no. 7:96

Question: *A Jew owns a village and by governmental decree he is required to pay a huge amount of money toward the local church. He refuses to pay. The church brought suit against him and rumor has it that the judge will sentence the Jew to pay the huge amount of 2,000 rubles. He asks whether he is permitted to negotiate a settlement to pay voluntarily a smaller amount.*

Responsum [*to Rabbi Yisrael Kara of Shtertz*]: . . . Since he knows that they are going to win the case and will attach his property for a larger amount, he is permitted to settle with them for a smaller amount so as to save his money.

The Butcher's Penalty
Teshuvot Maharsham, no. 1:61

Question: *A community penalized their butcher for certain indiscretions by forbidding him to open his store for a period of three months. If he were to violate this directive, his store would be closed permanently. He agreed to abide by the verdict. However, the gentile fast of Lent occurred during this three-month period, when no cattle are slaughtered by* shechitah, *since the Jewish community is very small and the gentiles don't consume any meat during the eight weeks of their fast. After the three months passed, the butcher reopened his store. Many people object, claiming that the weeks of Lent were not included in the three months penalty, since during these weeks no meat is sold anyway.*

Responsum [*to Rabbi Stockhammer of Leardina, Marmarosh, Hungary*]: An answer can be inferred from the following comment on *Bava Kama*: "We must ponder the question, when Bet Din sets a term for any given purpose, whether Shabbat and the festivals are included in that term. It seems to me that they are included, even though the activity for which Bet Din has appointed the term cannot be carried out on these days."

In our case, likewise, the days of the fast of the gentiles are included in the three months penalty.

The Borrowed Wedding Ring
Teshuvot Maharsham, no. 1:29

Question: *It happened in Talmitch that a bridegroom under the chupah [wedding canopy] gave his bride a ring that he had borrowed from a married woman. The woman lent him the ring as a* matanah al menat lehachazir—*a gift that is given with the understanding that it is to be returned. The marriage was consummated, but since then he has learned that there exists a doubt regarding the legality of the marriage. Should be marry her again?*

Responsum: The question revolves around the fact that the woman had no right to lend her ring without her husband's knowledge. However, in this case we may apply the rule that "a person is content if, without his knowledge, a mitzvah is done with his property." . . . Furthermore, according to *Even Ha'ezer*, no. 26, the consummation constitutes a de facto marriage. . . .

Even if the bride did not know that it was a borrowed ring, it is stated in *Teshuvot Chaim Shaal* 2:38, no. 54, that the *poskim* (halachic authorities) take a lenient view in this case. Therefore, in my opinion, he need not marry her again. . . . However, to be on the safe side, he should perform a second *kiddushin* before two witnesses, secretly, without any publicity. He should say that he is doing it merely to be exceedingly prudent, but certainly not as a halachic requirement.

RABBI AVRAHAM BORENSTEIN OF SOCHATCHOV—AVNEI NEZER
רבי אברהם בורנשטין מסוכצ׳וב — אבני נזר

born: Bendin, Poland, 1839
died: Sochatchov, Poland, 1910
Popularly known as Avnei Nezer, the title of his work.

The Avnei Nezer, son of Rabbi Zev Nachum Borenstein, rabbi of Biala, had been a child prodigy. When he was 13 years old he participated in his father's lectures for advanced talmudic scholars. The illustrious Kotzker Rebbe chose him as his son-in-law and he became one of the prominent chasidim of Rabbi Chanoch Henach of Alexander.

After serving as rabbi in a number of communities, he accepted the rabbinate of Sochatchov, a town west of Warsaw, where he remained for the rest of his life. He established an important yeshivah and responded to the numerous she'eilot that were sent to him from the entire country and beyond. His responsa were compiled into a nine-volume work, *Avnei Nezer*.[1] He also wrote the well-known *Eglei Tal*, a treatise on the thirty-nine labors that are forbidden on Shabbat. Rabbi Borenstein was one of the leading figures of Polish Jewry of the recent past.

Hand-Made or Machine-Made Matzot
Teshuvot Avnei Nezer, Orach Chaim, no. 2:536

Question: *What is your view regarding machine-made matzot?*

Responsum: [*to Congregation Adat Yeshurun of Dombrova*]: Your rabbi bitterly complained to me that you curtailed his salary and took other steps

Title page of *She'eilot uTeshuvot Avnei Nezer* by Rabbi Avraham Borenstein, the Sochatchover Rebbe and son-in-law of the towering chasidic leader, the Kotzker Rebbe, Rabbi Menachem Mendel. The eight letters following the names Avraham and Mendel are an abbreviation of *zecher tzaddik vekadosh livrachah lechayei haolam haba*, "of saintly and blessed memory for life everlasting." This was printed in Pietrkow, 1926.

that are detrimental to him, and that you did all this because he banned the use of machine-made matzot. Please be advised that I resent very much both the fact that you permitted the use of machine-made matzot and that you persecute your rabbi for forbidding them. Everyone knows that all the great rabbis of our country, the saintly Gerrer rebbe, the rabbis of Tchechanov and Kutno of blessed memory, positively prohibited them. How can anyone permit that which these personalities banned, although it must be said that there are many authorities who permit their use....

Therefore, your rabbi, who manned the breach and waged the battle for the mitzvah of God, should receive his full salary, now and in the future, and most certainly his salary should not be reduced. I admonish you in the most severe terms to reinstate the rabbi's salary and to abolish the bad custom of using machine-made matzot. You will be forgiven for the past and receive a rich reward for the future....

Wishing you peace and blessings.

Does a Hospital Room Need a Mezuzah?
Teshuvot Avnei Nezer, Yoreh De'ah, no. 2:380

Question: *Is a hospital room required to have a mezuzah, since there are patients who stay there for two or three months? Is it comparable to a room that was rented for more than thirty days, which is required to have a mezuzah?*

Responsum: ... In this case, the patients do not rent the hospital, they merely pay for their hospitalization. Thus, in no way can the hospital be considered as belonging to the patients who stay there....

According to most authorities, the reason that a rented house is required to have a mezuzah is that people think that the resident owns the house. This rationale does not apply to a hospital. For even if he owned the hospital, he would not be staying there if he were not sick. He is there because he is sick, for that is the purpose of a hospital, and no one will infer that he owns the hospital just because he is staying there....

Therefore, there is no basis for requiring a hospital to affix a mezuzah.

Buying Land in Eretz Yisrael
Teshuvot Avnei Nezer, Yoreh De'ah, no. 2:454

Question: *In recent times, many people have been buying land in Eretz Yisrael from which they can earn a livelihood within a few years. What is your view? Is this an obligation or not?*

Responsum: The early and later authorities have already decided that settling in Eretz Yisrael at the present time constitutes a mitzvah ... which is equivalent to all the mitzvot.... Now, if someone lives in Eretz Yisrael but his only source of income is the support he receives from abroad, then he still is not independent. This, it seems to me, is the reason that the great rabbis did not move to Eretz Yisrael. Nevertheless, even living under such conditions, it is a mitzvah ordained by the Torah. However, if by buying land in Eretz Yisrael they can earn a living from the land, then they are fulfilling the mitzvah to its fullest extent.

... To summarize: Halachically, if someone moves to Eretz Yisrael and has a source of income, then by living there he is fulfilling a mitzvah that is equivalent to all mitzvot, provided he settles there in an environment of observant Jews.... Through the observance of mitzvot in Eretz Yisrael, the *kedushah* (sanctity) and blessing will increase in the land. The more people observe mitzvot in Eretz Yisrael, the more blessing God will shower on its fruit. It is a mitzvah, even for people living outside Eretz Yisrael, to buy land there. Therefore, you, Jewish people of wealth, who have the means to bring this magnificent idea to reality, you are duty-bound to fulfill this great mitzvah. The reward for buying land in Eretz Yisrael will be immeasurably great.

Let us pray for God's help, that we may be successful and with the sound of rejoicing and thanks we shall go up to the House of God in the year *ki va ha'eit lechenenah.*[2] "For it is time to be gracious to her [Zion], for the appointed time has come" [Psalm 102:14].

Unfair Competition?
Teshuvot Avnei Nezer, Choshen Mishpat, no. 24

Question: *Concerning a man who for many years had the only store in town. Recently someone else* opened another store selling the same merchandise. The latter also owns a concession at the firing range, that is to say, he sells admission tickets allowing non-Jews to collect spent artillery shells after target practice. He threatens to sell these admission tickets only to those non-Jews who buy at his store.*

Responsum [*to Rabbi Eliezer Shemuel of Akinov*]: *You wrote me your reason for barring him from doing business. . . . However, it seems to me that if he retracts his threat and tells the non-Jews that he will sell them the admission tickets to collect shells even if they buy at the other store, and that he will not discriminate against people buying at his competitor's store, then we cannot prevent him from conducting his business.*

Of course, the storekeeper cannot be trusted on his word alone. He must sign an affidavit and, if possible, he should also make a deposition to that effect in front of two witnesses.

Lumber from a Demolished Church
Teshuvot Avnei Nezer, Choshen Mishpat, no. 99

Question: *In our town there was a church that has been torn down. A non-Jew bought the lumber from the church and used it in the construction of homes. We learned that there were two Jewish apostates involved in the building of the church. Thus, part of the church material belonged to these apostates, and as such it is forever barred from use. . . .*

Aside from the fact that we have a housing shortage, we are concerned about anti-Semitism, because the local priest said if we prohibit the houses he will declare a boycott against all Jewish shops. I tried to find a way to permit it.

Responsum [*after a thorough analysis of all the pertinent opinions*]: *. . . To summarize, once the church and its relics have lost their identity, then even the church articles belonging to a Jew are no longer forbidden.*

Sterilization
Teshuvot Avnei Nezer, Even Ha'ezer, no. 1:1

Question: *Concerning a woman whose life is endangered when giving birth. Her condition is becoming progressively worse with each delivery. The doctors warned her not to have marital relations unless she takes a medication that will render her sterile. Is she permitted to take this medication, seeing that her husband has not yet fulfilled the mitzvah of "Be fruitful and multiply," since they have three sons but no daughter?*[23]

Responsum [*to Rabbi Betzalel of Lubavitch*]: *. . . At any rate, it seems that there is no prohibition against taking the sterilization drug. She has no obligation to risk her life. . . . To summarize, I agree with you that she is permitted to take the medication that will render her sterile.*

RABBI YONATAN STEIF
ר׳ יהונתן שטייף

born: Gaya, Czechoslovakia, 1877
died: Brooklyn, New York, 1958

One of the great halachic authorities of the recent past, Rabbi Yonatan Steif received his talmudic schooling in the yeshivah of Pressburg, Hungary, under the leadership of Rabbi Simchah Bunam Sofer, known as Shevet Sofer, a grandson of the famous **Chatam Sofer**. Before long his brilliance was recognized, and he was asked to deliver talmudic discourses to advanced students. His first rabbinic position was in Guta, followed by a call to serve as rabbi of Ungvar, Czechoslovakia, where he remained for eleven years. In 1921 he was chosen to be the rabbi of the Hungarian capital Budapest and to serve as *Rosh Bet Din*.

During the Nazi deportations he was miraculously rescued as one of the 1,684 Hungarian Jews on the famous "Kastner train," which was taken via Bergen-Belsen to Switzerland as a result of Rabbi Michael Ber Weissmandl's ransom negotiations with Adolf Eichmann. Upon his arrival in the United States in 1946, he was immediately invited to be the spiritual leader of the fledgling congregation Adas Yere'im, founded by émigrés from Vienna.

Rabbi Yonatan's mastery of Talmud and Halachah was acclaimed by the entire spectrum of Torah-observant Jewry, and queries were directed at him by both chasidic and nonchasidic questioners. His kindness, modesty, and gentleness are remembered by all who knew and loved him.

Rabbi Yonatan Steif.

Must She Keep This Promise?
Teshuvot Rabbi Yonatan Steif, no. 80

Question: *Before their wedding, a boy and a girl solemnly pledged to one another never to remarry if one should predecease the other. But the husband has died and the wife wishes to marry a suitable man. Is she permitted to remarry?*

Responsum: Turei Zahav on *Yoreh De'ah* 231:3 explicitly states that a vow of this kind has no validity. . . . A man should not live without a wife, as it is written, "It is not good for man to be alone."[1] The same applies to a woman. Additionally, it can be argued that she made the pledge only to please her husband and preserve the harmony of her marriage. In a way, she was acting under duress.

We should also mention that according to the kabbalists, contrary to what one might expect, great benefit accrues to the soul of the deceased if his wife remarries. Therefore, it seems to me that the right thing for her to do is to visit her husband's grave and ask his forgiveness, if she decides to remarry. She should give charity in memory of her first husband's soul, and her pledge should be nullified. She is then permitted to remarry.

Should the Soldier Travel on Yomtov?
Teshuvot Rabbi Yonatan Steif, no. 160

Question: *A soldier is ordered to report for duty at his military base on Yomtov. Should he travel the day before Yomtov, thereby missing the opportunity of fulfilling the mitzvah of sukkah,*[2] *or should he rather stay at home, fulfill the mitzvah, and afterward travel to his destination on Yomtov? Would he be permitted to violate the Yomtov because of unavoidable government orders?*

Responsum: . . . It is preferable that he travel on the day before Yomtov. On Yomtov he is then exempt from the mitzvah of sukkah, because of circumstances beyond his control. Besides, we have a rule that wayfarers are exempt from the mitzvah of sukkah, and there is no mention anywhere that they are forbidden to start out on a trip even if this entails missing the mitzvah of sukkah. . . . The Torah exempts the soldier from the mitzvah of sukkah due to circumstances beyond his control.

Title page of *She'eilot uTeshuvot Rabbi Yonatan Steif.* The abbreviation following Rabbi Steif's name stands for *zeicher tzaddik vekadosh liverachah lechayei ha'olam haba,* "of blessed and sainted memory for life everlasting." The letters *yetzu* following "Brooklyn" are an abbreviation of *yishmereim tzuram vego'alam,* "May the Rock and the Redeemer protect her." Published in Brooklyn, New York, 1968.

Wearing Chasidic Garb?
Teshuvot Rabbi Yonatan Steif, no. 126

Question: *A person's father, while living in Poland, dressed in the chasidic manner. The father has changed to wearing modern-style clothes. Should the son continue to wear chasidic clothes as his forefathers did in Poland? By wearing modern clothes, isn't he violating the law of "Do not follow any of their customs"?*[3]

Responsum: . . . *Teshuvot Chatam Sofer, Orach Chaim* 159, explains that changing to modern-style clothes was not done for the purpose of emulating gentiles. It is therefore permissible. If it has become the accepted custom of Torah-observant Jews to dress according to the prevailing fashion, this does not constitute a transgression of "Do not follow any of their customs." Of course, if you are able to wear the type of clothing that traditionally was worn by *tzaddikim,* you should be commended.

Visiting the Sick by Telephone
Teshuvot Rabbi Yonatan Steif, no. 294

Question: *Do you fulfill the mitzvah of* bikur cholim, *visiting the sick, by calling the patient on the telephone?*

Responsum: There is no doubt that calling a sick person on the telephone is considered visiting him. **Rambam**[4] classifies the mitzvah of visiting the sick under the heading of "loving your neighbor." This being the case, any favor you do for your friend, even if you do it by telephone, is a manifestation of "loving your neighbor." Nevertheless, the essential mitzvah of visiting the sick should be done by personally going to see the patient.[5] Seeing the patient's suffering will stir your feelings more than merely talking to him on the telephone will. It will cause you to pray more fervently for him, and you will see more clearly what his needs are. . . .

Proper Pronunciation
Teshuvot Rabbi Yonatan Steif, no. 158

Question: *Is it essential that prayers be pronounced properly?*

Responsum: People who do not distinctly articulate their prayers rely on the Mishnah in *Berachot* 15a: "If you recited the Shema, enunciating the letters carelessly, you have fulfilled your duty." Because of the great familiarity with the *Shema*, it is very difficult to be careful to pronounce every word correctly. Nevertheless, it is a mitzvah to teach people to articulate the words distinctly, especially how to utter the Divine Name properly. . . . I have always been surprised to hear outstanding scholars from Poland omitting the letter *yud* when they utter the Divine Name. They probably heard it like that from their rabbis. We must try to find ways to justify them, and God forbid not to criticize them.

All the same, we certainly should instruct the chazzan to train himself to pronounce the Divine Name properly. He thereby honors God's great Name, blessed is He; and it is written, "for them that honor Me I will honor."[6]

The Torah Scroll Fell Down
Teshuvot Rabbi Yonatan Steif, no. 203

Question: *On Simchat Torah,*[7] *during the dancing with the Torah scrolls, one side of a scroll unwound and rolled to the floor. Some say that people inadvertently stepped on it. How can this sin be rectified?*

Responsum: Generally, when things of this nature happen it is customary that those who were present observe a fast day. . . . Perhaps God caused it to happen because they were not sufficiently respectful of the Torah, for example, by talking during the reading of the Torah or by leaving the synagogue during the reading. . . . They should correct their failings and accept upon themselves to mend their ways. They can then put their fears to rest. God will protect their homes and no harm or sickness will befall them. Serenity will reign within their walls. . . . Certainly the person who was carrying the Torah scroll when it fell should fast, and the congregation should at least give charity, each according to his means. Whoever knows that he stepped on the Torah scroll should fast or redeem his fast by giving charity, and God in His goodness will forgive us. The community should declare a public fast for anyone capable of fasting. People who are physically frail, and also women and the elderly, should redeem the fast by donating a few coins to charity. The contributions should be given to Torah institutions and to the poor people in Eretz Yisrael.

It also would be proper to have the Torah scroll inspected, since perhaps it was a sign from Heaven to have an error corrected in the writing of the Torah text.

RABBI MOSHE FEINSTEIN—REB MOSHE
הרב משה פיינשטיין — רב משה

born: Uzda, near Minsk, Russia, 1895
died: New York, 1986
Universally known as Reb Moshe.

Reb Moshe descended from a long line of famous talmudic scholars, and at an early age he excelled in his Torah studies. A child prodigy, blessed with an unfailing memory, he was chosen to deliver an original talmudic discourse at the dedication ceremonies of the yeshivah in Shklov, where he was a student under Rabbi Pesach Pruskin. He was only 12 years old at the time.

In 1920 the 25-year-old Reb Moshe was chosen rabbi of Luban. He valiantly led the struggle against religious persecution by the Communists. In 1936 he escaped from Stalinist terror and oppression and came to the United States, where he was invited to serve as *rosh yeshivah* of Yeshivat Tiferet Yerushalayim in New York. He held this office for the rest of his life.

Under his inspired leadership, the yeshivah flourished and guided thousands of rabbis and lay scholars to prominent positions in American Jewry.

Reb Moshe made his greatest impact on Torah life in his capacity as *poseik*. He was the universally acknowledged *gadol hador*, outstanding Torah scholar of our age. The most complex problems from near and far were addressed to him. With his encyclopedic knowledge and keen insight, he found answers to all the knotty questions that reached him.

His responsa reflect his vast erudition and his gentle and compassionate character. They were published in a six-volume work, entitled *Igrot Moshe* (Correspondence of Moshe).[1] His talmudic discourses have been published under the title of *Dibrot Moshe*, and recently a penetrating commentary on the Torah has appeared, entitled *Darash*

Rabbi Moshe Feinstein.

Moshe.[2] His responsa contain a number of landmark decisions that have affected the everyday life of Torah Jewry. They are accepted as authoritative Halachah by the widest spectrum of Jewish circles, and the expression, "Reb Moshe *paskened* . . . ," "Reb Moshe decided as follows . . . ," has become proverbial. A biography entitled *Reb Moshe* by Rabbi S. Finkelman has been published by Mesorah Publications.[3]

In 1962, after the death of Rabbi Aharon Kotler, the preeminent Torah scholar and leader of his day, the mantle of leadership fell on Reb Moshe's shoulders. The unassuming and humble man reluctantly took on the demanding task. With formidable wisdom, kindness, and unwavering faith, he guided Torah Jewry through turbulent times. He lives on in the hearts of an entire generation who knew and loved him.

Heart Transplants
Igrot Moshe, Yoreh De'ah, no. 174

Tammuz 1968

Question: *Would you please state your view concerning heart transplantation?*

Responsum: Regarding the recent development that several doctors have begun to transplant the heart of one person into a patient suffering from heart disease, I wish to give a clear and unequivocal answer that leaves no room for debate or argumentation.

The heart transplants that doctors have begun to perform of late clearly constitute the taking of two lives. They intentionally kill the donor, who is still alive, not only by the halachic definition of death, but even according to the doctors—for there are some who tell the truth and say that the donor is still alive. But deplorably, they are not concerned with this life because he has only a few hours or days to live. They also intentionally kill the heart patient. It is a known fact that many heart patients continue to live for many days and even years. By removing the heart and replacing it with a donor heart, the doctors have caused all patients to die within a few days, most within hours, and a few within a few days. And even regarding the patient in South Africa who is still alive six months after his transplant, they all agree that he cannot survive much longer. I am astonished about the governments of the various countries, that they permit these evil physicians to kill two persons each time, noting that not one patient has survived. They should have been dealt with as unmitigated murderers. For although the patient agreed to the operation, he did so in error, being misled by these evil physicians. Besides, the patient's agreement is

Title page of *Igrot Moshe* by Rabbi Moshe Feinstein, foremost halachic authority of our generation, "Rosh Yeshivah of Mesivta Tiferet Yerushalayim, New York; formerly of Luban, district of Minsk, Russia." Published in 1960 in New York.

worthless, since no one is permitted to commit suicide.

This responsum should be publicized in this exact wording, without additions or omissions.

Buying Insurance
Igrot Moshe, Orach Chaim, no. 2:111

Marcheshvan 1964

Question: *Is there any benefit or possible wrongdoing in buying insurance? Does it exhibit a lack of trust in God's ability to make a person wealthy so that he will have a large estate to leave to his heirs?*

Responsum: Man must strive to earn his livelihood. He may not say, "If I don't do anything, God will provide somehow." How does he know that he has earned this great merit? Besides, it is forbidden to rely on miracles. Although man should be mindful that whatever he earns from his labor derives from God, it is God's decree that He provides a livelihood only when it is earned through labor, as it says, "By the sweat of your brow you will eat bread."[4] . . . And so an insurance policy is like any business that one does to provide for his family. It is permitted to buy a policy because it is a form of providing for your family.

Since God enlightened the recent generations to design the concept of insurance so that people should have money for their old age and heirs, it is beneficial and appropriate to obtain it for all God-fearing and observant Jews who place their trust in God. The same holds true for fire, theft, and automobile insurance; there is no question of lack of faith.

Auditor for the Internal Revenue Service
Igrot Moshe, Yoreh De'ah, no. 159

Adar 1947

Question: *Is it permissible to accept a position as auditor for the Internal Revenue Service, because one may discover an offense by someone? Wouldn't informing the government be an act of betrayal, since the government metes out a harsher sentence than that imposed by Torah law?*

Responsum [*to Mr. David E. Bass*]: It is clear that whoever audits these books will find the offense. Furthermore, if this person does not take the position, the IRS will find another auditor, so that the lawbreaker's loss is no greater if the man accepts the position than if he did not, and someone else would take his place. Thus, by taking the job, he does not inflict any damage, and there is no prohibition involved.

Moreover, the auditor should consider that most of the returns he examines are correct. It is only a possibility that he finds a fraudulent tax return. We cannot forbid him to accept a job on the outside chance that he finds wrongdoing. . . . And if he does find an offense, he is obligated to report the truth and testify to facts of the case. It would bring dishonor on God's name if he did not testify.

Forced Baptism
Igrot Moshe, Yoreh De'ah, no. 129

Nisan 1961

Question: *A woman and her daughters were kept in hiding with a non-Jewish family during the years of the Holocaust. After they had stayed with them awhile, the non-Jew forced them to convert to Christianity, threatening to betray them to the Germans to be killed if they refused to convert. Unable to face up to this grave challenge, the woman agreed and was accepted into the Christian faith without the services of a cleric. The non-Jew himself sprinkled water on her and took her and the children to church. Immediately after the liberation they proudly returned to Judaism and they are fully observant Jews. Do they have to undergo any special procedures?*

Responsum [*to Rabbi Moshe Leiter*]: They are not considered apostates; they are not persons who abandoned their faith. . . . If she is in good health, it is recommended that she fast each year on that day, if she remembers the date. If she doesn't, she should fast on any day she wishes. The daughters, who were small at the time, do not have to fast, but they should strive to live according to the Torah way of life and to sanctify the name of God by setting a good example. That will be their atonement from He "who desires repentance."

A Statue for President Kennedy
Igrot Moshe, Yoreh De'ah, no. 54

Tevet 1964

Question: *The municipal authorities of a city want to erect a statue in honor of President Kennedy, who was assassinated. They invited the local rabbi, as the leader of the Jewish community, to participate in the memorial committee and to raise funds for this purpose in the Jewish community. Is there a halachic objection to this?*

Responsum [*to Rabbi Yitzchak Isaac Tzorn*]: The prohibition against making a statue, as set forth in *Yoreh De'ah* 141:4, is applicable only if the statue is for personal use. In this case the rabbi is permitted to participate for the sake of maintaining good relations with our neighbors, but even more so because he expresses thereby his high regard for the presidency. In summary, I do not see any reason for prohibiting this.

Teaching Mythology
Igrot Moshe, Yoreh De'ah, no. 3:53

Nisan 1960

Question: *Is a person who is employed as a teacher of ancient history permitted to lecture on pagan religion and mythology? Is it subject to the prohibition of "Do not turn to false gods"?*[5]

Responsum [*to Rabbi Yehudah Parnes*]: If he must teach a course of their religions and mythology, he should present it in a way that the students understand that it is meaningless nonsense, that any rational person has nothing but contempt for the foolishness these people believed in. There may even be some benefit in this. The students will begin to understand that even today there are ideologies that many people believe in that in reality are absurd, yet people follow them blindly; just as in the ancient past many generations erred by believing in paganism and millions of people adhered to it. Only the Jewish people, who were few in number, recognized the truth, accepted the Torah, and kept it through the ages. They gave their life for it, and the world ridiculed and despised them. Today all the nations of the world realize that Israel possessed the truth all along.

But we certainly may not lecture non-Jews about the religion they practice today in the country under whose protection we live in peace and tranquility, by the grace of God, and for whose welfare we must pray. Nevertheless, teaching about the irrational beliefs of the people of antiquity is a good thing and will have beneficial results.

Paper Cups for Kiddush?
Igrot Moshe, Orach Chaim, no. 39

Nisan 1968

Question: *Is it permitted to use paper cups when reciting* kiddush?[6]

Responsum [*to Mr. Aryeh Leib Bobbins*]: According to *Tosafot Berachot* 50 (listed under *Modim*), the cup used for *kiddush* should be in perfect condition. Thus, we are required to use a graceful cup for *kiddush*. A paper cup, which is a disposable item to be used only one time, lacks dignity and surely is not an appropriate vessel for *kiddush*. However, if no other cup is available, perhaps you may be lenient.

RABBI MORDECHAI YAAKOV BREISCH
רבי מרדכי יעקב ברייש

born: Skul, Galicia (Austria), 1895
died: Zurich, Switzerland, 1976

Even as a young child Mordechai Yaakov Breisch displayed an insatiable hunger for Torah. Growing into manhood, he studied under Rabbi Meir Arik of Tarnow and became a dedicated chasid of the Belzer Rebbe. After his marriage in 1920, he moved to Lemberg, and in 1928 he received a call to lead the congregation of Eastern European Jews in Duisburg, Germany. With the rise of the Nazis he was one of the first to feel the full fury of their hatred. He was beaten to within an inch of his life and was paraded along the main street of Duisburg, and then, in the presence of thousands, his beard was cut off. By God's grace, a high official rescued him from the howling mob and he was able to escape.

He emigrated to Switzerland and in 1934 was appointed rabbi of Agudat Achim, the congregation of Eastern European Jews in Zurich. He held this position until the end of his life. These were his most productive years; with great wisdom and tact, he exerted an overpowering influence on the community, raising its standards of observance and scholarship. In 1960, largely through his efforts and inspiration, the community opened a spacious new building to house the synagogue, day school, and Bet Midrash. He was recognized as an outstanding *poseik* and received inquiries on complex halachic problems from communities all over the world.

A compilation of his responsa, published under the title of *Chelkat Yaakov*,[1] contains numerous questions arising from advances in science, technology, and medicine—questions he solved ingeniously by finding parallels in the writings of the classic codes and responders. A measure of Rabbi Breisch's greatness is the fact that his decisions are accepted by the entire spectrum of Torah-observant Jewry.

Rabbi Mordechai Yaakov Breisch.

With Left Arm in a Cast, Where Should Arm Tefillin Be Placed?
Teshuvot Chelkat Yaakov, no. 2:43

Question: *A person broke his left arm and it is in a cast. Should he put his arm tefillin on his right arm?*[2]

Responsum [*to Yechezkel Halberstam of Tchechanov, now in Brooklyn*]: Clearly, he should place his arm tefillin on his left arm on top of the cast, and not on his right arm. The disqualification of the right arm is derived from "It shall be as a sign on *your hand*"[3] [Hebrew *yadechah*, which is written with a superfluous *hei* at the end of the word; our rabbis interpret this as meaning *yad keha*, the weaker hand, which is the left hand]. But the Gemara does not mention a cast or any other intervention as being unsuitable.... Thus, in our case, it is clear that he must place the tefillin on his left arm, even when it is in a cast, but not on his right arm, for then he would not have fulfilled the mitzvah at all.

Fertility Drug Made of Blood
Teshuvot Chelkat Yaakov, no. 2:5–6

Question: *Doctors can now administer to childless couples a drug made of blood plasma, which is said to promote conception. May this drug be taken?*[4]

Responsum [*to Rabbi Shemuel Zev Roth, Antwerp, Belgium*]: ... In this case we rely on the view of the Shach[5] to permit it.... In my opinion, in light of the great importance of the mitzvah of procreation of the Jewish people after the Holocaust, and in light of the harmful effects infertility has on harmonious family life, it is the duty of all rabbis to exert themselves to permit this, in keeping with the principles of the Torah and the *Shulchan Aruch*.

Take Appetite Depressant Pill before Yom Kippur?
Teshuvot Chelkat Yaakov, no. 2:58

Question: *The doctors have developed a pill that, when taken in the morning, prevents hunger pangs all day. Each capsule contains about two hundred small time-release granules, which desensitize the hunger feelings. Is it permitted to swallow such a capsule shortly before Yom Kippur so as not to suffer from hunger during the fast? Do we have to be concerned that the Torah states, "You must afflict yourselves"?*[6]

Responsum [*to Rabbi Yechezkel Halberstam of Tchechanov, now in Brooklyn*]: In my opinion this is plainly permissible. Since the capsule is taken before the onset of Yom Kippur and not on Yom

Title page of *Chelkat Yaakov* by Rabbi Mordechai Yaakov Breisch of Zurich, Switzerland, "Responsa dealing primarily with current problems arising from advances in science and technology as they affect our daily life." The letters before Zurich are an abbreviation of *av bet din*, Chief Rabbi. The letters after Zurich mean *Yishmereim tzuram vego'alam*, "May the Rock and the Redeemer protect her." Printed in Jerusalem, 1951.

Kippur itself, it is comparable to eating all one can take before Yom Kippur so that the time of digestion will last longer. As long as the food has not been digested, you don't feel hungry. Would it enter anyone's mind to prohibit this? The present case is analogous to this. The capsule contains tiny granules. The outer shell dissolves in the digestive juices of the stomach, releasing the small granules, which consecutively counteract the hunger feelings. The same happens with food. Some foods will digest faster than others. It certainly is not forbidden to eat foods that are slow to digest.... On the contrary, Rashi states (*Yoma* 81b), "Prepare yourself on the ninth of Tishri so that you will be able to fast on the tenth (Yom Kippur)." And in *Rosh Hashanah* 9a it says, "The more you eat before Yom Kippur, the better." Care should be taken, however, to make certain that the capsule does not contain any forbidden ingredients.

A Soldier's Dilemma
Teshuvot Chelkat Yaakov, no. 1:37-38

Question: *In 1940, Rosh Hashanah occurred on Thursday and Friday. As a result of the wartime conditions, many Jews were in the army in places where there are no prayer services and where they cannot listen to the sounding of the* shofar. *The military authorities grant them a furlough to return home for the two days of Rosh Hashanah on condition that each reports back to his unit on the day after Rosh Hashanah, which is Shabbat. Is a soldier permitted to go on furlough for two days in order to fulfill the mitzvot of Rosh Hashanah if he is forced to desecrate the Shabbat by having to travel back to base?*

Responsum: [After citing all pertinent sources, Rabbi Breisch offers a number of reasons why the soldier is permitted to accept the furlough, concluding:] There is yet another reason to permit him to accept the furlough: Because he may not have to return on Shabbat—perhaps the war will end and there will be peace in the world, or he might become sick. Therefore, the desecration of Shabbat is not certain. In view of all the aforementioned reasons, he is definitely permitted to take this furlough.

Guilt Feelings over a Brother's Death during the Holocaust
Teshuvot Chelkat Yaakov, no. 1:143

Question: *It happened during the Holocaust that the accursed Nazis evacuated a concentration camp since they feared the approaching American army. They hounded the emaciated inmates, goading them to march at top speed to prevent them from being liberated. It was a death march in which those who were too weak to continue were shot on the spot. Many times, during one of the brief rest stops, a prisoner would fall asleep and would not immediately respond to the marching orders. Instantly, the murderers would put a bullet through his head. This prompted the prisoners to devise a buddy system, taking turns sleeping so that one could wake up the other.*

One man, a Torah-observant Jew, was in this march together with his younger brother (may God avenge his blood). During a rest stop he told his brother to take a nap; he would watch over him and wake him up. However, he too fell asleep. And when the cries of "Los! Los!" (German for "Get moving!") were heard, in the scramble and the confusion he lined up with the others, and instantly the column began to move. When he remembered his brother, it was too late to go back as he surely would have been shot. He never heard from his brother again, and he is certain that they killed him. For the last thirteen years he has been reproaching himself for his brother's death, and he is depressed with feelings of guilt. He wants to know whether or not he must atone for this.

Responsum [*to Rabbi Avraham Meir Israel, formerly of Hunyad, Romania, now in New York*]: His guilt feelings stem from two sources: (1) that he failed to wake up his brother when he was aroused from his sleep, and (2) that he did not go back to wake him up after he had joined the column. The fact that he told him to take a nap is of no consequence. The brother was so exhausted that he would have gone to sleep anyway. Proof of this is the fact that he himself fell asleep.

Throughout halachic literature, the *poskim* discuss the question of whether forgetting is due to negligence or is an unintentional, unavoidable circumstance.... In our case, where he blames himself for not waking his brother, it is abundantly clear that this was not due to negligence. We are dealing here with prisoners who were overtired, weak, and totally exhausted from the long march and who were overcome by sleep; of course their sleep is an unavoidable circumstance. And when they are suddenly aroused from their sleep, their mind is not clear at first, and their actions are unavoidable.

Regarding his concern for not having gone back to wake him up after having joined the column.... This is analogous to the dispute in *Bava Metzia* 62a between Rabbi Akiva and Ben Peturei: "Two people are lost in the desert; one of them has a jug of water. If one drinks the water, he will make it to safety; if they share the water they will both die. Ben Peturei said, 'Let them both drink and die.' Rabbi Akiva replied, it is written, 'Let your brother live alongside you' (Leviticus 25:36)."[7] The implication is, "Your life takes precedence over your brother's life." Since the halachah is decided according to Rabbi Akiva, he surely should not have jeopardized his life....

I want to conclude by stating that in the present case the brother should have no pangs of conscience since this leads to grief and despair, which is an even greater sin, for it distresses him and prevents him from serving God. For we must serve God with gladness.

To remove any trace of guilt, let him make an effort to do the kind of mitzvot that relate to this case. For example, let him refrain from humiliating other people, since this is tantamount to shedding blood. If he can have children, he should not abstain, since this too is equal to bloodshed. Let him raise an orphan in his house. Let him support Torah scholars according to his means, as it is written, "The soul of a man is the lamp of God" (Proverbs 20:27). Let his heart rejoice in the fulfillment of the mitzvot of God.

Question Concerning Jewish Army Chaplain
Teshuvot Chelkat Yaakov, no. 2:76

Question: *A Jewish chaplain has a non-Jewish aide who assists him in the performance of his military duties. A Torah-observant soldier asked the chaplain to be appointed to this position. The chaplain is eager to assign the soldier to the post, since this would afford the soldier the opportunity to eat kosher food, put on tefillin, and pray every day. On the other hand, it is inevitable that occasionally the chaplain will have to order him to drive on Shabbat or to violate the Shabbat in other ways. Still, he would desecrate the Shabbat to a far lesser degree than on his regular army duties. The chaplain wants to know if he is permitted to appoint him as his aide and command him to violate the Shabbat when the need arises.*

Responsum: ... In summation, I want to state that not only is the chaplain permitted to appoint the Jewish aide, but he is thereby performing a mitzvah, saving him from transgressing many Torah laws. ... The chaplain should be careful that the aide performs for him on Shabbat only such labors that are required by the army, but no optional work. ...

RABBI YITZCHAK YAAKOV WEISS— MINCHAT YITZCHAK
הרב יצחק יעקב וייס — מנחת יצחק

born: Dohina, Galicia, 1902
died: Jerusalem, 1989

Rabbi Weiss, also called Dayan (Judge) Weiss, was one of the foremost *poskim* of our generation. Before World War II he served as *Av Bet Din* (Chief Judge) of Grosswardein, Romania, and after the war he was a member of a special Bet Din convened to deal with *agunah* problems. In 1949 he was elected head of the Bet Din of Manchester, England, a post he held for twenty years. In 1972 Dayan Weiss was called to lead the Bet Din of the Eidah Chareidit community in Jerusalem, a position he maintained until his death on June 14, 1989.

He gained great renown for his brilliance and erudition, and he received halachic queries from all parts of the world. His responsa reflect the vastness of his talmudic knowledge and his prodigious familiarity with the writings of early and recent *poskim*. These responsa, all of which are contained in the nine-volume set of *Minchat Yitzchak*,[1] include decisions on many halachic applications to problems arising from modern technology and medicine, as well as decisions on burning questions that evolved in the wake of the Holocaust. He was recognized as a leading *poseik* by the full range of the Torah world, regardless of political or ideological orientation.

Rabbi Yitzchak Yaakov Weiss.

Tefillin on Tattooed Arm?
Minchat Yitzchak, no. 3:11

Question: *A man, while serving in the military, had his left arm tattooed, and in the place where the arm tefillin are put there is an image of a naked woman.*

The design cannot be removed. Now he is a baal teshuvah *(returnee to Torah observance) and has begun to pray. He wants to know if he may place the tefillin on his left arm, on this image, or should he put it on his right arm?*[2]

Responsum: In my opinion, he should put the tefillin on his left arm. Even if the image extends over the entire biceps, a large part of it can be kept covered continually, and he should expose only the area where the hand tefillin is placed, in such a way that the entire image is not quite visible. He should have the tefillin made in the smallest size that is halachically permitted. While reciting the *berachah*, he should keep the entire area covered. I have heard it said that it is possible to have a tattoo removed by an expert.

Incident in a Concentration Camp
Minchat Yitzchak, no. 6:55

Question: *Concerning a tragic incident that happened to the questioner during the Holocaust, in a concentration camp in the accursed Germany. He had a Jewish* kapo, *an overseer, appointed by the evil S.S. to supervise the work [of the prisoners]. Most of these* kapos, *regrettably, were vicious bullies who beat their unfortunate brothers without mercy. Many actually killed prisoners. The questioner one time was beaten by a* kapo *to within an inch of his life. Thereupon he went and informed against the* kapo *to the S.S. They put this* kapo *into prison and beat him to death. The* kapo's *death was thus a direct result of the man's denunciation. Now, many years later, the man has terrible pangs of conscience, fearing that he is guilty of the* kapo's *death. Does he need atonement?*

Responsum: . . . The man who beat him continually struck his fellow Jews savagely. He also hit the questioner to within an inch of his life. Thus, the *kapo* is considered a *rodeif*[3] under the laws set forth in *Choshen Mishpat* 12 and 425:1. If the questioner had not denounced him, he would have continued his evil deeds.

On the other hand, we must consider that the *kapo* was forced to do this by the German *resha'im* (evildoers), may their name be blotted out, in line with their policy of ordering one man to kill another, and then they would kill the killer.

The questioner should accept on himself an act of repentance that a great *tzaddik* will outline for him. May the Holy One, blessed is He, protect us that we will never have to ask such questions and that we will merit the coming of Mashiach, speedily, in our days.

Girl Born of Non-Jewish Mother
Minchat Yitzchak, no. 7:90

Question: *After the end of World War II a Jewish man married a non-Jewish woman and had a daughter by her. The mother died in childbirth. He became a* baal teshuvah *(returnee to Torah observance) and married an observant woman, so his daughter was raised in a strictly Orthodox atmosphere. She is a God-fearing girl, but she has not been told of her origins. Thus she has not undergone conversion with* tevilah *(immersion in a mikveh).*[4]

Now she is engaged to be married. Her relatives and friends say that if she should be informed that she has to undergo conversion, the shock might affect her health, since she has a very sensitive dis-

Title page of *She'eilot uTeshuvot Minchat Yitzchak* by Rabbi Yitzchak Yaakov Weiss, Rabbi of Manchester, England, and Jerusalem. This volume was printed in London in 1951.

position, not to mention the risk that her engagement might be broken. Should she be told?

Responsum: [After citing all the opinions of early and later authorities on similar cases, Rabbi Weiss concludes:] Because of all these reasons, I would not permit her to get married unless she is told that she is not Jewish and she is converted according to Halachah and declares her acceptance of the yoke of mitzvot before a Bet Din, and undergoes immersion in a mikveh.

Faith Healers
Minchat Yitzchak, no. 6:80

Question: *Please forgive me for asking, but I need an answer very urgently. I have learned of a healer in Manila, the Philippines—the cleric, Reverend Tony Agapo, who cures all diseases and plagues and performs surgery without making incisions, just with his hands. It is incredible, but it is a fact. He has healed thousands of people in this manner without using instruments or medicines. After the operation, he moves his hand over the incision a few times, and no scar is visible.*

My question is whether a patient who is seriously ill with an incurable disease may go to this cleric to be healed, since his therapy is against nature, and there is the suspicion that he mentions the name of his deity. Possibly it is forbidden, even to save a life. But with this cleric we don't know whether he uses religious incantations or sorcery. He does not speak about religion; he merely says that one has to believe in God, that He is a true healer. Please answer quickly. It is very urgent.

Responsum: [After a thorough and lengthy analysis of the she'eilah, he concludes:] All authorities agree that it is forbidden, even in a life-threatening situation. May the Healer of the sick protect us that we should not need any of this. "You must remain totally faithful to God your Lord" (Deuteronomy 18:13). We should use only qualified physicians, prayer to God, and charity. These will surely help.

P.S. I received a letter from Rabbi Meir Katz in which he enclosed a letter from the above-mentioned cleric under the letterhead "Spiritual Church of Science," in which the cleric writes that he is only a tool of the "Lord," and that we see in him the power of the "Lord," and that part of his therapy is to use the patient's faith in the "Lord." Rabbi Katz adds that although he does not specifically mention who is meant by the "Lord," it is clear that it refers to the founder of their religion. How right were our sages in forbidding us to be cured by a cleric in an unnatural way, even in life-threatening situations. May God send a complete recovery to all the sick in Israel.

Exaggerations at Fund-Raising Appeals
Minchat Yitzchak, no. 3:97

Question: *Regarding fund-raising appeals where the donations are announced. Is one allowed to announce an amount that is greater than what he intends to donate, for the purpose of inducing someone else to give more?*

Responsum: This is clearly forbidden. The Gemara in *Sukkah* 29a states that people's possessions are confiscated by the government in Divine retribution for four sins, one of them being "for publicly announcing charitable contributions and not paying them." Maharsha[5] explains this to mean that prominent members of the community announce a large amount and don't pay all of it with the excuse that they meant only to make others give. . . . So you see, this has been the custom since time immemorial, and our sages frowned on it, including it among the four failings for which a severe punishment is exacted.

Conflict between Yeshivah Students and Parents
Minchat Yitzchak, no. 9:103

Question: *Concerning a number of yeshivah students who are studying diligently, whose parents urge them to leave the yeshivah and enter college or the university. The parents offer the excuse that they are concerned about their sons' material well-being, hoping that they will get lucrative positions. Must the students heed their parents' wishes?*

Responsum: It is clear that the sons are not obligated to listen to their parents. I direct my remarks to the students and say to them, "Don't listen to your parents in matters that concern the foundation of our religion and the basis of Torah. Parents have no right to interfere with their sons' Torah studies."
... To the parents I say, "Please have mercy on the souls of your children who study the pure Torah. Don't make them interrupt their studies, on which the existence of the whole world depends. Through its strength we shall leave this bitter exile.... It is a source of great merit for you if your children study Torah. You will share the reward that is set aside for the learners of Torah and their supporters. Together, may we see the light of Mashiach."

Report Careless Drivers to the Police?
Minchat Yitzchak, no. 8:148

Question: *Is it permissible to report to the police a careless driver who threatens the lives of other people? Generally, speeders are fined or their driver's license is suspended for a period of time, as a means of teaching them not to endanger human life.*

Responsum: The **Rambam** in paragraph 9 of *Hilchot Choveil uMazik* (The Laws Regarding Bodily Harm) states that you are forbidden to denounce a Jew—even a sinner—to the non-Jewish authorities, even if this person caused you a great deal of distress. But in paragraph 11 the Rambam qualifies this statement, stating that you are permitted to denounce to the non-Jewish authorities anyone who causes distress to the entire community. ... It is clearly evident to what extent the sages wanted to protect the community against sorrow and distress. ... It is clear that a driver who exceeds the speed limit, and thus cannot stop his car when it is necessary, has the legal status of *rodeif*, "a pursuer with the intent to kill." If, after he has been duly warned, he continues to drive recklessly you are permitted to report him to the police. The same applies to drivers who do not obey traffic signs or who pass other cars in a hazardous fashion, or who drive without having obtained a driver's license. Although they do not willfully endanger other people's lives, they are in the category of *rodeif*. ...

This includes also drivers who park their cars in a way that poses a hazard to pedestrians or who park on the sidewalk, thereby forcing pedestrians to walk in the street. These are classified as people "who dig a hole in a public domain," and who are liable according to the *Shulchan Aruch, Choshen Mishpat* 410. It is a mitzvah to remove any public hazard, and many *poskim* state that failure to remove such perils is a violation of the Torah law, "Do not allow a dangerous situation to remain in your house" (Deuteronomy 22:5).

However, before a driver is reported to the authorities he should be given a warning.

RABBI MENASHE KLEIN—UNGVARER RAV
רבי מנשה קליין

born: Irlava, near Ungvar, Czechoslovakia, 1925

Rabbi Menashe Klein is a descendant of Rabbi Yomtov Lipmann Heller who wrote the famous commentary *Tosefot Yomtov* on the Mishnah, and of the illustrious kabbalist and philosopher, the Maharal of Prague. He studied Torah in the Yeshivah of Ungvar under Rabbi Kahane and Rabbi Chaim Tzvi Mannheimer, a disciple of the **Chatam Sofer.** In 1944, while still a youngster, he was carried off to Auschwitz where his body and soul were seared by the agony and horror that the maniacal Nazi tormentors inflicted on him. There in the dungeon of death he forged a bond of friendship with a young man who would one day become the winner of the Nobel Peace Prize, Elie Wiesel. It is a friendship that has endured until today. Miraculously surviving his experience at the hands of the cruel enemy, he was liberated in Buchenwald by the American forces led by General Dwight D. Eisenhower. Arriving in the United States in 1946, he entered the yeshivah of the Klausenburger Rebbe, Rabbi Yekutiel Halberstam, himself a Holocaust survivor, who granted him *semichah* (rabbinical ordination). He also studied under two of the foremost halachists of our age, Rabbi Aharon Kotler and Rabbi Yisrael Kanievsky, popularly called "The Steipler." An eminent Torah scholar, chasidic leader, and spellbinding orator, Rabbi Klein began to attract a wide following; with his warmhearted personality he soon established a flourishing congregation and a yeshivah for advanced talmudic studies, named Yeshivah Bet She'arim, in the Borough Park section of Brooklyn, New York. On a hill overlooking Jerusalem he built a large complex of modern apartment buildings for Torah scholars, named Kiriat Ungvar, perpetuating the memory of the victims of the Holocaust from that city. An

Rabbi Menashe Klein.

imposing synagogue and study hall in the center of the neighborhood were consecrated by Elie Wiesel as a tribute to his slain parents.

Rabbi Menashe Klein, a world-renowned *poseik*, daily receives she'eilot from all parts of the world, and dispenses counsel and aid to all those who seek it. Four thousand of his teshuvot have been published in a ten-volume work entitled *Mishneh Halachot*,[1] many dealing with halachic problems arising from the advances in science and technology. A man of indomitable spirit, he personifies the victory of the Jewish people over the forces of darkness—the burning bush that will not be consumed.

Use Postage Stamp on Which God's Name Appears?
Mishnah Halachot, nos. 5:119 and 5:121

Question: *The United States Postal Service has issued a postage stamp inscribed with the words, "In the beginning God. . . ." Are we permitted to discard an envelope on which this stamp has been placed? Should we be concerned that by using such stamps we cause the Divine Name to be erased when the stamp is cancelled?*[2]

Responsum: . . . Of course, if you can be careful not to throw such envelopes into the trash, you are to be commended, but those who cannot be vigilant about it are not committing a sin. . . .

According to the postal law, each stamp must be cancelled, and thereby the Divine Name is erased. The questioner wants to compare the problem concerning this stamp to a case in *Igrot Moshe* by Rabbi **Moshe Feinstein** where he rules that it is forbidden to bring tefillin to a patient who is suffering from a contagious disease and is under quarantine in a hospital. He bases his ruling on the fact that by law all articles in the possession of such patients must be incinerated. Therefore, bringing tefillin to the hospital amounts to intentionally destroying them. . . . The questioner contends that similarly, by using the stamp imprinted with God's name, you cause that name to be blotted out when the stamp is cancelled. . . .

Conversely it can be argued that the burning of the tefillin is beyond the patient's control. It is not the patient who is burning them, it is the non-Jewish worker at the hospital incinerator who is doing it. Certainly, when the patient is fulfilling the mitzvah of tefillin, he should not be concerned that eventually they will be destroyed. . . . And if this patient is a man who never in his life has put on tefillin and now that he is sick wants to repent, should we allow him, God forbid, to die without ever having put on tefillin? And even if he is a man who regularly puts on tefillin, should we prevent him from continuing to do so because of a gentile decree? . . . When we were in the German (may their name be blotted out) concentration camps, we carried our tefillin with us and we did all we could to put them on whenever possible. Yet we were fully convinced that if they would catch us they would destroy the tefillin. This did not deter us from finding ways of putting them

Title page of *Mishneh Halachot*, responsa by Rabbi Menashe Klein of Ungvar, *rosh yeshivah* of Yeshivah Bet She'arim, Brooklyn, New York. Published in Brooklyn in 1983.

on—and how many beatings did we suffer for it. But no one dreamt of refraining from putting on tefillin because they might be burned or disgraced. To the contrary, when we find ourselves in trouble and distress we must do all in our power to fulfill this mitzvah, and if the non-Jews treat the tefillin with contempt, God will avenge the insult.

Teshuvot Achiezer 3:36 states that it is not forbidden to erase the Divine Name if it is written in the vernacular, but we may not cause the name to be disgraced.... Therefore, in the present case, the stamp should not be used. Although the Divine Name written in English may be erased or burned, we may not cause it to be disgraced.

Letter with Uncancelled Stamp
Mishnah Halachot, no. 6:288

Question: *Are you allowed to use a stamp that erroneously was not cancelled? I heard that whenever the Chafetz Chaim[3] sent a letter through a messenger, he tore up a stamp so as not to cause a loss to the government.*

Responsum: You cannot cite the incident with the Chafetz Chaim as an analogy to the present case. When the Chafetz Chaim used a messenger to deliver a letter, he was not required to pay the government, for the government does not demand that anyone forwarding a letter must buy a stamp. It only requires a letter sent through the mail to have a stamp affixed to it. The saintly Chafetz Chaim tore the stamps only to sanctify the name of God.

In our case, if someone sent a letter, [after] placing a stamp on it, the stamp represents the price for the delivery of the letter, and the sender received the value for his stamp. The fact that the stamp was not cancelled was due to the negligence of the postal employee.... Since the postal service is a branch of the U.S. Government, we are concerned here with the rule of *dina demalchuta dina*, "the law of the government is binding." This certainly applies to the U.S. Government and other countries where all citizens are equal under the law.... Therefore, he must tear up the stamp and may not use it.

Tragic Incident during the Holocaust
Mishnah Halachot, no. 6:314

Question: *During the Nazi occupation of Poland, the Nazis, in an attempt to collect all furs owned by Jews, announced that whoever did not hand over his furs would be shot. Three Jewish elders were assigned to run the collection. They were warned that they would pay with their lives if anyone was found hiding a fur. After all the furs were surrendered, the Germans made a search and found one fur hat. The owner was shot on the spot. The three Jewish elders were beaten and tortured, so that one died of his injuries, the second one hovered between life and death, and the third one was still conscious. This third elder was the father of the person who is submitting the present question.*

As the son was watching his father's agony, the Nazi soldier (may his name be blotted out) said to the son, "If you'll give me your gold watch, I'll shoot your father with my gun so that he won't have to suffer any longer." The son handed him his watch and the Nazi killed the father. Now the son is deeply depressed, thinking that he may have done wrong by bringing about his father's death. He thinks that God might have performed a miracle and saved his father, and that he caused his death.

Responsum: Woe is us that things like that happened in our lifetime, and what is even more painful is that we have almost forgotten everything that these accursed *resha'im*, may their name be blotted out, have done. They murdered the best of our people; hardly anyone escaped. And although we are all survivors of the Holocaust, tormented and aching from head to toe, we are beginning to forget. May God forgive me for writing these lines, but no one can escape reliving his agony when he sees what these accursed creatures have done. Every day their perfidy becomes more clear, and I myself have tasted this cup of bitterness, as you know....

We may bring a parallel to our case in the Gemara in *Avodah Zarah* 18a, which relates the story of Rabbi Chaninah ben Teradyon, whom the Romans wrapped in a Torah scroll which they set afire after placing woolen sponges on his chest to retard his death.... The executioner said to him, "Rabbi, if I stoke up the fire and remove the sponges to hasten the end of your agony, will you promise me everlasting life?" He replied, "Yes." "Swear it to me." He swore. The Roman immediately stirred up the fire and removed the sponges. As the rabbi died, the executioner himself jumped into the pyre. Then a Heavenly Voice was heard saying, "Rabbi Chaninah and his executioner are ready to enter the World to Come."

This story proves that since Rabbi Chaninah was about to die, he was permitted to ask the executioner to remove the sponges and advance his death....

We can also adduce a proof from the death of the occupants of Masada, who killed one another to avoid being wiped out by the attacking Romans, as we are told by Josephus.[4]

In my opinion, since the father would have been killed in any event, the son, by saving his suffering father from excruciating pain, performed a mitzvah. However, no inference should be drawn from this, God forbid, for permitting hastening the death of a sick person, or euthanasia, for this is tantamount to murder. It applies only in the case where a person was being killed.

May it be His will to avenge the blood of the Jewish people that has been spilled, and to awaken those who are asleep in the dust with the coming of Mashiach.

Kidney Transplants
Mishnah Halachot, no. 6:324

Question: *The questioner's brother needs a kidney transplant. According to the doctor, the best results are obtained with a kidney donated by a brother or sister. Is he obligated to donate his kidney to his brother? If he has no halachic obligation, does he have a moral obligation to donate his kidney, or is he forbidden to do so?*

Responsum: The Gemara in *Sanhedrin* 73a states, "If you see your fellow drowning in a river or attacked by wild beasts or assaulted by robbers, it is your duty to save him, in compliance with the verse, 'Do not stand still when your neighbor's life is in danger'" (Leviticus 19:16). The Gemara expounds, "as long as you don't endanger your own life in the process. If your own life is at risk you are exempt from rescuing him." . . .

Perhaps the story of Esther has a bearing on this case. Mordechai asked her to go to the king and to plead for her people. She replied that any man or woman who enters the king's inner court without being called is killed. Mordechai answered, "You don't think that you have a better chance to escape than the rest of the Jews. And who knows—maybe it was just for a time like this that you became Queen" (Esther 4:13-14).

It seems that their argument centered on this: Esther thought that it is prohibited to risk your life to save others, whereas Mordechai thought that you are obligated to risk your life in order to save the entire Jewish people.

[Rabbi Klein proceeds to probe the question from a number of vantage points.] . . . To summarize: It is a mitzvah to jeopardize your life in order to save an entire community or to save a Torah scholar and certainly one's own teacher. If the victim and the rescuer are of equal stature, and surely if the victim is of lower stature than the rescuer, he is forbidden to risk his life to save him; thus he has no moral obligation either. . . .

A similar case happened with one of the students of our yeshivah here in Brooklyn. His wife suffered from the same kidney disease. Her sister, who also was married to a student of our yeshivah, offered to donate a kidney to her sister. I did not rule on whether it is permitted or forbidden to donate an organ, since the patient's husband only asked me whether surgery should be performed on his sick wife, and this is surely permitted.[5]

I have written you some of the arguments that can be made in favor of donating an organ and some of the arguments that tend to prohibit it. I cannot make a definitive ruling on this matter unless you consult at least two other prominent *poskim*, such as my friend Rabbi Shlomoh Zalman Auerbach and my friend Rabbi **Yaakov Weiss**, or my friend Rabbi Eliyashuv. These are life-and-death decisions. . . .

Practice Birth Control?
Mishnah Halachot, no. 5:210

Question: *Is it permissible to practice birth control after you have fulfilled the mitzvah of "Be fruitful and multiply" by having both a son and a daughter? The argument is advanced that thereby the wives are spared the distress of childbirth, and by having fewer children the husband is not required to work so hard and can devote more time to Torah study.*

Responsum: My dear student, it pains me to write about such matters and my heart grieves when I see that even advanced yeshivah students, who are meticulous in the observance of all mitzvot, search for leniencies when it comes to this issue. . . . Their arguments do not hold water. They simply want to follow the prevailing trends of the surrounding culture. . . .

The argument that it is difficult to earn enough to support many children is a fallacy. God provides for every creature from the mighty bison to the lowly flea and gives sustenance to every Jewish soul. Our sages say in *Niddah* 35b that every baby that is born brings his loaf of bread with him. We say in *Birkat Hamazon* (Grace after Meals), "He gives nourishment to all flesh, for His kindness is eternal . . . because He is God Who nourishes and sustains all. . . ."

They claim that they are concerned with the distress of the wife. Of course a husband should worry about the state of his wife's health and well-being, but not to the point of permitting things that are forbidden. And what if she is distressed because she has to fast on Yom Kippur; should she therefore not fast? The truth is that we see many women who complain about the hardships involved in raising children while at the same time they go to work from morning until night without voicing any discontent—because they receive a salary. At weddings or bar mitzvah parties they will stay up dancing until late in the night without grumbling, but when they must get up at night occasionally to soothe a crying baby they find it distressful. . . . They merely want to live according to the dictates of the current styles and mores.

The men contend that by practicing birth control they will not have to work so hard and will be able to devote more time to Torah study. This too is erroneous. I say, if you want to study more Torah, don't go to weddings and banquets—study instead. Don't go to endless meetings—study instead. Don't talk on the telephone for hours on end, don't read newspapers and magazines. If you add all these wasted hours and study instead, taking time out to study with your children every day and thereby relieve your wife's burden somewhat, then you will be blessed with a long life together with your family. [There follows a detailed analysis of the halachic views regarding various methods of contraception.]

Discovery of a Valuable Book
Mishnah Halachot, no. 6:284

Question: *Reuven owed Shimon $3.00 and paid the debt by giving him the book* Ne'ot Yaakov *by Rabbi Yaakov Algazi. They agreed verbally that since the exact value of the book was unknown to either of them, each would forgive the other, whether it was worth more or less than the amount of the debt. After examining the book, Reuven discovered that it contained handwritten marginal notes, and after further investigation he found that this book had belonged to the illustrious Rabbi* **Chaim Yosef David Azulai,** *and it was he who had written the marginal notes. An inscription on the title page read: "Received as a gift . . . , signed Chaim Yosef David Azulai." An expert on manuscripts told him that the book was worth about $1,000. He wants to know whether or not he is obligated to return the book to Reuven.*

Responsum: It seems to me that he does not have to return the book, on the basis of the Bet Yosef's remarks in *Choshen Mishpat* 209 that the laws of overreaching do not apply to articles for which there is no established market price. . . . In our case the value of the manuscript is not clearly established, as it depends on finding a buyer who is interested in antique manuscripts. . . . To summarize, he need not return the book.

Bar a Photographer from Taking Your Picture?
Mishnah Halachot, no. 7:114

Question: *Are you permitted to stop a photographer from taking your picture?*

Responsum: Although in the entire world, taking photographs has become an accepted practice, nevertheless the sages don't favor it.[6] . . . Therefore, certainly if someone wants to be stringent about it, he may refuse to have his picture taken.

Teshuvot Yavetz 1:170 [see page 114] relates that his father, the **Chacham Tzvi,** was invited by the Sephardi community of London, where he was given a royal reception. On that occasion they asked him to pose for a portrait and he refused, although most *poskim* see no prohibition in making an oil painting, especially if it is only of the face. Surreptitiously they did obtain a sketch of him from which the artist made a painting. . . . If it is prohibited to reproduce someone else's writings without his permission, surely taking his picture should require his permission. The government, too, by law has the right to forbid the taking of photographs for security reasons, and surely a *tzaddik* may bar a photographer from taking his picture.

GLOSSARY

Acharonim: Rabbinic sages from the fifteenth century to the present.

aggadah: The nonlegislative part of the Talmud. It comprises ethics, history, allegories, and parables.

agunah: A woman whose spouse is presumed dead and who seeks clarification of her marital status. Also, a woman tied to an absent husband.

aron hakodesh: Holy Ark containing Torah scrolls.

Av Bet Din: Chief Justice.

aveirah (-ot): Sin, transgression.

baal teshuvah: Returnee to Torah observance.

berachah: Blessing.

Bet Din: Rabbinical Court.

Bet Hamikdash: The Holy Temple.

Bet Midrash: A hall for Torah study.

bimah: Platform for the reading of the Torah.

brit (milah): Circumcision ceremony.

chametz: Leavened dough or bread, forbidden on Passover.

Chasidism, chasidut: A movement of religious revival, founded by Rabbi Yisrael Baal Shem Tov, South Poland, 1700–1760.

chasidim: Followers of a chasidic rebbe.

chazzan: Cantor.

Choshen Mishpat: One of the four sections of the *Shulchan Aruch*, the comprehensive Code of Jewish Law, written by Rabbi Yosef Karo, 1488–1575. *Choshen Mishpat* deals with business and financial law.

Chumash: Five Books of the Torah, Pentateuch.

chupah: Wedding canopy.

dayan (-im): Rabbinical judge.

etrog: Citron, one of the four species of the lulav-bundle that is waved on Sukkot.

Even Ha'ezer: One of the four sections of the *Shulchan Aruch*, the comprehensive Code of Jewish Law, written by Rabbi Yosef Karo, 1488–1575. *Even Ha'ezer* deals with the laws of marriage and divorce.

Gemara: Talmud.

get: Religious divorce.

Haggadah: Service on Passover night.

Halachah (-ot): Torah and rabbinic law.

HaShem: God; literally, the Name.

Haskalah: The so-called Enlightenment.

Kabbalah: Jewish mysticism.

Kaddish: Prayer recited by mourners.

kashrut: Laws of kosher food.

ketuvah (-ot): Marriage contract; describes the husband's obligations.

Kiddush: Blessing recited over wine before the Shabbat or holiday meal.

kohen: Priest; descendant of Aaron.

mamzer: Child born from a forbidden union.

maror: Bitter herbs eaten at the Passover seder.

Mashiach: Messiah, the anointed one.

mechitzah: Partition (in synagogue) separating men and women.

megillah: Scroll made of parchment on which the Book of Esther is written. It is read on Purim.

melamed: Torah teacher of young boys.

menorah: Candelabra; a seven-branched menorah was used in the Temple; an eight-branched menorah is used on Chanukah.

meshumad: Apostate; a Jew who renounced his faith and converted to another religion.

mezuzah (-zot): Parchment scroll affixed to doorpost on which the Shema is written.

mikveh: Ritualarium; ritual bath.

milah: Ritual circumcision.

Minchah: The afternoon prayer.

minhag: Custom.

minyan: Quorum of ten adult males required for communal prayer.

mitzvah (-vot): Torah commandments.

mohel: Person performing the milah.

Orach Chaim: One of the four sections of the *Shulchan Aruch*, the comprehensive Code of Jewish Law, written by Rabbi Yosef Karo, 1488–1575. *Orach Chaim* deals with the laws of daily prayers, Shabbat, and festivals.

Pesach: Passover.

poseik: Authority on Halachah.

Rav: Rabbi.

Rabbeinu: Our teacher.

rebbi: Teacher, mentor.

resha'im: Evil-doers.

Rishonim: Early rabbinic sages from the tenth to the fifteenth centuries.

rosh (rashei) yeshiva: Dean(s) of a yeshivah.

Savoraim: Talmudic sages of the sixth century, successors to the Amoraim, the collective authors of the Talmud.

sefer Torah: Torah scroll.

Shacharit: The morning prayer.

Shechinah: Divine Presence.

she'eilah (-lot): Question, query.

(the) Shema: Hear O Israel, the first words of fundamental Jewish prayer declaring faith in God.

shochet: ritual slaughterer.

Shulchan Aruch: Comprehensive code of Jewish Law compiled by Rabbi Yosef Karo.

siddur: Prayer book.

sukkah: Thatched hut, booth; used as temporary dwelling on Sukkot.

Sukkot: The festival of Tabernacles.

tallit: Prayer shawl.

tefillin: Phylacteries.

teshuvah (-vot): Responsum (-sa).

Tetragrammaton: The four Hebrew letters representing the Name of God that is ineffable.

tevilah: Immersion in a mikveh.

Tosafot: Collection of commentaries on the Talmud printed on the outside margin of the Talmud page.

tzaddik: Righteous man.

tzedakah: Charity.

tzitzit: Tassels attached to the four corners of a tallit.

yahrzeit, yahrtzeit: Anniversary of a death.

yeshivah (-ot): Torah school(s).

Yomtov: Jewish holiday.

Yoreh De'ah: One of the four sections of the *Shulchan Aruch*, the comprehensive Code of Jewish Law compiled by Rabbi Yosef Karo. *Yoreh De'ah* deals mainly with dietary laws.

NOTES

I. THE RESPONSA OF THE GEONIM: 589–1038

Rav Poltoi Gaon

1. "After him [Mar Yosef] Mar R. Poltoi . . . ruled for sixteen years (842–858) from the year 153 [of the Seleucid Era]." In *The Iggeret* (*Letter*) *of Rav Sherira Gaon* (Jerusalem: Rabinowich, 1988), p. 142.
2. The term *Ashkenazi* denotes Jews from France, Germany, Central Europe, and Russia.
3. This responsum gives indication that Ashkenazi Jews in the middle of the ninth century were busily engaged in trading in faraway Babylonia.

Rav Netronai Gaon

1. Rav Netronai succeeded Rav Sar Shalom as Gaon of Sura in 853, and was succeeded by Rav Amram Gaon in 858.
2. Genesis 17:8.

Rav Amram Gaon

1. Rav Amram Gaon wrote the *Seder Rav Amram Gaon*, the complete order of prayers, as part of a responsum. It is the first *siddur* (prayer book) ever issued. See *The Iggeret of Rav Sherira Gaon*, (Jerusalem: Rabinowich, 1988) p. 146.
2. From *Otzar HaGeonim*, vol. 7.

Rav Nachman Gaon

1. Dr. Joel Müller, Berlin, 1891.
2. According to Halachah the only evidence acceptable in court is the testimony of two qualified witnesses. Circumstantial evidence is not admissible. An exception is made in certain cases when an innocent, unpremeditated statement of even one non-Jew is accepted in evidence. Such statements are termed *meisiach lefi tumo*, which means speaking innocently, casually. In the present case, without the *meisiach lefi tumo* testimony to the effect that she had not been violated, the kohen's wife would not be permitted to return to her husband.
3. According to Professor David Miller of the Department of Arabic Languages at the Vienna University.

Rav Sherira Gaon

1. The Ran cites this method in his commentary on the Rif about this mishnah.
2. Jerusalem, 1988.
3. Rava and his colleague Abbaye were the heads of the fourth generation of Amoraim (teachers of Talmud) in Babylonia. Rava lived past the age of 70 and is cited in the Talmud 2000 times.
4. Rav Hai was born in 939 C.E. and was appointed as *Av Bet Din* in 986.

Rav Hai Gaon

1. *Pesikta Rabbati* 22.
2. Exodus 20:7.
3. A reference to Leviticus 21:18, which states: "Thus, any blemished priest may not offer a sacrifice."

II. THE RESPONSA OF THE RISHONIM: 1038–1492

Rabbi Moshe Ben Maimon—Rambam (Maimonides)

1. First published in Constantinople, 1536, and republished under the title *Pe'er HaDor*, Amsterdam, 1765.
2. Deuteronomy 20:19.
3. Proverbs 6:23.
4. On Shabbat and Yomtov we are forbidden to handle *muktzeh*, any article that is intended for a use that is forbidden on Shabbat. Thus, a hammer, a pen, or a candle are *muktzeh*. Objects that cannot be considered a vessel, such as wood, pebbles, chunks of metal, and the like, are also *muktzeh* and may not be handled (*Orach Chaim*, 308).
5. Isaiah 1:25.

Rabbi Meir of Rothenburg—Maharam

1. *Teshuvot Maharam*, Cremona, 1557; Prague, 1608; Lemberg, 1860; Berlin, 1891.
2. *Gittin* 4:6.
3. It commemorates the destruction of the first and second Temples in 423 B.C.E. and 69 B.C.E. respectively (M. Kantor, *The Jewish Time Line Encyclopedia*, Jason Aronson, Inc., Northvale, N.J., 1989).
4. Rabbi Meir of Rothenburg speaks from painful personal experience as described in the biography at the beginning of this chapter.
5. Isaiah 66:24.
6. Rabbeinu Gershom, *Meor haGolah*, Light of the Diaspora, 960?-1040?, was the most prominent leader of Ashkenazi Jewry of his time. He lived in an era when the Christian Church forced conversions by threatening Jews with death or expulsion. Many chose death rather than abandon their faith. Rabbeinu Gershom's only son was forced to convert to Christianity. When he died before being able to return to Judaism, Rabbeinu Gershom observed a two-week period of mourning: one week for the loss of his life, and the second for the loss of his soul.

Rabbi Shelomoh ibn Aderet—Rashba

1. Spain, 1180–1263, author of *Shaarei Teshuvah*, Gates of Repentance.
2. Rabbi Moshe ben Nachman (Nachmanides), Spain, 1194–1270.
3. Rabbi Moshe ben Maimon (Maimonides), Spain and Egypt, 1135–1204.
4. Died Spain, c. 1340.
5. Rabbi Yom Tov Ashvili, Spain, c. 1260–1328.
6. Constantinople, 1513; Bologna, 1539; Livorno, 1657, 1778; Salonica, 1803; Livorno, 1825; Warsaw, 1865.
7. Most recent, Jerusalem, 1973, to tractate *Ketuvot*.
8. Leavened; the questioner is concerned with the fact that ripe wheat kernels might become *chametz* if rain falls on them, since they no longer need the soil. It is best to harvest the wheat used for matzot while the kernels are still slightly green. On Seder nights we eat *matzah shemurah*, matzoh that is specifically supervised from the time of harvesting.
9. Genesis 49:1.
10. Genesis 49:10.
11. Haggai 2:9.
12. Exodus 4:8,9.
13. Rabbi Yonatan Eibschutz (Germany c. 1690–1764) finds an amazing allusion to this in the verse, "The blood will be a sign for you on the houses" (Exodus 12:13). The fact that in connection to the plague of blood the word *acharon*, "the last," is mentioned, and it is followed by another plague, is proof "on the houses," that "the last house" in *Haggai* 2:9 does not mean that there will be no third Temple; *acharon* in this case translates "the latter." There certainly will be a third Temple.
14. Genesis 38:7; see Rashi's commentary.
15. Psalm 127:3.

Rabbi Asher ben Yechiel—Rosh

1. Constantinople, 1522; Venice, 1552.
2. In his introduction to *Bet Yosef*.
3. Leviticus 19:3.
4. The Bet Din in Castile (Northern Spain) was authorized by the government to adjudicate civil and criminal cases, impose penalties, and even administer capital punishment. Rosh agreed to the use of the death sentence for informers and for people who brought to the authorities false charges against Jews.
5. Leviticus 19:16.
6. Judges 5:31.
7. After his arrival from Germany, Rosh was invited to serve as the rabbi of Toledo and had to familiarize himself with the local customs.

Rabbi Yom Tov ibn Ashvili—Ritva

1. Jerusalem, 1959.
2. Livorno, 1838.
3. Rambam, *Hilchot Ishut*, Book 4, Laws of Marriage and Divorce 14:8.
4. Note his deep humility; literally, "I am the tail of these great lions."
5. *Shavuot* 40b.
6. The Geonic era spanned four and a half centuries, from 589 to 1038 C.E.
7. *Hilchot Sefer Torah*, Laws of the Torah scroll 1:2 and 10:1.
8. A town in the district of Aragon, near Saragossa.
9. Jeremiah 3:22.

Rabbi Nissim Girondi—Ran

1. Rome, 1545; most recently an annotated edition, Jerusalem, 1984.
2. Constantinople, 1533; Jerusalem, 1874.
3. The Torah (Exodus 22:6–14) recognizes four categories of *shomerim*, guardians, or persons into whose care other people's money or belongings have been entrusted: (1) *shomer chinnam*, unpaid guardian; (2) *shomer sachar*, paid guardian; (3) *socher*, renter; and (4) *sho'el*, borrower.
4. Majorca is an island off the eastern coast of Spain.
5. The rules of *shechitah* are alluded to in the verse, "You may slaughter any of the cattle or sheep that God will have given you in the manner that I have prescribed" (Deuteronomy 12:21). *Shechitah* is accomplished by cutting the throat of an animal with a flawlessly sharp knife, in

NOTES

swift strokes, without applying pressure. It is the most humane and painless form of slaughter and is applied by a shochet who must be a respected Torah scholar well versed in the many laws of *shechitah* as they are delineated in Tractate *Chullin* and in *Shulchan Aruch*, *Yoreh De'ah*.

Rabbi Yitzchak ben Sheshet Perfet—Rivash

1. Riva di Trani 1554; Lemberg, 1805.
2. The Marranos were Spanish Jews who were forced to convert to Christianity but secretly continued to practice their Jewish faith. Many Jews escaped to Moslem countries and to the Netherlands, where they found freedom, but many others (mostly the wealthy) chose to remain in Spain and lived a double life of publicly professing to be Christians while secretly practicing Judaism. There were 200,000 of them in the Aragon and Castile provinces of Spain, and thousands more in other regions. The name "Marranos" is a pejorative used by the Spaniards; it means "swine." The Hebrew term is *anussim* (the forced ones) or *conversos*. Rivash, who fled in the wake of the massacres of 1391, was deeply involved in the problems arising from the Marranos phenomenon. This teshuvah is one such problem.
3. That is, the land of forced baptism, Spain.
4. Responsa are not restricted to questions of Halachah. They encompass the full range of the Jewish experience. The present teshuvah is an illustration of a rabbi's answer to a philosophical question. Such questions are the subject of many responsa.
5. A major work on Jewish philosophy, first published in 1190.
6. Wine that has been produced by a non-Jew or Jewish wine that has been touched by a non-Jew is forbidden for drinking. Such wine is called *stam yeinam*, ordinary, non-Jewish wine. *Yayin nesech*, wine for libation, is the source of this prohibition, since there is the apprehension that the wine was produced to be used in non-Jewish religious worship. If kosher wine has been boiled until its quantity is reduced by evaporation, the so-called *yayin mevushal*, and such wine is touched by a non-Jew, it may be used for drinking. In the present case the wine in the vat had not been touched by the non-Jew, who had only indirect contact with the wine by holding the Jew's hand.

Rabbi Shimon Duran—Rashbatz

1. Amsterdam, 1738.
2. A small settlement in the Sahara Desert, in eastern Algeria, 250 miles south of the Mediterranean coast.
3. A town on the Mediterranean coast, about 100 miles east of Algiers.
4. Rabbi Moshe ben Maimon, Maimonides, Spain, Egypt, 1135-1204.
5. Rabbi Meir of Rothenburg, Maharam, Germany, 1215-1293.
6. On the Moslem festival *Id al-Adha*, a sheep is sacrificed by each family in commemoration of Abraham's binding of Isaac, which is described in Genesis 22. This festival is celebrated on the tenth of the month *Dhu al-Hidjja* of the Moslem calendar. Since the Moslem calendar retrogresses, there is no corresponding secular date.
7. According to *Sanhedrin* 56b, the following seven mitzvot were given to the descendants of Noah, and thus to all mankind: (1) the administering of justice; and the prohibitions (2) against blasphemy, (3) against idolatry, (4) against murder, (5) against illicit intercourse, (6) against robbery, and (7) against eating flesh from a living animal.
8. Rav Yehudah and Rava were Amoraim, sages of the Talmud. Rava became the foremost Talmudic authority in 338 C.E.
9. This Gemara relates that, initially, every father taught his son. Children who had no father would not learn Torah. Then Rabbi Yehoshua ben Gamla established that every town and village should appoint teachers for the young and that children should enter classes when they were 6 or 7 years old.
10. Rabbi Moshe ben Nachman (Nachmanides), Spain, 1194-1270.
11. *Ketuvot* 110b.
12. *Ketuvot* 111a.
13. Psalm 102:15.
14. *Kiddushin* 40a.
15. The author of this responsum, Rabbi Shelomoh Duran (Rashbash, Algiers, 1400-1467) was the son of the Rashbatz and succeeded his father as rabbi of Algiers. Like his father, he wrote many responsa.

Rabbi Yisrael Brunna—Mahari Brunna

1. A city about 70 miles north of Vienna; it is now part of Czechoslovakia.
2. A city in Bavaria, Germany, about 70 miles north of Munich.
3. Salonica, c. 1798.
4. *Sotah* 14a.
5. Rabbi Yaakov Weil, who died c. 1455, was rabbi of Augsburg and Erfurt, Germany, author of *Teshuvot Mahari Weil* (Venice, 1523), and the mentor of Mahari Brunna.
6. *Nazir* 62a.
7. I Samuel 6:8-12.
8. *Kiddushin* 66b.
9. *Eiruvin* 69b.
10. Proverbs 21:27.
11. II Chronicles 5:15.
12. *Chullin* 24b.

13. From the Shacharit (morning) service.
14. Rabbi Yaakov Weil.
15. Rabbi **Meir of Rothenburg**, Germany, 1215–1293.
16. *Gittin* 45a.
17. *Gittin* 45a, under the word *delo*.
18. *Gittin* 58a, under the words *kol mamon*.

Rabbi Yosef Colon—Maharik

1. Cremona, 1557.
2. Jerusalem, 1988.
3. During the raging of the plague epidemic in Europe during the fourteenth and fifteenth centuries, the Jews were not affected as seriously as the general population because of their observance of kashrut and the laws of personal cleanliness. As a result, they were accused of poisoning the wells and were tortured in order to force them to confess. Thousands were massacred, and many communities were expelled.
4. Deuteronomy 29:18.
5. Isaiah 51:17.
6. A region of northern Italy.
7. Leviticus 18:3. This is an explicit commandment not to emulate the gentiles.

Rabbi David ibn Zimra—Radvaz

1. Venice, 1749.
2. Amsterdam, 1713.
3. Zalkava, 1862.
4. Lemberg, 1883.
5. The Karaites (*Kara'im*) are a sect of Jews founded in 764 C.E. by Anan ben David, whose pride was hurt when his younger brother Chananiah was appointed *Reish Galuta* (exilarch, political leader of Babylonian Jewry). Anan, filled with hatred toward the rabbis, invented a new religion that denied the validity of the entire Oral Law as recorded in the Talmud and that claimed to accept only the Scriptures. The name *Kara'im* means people of the Scriptures. The movement, which began in eighth-century Persia, spread to Egypt, Syria, and later Russia by way of Turkey. The Karaites were forbidden not only to kindle fire on Shabbat but even to warm themselves or to leave their homes. They did not observe the mitzvot of tefillin and mezuzah and many other precepts that are delineated in the Oral Law. After the tenth century the movement gradually disintegrated because of countless differences that existed between the various Karaite groups. Karaites still exist today; about 7,000 live in or near Ramle, Israel, and some 5,000 in the Soviet Union.
6. The reference is to Deuteronomy 23:3: "A *mamzer* must not enter the assembly of God," which means "into God's marriage group." A person is considered a *mamzer* only if he or she is born of an adulterous or incestuous union, not merely born out of wedlock. The underlying problem of this she'eilah is this: A Karaite *get* is invalid according to Halachah. Now, if Karaite marriage (kiddushin) is recognized by Halachah, then a woman who obtained a Karaite divorce is halachically still married to her husband. If this woman remarries, she is comitting adultery and her offspring is a *mamzer*. Radvaz, in his response, rules that a Karaite marriage has no validity, and no divorce is needed to dissolve such a "marriage"; thus, a child born of such a union is merely a child born out of wedlock, but he certainly is no *mamzer* and thus he may marry a Jewish woman.
7. This is an excerpt of a teshuvah of historic importance. It is a landmark decision, tracing the Ethiopian Jews' ancestry to the tribe of Dan. The recent decisions by the Chief Rabbinate of Israel concerning Ethiopian Jews were based on this teshuvah. Kush is usually identified as Ethiopia (see Numbers 12:1, commentary of Targum Yonatan and **Rashbam**).
8. Karaites: see note 5.
9. The legality of a marriage is determined by the presence of two valid witnesses.
10. Rambam was named Nagid, "prince" of Egyptian Jewry, a title conferred on his son R. Avraham and five generations of Rambam's descendants. The *nagid* appointed the *dayanim* (judges) for all Egyptian communities and acted as arbitrator in disagreements arising between the judges and the community.
11. According to the laws of kashrut, meat and dairy products may not be eaten or cooked together, nor may we derive any benefit from such mixed foods. We must also bear in mind that all things forbidden by the Torah that become mixed with permitted food of a different species are neutralized by sixty times their own bulk. In the present case, the sugar is only fifty times the quantity of the milk, and this fact gave rise to the she'eilah. (See **Rambam**, *Ma'achalot Asurot* [Forbidden Foods] 9:1 and 15:17.)
12. It should be remembered that Radvaz lived in Egypt. Evidently, mummies were thought to have therapeutic powers.

III. THE RESPONSA OF THE EARLY ACHARONIM: 1492–1648

Rabbi Meir Katzenellenbogen—Maharam of Padua

1. Poland, 1530–1572.
2. Venice, 1553.
3. Rabbi Yisrael Isserlin, Germany, 1390–1460.
4. One who renounces Judaism, converting to another religion.
5. II Kings 18:1–3. Chizkiyah (Hezekiah) was a very righteous king, and his father Achaz was evil in the sight of God. Still, he is called Chizkiyah ben Achaz (son of Achaz).

Rabbi Yosef Karo—Beit Yosef, Shulchan Aruch

1. Smyrna, 1795.
2. Taken from Song of Songs 3:6.
3. Rabbi Moshe ben Maimon (Maimonides), Egypt, 1135–1204.
4. Rabbi Nissim, Safed, 1488–1575, prominent Talmudic commentator.
5. The four *chayot*, "living creatures," mentioned in the mystical *Maaseh Merkavah*, in Ezekiel 1:10, are man, lion, ox, and eagle.
6. Rabbi Asher ben Yechiel, Germany and Spain, 1250–1327, was the author of an important halachic code.
7. Rabbi Yaakov Baal Haturim, Spain, 1275–1340, great halachic codifier.
8. Rabbi **Yitzchak ben Sheshet Perfet**, Spain, Algiers, 1326–1407, leading authority of his time and author of responsa. See page 32.
9. Leviticus 19:15.

Rabbi Moshe di Trani—Mabit

1. Spain, Safed, 1488–1575.
2. Venice, 1629.
3. Venice, 1553.
4. Venice, 1576.
5. The literal translation of *kiddushin* is consecration. When the groom places a ring on his bride's finger, he declares, *Harei at mekudeshet li betabaat zo kedat Moshe ve Yisrael*, "Behold, you are consecrated to me by means of this ring according to the law of Moshe and Yisrael." Although it is the universal custom for the groom to give a ring to his bride, any article of value may be used for *kiddushin*. Since Reuven gave her a cluster of grapes, the question is whether she requires a *get* (religious divorce) to sever this "marriage."
6. Our sages derive from Exodus 22:6–14 the laws dealing with the four *shomerim* [guardians], the four categories of custodianship of those who have been entrusted with other people's property: the unpaid guardian, the paid guardian, the renter, and the borrower. Since the borrower has the full use of the borrowed article without paying for it, he is liable for everything, even for unavoidable accidents.
7. The responsa of Rabbi Moshe Nachman (Nachmanides), Spain, 1195–1270.
8. Marranos, also called *anussim* (the forced ones) or *conversos*, were the Jews of Spain who during the fourteenth and fifteenth centuries were forced to convert to Christianity but secretly remained faithful to the Torah. The Inquisition relentlessly sought out these *anussim*, and after being tortured they were burned alive.
9. Rabbi **Yitzchak ben Sheshet Perfet**, Spain and Algiers, 1326–1407.

Rabbi Shemuel di Medina—Maharashdam

1. Salonica, 1596.
2. The question is prompted by the concern over the prohibition of *hotza'ah*. One of the thirty-nine main labors forbidden on Shabbat is to carry anything from a private into a public premise, as, for example, from a house into the street or from the street into a house. The questioner wonders whether or not by going out wearing this garment one is violating the prohibition of *hotza'ah*.
3. *Chacham*, wise man, is the title for rabbi used by Sephardi Jews (Jews from Spain and the Mediterranean and Middle Eastern countries).
4. The juxtaposition of the sections of the Unloved Wife and that of the Rebellious Son in Deuteronomy 21:15–21 implies that the children of a hated wife will have flawed character traits.
5. The Torah delineates the laws of the *nazir* in Numbers 6:1. A *nazir* must abstain from eating grapes and raisins and drinking any grape beverage, and he may not cut his hair nor have contact with the dead. If a person vows, "I will be a *nazir*," his term of *nezirut* abstention is for thirty days. But if he says, "I will be a *nazir* like Samson," as in the present case of the brother, he remains a *nazir* forever; his vow cannot be annulled.
6. Leviticus 19:16.
7. Exodus 22:5.
8. The Torah, in Exodus 22:6–15, recognizes four categories of *shomerim*, or guardians, people entrusted with the property of others: *shomeir chinam*, an unpaid guardian; *shomeir sachar*, a paid guardian; *socheir*, a renter; and *sho'eil*, a borrower.

Rabbi Moshe Alshich—Alshich Hakadosh

1. Venice, 1605.
2. Constantinople, 1595.
3. According to Halachah, property is transferred by means of *kinyan*, a mode of acquisition. The transfer is effected, not by money changing hands, but by a symbolic barter, as for example by *kinyan sudar*, literally "acquisition of a scarf," during which a scarf is symbolically grasped by both parties to the transaction. The underlying principle of this form of acquisition is that the buyer should give the seller an article of some utility, no matter how small its value, and say to him, "Acquire this article in exchange for the . . . you sold me for so and so much." The moment the seller lifts the article, taking possession of it, the buyer acquires title to the property, although he has not paid for it. Then neither party may renege (**Rambam**, *Hilchot Mechirah*).
4. The word *ploni*, meaning so-and-so or such and such, occurs in the Bible in I Samuel 21:3, II Kings 6:8, and Ruth 4:1. According to Rashi it is related to the word *yipalei*, "it is concealed," as in Deuteronomy 17:8. Ploni

thus signifies a person or place whose identity is unknown. The term ploni or Ploni ben Ploni is used in rabbinic writings to denote "John Doe" or X.

5. The *kehillah* (Jewish community) provided public services, such as education, support of the needy, support of the rabbi and the synagogue, mikveh, cemetery, and many others. It possessed the power of taxation and used the oath and the *cherem* (power of excommunication) as a means of enforcing its powers of taxation. A Jew in reporting his taxable income had to take an oath that the information he reported was true. Taking a false oath is a very grave sin. The threat of excommunication was an important deterrent against those who refused to pay their taxes.

6. The Torah commands, "On the first day [of Sukkot] you must take for yourself a fruit of the *hadar* tree [*etrog*], branches of *tamar* [palm trees, *lulav*], boughs of the *avot* tree [myrtle branches, *hadassim*], and willows that grow near the brook [*aravot*]" (Leviticus 23:40). In fulfillment of this mitzvah, the Four Species are taken in hand every day of Sukkot, except on Shabbat. They consist of the *lulav*, three *hadassim*, and two *aravot*, together with the *etrog*. After reciting the blessings, we wave the bundle in the six directions.

Rabbi Shelomoh Luria—Maharshal

1. *Bava Kama*, Prague, 1618; other volumes at later dates and various locations.
2. Lublin, 1575.
3. Leviticus 19:31 and Deuteronomy 18:11. *Ov* is a method of communicating with the dead; see I Samuel 28:3-9. The sorcerer makes a voice seem to appear from under his arm (*Sanhedrin* 65b). *Yidoni* involves the sorcerer's placing the bone of a bird in his mouth to produce sounds.
4. Deuteronomy 18:13. Rashi interprets this phrase to mean: "Put your hope in Him and do not investigate the future."
5. The Fast of the Ninth of Av, which commemorates the destruction of the First as well as the Second Temple.
6. The Torah commands us to wear the *tzitzit* (fringes), "that you may see them and remember all of God's commandments and perform them" (Numbers 15:39).

Rabbi Betzalel Ashkenazi—Shittah Mekubetzet

1. *Bava Kama*, Amsterdam, 1752; *Nazir*, Livorno, 1774.
2. Venice, 1590.
3. This teshuvah deals with the concept of *meisi'ach lefi tumo*.
What is meant by this phrase?
The Gemara in *Yevamot* 47a rules that testimony of a non-Jew is not accepted in a Bet Din because it is unreliable. However, if there is reason to believe that the non-Jew is telling the truth, his testimony is valid. For example, if a non-Jew makes a casual, offhand remark, his statement is obviously true and is admissible in Bet Din. He is termed *meisi'ach lefi tumo*, making a statement in ignorance of its legal bearing (*Yevamot* 121b).
Such testimony can be of crucial importance in establishing the death of a missing husband and freeing his wife from her status of *eishet ish* (married woman). Without evidence of her husband's death, the wife remains an *agunah*, a woman tied to an absent husband and unable to remarry. The rabbis explored all possible legal avenues to help these unfortunate women. The responsa literature is replete with attempts at solving *agunah* cases, such as this teshuvah.

4. An allusion to Psalm 79:12.
5. The autonomous Jewish communities exercised governmental powers, among which was taxation. The Jewish community provided public services, such as education, health care, synagogues, courts, etc. (Rema, *Choshen Mishpat* 37:22).
6. Alimony settlement, a minimum of two hundred dinars, to which she is entitled by virtue of her marriage contract.

Rabbi Avraham di Boton—Lechem Mishneh, Lechem Rav

1. Venice, 1609.
2. Smyrna, 1660.
3. Rabbeinu Tam in Tosafot on *Kiddushin* 9a, under the word *vehilcheta*, states that the marriage should be consecrated with an article of known value, such as a ring. Pearls or jewels should not be used because the bride can easily overestimate their value. Therefore it is customary to use a plain wedding ring.
4. *Eirusin* (betrothal), also called *kiddushin* (consecration), is the part of the wedding ceremony when a special *berachah* is pronounced after which the bride accepts the ring from her groom.
5. According to Halachah, a child of a Jewish father and a non-Jewish mother is not a Jew.
6. Rabbi **Shimon Duran**, Algiers, 1361-1444.

Rabbi Meir of Lublin—Maharam Lublin

1. Venice, 1618.
2. Venice, 1619.
3. Rabbi Yonah of Gerona, Spain, 1180-1263, in his work *Orechot Tzaddikim*, Chapter 26, prescribes the following regimen as penance for a murderer: He is to go into exile for a period of three years; he should receive lashes in each city and proclaim, "I am a murderer"; he should not eat meat or drink wine; he should bind to his neck the arm and hand with which he killed; he should

walk barefoot; he should weep over his sin and fast each day for the duration of his exile; after that he should fast Mondays and Thursdays for one more year; if people vilify him, he is to remain silent; he is not to walk for pleasure; on his wanderings he should lie down in front of the synagogue so that the congregants will step over him, but they should not step on him.

4. *Makkot* 2:2. Since the victim was not in the line of the throw when the killer released the stone, he is not exiled.

5. The unintentional murderer insisted on doing penance because God caused a man to die through him. Although he was not to blame, he has feelings of guilt because, as the old proverb says, "Out of the wicked comes forth wickedness" (I Samuel 24:14).

6. A Jew who was forced to convert to Catholicism but observed the Jewish faith in secret. During the sixteenth century, Jews in Italy suffered greatly from the oppressive decrees issued by the various popes. The fact that this she'eilah was asked of Maharam Lublin, who lived in Poland, attests to the high esteem in which he was held in communities as far away as Italy.

7. A region in east central Europe, now southwest Poland.

8. Rabbi **Yosef Colon**, Italy, 1410–1480, author of *Teshuvot Maharik*.

9. Rabbi **Asher ben Yechiel**, leading halachist and codifier, lived in Germany and Spain, c. 1250–1327; see page 23.

Rabbi Yoel Sirkes—the Bach

1. Tur is the popular name of *Arba'ah Turim*, the four-part seminal code of Halachah and the forerunner of the Shulchan Aruch. It was written by Rabbi Yaakov Baal HaTurim, Germany, Spain, c. 1275–1343.

2. Early responsa, Frankfort, 1697

3. Later responsa, Koritz, 1785.

4. The practice of using the services of a *shadchen*, a marriage broker, dates back to the days of the Patriarchs, when Avraham's servant Eliezer arranged the match between Yitzchak and Rivkah (Genesis 24). Matchmaking is considered a mitzvah and may be done on Shabbat (*Shabbat* 150a). **Maharam Rothenburg** writes in his responsum no. 498 that in Austria it was the custom to pay the matchmaker's fee after the wedding, whereas in the Rhineland it was paid after the engagement. The standard fee for a *shadchen* was two or three percent of the dowry ("Enactments of the Vaad Arba Aratzot," in *Anshe Shem* by Buber, p. 225). Today the use of a *shadchen* in introducing singles for a prospective match is still very much in vogue.

5. A cymbal, or a pair of concave metal plates clashed or beaten to produce a musical sound.

6. Albrecht Wenzel Eusebius von Wallenstein, 1583–1634, Duke of Friedland and Mecklenburg. He was an Austrian general during the Thirty Years' War, a war between Catholics and Protestants which lasted from 1618 to 1648.

Rabbi Yaakov Sasportas

1. Amsterdam, 1734.

2. Amsterdam, 1737.

3. One of the foremost scholars of his time, Rabbeinu Gershom lived in Germany, c. 960–1040. He is best known for his enactments, which are accepted as law by all Ashkenazi Jews. For example, he issued a ban against polygamy and against divorce without the wife's consent.

4. The priestly blessing appears in the Torah: "May God bless and keep watch over you. May God make His Presence enlighten you and be gracious to you. May God direct His Providence toward you and grant you peace" (Numbers 6:24–27). In Eretz Yisrael it is customary for the kohanim to bless the congregation every day. Outside Eretz Yisrael the priests bless the congregation on Yomtov only (*Orach Chaim* 128:42).

5. Deuteronomy 13:9.

Rabbi Shmuel Abohab—Dvar Shmuel

1. Venice, 1702.

2. The various segments of prayer are usually concluded by the recitation of the Kaddish. Many of these Kaddish recitations are the privilege of mourners, or of those observing *yahrtzeit*, the anniversary of the death of a parent. It is a basic requirement that a minyan (a quorum of ten adult males) be present during the recitation of the Kaddish.

Kedushah, or Sanctification, is a prayer of surpassing importance. In it we emulate the angels in singing God's praises by proclaiming, "Holy, holy, holy is God the Master of Legions, the whole world is filled with His glory." With our feet together we rise up on our toes to indicate that we strive to free ourselves from our earthly bonds and combine our prayer with that of the angels. Like the Kaddish, the Kedushah may be recited only in the presence of a minyan.

3. Numbers 6:22. The verses 22–26 delineate the well-known priestly blessing: "May God bless you and keep watch over you, ... " The introduction of "*This* is how you must bless ... " teaches us that it must be said in Hebrew to the exclusion of other languages.

4. Shemoneh Esreih, also called Amidah, is one of the principal parts of the daily prayer and is recited three times each day during the morning (Shacharit), afternoon (Minchah), and evening (Maariv) services. On weekdays it consists of nineteen blessings in which we praise God and ask Him for insight, forgiveness, redemption, healing for the sick, years of prosperity, the ingathering of the exiles,

restoration of justice, the downfall of God's enemies, reward for the righteous, and the rebuilding of Jerusalem. We conclude by thanking God for His miracles and praying for peace. It is a prayer that is said silently while standing erect and with utmost concentration. It is then repeated aloud by the chazzan.

5. Italy was the center of the Renaissance, the revival of art and letters in Europe. It began in the fourteenth century and gradually spread to other countries. Much of the art of the great painters and sculptors of that era was based on biblical themes.

6. Psalm 106:35.

7. Micah 4:5.

8. Amoraim are the collective authors of the Talmud.

Rabbi Yair Chaim Bachrach—Chavat Yair

1. *Pilpul*, literally "pepper," is an ingenious approach to the study of Talmud, whereby questions are answered in brilliant flashes of insight rather than through systematic analysis.

2. Frankfort on-the-Main, 1699.

3. This question is motivated by Deuteronomy 20:19, "You must not destroy its trees, wielding an ax against any food-producing tree." This law forbidding the destruction of fruit trees applies to the destruction of any article of value. It is called the law of *bal tash'chit*, "don't destroy."

4. The reference is to Exodus 35:22, which lists *kumaz*, body ornaments, as one of the pieces of jewelry the women donated to the Tabernacle. According to Rashi, *Shabbat* 84a, *kumaz* is a gold genital shield for women.

IV. THE RESPONSA OF THE LATER ACHARONIM: 1649-PRESENT

Rabbi Tzvi Ashkenazi—Chacham Tzvi

1. Amsterdam, 1712.

2. A major philosophic work by Rabbi Yehudah Halevi, Spain, c. 1080-c. 1145, first published in Fano, Italy, 1506.

3. Hence the Hebrew word *matbei'a* for coin.

4. Prague, 1565-1630.

5. A compendium of the 613 mitzvot of the Torah, giving kabbalistic interpretations of the laws. *Shelah* is the acronym of the initials of *Shenei Luchot Habberit*, "The Two Tablets of the Covenant" (Amsterdam, 1648).

6. Possibly an allusion to Baruch Spinoza, the Jewish philosopher who had been excommunicated in Amsterdam in 1656 for his pantheistic, anti-Torah writings.

7. With regard to Shabbat, a private domain is a place that is surrounded by partitions, whereas streets and market squares are considered public domain. On Shabbat it is forbidden to move or carry any object in a public domain. A detailed discussion of these halachot can be found in *Shulchan Aruch*, *Orach Chaim* 345-396, with commentary by Mishnah Berurah. They are treated in simplified form in *Kitzur Shulchan Aruch*, Chapters 81-84, available in English translation.

8. Most authorities consider this to be the variety of lettuce known as Romaine lettuce. Some authorities hold that the variety known as crisp, head, or iceberg lettuce (*latuca sativa*) may be used for maror. Since often there are small insects found on Romaine lettuce, its leaves should be carefully inspected before being used.

9. The Chacham Tzvi lived and studied many years among Sephardi Jews and was thoroughly familiar with their customs and languages.

10. A *kazayit* is a quantity the size of an olive, which is the equivalent of one fluid ounce.

11. In English it is called endive (*chicorium endivia*).

12. The beauty of an *etrog* is manifest in its shape, its size, its freedom of even the smallest spot, the texture and the regularity of the ridges of its skin. People who want to perform the mitzvah in its most beautiful way will spend a great deal of money to obtain a *hadar*, a flawless *etrog*.

13. Rabbi Moshe Mintz, Germany, 1415-1485, author of *Teshuvot Maharam Mintz*, Cracow, 1617.

14. Rabbi **Yosef Colon**, Italy, 1410-1480; author of *Teshuvot Maharik*, Cremona, 1557.

Rabbi Yaakov Reischer—Shevut Yaakov

1. Prague, 1689.

2. Dessau, 1692.

3. Wilhelmsdorf, 1729.

4. Halle, 1710; Offenbach, 1719; Metz, 1789.

5. Upon seeing exceptionally strange-looking people or animals, we say the *berachah*, "Blessed are You, Lord our God, King of the Universe, Who make creatures different."

6. Genesis 5:2.

7. The questioner is concerned with the prohibition of *amirah lenochri*: anything we are forbidden to do on Shabbat we may not tell a non-Jew to do for us. In the case of the letter, on Shabbat we are not permitted to carry anything from a house into the street or vice versa.

8. Reference is made to the Book of Daniel where we are told (Chapter 3) that Chananiah, Mishael and Azariah, the three exiles from Judah, re-named Shadrach, Meshach and Abed-nego, servants of King Nebuchadnezzar, chose death in a fiery furnace rather than to bow down to the king's statue of gold. God saved them and not a hair on their heads was singed.

9. *Shabbat* 33b.

10. Jeremiah 15:2 and 43:11.

11. Judges 4:17.

NOTES

Rabbi Yechezkel Katzenellenbogen—Kenesset Yechezkel

1. Altona, 1732.
2. Paritzk, 1786.
3. The *Shulchan Aruch*, the universally accepted code of Jewish law, was written by Rabbi **Yosef Karo**, who was born in Spain in 1488 and died in Safed, Eretz Yisrael, in 1575. His rulings are based primarily on decisions of Sephardi authorities.
4. Rema is the abbreviation of the initials of Rabbi Moshe Isserles, who was born in Cracow, Poland, in 1520 and died there in 1572. He wrote the famous glosses on those paragraphs of the *Shulchan Aruch* in which he differs with the author, stating the Halachah as it has been decided by the Ashkenazi authorities. It should be noted that the halachic differences of these two towering personalities concern only customs and traditions. On all fundamental principles and laws of Torah, the Sephardi and Ashkenazi communities are indivisibly united.
5. If the child is in good health, the mitzvah of *milah* must be performed on the eighth day: "Throughout all generations, every male shall be circumcised when he is eight days old" (Genesis 17:12). Even if the eighth day occurs on Shabbat, the *milah* is performed on that day. If the infant is sick, however, the *milah* is postponed. In addition, *milah* must be performed in the daytime. Therefore, if it is performed at night or before the infant is eight days old, the obligation of *milah* was not fulfilled, and a symbolic drawing of a drop of blood must be done (Shach on *Yoreh De'ah* 262, *Shaagat Aryeh* 53).
6. Rif is the acronym of Rabbi Yitzchak alFasi (of Fez, Morocco), 1013–1103, author of *Sefer Hahalachot*, a summary of the halachic portions of the Talmud. It is the forerunner of the **Rambam's** *Mishneh Torah* and the *Shulchan Aruch*.
7. Rosh is the abbreviation of **Rabbeinu Asher ben Yechiel**, 1250–1327, author of an important halachic code that follows the talmudic tractates.
8. Rashi, Rabbi Shelomoh Yitzchaki, 1040–1105, greatest of all commentators, wrote commentaries on the Torah, Bible, and Talmud.
9. The Book of Esther, written on a parchment scroll; it is read on Purim to commemorate the miraculous rescue of the Jewish people in ancient Persia from the hands of the wicked Haman.

Rabbi Yaakov Emden—Yavetz

1. Altona, 1739.
2. Altona, 1752.
3. Altona, 1745.
4. The Torah states, "But Saturday is the Shabbat to God your Lord. Do not do anything that constitutes work" (Exodus 20:10). Our sages enumerate (*Shabbat* 73a) thirty-nine categories of principal labors, including carrying, lighting a fire, cooking and other food preparation, writing, sewing, building, plowing, harvesting, and other agricultural activities.
5. According to Halachah, the child of a Jewish mother and a non-Jewish father is Jewish; the child of a Jewish father and a non-Jewish mother is non-Jewish.
6. Exodus 20:20.
7. **Chacham Tzvi,** R. Tzvi Ashkenazi, 1660–1718.

Rabbi Yechezkel Landau—Noda biYehudah

1. Prague, 1776 and 1811.
2. Prague, 1791.
3. Prague, 1827.
4. Prague, 1794.
5. In the case of a rabbinical prohibition, *Magein Avraham* permits you to ask a non-Jew to do the prohibited labor, but only if a serious loss is prevented thereby (*Shulchan Aruch, Orach Chaim* 307). But you may not ask a non-Jew to do a biblically forbidden labor for you, not even for the prevention of a serious loss.
6. Kohanim are the channel through which God's blessings flow unto the Jewish people. The kohanim, descendants of Aharon HaKohen, recite the priestly blessing on the festivals. It has the following text: "May God bless you and keep watch over you. May God make His Presence shine upon you and grant you grace. May God direct His Providence toward you and grant you peace" (Numbers 6:21–26).
7. Reincarnation is the kabbalistic concept, termed *gigul neshamot*, whereby souls who have committed sins during their life are returned to earth in a new body to atone for the sins of their previous life.
8. Deuteronomy 4:15.
9. Genesis 25:32.
10. Rabbi Yechezkel Landau was well versed in the most profound kabbalistic mysteries, but he kept his knowledge concealed from the world. In *Noda BiYehudah, Mahadura Tanina, Orach Chaim* 109, he writes, "The truth is that I don't engage in the study of mysticism. I wish I could study as much Talmud and the books of law as I should, books that are needed for practical application. They are our life and about them we should meditate."
11. *Moreh Nevuchim*, "Guide of the Perplexed," by **Rambam** (Maimonides) is a seminal work on Jewish philosophy, written in Arabic and first published in 1190 under the title *Dalalat al Hairin*.

Rabbi Chaim Yosef David Azulai—Chida

1. Vilna, 1853, in three volumes, comprising the names of over 1,300 scholars and the titles of over 2,000 books.
2. Livorno, 1789.
3. Livorno, 1798.
4. The Chida was a Sephardi Jew.

5. An ancient chant that is sung at the conclusion of the seder, according to Ashkenazi usage. Its deceptively simple lyrics are allusions to profound philosophical concepts.

6. Rabbi Yitzchak Luria Ashkenazi, illustrious kabbalist, lived in Safed, Eretz Yisrael, 1534–1572.

7. Germany, c. 1160–c. 1238. Author of the well-known *Sefer HaRokeach* (Fano, 1505), a work on Halachah, customs, and ethics.

8. Rabbi Yitzchak Luria Ashkenazi, illustrious kabbalist, lived in Safed, Eretz Yisrael, 1534–1572.

9. Ecclesiastes 7:20.

10. The Chida wrote this responsum as a young man. Attached to the end of it is the critical commentary by his teacher Rabbi Yonah Navon. It affords us a rare insight into a loving master–student relationship. It shows the master gently correcting the impetuous young student's errors while at the same time encouraging him. A facsimile of the original teshuvah, which was discovered only in 1961, appears at the beginning of the volume *Yosef Ometz*.

11. In Jerusalem, Purim is observed on the fifteenth day of Adar. All other communities observe the festival on the fourteenth of Adar (*Megillah* 2b,3a).

12. The Megillah is not read on Shabbat as a precaution lest people carry the scroll to the synagogue on Shabbat, when carrying is forbidden. For the same reason the *shofar* is not sounded when Rosh Hashanah occurs on Shabbat, and the *lulav* is not taken when Sukkot falls on Shabbat (*Megillah* 4b, *Sukkah* 42b, *Rosh Hashanah* 29b).

13. In rabbinic literature the names Reuven and Shimon are chosen to represent any two parties to a legal dispute or business transaction, in the same way that the terms Mr. X and Mr. Y are used. If the parties are women the names Rachel and Leah are used.

Rabbi Akiva Eiger

1. In 1985 a new comprehensive edition was published in Eretz Yisrael.

2. For an excerpt of this responsum, see page 59.

3. Rabbeinu Gershon (c. 960–c. 1040) was one of the earliest and most prominent scholars of Ashkenazi Jewry. His yeshivah in Mainz was the first Torah academy in Europe. He is best known for his *takkanot* (enactments), which were accepted by all Ashkenazi Jews. Two of these enactments brought about major changes in Jewish life: his prohibition against polygamy, and his ban against divorce without the wife's consent. The words *Me'or HaGolah* (The Light of the Diaspora), are a title appended to Rabbeinu Gershon's name, and are indicative of the great esteem in which he was held.

4. *Moredet*, rebellious wife, is the halachic term for a wife who denies her husband conjugal relations in order to torment him in revenge for a marital dispute they had, and who refuses to be reconciled. If she persists in spite of repeated warnings by the Bet Din, her husband may divorce her without her consent (*Even Ha'ezer* 77:2) and she forfeits her *ketuvah* (alimony settlement). In this instance the ban of Rabbeinu Gershon forbidding a husband to divorce his wife without her consent does not apply (see previous note).

5. Sma is the acronym formed of the first letters of *Sefer Me'irat Eynaim*, an important commentary on the *Shulchan Aruch, Choshen Mishpat*, by Rabbi Yehoshua Falk Katz of Lemberg, Poland. He died in 1614.

Rabbi Moshe Sofer (Schreiber)—Chatam Sofer

1. On the four sections of the *Shulchan Aruch*, 1377 responsa: *Orach Chayim*, Pressburg, 1855; *Yoreh De'ah*, Pressburg, 1841; *Even Ha'ezer*, Pressburg, 1858; *Choshen Mishpat*, Pressburg, 1862.

2. Drohbitch, 1896.

3. Vienna, 1896.

4. Emperor Joseph of Austria-Hungary.

5. From the Nishmat prayer in the Shacharit service of Shabbat.

6. The Gemara compares men and women singing in unison to "a flame on flax fiber (which ignites very easily)." Rashi explains that the men would be paying attention to the women singing, which is forbidden because a woman's singing inflames a man's passion.

7. Exodus 22:24.

8. This advice to the local rabbi not to treat the guilt-ridden woman too harshly is a beautiful example of the Chatam Sofer's wisdom and keen understanding of human nature.

Rabbi Yehudah Assad

1. Lemberg, 1873.

2. A favorite classic written by Rabbi Yehudah HeChasid, who lived in Germany c. 1150–1217.

3. Sephardi Jews, however, who do not have this tradition, name their children after living relatives.

4. We are forbidden to erase God's name. The Talmud infers this from Deuteronomy 12:3–4: "You must tear down their altars [of the idol worshipers], . . . obliterating their names from that place. 'Do not do this to God your Lord.' This is a prohibition addressed to one who would blot out the name of God from any writing" (*Makkot* 22a).

Rabbi Moshe Schick—Maharam Schick

1. Rabbi **Moshe Sofer,** Pressburg, Hungary, 1762–1839.

2. Munkatch, 1880.

3. Munkatch, 1881.

4. Lemberg, 1884.
5. Lemberg, 1884.
6. Although Maharam Schick was passionately opposed to any deviation from traditional religious practice, he recognized the immense benefits to be gained by reaching the alienated Jews through sermons delivered in the local language.
7. Leviticus 19:17.
8. Deuteronomy 19:21.
9. Genesis 9:6.
10. Deuteronomy 19:21.
11. Deuteronomy 13:6.

Rabbi Avraham Shemuel Binyamin Sofer (Schreiber)—Ktav Sofer

1. Pressburg, 1879.
2. Rambam, *Hilchot Teshuvah*, Laws of Repentance 1:3 and 7:3.
3. Leviticus 25:17.
4. Mishnah *Bava Metzia* 2:11.
5. Psalm 119:72.
6. An idiomatic expression taken from Ruth 4:7, "Now this is as formerly done in Israel." It means ". . . done by the Jewish people."

Rabbi Moshe Weinberg of Volbrum—Ohel Moshe

1. Pietrkow, 1908.
2. Halachah treats breaking an engagement as a serious matter. It is the subject of a great number of responsa.

Rabbi Yosef Shaul Halevi Nathanson—Sho'eil Umeishiv

1. Followers of the Haskalah movement (Jewish "enlightenment").
2. Lemberg, 1865–1879.
3. Lemberg, 1875.
4. From the verse "Now write for yourselves this song . . ." (Deuteronomy 31:19) is derived the mitzvah for each Jew to write (or have written for him) a Torah scroll.
5. *Treifah*, literally "torn off," denotes an animal that has a lesion or wound that will eventually kill it. After the *shechitah*, the lungs and other organs are carefully examined to make sure the animal is kosher.

Rabbi Naftali Tzvi Yehudah Berlin—Netziv

1. Warsaw, 1892, 1894.
2. To rabbis in New York, Baltimore, Cincinnati, and Charleston, South Carolina.
3. Vilna, 1879, 1880.
4. The meat of the hindquarter of the animal is not sold as kosher, since rendering it kosher would entail the extremely tedious process of excising the forbidden *cheilev* (certain fats) and the *gid hanasheh* (sciatic nerve), which is described in Genesis 32:33: "Therefore the children of Israel shall not eat the *gid hanasheh*."
5. The Torah is read in public during the Shacharit and Minchah services of Shabbat and of fast days, and during Shacharit of Yomtov, Chol HaMoed, Rosh Chodesh, Chanukah, Purim, and every Monday and Thursday.
6. Moving the reading platform from the center to the front of the synagogue was one of the first changes introduced by the Reform movement. The rabbis perceived even the slightest deviation from tradition as opening the floodgates to the new movement, leading to emancipation and eventual assimilation.
7. An allusion to Isaiah 5:5.
8. *Hilchot Tefillah*, Laws of Prayer, 11:3.
9. The concern is whether the steam will cause the flour to leaven. Even the slightest leavening renders the flour *chametz*, which is forbidden on Passover.
10. Proverbs 3:17.

Rabbi Yitzchak Elchanan Spector

1. Chibbat Tzion, "Love of Zion" was a 19th-century religious movement aimed at resettling Jews in Eretz Yisrael. It originated in Eastern Europe under the leadership of Rabbi Shmuel Mohilever, an eminent Torah scholar. Its members were known as Chovevei Tzion, "Lovers of Zion."
2. Vilna, 1889.
3. A city in present-day eastern Turkey, near the Russian city of Yerevan.
4. *Agunot*, plural of *agunah*, refers to women whose spouses are presumed dead and who seek clarification of their marital status.
5. The Mishnah (*Shavuot* 8:1) identifies four *shomerim*, that is, four classes of guardians entrusted with the care of other people's property: (1) the unpaid *shomeir*; (2) the paid *shomeir*, one who gets paid for watching an article (this includes one who accepts an article as a broker or seller with the intention of profiting by its sale, as in the present case); (3) the renter; and (4) the borrower.

Rabbi Yitzchak Aharon Ettinger—Mahari Halevi

1. Zalkova, 1828, 1829.
2. Lemberg, 1893.
3. A man or woman who is mentally unbalanced cannot give or receive a religious divorce.

Rabbi Yosef Chaim Al Chakkam of Baghdad—Ben Ish Chai

1. Sages of the Mishnah, seven generations (35 B.C.E.–200 C.E.) from the days of Hillel and Shammai to the era of Rabbi Yehudah HaNasi.

2. Rabbi Yitzchak Luria, Tzefat (Safed), 1534–1572, a great teacher of Kabbalah, who transmitted his teachings orally. Rabbi Chaim Vital, his foremost disciple, recorded the Ari's discourses and published them in *Etz Chaim* and other works.

3. Jerusalem, 1973.

4. Before eating bread we recite the blessing of Ha-Motzi: "Blessed are You, God, our Lord, King of the universe, Who brings forth bread from the earth."

5. Leviticus 17:7–9.

6. Our sages enumerate thirty-nine principal labors we are forbidden to perform on Shabbat, one of which is *hav'arah*, igniting a fire. One of the conditions for being guilty of violating these laws is that the work must be done for its own purpose. Work that is not done for its own purpose—*melachah she'einah tzerichah legufah*—is exempt. For example, if you dig a hole on Shabbat but you have no need for the hole, you only need the earth you scoop out, then your digging was not done for its own purpose, namely, to obtain a hole. Therefore, you are exempt. In the present case, likewise, the traveler did not light the candle for its own purpose of producing light, but in order to trick the Arabs into thinking that he was a non-Jew.

7. *Shabbat* 73a.

8. The laws of Shabbat are suspended where human life is threatened. Indeed, it is a mitzvah to desecrate the Shabbat for a person who is dangerously ill. Saving a human life supersedes everything. In many cities in the United States, Israel, and other countries, "*Hatzalah*" ambulances staffed by Shabbat-observant volunteers will drive on Shabbat to make emergency calls, saving many lives.

9. Leviticus 19:14. This means that you are forbidden to cause another person to commit a sin.

10. *Hilchot Shemittah Veyoveil* 13:6

Rabbi Shalom Mordechai Schwadron—Brezaner Rav, Maharsham

1. Jerusalem, 1974.

2. On Yom Kippur, when food is given to a woman who is pregnant or to a sick person, we say to them, "If you are sure that you may be in danger if you do not eat as much as you require, then you may eat in the ordinary manner until you are satisfied. However, if it is possible to eat less than the required quantity at one time, then act as follows: Eat at one time no more than the quantity of two thirds of an egg, and rest somewhat. Then eat a similar quantity again." Thus he may eat even many times. When drinking, they should swallow less than a mouthful at one time (*Kitzur Shulchan Aruch* 133:15).

3. Moslems circumcise their children at 13 years of age. They emulate their progenitor Yishmael, the son of Avraham, who was 13 years old when he was circumcised. See Genesis 17:25.

Rabbi Avraham Borenstein of Sochatchov—Avnei Nezer

1. Pietrkow, 1926.

2. An allusion to Psalm 102:14. The numerical value of the Hebrew words amounts to 642, and the year 5642 parallels the secular year 1882. It is a common practice to write the Hebrew year in the form of a Biblical phrase with a hope-inspiring message whose numerical value matches that of the given year. Often the text is slightly altered in order to achieve the correct value, as was done in this case.

3. According to Halachah, a man has fulfilled his mitzvah when he has produced one son and one daughter.

Rabbi Yonatan Steif

1. Genesis 2:18.

2. We are commanded to live in a sukkah (thatched hut) during the festival of Sukkot to commemorate the clouds of glory that enveloped the Israelites in the desert, "so that future generations will know that I had the people of Israel live in huts when I brought them out of Egypt" (Leviticus 23:43). For a detailed discussion of the laws and symbolism of the sukkah, see *Orach Chaim* 626–644 and *Kitzur Shulchan Aruch* 134–135.

3. Leviticus 18:3. This commandment forbids emulating gentiles, lest "you fall into a deadly trap by trying to follow them" (Deuteronomy 12:30).

4. *Hilchot Eivel* 14:1.

5. *Bava Metzia* 30b.

6. I Samuel 2:30.

7. The last day of Sukkot is called Simchat Torah, the Rejoicing of the Law. The reason for our happiness is that on that day we complete the annual cycle of weekly Torah reading and begin anew with *Bereishit*: "In the beginning . . ." In a great outpouring of joy, amid singing and dancing by young and old, the Torah scrolls are carried in circuits, called *hakafot*, around the *bimah*. We celebrate the fact that the Torah and the Jewish people live on forever. For the Torah is "more precious than the finest gold and gems" (Proverbs 3:15). "For to us it is strength and light."

One can easily imagine the consternation that must have gripped the congregation when at the height of their joyous celebration the shocking incident occurred that is the subject of the present she'eilah.

Rabbi Moshe Feinstein—Reb Moshe

1. New York, 1959; B'nei B'rak, Israel, 1981.

2. B'nei B'rak, Israel, 1988.

3. Brooklyn, New York, 1986.
4. Genesis 3:19.
5. Leviticus 19:4.

Rabbi Mordechai Yaakov Breisch

1. Jerusalem, 1951; London, 1959, four volumes.
2. The arm tefillin are placed on the left biceps. Someone who writes left-handed puts the arm tefillin on *his* weaker arm, which is the right arm.
3. Exodus 13:16.
4. The consumption of blood is forbidden by the Torah: "Do not eat any blood, whether from a mammal or a bird, no matter where you may live. Any person who eats blood shall have his soul cut off from his people" (Leviticus 7:26–27). "This is because the life force of the flesh is in the blood . . ." (Leviticus 17:11).
5. Rabbi Shabbetai HaKohen, Lithuania and Moravia, 1622–1663, author of *Siftei Kohen* (abbreviated Shach), a monumental commentary on *Shulchan Aruch, Yoreh De'ah*. The reference Rabbi Breisch makes to this commentary is to no. 155:13, where the Shach states that eating forbidden foods in a way that does not give enjoyment (such as swallowing a pill) is permitted.
6. "Affliction" includes refraining from eating, drinking, washing, anointing, wearing shoes, and having marital relations.
7. The Maharsha (R. Shmuel Eliezer Eidels, Poland, 1555–1631) explains that *imach*, "alongside" (literally "with you"), implies that your brother's position is subordinate to yours. In other words, after making sure that *you* stay alive, see to it that your brother stays alive alongside you.

Rabbi Yitzchak Yaakov Weiss—Minchat Yitzchak

1. Jerusalem, 1985–1989.
2. It is a Torah command to put on tefillin every weekday. The arm tefillin represent our resolve to submit our hearts and strength to God. The head tefillin represent our resolve to dedicate our intellect to Him. It is written, "Place these words of Mine on your heart" (Deuteronomy 11:18), which means that it must be put physically opposite the heart. Therefore, we must place the arm tefillin on the biceps of the left arm and incline it slightly toward the heart. The head tefillin are placed on the head midway between the eyes, in such a way that the lower edge of the tefillin is not lower than the place where the hair begins to grow.
3. A *rodeif*, "pursuer," is a person who is chasing after someone, trying to kill him. Every Jew has the responsibility to save the intended victim, even by taking the pursuer's life.
4. According to Torah law, anyone born of a Jewish mother or converted according to Halachah is a Jew. This girl, having been born of a non-Jewish mother, requires *giur* (conversion).
5. Rabbi Shemuel HaLevi Eidels (1555–1631), who wrote a commentary on Talmud, Rashi, and Tosafot, which is now printed in all standard editions of the Talmud. He served as rabbi in Chelm, Lublin, and Ostraha, all in Poland.

Rabbi Menashe Klein—Ungvarer Rav

1. Brooklyn, 1970–1983.
2. We are forbidden to destroy anything associated with the worship of God and to erase God's name (*Makkot* 22a). Our sages derive this from the juxtaposition of two verses. Referring to the idolatrous nations occupying the Promised Land, the Torah states: "You must tear down their altars, break up their sacred pillars, burn their Ashera trees, and chop down the statues of their gods, obliterating their names from that place. You may not do this to the Lord your God" (Deuteronomy 12:3,4).
3. Rabbi Yisrael Meir HaKohen Kagan, known as the Chafetz Chaim, after the title of one of his works, lived in Lithuania from 1839 to 1933. He was the spiritual leader of his entire generation.
4. Flavius Josephus (Yosef ben Mattityahu) (37 C.E.–c. 105 C.E.), historian and Jewish general, defended the Galilee during the war against Rome (66 C.E.). His works, written in Greek, are among the principal sources of historical data of post-Biblical events in Jewish history. He wrote "Antiquities" (from Creation to the Herodian era); "The War of the Jews" (from the Maccabees to the fall of Judea); and "Apion," a defense of Judaism against the attacks by his adversary Apion, one of the first anti-Semitic authors living in Alexandria in the first century C.E.
5. There is a very moving sequel to this story. The kidney transplant was performed successfully and the sick sister, who had been childless after being married for fifteen years, subsequently gave birth to a healthy son. The *brit* occurred on Yom Kippur and was performed by Rabbi Menashe Klein.
6. Their concern is the prohibition of "Do not make a representation of anything that is with Me" (Exodus 20:20), forbidding the making of statues of angels. The Gemara in *Rosh Hashanah* 24a applies this prohibition to making replicas of objects used in the Holy Temple.

APPENDIX OF ADDITIONAL PROMINENT HALACHIC AUTHORITIES

The responsa literature, She'eilot uTeshuvot, often abbreviated Sh'uT, plays a pivotal role in the process of halachic decision-making. At the same time it affords us an insight into the life and times of the various Jewish communities over the past 1,000 years. Over the centuries our heritage has been enriched by many thousands of these works of teshuvot, written by *meshivim*, responders, who combined phenomenal brilliance with gentle sensitivity. These were the eminent Torah leaders of their generations, and through their writings their influence is felt to this day.

During the process of compiling an anthology, many difficult choices must be made. Without a doubt the personalities whose works have been selected for this volume rank among the foremost Torah scholars of all time. However, many sages of eminent stature could not be included because of the limitations of space. For this reason we have compiled the following appendix, which lists the names, major works, and biographical data of a number of other great responders whose teshuvot have enlightened and guided not only their own communities but Jews throughout the world.

The names are arranged alphabetically, according to first names.

R. Aharon Shmuel Kaidanover—Maharshak
רבי אהרן שמואל קידנובר—מהרש"ק
She'eilot uTeshuvot Emunat Shmuel (Frankfort on the Main, 1663)
born: Vilna, 1614
died: Chmelnik, Poland, 1676

R. Aryeh Leib Ginzburg—Shaagat Aryeh
רבי אריה ליב גינסבורג—שאגת אריה
Shaagat Aryeh (Frankfort on the Oder, 1746)
born: Weisun, near Minsk, Russia, 1695
died: Metz, France, 1785

R. Chaim Benvenisti
רבי חיים בנבנשת
She'eilot uTeshuvot R. Chaim Benvenisti (Constantinople, 1743)
born: Constantinople (now Istanbul), Turkey, 1603
died: Smyrna (Izmir), Turkey, 1673

R. Chaim Halberstam of Sanz
רבי חיים הלברשטם
Teshuvot Divrei Chaim (Lemberg 1875)
born: Tarnograd, Poland, 1793
died: Sanz, Poland, 1876

R. Chaim Ozer Grodziensky
רבי חיים עוזר גרודזנסקי
Teshuvot Achiezer
born: Ivye, Lithuania, 1863
died: Vilna, Lithuania, 1939

R. Chisdai HaKohen Perachia
רבי חסדאי הכהן פרחיא
She'eilot uTeshuvot Torat Chesed (Salonica 1723)
died: Salonica, 1678

R. Elazar Shapira of Munkatch
רבי אלעזר שפירא
Teshuvot Minchat Elazar (Munkatch 1902)
born: Stryzhov, Hungary, 1871
died: Munkatch (Czechoslovakia, now USSR), 1937

R. Eliezer ibn Archa
רבי אליעזר אבן ארחא
She'eilot uTeshuvot R. Eliezer ibn Archa (Jerusalem 1978)
born: Safed?, Eretz Yisrael
died: Hebron, Eretz Yisrael, 1651

R. Eliyahu ben Yehudah Kovo
רבי אליהו בן יהודה קובו
Teshuvot Aderet Eliyahu (Constantinople 1739)
born: Salonica, c. 1630
died: Salonica, 1688

R. Eliyahu Mizrachi — Ra'am
רבי אליהו מזרחי — רא"ם
Teshuvot R. Eliyahu Mizrachi (Constantinople 1561)
born: Constantinople (now Istanbul), Turkey, 1450
died: Constantinople (now Istanbul), Turkey, 1525

R. Ezriel Hildesheimer
רבי עזריאל הילדסהיימר
Teshuvot R. Ezriel Hildesheimer
born: 1820
died: Berlin, Germany, 1899

R. Levi ibn Chaviv — Ralbach
רבי לוי אבן חביב — רלב"ח
She'eilot uTeshuvot Ralbach (Venice 1565)
born: Zamora, Spain, c. 1485
died: Jerusalem, c. 1545

R. Menachem Azaryah of Fano — Rama of Fano
רבי מנחם עזריה מפאנו — רמ"ע מפאנו
Teshuvot Menachem Azaryah (Venice 1600)
born: Fano?, Italy, 1548
died: Mantua, Italy, 1620

R. Menachem Mendel Krochmal
רבי מנחם מענדל קרוכמל
Teshuvot Tzemach Tzedek (Amsterdam 1675)
born: Cracow, Poland, c. 1600
died: Nikolsburg, Moravia, 1661

R. Moshe Alashkar — Maharam Alashkar
רבי משה אלאשקר — מהר"ם אלאשקר
Teshuvot Maharam Alashkar (Sabbionetta 1554)
born: Spain, 1460
died: Jerusalem, 1542

R. Moshe Galante — Maharam Galante
רבי משה גאלאנטי — מהר"ם גאלאנטי
She'eilot uTeshuvot Maharam Galante (Venice 1608)
born: Rome, Italy, c. 1520
died: Safed, Eretz Yisrael, c. 1610

R. Moshe Mintz — Maharam Mintz
רבי משה מינץ — מהר"ם מינץ
Teshuvot Maharam Mintz (Cracow 1617)
born: Mainz, Germany, c. 1415
died: Posen, Poland, c. 1485

R. Yaakov bei Rav
רבי יעקב בי רב
Teshuvot R. bei Rav (Venice 1663)
born: Maqueda, Spain, 1475
died: Safed, Eretz Yisrael, 1546

R. Yaakov HaLevi Patras — Mahari
רבי יעקב הלוי פטרס — מהר"י
She'eilot uTeshuvot Rabbi Yaakov — Mahari (Venice 1614)
born: Greece, c. 1560
died: Zante, Greece, 1636

R. Yaakov Weil — Mahariv
רבי יעקב וויל — מהרי"ו
She'eilot uTeshuvot Mahariv (Venice 1523)
died: Germany, c. 1455

R. Yaakov Moelin — Maharil
רבי יעקב מולין — מהרי"ל
Teshuvot Maharil (Venice 1549, Jerusalem 1977)
born: Mainz, Germany, c. 1365
died: Worms, Germany, 1427

R. Yehoshua ben Yosef of Cracow
רבי יהושע בן יוסף מקרקא
Teshuvot Pnei Yehoshua (Amsterdam 1715)
born: Vilna, Lithuania
died: Cracow, Poland, 1648

R. Yehoshua (Rephael) Benveniste
רבי יהושע בנבנשת
She'eilot uTeshuvot Shaar Yehoshua (Jerusalem 1982)
born: Constantinople (now Istanbul), Turkey, c. 1590
died: Constantinople (now Istanbul), Turkey, c. 1668

R. (Don) Yitzchak Abarbanel
רבי (דון) יצחק אברבנאל
in *She'eilot R. Shaul HaKohen* (Venice 1574)
born: Lisbon, Portugal, 1437
died: Venice, Italy, 1508

APPENDIX

R. Yitzchak of Posen
רבי יצחק מפוזן
Teshuvot R. Yitzchak MiPosna (Jerusalem 1982)
died: Posen, Poland, 1685

R. Yomtov Tzahalon—Maharit Tzahalon
רבי יום טוב צהלון— מהרי"ט צהלון
Teshuvot Maharit Tzahalon (Venice 1694, Jerusalem 1980)
born: Safed, Eretz Yisrael, c. 1559
died: Safed?, Eretz Yisrael, 1620

R. Yosef Dov Soloveitchik—Beit HaLevi
רבי יוסף דוב סולובייצ'יק—בית הלוי
Beit HaLevi (Vilna 1863)
born: Nisviz, Poland, 1820
died: Brisk, Poland, 1892

R. Yosef Rosen of Rogatchov
רבי יוסף רוזן
Tzofnat Pane'ach
born: Rogatchov, Russia, 1858
died: Vienna, Austria, 1936

SUBJECT INDEX

Abortion, 115, 133
Agnostic doctor, 86
Agunah(-ot), 35, 59, 73, 87, 123, 148, 158
Anussim, *see Marranos*
Apostates, 4, 18, 52, 134, 136, 144
Asceticism, 94

Bans, 120
Baptism, forced, 170
Birth control, 183
Brit Milah, *see Milah*

Cantor, *see Chazzan*
Chazzan, 15, 41, 77, 78
Captives, 6, 18, 64
Chametz, 21
Chanukah, 110
Charity/tzedakah, 107, 128, 150
Chasidic garb, 166
Chol HaMoed, 3
Christianity, 21
Chukat Hagoy, *see Emulating non-Jew*
Circumcision, *see Milah*
Competition, 22, 152
Conscience, pangs of, 72, 82
Conversion, 21, 177
Conversos, *see Marranos*

Disputation/religious, 21
Disputes/financial, *see Financial disputes*
Disrespect of rabbis, 44
Divorce, *see Domestic disputes*
Domestic disputes, 27, 28, 36, 37, 41, 67, 71, 98, 106, 108, 111, 121, 124, 130, 149, 151, 159
Dream, interpretation of, 156
Driving, dangerous, 179
Drowning victim, 123

Egyptian mummies, *see Mummies*
Emulating non-Jews, 44, 94

Engagement, breaking of, 88, 140, 152
Eretz Yisrael, 30, 37, 39, 43, 157, 163
Etrog, 68, 103
Ethiopian Jews, 47

Family problems, *see Domestic disputes*
Fertility drug, 22
Financial disputes, 19, 22, 25, 26, 27, 41, 44, 47, 56, 59, 60, 64, 65, 66, 69, 71, 74, 76, 79, 83, 84, 86, 87, 90, 97, 102, 103, 106, 113, 122, 125, 127, 130, 137, 142, 143, 149, 151, 152, 153, 163, 184
Fund-raising appeals, 178

Gambling, 22, 27
Genizah of Cairo, 9, 14
Graves, 128

Healing, 156, 178
Heart transplants, *see Transplants*
Holocaust, 170, 174, 177, 182
Horse races, 40
Hunting, 118
Husband/wife, friction, *see Domestic disputes*

Iggeret of Rav Sherira Gaon, 7
Inheritance, 76, 153
Insurance, 169
Intermediate days, *see Chol HaMoed*
Internal Revenue service, 170

Jew/gentile relations, 33, 41, 83, 94, 137, 138, 140, 141, 160, 164

Kabbalah, 104
Karaites, 47
Kashrut—meat, 30, 153
Kashrut—wine, 33
Kennedy memorial, 170
Kiddush, 171

Kidney transplants, *see Transplants*
Kohen, 9, 117

Landlord/tenant disputes, *see Financial disputes*

Marranos, 33, 61, 78, 82, 91
Marriage, 31, 55, 57, 58, 63, 78, 117, 138, 157, 161
Marriage broker, *see Shadchen*
Mashiach, 21
Matzot, 146, 162
Medical care/fees, 47
Messiah, *see Mashiach*
Messiah (false), 21
Mezuzah, 163
Milah, 16, 110, 117
Minyan, 104, 111
Missionaries, 132
Moslems, 24, 36, 160
Mummies, 48
Murder, 82, 84, 128, 134
Mythology, 171

Naming child, 129, 156
Neighbors, disputes between, 56

Oral Law (history of), 7

Passover, 103
Penalty, 161
Philosophical questions, 33, 101, 118
Phylacteries, *see Tefillin*
Pirates, 64, 74
Portraits, 114, 184
Postage stamps, 181, 182
Prayer, *see Synagogue*
Prisoners, *see Rescue*
Promises, *see Vows*
Pronunciation, proper, 167

Quarrels—neighbors, 62
Quarrels—father/son, 24, 60, 178

Rabbis/judges—disrespect, 44
Rabbis/judges—appointing, dismissing, 56, 75, 109, 143
Ransom, 25, 41, 83, 113

Repentance, 28
Rescue, 41, 42, 51

Sanctification of God's Name, 107
Sefer Torah—scroll, 16, 27, 130, 142, 167
Sefer Torah—mantle, 97
Shabbat, 15, 33, 63, 72, 102, 107, 113, 114, 135, 155
Shabbetai Tzevi, 91, 92
Shadchen, 86, 157
Shochet, 15, 87, 153
Siamese twins, 105
Slanderer, 24
Slave/slave girl, 16, 21, 55, 95
Soldier, 166, 174, 175
Sorcerers, 71
Sterilization, 164
Sugar, processing of, 48
Superstitions, 97, 178
Synagogue/prayer, 24, 38, 41, 43, 55, 61, 79, 83, 88, 93, 95, 97, 111, 127, 130, 131, 133, 135, 140, 142, 145, 146

Taxes—levies and exemptions, 43, 45, 68, 75, 151
Teachers, 37, 40
Tefillin, 173, 176
Testing servant, 156
Theft, 28, 29, 103
Tombstone, 121
Torah scroll, *see Sefer Torah*
Transplants, heart, 169
Transplants, kidney, 183
Trees, destruction of, 14
Tuition, 52
Twins, 40
Tzedakah, *see Charity*

Visiting the sick, 167
Vows, promises, 30, 52, 53, 61, 63, 148, 165

Water, drinking, 145
Wills, 67
Witnesses, 34, 80

Yom Kippur, 160, 173

Zohar, 160

INDEX OF AUTHORS AND PERSONALITIES

Abarbanel, (Don) Yitzchak, 202
Acharonim, xvii, xviii, 49, 99
Achiezer, Teshuvot, 181, 201
Aderet Eliyahu, 202
R. **Aharon di Trani**, see Mabit
R. **Aharon Kotler**, 99, 169, 180
R. **Aharon Shmuel Kaidanover**, see Maharshak
R. **Akiva Eiger**, 99, **123-125**,* 135
R. **Alexander Wimpen**, 18
Alshich Hakadosh, 54, **66-69**
Alshich, R. Moshe, see Alshich Hakadosh
R. **Amram Gaon**, 1, **5**, 23
R. **Aryeh Leib Ginzburg**, see Shaagat Aryeh
Ari Hakadosh, 49, 66, 70, 73, 121, 154, 156
R. **Asher ben Yechiel**, see Rosh
R. **Asher of Cracow**, 81
Avnei Nezer, **162-164**
R. **Avraham Borenstein**, see Avnei Nezer
R. **Avraham di Boton**, **77-80**
R. **Avraham b. Rambam**, 47
R. **Avraham Shmuel B. Sofer**, see Ktav Sofer

Baal HaTurim, see Tur
Bach, 49, **85-88**
R. **Bachya**, 20
Beit HaLevi, 203
Beit Yosef, see R. Yosef Karo
Belzer Rebbe, 172
Ben Ish Chai, **154-157**
R. **Betzalel Ashkenazi**, see Shittah Mekubetzet
Brezaner Rav, see Maharsham
R. **Bustenai**, 1

Chacham Tzvi, 99, **101-104**, 112, 184
Chafetz Chaim, 182
R. **Chaim Benvenisti**, 201
R. **Chaim Halberstam of Sanz**, 129, 201
R. **Chaim Ozer Grodziensky**, 201

R. **Chaim Tzvi Mannheimer**, 180
R. **Chaim Vital**, 66, 154
R. **Chaim Volozhiner**, 144
R. **Chaim Yosef David Azulai**, see Chida
Chacham Tzvi, 99, **101-104**, 112
R. **Chanan of Ashkana**, 1
R. **Chaninah**, 8
R. **Chanoch Henach of Alexander**, 162
Chatam Sofer, 99, **126-128**, 129, 132, 134, 135, 146, 151, 165, 166, 180
Chavat Yair, **96-98**, 107
Chelkat Yaakov, see R. Mordechai Yaakov Breisch
Chida, **119-122**
R. **Chisdai Crescas**, 32
R. **Chisdai Perachia**, 201
Colon, R. Yosef, see Maharik

R. **David Halevi**, 85
Divrei Chaim, see R. Chaim Halberstam of Sanz
Dvar Shmuel, **93-95**

Ein Yitzchak, see R. Yitzchal Elchanan Spector
R. **Elazar Shapira, Munkatch**, see Minchat Elazar
Elie Wiesel, 180
R. **Eliezer ibn Archa**, 201
R. **Eliyahu Kovo**, 202
R. **Eliyahu Mizrachi**, 202
Emden, R. Yaakov, see R. Yaakov Emden
R. **Ezriel Hildesheimer**, 202

Geonim, xvii, 1-2
R. **Gershon Meor Hagolah**, 124

R. **Hai Gaon**, 1, **9**, 23
Hildesheimer, R. Ezriel, see R. Ezriel Hildesheimer

---

*Page numbers in boldface refer to the author's own chapter.

Iggeret, *see Rav Sherira Gaon*
Igrot Moshe, *see R. Moshe Feinstein*

Kaidanover, Aharon Shmuel, *see Maharshak*
Karaite sect, 8, 47
Karo, R. Yosef, *see R. Yosef Karo*
Kenesset Yechezkel, 109–111
Klausenburger Rebbe, 180
Kotzker Rebbe, 162
Ktav Sofer, 126, **135–138**

Lechem Mishneh, *see R. Avraham di Boton*
Lechem Rav, *see R. Avraham di Boton*
R. Levi ibn Chaviv, 62, 202

Mabit, 58–61, 77, 124
Magen Avraham, 99
Maharal of Prague, 180
Maharam Alashkar, 202
Maharam di Boton, 77
Maharam Galante, 202
Maharam Lublin, 81–84
Maharam Padua, 51–53, 70
Maharam Rothenburg, 17–19, 23, 36, 41, 78, 111
Maharam Schick, 132–134
Maharashdam, 62–65, 77, 79, 80
Mahari Assad, *see R. Yehudah Assad*
Mahari Brunna, 39–41
Mahari HaLevi, 150–153
Mahari Mintz, 51, 202
Mahari Weil, 39, 41, 202
Maharik, 42–45, 74, 83, 104, 108, 130
Maharil, 202
Maharit Tzahalon, 203
Maharsha, 178
Maharshak, 201
Maharshal, 70–72, 111
Maharsham, 158–161
Maimonides, *see Rambam*
Mar Acha, 8
R. Mari Sorgo, 8
Masat Binyamin, 109
Megaleh Amukot, *see R. Natan Shapira*
R. Meir Arik, 172
R. Meir Katzenellenbogen, *see Maharam Padua*
R. Meir of Lublin, *see Maharam Lublin*
R. Meir of Rothenburg, *see Maharam Rothenburg*
R. Menashe Klein, 180–184
R. Menashe ben Yisrael, 89

R. Menachem Mendel Krochmal, *see Tzemach Tzedek*
R. Mendel Bess, 96
R. Michael Ber Weissmandl, 165
Minchat Elazar, 201
Minchat Yitzchak, 176–179
Mishneh Halachot, *see R. Menashe Klein*
R. Mordechai Banet, 129
R. Mordechai Yaakov Breisch, 172–175
R. Mordechai Zev Ettinger, 150
Moreh Nevuchim, 118
R. Moshe Alashkar, 202
R. Moshe Alshich, *see Alshich Hakadosh*
R. Moshe Bei Rav, 54
R. Moshe ben Maimon, *see Rambam*
R. Moshe Chagiz, 121
R. Moshe Cordovero, *see Remak*
R. Moshe Feinstein, 99, **168–171**, 181
R. Moshe Galante, *see Maharam Galante*
R. Moshe Isserles, *see Rema*
R. Moshe Mintz, *see Maharam Mintz*
R. Moshe Weinberg, *see Ohel Moshe*

R. Nachman bar Mar Tzadok, 1, 6
R. Naftali Tzvi Yehudah Berlin, *see Netziv*
Nathan of Gaza, 89, 92
R. Natan Adler, 126
R. Natan Shapira, 81
R. Netronai Gaon, 1, **4**
Netziv, 144–146
R. Nissim Girondi, *see Ran*
Noda biYehudah, 116–118

Ohel Moshe, 139–140
Or HaChayim, 119
Oliver Cromwell, 89

Pnei Yehoshua, 202
R. Peretz HaKohen, 32
R. Pesach Pruskin, 168
R. Poltoi Gaon, 3

Ra'ah, 26
Ra'am, *see R. Eliyahu Mizrachi*
Radvaz, 46–48, 73
Ralbach, 202
Rama of Fano, 202
Rambam (Maimonides), 11, **13–16**, 20, 23, 24, 26, 27, 28, 33, 36, 47, 55, 57, 58, 64, 78, 80, 88, 136, 142, 146, 157
Ramban (Nachmanides), 26, 35

INDEX OF AUTHORS AND PERSONALITIES

Ran, Rabbeinu Nissim, 18, **29–31**, 32, 56
Rashba, **20–22**, 23, 26, 28, 52, 78, 106
Rashbash, 35, 37
Rashbatz, **35–38**, 79
Rashi, 23, 26, 42, 70, 111, 126, 174
Ravad, 23
Rema, 49, 51, 70, 125, 137, 147
Remak, 54
Rif, 12, 23, 26, 29, 57, 88, 111
Rishonim, xvii–xviii, 11
Ritva, 20, **26–28**
Rivash, **32–34**, 35, 57, 61, 78, 123
Rogatchover, *see Tzofnat Pane'ach*
Rosh, 11, **23–25**, 56, 57, 84, 88, 111, 114, 139, 145
Rudolph, Emperor, 17

R. Saadya Gaon, 1
She'eilot R. Shaul HaKohen, *see Abarbanel*
Shaagat Aryeh, 201
Shaar Yehoshua, 202
Shabbetai Tzevi, 89, 92, 93, 112
R. Shalom Mordechai Schwadron, *see Maharsham*
R. Shemuel di Medina, *see Maharashdam*
R. Sherira Gaon, 1, **7–8**
R. Shimon Duran, *see Rashbatz*
R. Shlomoh HaMeiri, 1
Shelah HaKadosh, 49, 81, 102
R. Shelomoh ibn Aderet, *see Rashba*
R. Shelomoh Kluger, 129, 141
R. Shelomoh Molcho, 54
R. Shelomoh Taitatzak, 66
R. Shelomoh Tarbot, 42
Shevut Yaakov, **105–108**
Shittah Mekubetzet, 46, **73–76**
Sho'eil Umeishiv, *see R. Yosef Shaul Nathanson*
Shulchan Aruch, *see R. Yosef Karo*
R. Shmuel Abohab, *see Dvar Shmuel*
R. Shmuel of Evreux, 17
Sma, 125
Sochatchover Rebbe, *see Avnei Nezer*
Soloveitchik, R. Yosef Dov, *see Beit HaLevi*
Steipler, the, 180

R. Tam, 23, 78
Tashbatz, *see Rashbatz*
Terumat Hadeshen, 39
Torat Chesed, Sh uT, *see R. Chisdai Perachia*
Tur, Baal HaTurim, 24, 94–95
Tzemach Tzedek, 85, 202

Tzofnat Pane'ach, 203
R. Tzvi Ashkenazi, *see Chacham Tzvi*

Vilna Gaon, 99

R. Yaakov Baal HaTurim, *see Tur*
R. Yaakov bei Rav, 202
R. Yaakov Emden (Yavetz), 99, 101, 109, **112–115**, 184
R. Yaakov Ornstein, 150
R. Yaakov HaLevi Patras, 202
R. Yaakov Moelin, *see Maharil*
R. Yaakov Pollak, 51
R. Yaakov Reischer, *see Shevut Yaakov*
R. Yaakov Sak, 101
R. Yaakov Sasportas, **89–92**, 112
R. Yaakov Weil, *see Mahari Weil*
R. Yair Chaim Bachrach, *see Chavat Yair*
Yavetz, *see R. Yaakov Emden*
R. Yehoshua Benveniste, *see Shaar Yehoshua*
R. Yehoshua of Cracow, *see Pnei Yehoshua*
R. Yehudah Assad, **129–131**
R. Yechezkel Katzenellenbogen, *see Kenesset Yechezkel*
R. Yechezkel Landau, *see Noda biYehudah*
R. Yechiel of Paris, 17
R. Yeshayah Horowitz, *see Shelah*
R. Yeshayah of Pshedburzh, 139
Yeshuot Malko, 139
R. Yisrael Isserlin, *see Terumat Hadeshen*
R. Yisrael Kanievsky, 180
R. Yitzchak (Don) Abarbanel, *see Abarbanel*
R. Yitzchak Aharon Ettinger, *see Mahari HaLevi*
R. Yitzchak of Posen, 203
R. Yitzchak ben Sheshet Perfet, *see Rivash*
R. Yitzchak Elchanan Spector, **147–149**
R. Yitzchak Luria, *see Ari Hakadosh*
R. Yitzchak Rappaport, 119
R. Yitzchak Yaakov Weiss, *see Minchat Yitzchak*
R. Yoel Sirkes, *see Bach*
R. Yomtov Lipmann Heller, 180
R. Yonah Navon, 119, 122
R. Yonatan Eibschutz, 99, 109, 112
R. Yonatan Steif, **165–167**
R. Yosef Chaim of Baghdad, *see Ben Ish Chai*
R. Yosef Colon, *see Maharik*
R. Yosef Dov Soloveitchik, *see Beit HaLevi*
R. Yosef Karo, 24, 46, 51, **54–57**, 58, 66
R. Yosef Rosen of Rogatchov, *see Tzofnat Pane'ach*
R. Yosef Shaul Nathanson, 129, **141–143**

Finkel

AUTHOR

The Responsa Anthology

TITLE

DATE DUE	BORROWER'S NAME

Finkel
The Responsa Anthology

TEMPLE EMANU-EL
HaSifriyah
Haverhill, MA 01830